Critical S

Critical Sexual Literacy

Forecasting Trends in Sexual Politics, Diversity and Pedagogy

Gilbert Herdt, Michelle Marzullo and Nicole Polen Petit

ANTHEM PRESS

Anthem Press
An imprint of Wimbledon Publishing Company
www.anthempress.com

This edition first published in UK and USA 2021
by ANTHEM PRESS
75–76 Blackfriars Road, London SE1 8HA, UK
or PO Box 9779, London SW19 7ZG, UK
and
244 Madison Ave #116, New York, NY 10016, USA

British Library Cataloguing-in-Publication Data
A catalogue record for this book is available from the British Library.

Library of Congress Control Number: 2021942102

ISBN-13: 978-1-83998-066-4 (Hbk)
ISBN-10: 1-83998-066-4 (Hbk)
ISBN-13: 978-1-83998-069-5 (Pbk)
ISBN-10: 1-83998-069-9 (Pbk)

Cover image: Alexas_Fotos / Pixabay.com

This title is also available as an e-book.

We wish to acknowledge the scholars and activists—past, present and future—who work against all odds with much personal sacrifice to carve out the field of critical sexuality studies.

CONTENTS

Acknowledgments   xi

1 Introduction: What We Mean by Critical Sexual Literacy   1
   Gilbert Herdt and Michelle Marzullo

Part One   Sexual Literacy in Education and Research

2 Critical Pedagogy in Sexuality Education: Moving Toward Student
   Sexual Literacy as a Human Right   13
   Lisa M. Vallin

3 Situational Analysis and Critical Sexuality Studies   23
   Adele E. Clarke and Christoph Hanssmann

4 Dispelling the Myths about Sexuality Education   33
   Hon. Helen Clark

5 Advocating Black Sexual Literacy in U.S. Sexuality Education Efforts   35
   Jermisha J. Frazier

6 Reading MacKinnon in San Francisco   43
   Rita M. Melendez

7 Arguing for Sexual Literacy in Fieldwork Preparation   49
   Jerika Loren Heinze

8 Celebrating Black Sexual Freedom: Prioritizing Accurate Research of Black
   Sexuality   57
   Ericka Burns

9 Vnokecetv: Two-Spirit Love at the BAAITS Powwow   67
   Roger Kuhn

10 White Fragility and Decolonizing Sexuality Research   73
    Satori Madrone and Carole Clements

11 Doing Critical Sexuality Studies   79
    Michelle Marzullo

Part Two Sexual Literacy in Policy and Social Discourse

12 Moral and Sex Panics: Barriers to Sexual Literacy 93
Gilbert Herdt

13 Sexual Literacy Barriers for Intersex People 105
Angela Towne

14 Childhood and Sexual Literacy 113
Allison Moore and Paul Reynolds

15 Let's Cancel the Circular Firing Squad: Arguing against Cancel Culture in the Classroom Toward the Sexual Literacy Journey 123
Nicole C. Polen-Petit

16 Sexual Literacy and Sports: Moving Beyond the Binary in Favor of Evidence-Based Policies 131
Lisa Rapalyea

17 Navigating Surrogacy as a Gay Man: A Personal and Professional Sexual Literacy Journey 143
Elliott Kronenfeld

18 Sexually Fluid and Straight People in the Therapeutic Context 153
Caroline Paltin

19 Reconsidering the Sexual Context of Non-Consensual Sexual Interactions 163
Janna Dickenson and Rebecca K. Blais

20 The Global Gag Rule Expanded 175
Caitlin E. Gerdts

21 A Reckoning: Marxism, Queer Theory and Political Economy 183
Holly Lewis

Part Three Sexual Literacy in Diverse Communities

22 Becoming Critically Glocal: Beyond North and South, Individuals and Cultures in Understanding Sexual Literacies 195
Margaret Jolly

23 Sexual Risks in Migrations to Reach Western Europe 205
Lynellyn D. Long

24 Impact and Expansion of Social Networking on Sexual and Gender-Diverse Young People's Sexual Literacy 213
Alexander L. Farquhar-Leicester

25 Social Media and Sexual/Gender Diversity among Young People in Thailand 219
Jan-Willem de Lind van Wijngaarden

26 Queer Visibility and Recognition Online   223
    Daniel Cockayne and Jen Jack Gieseking

27 Errancy and Karma in Thailand: Glocal Sexual Health Literacy in the
    Name of the Aesthetic of Existence   229
    Narupon Duangwises

28 A Palm Springs Postcard: Understanding Sexual Literacy among Older
    Gay Men   235
    Brian de Vries

29 Glocality in the U.S. LGBT Rights Struggle   241
    Sean Cahill

30 Lifelong Sexual Literacy: A Universal Human Right for Sexual Minorities
    and Majorities   249
    Gilbert Herdt and Stefan Lucke

Part Four   Sexual Literacy in Health, Well-Being and Practice

31 Sexual Literacy and Health: A Global Challenge   259
    Deevia Bhana, Ekua Yankah and Peter Aggleton

32 Reproductive Rights and Justice: Thinking through the Connections,
    Contradictions and Complexities   267
    Elisabeth Berger Bolaza

33 LGBT Minority Stress through a Glocal Lens   277
    Sean G. Massey

34 Redefining Sexual Competence   287
    Stefan Lucke

35 The Medicalization of the DSM: Reconceptualizing Human Sexuality
    and Gender   297
    Megan Neitling

36 *"Our Body Is Our Own Body"*: The Collective Bodies of Public Health   305
    Katherine Lepani

37 COVID-19: Sexual and Reproductive Health   313
    Terry McGovern, Kathryn Gibb and Batul Hassan

38 Advocating for Sexual Literacy   323
    Allison Moore and Paul Reynolds

Contributors   333
Index   339

ACKNOWLEDGMENTS

We acknowledge with great thanks and appreciation the tremendous work of Charissa Maria, MSc, Indonesia. She has been a wonder to work with and a major help in the final style editing of this original project and we are so grateful to her.

Chapter 1

INTRODUCTION: WHAT WE MEAN BY CRITICAL SEXUAL LITERACY

Gilbert Herdt and Michelle Marzullo

Sexual literacy is a form of critical thinking focused on the knowledge, skills and actions needed to achieve sexual well-being across the life course. This interdisciplinary field of practice is not just about pedagogy only framed as "sex education" via institutional learnings in school (though we do regard that mode of delivery as very significant). Sexual literacy in our rendering is driven by evidence-based investigations, learnings and diagnoses of real-world power systems. In this view, sexuality is seldom seen in positive terms and is more broadly embedded in systems that constrain, limit and even distort sexual well-being (psychosexual, social and interpersonal intimacy). These are the terrains that the essays in this volume traverse.

We write in a time of the broadening and tragic global COVID-19 pandemic. The untold number of casualties and suffering inherent to any plague is staggering and this is the worst in more than a century. The pandemic of 2019 has, in a certain way, reminded humanity of who is in "control": nature. That is troubling for Western civilization, especially its political and corporate leaders, who have come to believe that nature could be controlled by humans for their profit and pleasure (Merchant, 2006).

This anthology project began in 2018, long before we knew that a worldwide pandemic was on the horizon, and we have marveled at how the very issues confronted in these remarkable essays actually played out in the societal distress, disorder, and inequalities that the pandemic reveals. Much as the HIV pandemic once defined a generational perspective for LGBTQ people, exposing the structural violences that cause fault lines and vulnerabilities of sexual identity across societies (Farmer, 2003; Herdt & Lindenbaum, 1991), the COVID-19 pandemic is redefining for the general population what it means to be human, to be social and sexual, gendered and reproductive (Logie & Turan, 2020). Those dying from COVID-19 are older, with over half of all deaths in people over the age of 80, who have little to no access to healthcare and have high incidences of illnesses that are related to poverty (such as diabetes, obesity and asthma) and who are forced to make life-or-death decisions about going to work or starving, protecting themselves or their families, or being infected. Like the HIV/AIDS pandemic, currently, the COVID-19 pandemic in the United States shows disproportionate incidences of infection killing Black and Brown people at far higher rates. These patterns are not accidental, incidental or natural: they are the product of widespread institutional and discursive stigmatization and structural violence (Galtung, 1969; Lee, 2019).

Structural violences dramatically "spotlight fissures of structural inequality" (Bowleg, 2020, p. 917; Logie & Turan, 2020; McGovern, Gibb, & Hassan, this volume; Treichler, 1987). Many of the terrible lessons learned during the HIV/AIDS pandemic over nearly 40 years, which were a remarkable impetus to sexuality studies, still hold today in the COVID-19 pandemic. Of course, the HIV/AIDS pandemic is also still very much with us now exacerbated by this new pandemic. At this time, we would especially draw attention to the massive health crises across nations, laying bare precisely those human beings whom we value and protect and those who we have not invested in protecting at all. In this environment, the world is changing in ways that are hard to predict yet the project of sexual literacy is as urgent today as ever before since it is a project that engages the very core of how we as humans organize our societies, learn about ourselves and value each other.

Genealogy of Sexual Literacy

Sexual literacy is the notion of socializing people through knowledge and skills enabling them to achieve greater health, harmony and sexual happiness. As a project, it is a modernist utopian idea rising out of globalization and worldwide human rights efforts (Herdt & Howe, 2007; Moore & Reynolds, 2018). What constitutes the praxis of sexual literacy? A simple formula helps guide us: $K + S + A = SWB$, wherein sexual knowledge based in evidence (K), plus skill sets based in communication (S), plus actions that are either pro-social behaviors or agentic (A) create sexual well-being (SWB; see Herdt & Polen-Petit, 2021). Sexual literacy extends to three core areas of contemporary concern: (1) individual sexuality, identities and intimate expressions; (2) gender, role and bodily integrity; and (3) institutional relationships, with sexual and gender performatives resonant within social and cultural domains.

In this formulation, sexual literacy is "a radical approach that seeks to transform the social and cultural relations under which sexuality is understood" (Moore & Reynolds, 2018, p. 200). Sexual literacy in this volume refers to a broad social, research and political endeavor that imparts individuals with "the knowledge necessary to promote and protect sexual wellness and the rights of oneself and intimate others" (Stein & Herdt, 2005, p. 1): it is a social justice project, a process for doing and a concept that may be used as a lens for conceptualizing research studies, educational efforts (individual, community and institutional) and advocacy interventions. Sexual literacy was first conceptualized around 2003 in praxis by Gilbert Herdt as he directed and founded the now-defunct San Francisco-based National Sexuality Resource Center (NSRC) and oriented that work around

> a positive, integrated and holistic view of sexuality from a social justice perspective. We believe that every person should have the knowledge, skills and resources to support healthy and pleasurable sexuality—and that these resources should be based on accurate research and facts. We examine how race, gender, culture, ability, faith and age intersect with and shape our sexual beliefs. We know that sexuality education and learning should be lifelong. We call this sexual literacy. (Moore & Reynolds, 2018, p. 199)

This definition of sexual literacy is distinguished from more narrow conceptions of it as seen in sexual health and wellness promotion because it goes beyond a narrow biomedical focus on sexually transmitted infections (STIs), pregnancy prevention, reproductive health issues and social determinants of health to be not only inclusive of these but also interested in broader influences that incarnate notions of sex and sexuality (Moore & Reynolds, 2018). The concept of sexual literacy has also been used in a limited way to examine sexuality education delivery for adolescents (see Sears, 1997). Sexual literacy as a project goes well beyond traditional pedagogical forms and delivery as well as public health-based sexual health and wellness efforts.

Similar to Herdt's intention to radically transform sociocultural relations around sexuality, Jonathon Alexander's (2008) work focused on unpacking what critical literacy and pedagogy mean in critical sexual literacy by drawing on Foucauldian discourse analysis (Arribas-Ayllon & Walkerdine, 2008) and Queer/lesbigay studies. Alexander leverages discourse as the "how" of sexual literacy, such that to be critically sexually literate requires an "understanding of the ways in which sexuality is constructed in language and the ways in which our language and meaning-making systems are always-already sexualized" (cited in Moore & Reynolds, 2018, p. 201).

Such power relations within sexuality studies are often discussed using the term created by Gayatri Spivak called *epistemic violence* ([1965] 1988), which articulates a concept for attending to how non-elite people are not only kept from power, via social and language practices backed by repressive political actions—such as arrest or criminalization—but are also kept from being allowed to express themselves fully, on their own terms. Instead, they are cajoled by a hegemonic regime (e.g., those holding power, those maintaining the status quo or defining what certain terms mean and how certain behavior should be expressed) to use hegemonic words, concepts and hence ways of thinking and behaving regarding all things, including those related to sex, sexuality and gender. A shorthand for discussing the impact of epistemic violence is to say that non-elites are kept from being able to speak.

If sexualities are relayed through language, and thus literacy, then this process of learning includes not only the reading and writing of a language but also the logic and ideological systems that are relayed through language regarding sex and sexuality that directly implicate how we conceptualize power systems and construct: pedagogical interventions, the objects of our research, certain sexuality problematics as in need of policy intervention (or not) and communication about sexuality across multiple levels from intrapersonal to transnational across space and time.

Key Characteristics of Sexual Literacy

Drawing on this conceptual genealogy, the key characteristics of sexual literacy are the following:

1. Sex-positive and value-driven, conceiving sexuality research and education as a means of political engagement that ethically orients around basic human well-being across the life course.

2. Guided by sex and sexuality as core organizing principals that are always-already holistic and integrative, such that humans use these concepts to form their cultures, socialities, intimacies and selves.

3. Rendered in discourse across geographically, spatially and temporally nuanced contextual articulations of freedom that fundamentally promote and protect bodily sovereignty and sexual citizenship for all, inclusive of the rights of oneself and intimate others.

4. Driven by learnings and messages about sex and sexuality that draw on intimate, physical sexual experiences and personal interpretation as well as upon media, cultural, institutional and other broad discourses that influence understandings of sex and sexualities.

5. Aimed at the lifelong process of individuals to both support their agency in living and ability to articulate their sexual selves to live their best lives and to potentially dialectically advance sexual literacy in context and through time.

We use these characteristics to broadly outline the organization of this anthology understanding that no one project can capture the entirety of the ongoing project of sexual literacy—we all play our parts in our respective geographic locations, discursive registers and fields of practice situated as we are in the glocal complexities that inform our work and personal lives.

Glocal as a Complexifier for Examining Power and Sexuality

If we are to understand sexuality as practiced, felt and understood in settings rife with power imbalances around the world then we must tangle with contextual meanings of sexuality. The concept of "glocal" was used as an orienting concept in soliciting the chapters in this anthology to provide a focus on the nuances of the broad terrain between local knowledges, shared experiences and broader messages around sexuality and gender that shape and inform sexual expression (i.e., meanings and skills) whether individual (intrapsychic), interpersonal (between two people), institutional (social and cultural) or political manifestations (such as within a region or nation, cross border, transnational, corporate or codified in laws and policies). Not all authors directly applied the term *glocal* in their writing, but all did actively think through a lens of glocal sexual literacy vis-à-vis their terrain of engagement.

Glocal is a term used to express the multiplicities of experiences within and between the most high-level ways of conceiving power via sociocultural influence *with* the localities that we inhabit. This is not to collapse the various scales that might be attendant on the nuance of a particular sexual/gendered issue or problematic. Rather, glocal investigation pays attention to the flux between these distinct points of abstraction (individuals, institutions, communities, ideologies, logics, locations, temporalities) that refract, ground and influence behaviors and meaning-making discourses around sex and sexualities as major organizing concepts for human interrelations. Our conceptualization of glocal is different from early critiques of the concept of the global/local split that would variously valorize the global as all promising (see Friedman, 1999, for an example of this valorization of globalization, and Ong, 1999, for a critique) or situate the local as the always-already timeless "authentic" (Fillitz & Saris, 2015) or the only/best way to guard against global, imperial, neocolonialist and/or neoliberal power machinations (Pratt & Rosner, 2012). In our usage, glocal is a rejoinder against the simplified dualities in the ever-renewing slashed-binaries that invoke modernity's winners and losers: global/local, hegemonic/powerless, man/woman, heterosexual/homosexual, cisgender/transgender, young/old, literate/illiterate, White/Black, rich/poor, healthy/ill and others the reader would add.

Glocal as a complexifier attenuates the important and ever-relevant "epistemic violence" in research and advocacy to avoid reductive or binary invocations as the "answer," to pay attention that we do not fall into the colonialist trap of "West is best" thinking about sexuality in settings around the world, and to continually focus us on locating the locus of power relations on issues of sexuality and gender by looking at the knowledge systems (or ways of thinking) that are invoked in a given situation. This of course means that those engaging sexual literacy think through not only what and where our studies engage but who is actually making this work—perspective and social location matter in sexual literacy research, education and advocacy work. Thus, the contributors to the volume are diverse in terms of disciplinary and field background, of personal positionality, of global location—many people "speak" in this collection though no collection can be exhaustive of all the voices and positionalities currently engaging sexual literacy work globally.

Sexuality that is rendered in this more embedded glocal perspective is not simply the result of internal drives or specific body parts (Petchesky, 2004). Nor is it only the product of assumed sets of technologies, surveillance, economic and regulative norms that enable control, focus attention, distract or organize sexuality via discourses (Foucault, [1975] 1977). A glocal lens on sexual literacy work is the product of intersectional transactions and meaning-making that continuously create and reproduce microcosms of meaning, desires, skills as well as broad and intimate power relationships (see Erel, Haritaworn, Gutiérrez Rodríguez, & Klesse, 2010, for excellent examples of such glocal critical sexuality studies (CSS)). These microcosms develop in contextually specific ways in our increasingly "glocal" betwixt, between and becoming (Alexander, 2005) transcendence of meanings and practices. In this volume, we are interested in explicitly forming up an approach to critical sexual literacy studies attendant to situational contexts and power "locations" that may be found geographically, digitally, in intimate ephemeral interactions, repetitive rituals, codifications and identifications, and so on.

Critical Sexual Literacy

Adding an explicit focus and expectation of analyses of power relations in glocal contexts, our approach extends earlier ideas about sexual literacy to now be considered "critical sexual literacy." This way of doing sexual literacy as critical sexual literacy draws on CSS examinations of power and privilege as a focus for research, education and advocacy on sexuality (see Erel et al., 2010; Fahs & McClelland, 2016; Plummer, 2012, 2019). This approach attempts to provide a more dynamic way to do critical sexuality research using situational analyses (see Clarke & Hanssmann, this volume) as a remedy for producing work that presents people as static and timeless or that presents either/or social analysis of the hegemony of globalization or provincial local sexual forms, movements, roles, social practices and attitudes. Critical sexual literacy that employs a glocal lens aims to be more nuanced, temporally accurate and critical to allow room for understanding the positive and negative impacts of power relations on sex and sexuality as well as making room for dealing with contradictions and meanderings; the mediocre and mundane; the beautiful, dangerous and sublime.

The chapters here examine myriad instances of intimate sexual meanings, behaviors, relationships and expressed sexuality identities as these are controlled by, contained, contested, expressed and/or transformed within contexts that name power relations. By exploring and amplifying the variety of ways to engage contextual power, the anthology supports the expansion of sexuality research, pedagogy and policy formation from individuals through institutions.

In doing sexuality studies in this way, we recognize that interdisciplinary research and policy formation always-already operates in ever-evolving glocal fields. Doing this work is part innovation, part revolution and part improvisation. Our pedagogical approach is anchored in historical sexuality studies; this begins with the stunning work of Alfred Kinsey and colleagues (1948) after World War II, the work of feminists (Meyerowitz, 1993; Pratt & Rosner, 2012), sociologists John Gagnon and William Simon who built upon Kinsey in the 1970s and a variety of very important lesbian, gay and queer theorists urging us to deconstruct sexual and gender normativities in the contexts of race, class and other power formations such as Michel Foucault, Judith Butler, Eve Kosofsky Sedgwick, David Halperin, Michael Warner, Roderick A. Ferguson, José Esteban Muñoz, Lisa Duggan, Elizabeth Freeman, Jack Halberstam, David Eng, Jasbir K. Puar, Mignon Moore, Jennifer Nash and so many others who intensified the historical formation of queer theory in the 1990s and since (Eng, Halberstam, & Muñoz, 2005; Gagnon & Parker, 1995; Moore, 2011; Plummer, 2012, 2019). Retrospectively, it is clear that the later studies advanced in tandem with the momentous global human rights movement that centered issues of sex, sexuality, gender and reproductive freedom (Aggleton & Parker, 2010; Correa, Petchetsky, & Parker, 2008), though not in a linear or orchestrated way (Gerber & Gory, 2014). The heritage of these remarkable transformations in CSS, sexual science, empirical and humanities-based studies and human rights, in the late twentieth century reveals many of the complex conundrums of power that drive sexual study in the twenty-first century and which the authors in the volume take up through the lens of critical sexual literacy.

Section Overview

What are the kinds of problems and solutions that applied critical sexual literacy work engages? How do we value one another and what political stakes are revealed when we do put one person over another? How do sexual identities and behaviors become authentic, meaningful and important to comprehend in specific times and contexts? How does such work push forward pedagogy and allow forecasting the circumstances of tomorrow inasmuch as we can foresee? To get at these questions, this volume uses the multifaceted characteristics of sexual literacy to engage critically and situationally across glocal factors, augmenting our ability to forecast sexuality issues (Clarke & Haussmann; Cahill, this volume).

Education and Research

The first section frontloads the main concerns of critical sexual literacy with the production of accurate pedagogy that draws on a sex-positive ethos and is value-driven to conceive critical sexuality research and education as a means of political engagement that ethically orients around basic human well-being across the life course. This section offers chapters that aim to examine critical sexual literacy research methodologies in CSS (Clarke & Hanssmann; Marzullo), decolonizing research and advocacy efforts (Kuhn; Madrone & Clements; Heinze) and in research that recognizes and aims to overcome racist bias in sexuality research (Burns). Since education is connected to research in so much as accurate sexuality education relies on accurate research, this section also engages in dispelling myths about sexuality education (Clark) to ensure that teaching and communication on "sex, power, and politics" remain connected to "interpersonal forms of power" (Melendez). Implicit in our definition of sexual literacy is the embrace of the concept of *critical pedagogy*, thus this section ends by linking critical pedagogy to sexual literacy as a fundamental human right (Vallin).

Policy and Social Discourse

The second section of the anthology organizes around the characteristics of sexual literacy as rendered in discourse across geographically, spatially and temporally nuanced contextual articulations of freedom that fundamentally promote and protect bodily sovereignty and sexual citizenship for all, inclusive of the rights of oneself and intimate others (see Josephson, 2016; Petchesky, 2000). Thus, we see scholars and educators as well as clinical and policy practitioners writing in this section. Sexual literacy in many contexts is indeed fought against and sometimes in ways that cloak the actual intentions of actors seemingly fighting for or against a specific issue with direct impacts on individuals given the inaccurate information, logics or discourses relayed around sexuality and gender issues. In this section, contributors navigate topics such as non-consensual sexual interactions (Dickenson & Blais) and sex panics (Herdt). They also show how sexuality educators struggle to accurately educate on childhood sexuality (Moore & Reynolds), in higher educational settings given the pervasiveness of "call out" or "cancel" culture (Polen-Petit) and with sexual minorities such as intersex people (Towne).

This section also investigates contexts that traverse terrains like sports (Rapalyea), surrogacy clinics (Kronenfeld), mental health therapy offices (Paltin) and health clinics (Gerdts) that become areas for haltingly advancing freedom and protecting bodily sovereignty. If we take context seriously in sexuality works then we must integrate the materiality of existence beyond the materiality of bodies and health, so thinking about how macro-level political economy impacts the kinds of works that critical sexual studies engage and what this means about our futures ends this section (Lewis).

Diverse Communities

Glocality in practice subsumes discourses on diversity, intersectionality and other ways of accounting for difference and power to focus on the contextual influences in which people navigate their desires, intimacies, rights-claims and sexual identities/behaviors. This section is guided by sex and sexuality as core organizing principles that are holistic and integrative such that humans use sex to form their cultures, socialities, intimacies and selves in ways that are always-already authentically invoked at the individual level, even if changeable over time. Scholars in this section examine the meaning of critical sexual literacy across vast terrains such as between the hemispheres of Global North and Global South (Jolly), via migration journeys (Long) and within online mediations (Wijngaarden; Cockayne & Gieseking). Religious ritual and ideologies impact our desires, intimacies, and sexual and gendered identities across various cultures; this is specifically examined in an article discussing global sexual health interpretation in Thailand (Duangwises). Sexual identities that have become politicized into minority/majority rhetorics exercise real power over the lives of many as exemplified in three chapters that end this section (DeVries; Cahill; Herdt & Lucke).

Health, Well-Being and Practice

We end this collection on the topic of health and wellness to reinforce two points about sexual literacy. First, we must not limit the investigation of sex and sexuality to merely biomedical or health concerns, thus the positioning of this topic as last; nor should we ever be so reductionist that we use the medical model to foreclose health outcomes as if separate from powerful discursive messages and sociocultural constructions of sexuality and gender. As we note above, sexual literacy is driven by learnings and messages about sex and sexuality that draw on intimate, physical sexual experiences and personal interpretation as well as upon media, cultural, political, institutional and other broad discourses. Sexual literacy is ultimately aimed at the lifelong process of individuals to both support their agency in living and articulating their sexual selves to live their best lives and (if they wish) to engage in efforts to change society, to potentially advance sexual literacy in context and through time.

Thus, we close this volume with chapters that focus on works being done on health, well-being and practice, which provide us a road map for how to engage (and what to avoid) in the future. Basic concepts are offered as examined through the lens of critical sexual literacy like health (Bhana, Aggleton & Yankah), reproductive rights and justice (Bolaza), LGBT minority stress (Massey) and sexual competence (Lucke). Three chapters in this section draw our attention to higher registers that ask us to identify broader influences shaping our views of sexuality: medicalization driving mental health diagnoses (Neitling), collectivities in public health discourse (Lepani) and structural violences that are actively shaping sexual and reproductive health during the COVID-19 pandemic (McGovern, Gibb & Hassan). The volume ends with an article on sexual literacy that suggests a framework and agenda for doing this work in the future (Moore & Reynolds).

Conclusion

We consider the outcome of sexual literacy efforts as allowing individuals to open a set of knowledge and lifelong abilities and skills, including emotional, analytical and critical thinking and reflection; to perform and achieve sexual well-being across the course of life; and to ultimately impact the ways in which we interact with each other across societies through time. The most optimal outcome of our approach is to enable every individual to attain sexual well-being, if not sexual happiness. While critical sexual literacy today is an academic enterprise in its conceptual foundations, these new essays leap well beyond the academy by critiquing and then advocating for the achievement of full sexual literacy for all persons, regardless of their roles and positions across the globe. While this seems obvious in practical terms, as we have previously mentioned, the pathways to advocating critical sexual literacy face very different barriers across scales of engagement. Our goal in studying glocal contexts of sexuality in a critical way has been to understand how the challenges, risks and rewards of achieving sexual literacy change are really worth it, because we are all worth it.

References

Aggleton, P., & Parker, R. (2010). *Routledge handbook of sexuality, health and rights*. London: Routledge.

Alexander, J. (2008). *Literacy, sexuality and pedagogy: Theory and practice for composition studies*. New York: Utah State University Press.

Alexander, M. J. (2005). *Pedagogies of crossing: Meditations on feminism, sexual politics, memory and the sacred*. Durham, NC: Duke University Press.

Arribas-Ayllon, M., & Walkerdine, V. (2008). Foucauldian discourse analysis. In Carla Willig and Wendy Stainton-Rogers (Eds.), *The Sage handbook of qualitative research in psychology* (pp. 91–108). Thousand Oaks, CA: Sage.

Bowleg, L. (2020). We're not all in this together: On COVID-19, intersectionality and structural inequality. *American Journal of Public Health, 110*(7), 917.

Correa, S., Petchesky, R., & Parker, R. (2008). *Sexuality, health and human rights*. New York: Routledge.

Eng, D. L., Halberstam, J., & Muñoz, J. E. (2005). What's queer about queer studies now? *Social Text, 84–85*(23), 1–18.

Erel, U., Haritaworn, J., Gutiérrez Rodríguez, E., & Klesse, C. (2010). On the depoliticization of intersectionality talk: Conceptualizing multiple oppressions in critical sexuality studies. In Y. Taylor, S. Hines, & M. E. Casey (Eds.), *Theorizing intersectionality and sexuality* (pp. 56–77). New York: Palgrave Macmillan.

Fahs, B., & McClelland, S. I. (2016). When sex and power collide: An argument for critical sexuality studies. *Journal of Sex Research, 53*(4–5), 392–416.

Farmer, P. (2003). *Pathologies of power*. Berkeley: University of California Press.

Fillitz, T., & Saris, A. J. (2015). *Debating authenticity: Concepts of modernity in anthropological perspective*. Oxford: Berghahn Books.

Foucault, M. ([1975] 1977). *Discipline and punish [Surveiller et punir]* (A. Sheridan, Trans.). New York: Pantheon. (Original work published 1975.)

Friedman, T. (1999). *The lexus and the olive tree: Understanding globalization*. New York: Picador.

Gagnon, J., & Parker, R. (1995). Conceiving sexuality. In R. G. Parker & J. H. Gagnon (Eds.), *Conceiving sexuality* (pp. 3–16). New York: Routledge.

Galtung, J. (1969). Violence, peace, and peace research. *Journal of Peace Research, 6*(3), 167–191.

Gerber, P., & Gory, J. (2014). The UN Human Rights Committee and LGBT rights: What is it doing? What could it be doing? *Human Rights Law Review, 14*(3), 403–439.

Herdt, G., & Howe, C. (2007). *21st century sexualities: Contemporary issues in health, education and rights.* New York: Routledge.

Herdt, G., & Lindenbaum, S. (1991). *The time of AIDS.* Thousand Oaks, CA: Sage.

Herdt, G., & Polen-Petit, N. C. (2021). *Human sexuality: Self, society and culture* (2nd ed.). New York: McGraw Hill.

Josephson, J. (2016). *Rethinking sexual citizenship.* New York: State University of New York Press.

Kinsey, A., Pomeroy, W., & Martin, C. (1948). *Sexual behavior in the human male.* Philadelphia, PA: W.B. Saunders.

Lee, B. X. (2019). *Violence: An interdisciplinary approach to causes, consequences, and cures.* Hoboken, NJ: Wiley-Blackwell.

Logie, C. H., & Turan, J. M. (2020). How do we balance tensions between COVID-19 public health responses and stigma mitigation? Learning from HIV research. *AIDS and Behavior, 24,* 2003–2006.

Merchant, C. (2006). The scientific revolution and the death of nature. *Isis, 97,* 513–533.

Meyerowitz, J. (1993). Beyond the feminine mystique: A reassessment of postwar mass culture, 1946–1958. *Journal of American History, 79*(4), 1455–1482.

Moore, A., & Reynolds, P. (2018). *Childhood and sexuality: Contemporary issues and debates.* London: Palgrave Macmillan.

Moore, M. (2011). *Invisible families: Gay identities, relationships, and motherhood among Black women.* Berkeley: University of California Press.

Ong, A. (1999). *Flexible CITIZENSHIP: The cultural logics of transnationality.* Durham, NC: Duke University Press.

Petchesky, R. (2000). Sexual rights: Inventing a concept, mapping an international practice. In R. Parker, R. M. Barbosa & Peter Aggleton (Eds.), *Framing the sexual subject: The politics of gender, sexuality and power* (pp. 81–103). Berkeley: University of California Press.

Petchesky, R. (2004). *Sexual rights across countries and cultures: Conceptual frameworks and minefields* [Policy Brief]. Sexuality Policy Watch. http://www.sxpolitics.org/wp-content/uploads/2009/03/sexual-minorities1.pdf

Plummer, K. (2012). Critical sexuality studies. In G. Ritze (Ed.), *The Wiley-Blackwell companion to sociology* (pp. 243–268). Hoboken, NJ: Wiley-Blackwell.

Plummer, K. (2019). Critical sexuality studies: Moving on. In G. Ritzer & W. W. Murphy (Eds.), *The Wiley Blackwell companion to sociology* (2nd ed., pp. 156–173). Hoboken, NJ: Wiley-Blackwell.

Pratt, G., & Rosner, V. (2012). *The global and the intimate: Feminism in our time.* New York: Columbia University Press.

Sears, J. T. (1997). Centering culture: Teaching for critical sexual literacy using the sexual diversity wheel. *Journal of Moral Education, 26*(3), 273–283.

Spivak, G. C. ([1965] 1988). Can the subaltern speak? In C. Nelson & L. Grossberg (Eds.), *Marxism and the interpretation of culture* (pp. 271–316). Urbana: University of Illinois Press. (Original work published 1965.)

Stein, T., & Herdt, G. (2005). Editorial: Welcome to SRSP 2005. *Sexuality Research and Social Policy: Journal of the National Sexuality Resource Center, 2*(1), 1.

Treichler, P. (1987). AIDS, homophobia and biomedical discourse: An epidemic of signification. *AIDS: Cultural Analysis/Cultural Activism, 43*(Winter), 31–70. https://www.jstor.org/stable/3397564

PART ONE

SEXUAL LITERACY IN EDUCATION AND RESEARCH

Chapter 2

CRITICAL PEDAGOGY IN SEXUALITY EDUCATION: MOVING TOWARD STUDENT SEXUAL LITERACY AS A HUMAN RIGHT

Lisa M. Vallin

Within the last decade, sexuality education has gained new significance and has been recognized as a crucial component for promoting health and wellness in several of the United Nations' Sustainable Development Goals (SDGs): Quality Education (SDG 4), Gender Equality (SDG 5) and Good Health and Wellbeing (SDG 3) principles all grounded in human rights. In 2018, UNESCO launched its campaign, "Comprehensive sexuality education: A foundation for life and love," advocating for quality comprehensive sexuality education as a human right and a means to promote sexual literacy—a term that describes the knowledge and skill sets needed to continue learning and to perform learning in ways that enhance intimate and erotic relationships and well-being, pleasure and rights (Herdt, 2007; Herdt & Polen-Petit, 2013). Empowering young people with quality sexuality education is not only reflective of human rights, it is an investment in healthy democratic societies (Magar, 2015). Thus, sexuality is perhaps one of the most fundamental aspects of human life. This complex phenomenon that helps us navigate our personhood, affirms our identities and expresses feelings and behaviors that bring central meaning to our lives. Sexuality permeates every aspect of society; therefore, education about sexuality is of central importance—it is a necessary human right.

This chapter focuses on sexuality education within the United States, a country long divided over the issue of sexuality education and that has not done well in providing sexual literacy for its people. It first provides historical context of sexuality education and then proceeds to discuss pedagogical practices that have largely been omitted in discussions about sexuality education. It concludes by exploring the use of critical pedagogy with an emphasis on love as a particularly effective approach for the promotion of sexually literate youth and sexuality education as a human right for all.

Historical Context of Sexuality Education in the United States

What one can and cannot not to teach about sex and sexuality has always been problematic in the United States. Sexuality education remains a highly contentious and politically charged issue. By contrast, in northern European countries such as the Netherlands, Switzerland and the Scandinavian countries, sexuality is not culturally or politically controversial (Schalet, 2004); rather, sexuality is viewed as a natural part of life, including young peoples' sexual development. European adolescents are expected to engage in sexual behaviors as they progress toward adulthood and are thus regarded as being capable of making well-informed decisions about their sexuality. This expectation is reflected in both social and legal rights (Mcgee & Mcgee, 1998; Schalet, 2004). Although adolescent sexuality is not necessarily celebrated or encouraged in Northern Europe, it is culturally recognized, supported by universal health care and backed by legal notions of gender equality, at least up to a point. As a result, the utilization of regular proactive reproductive health care is more pervasive (Dereuddre, Van de Putte, & Bracke, 2016; Santelli & Schalet, 2009) and results in fewer unwanted pregnancies and sexually trans-mitted infections (STIs). For decades, the Netherlands has consistently reported some of the lowest rates of teen pregnancies, births, abortions and STIs, whereas the United States has struggled with some of the highest rates (Brugman, Caron, & Rademakers, 2010).

Youth's sexuality in America is generally regarded with anxiety and discomfort. Adolescent sexuality is often taboo both in the home and at school, and the topic is surrounded by myth and folklore about raging hormones, poor parenting, STIs, unwanted pregnancies, sexual coercion, violence and abuse (Schalet, 2000). Unlike in Northern Europe, where young people are considered to be fully capable of making decisions about their sexuality, young people in the United States are not only viewed as incapable of making sexual decisions, but adolescent sexual activity overall is widely considered to be morally wrong (Schalet, 2004). The notion of youth is laced with sentiments of purity and innocence that are seen as needing to be protected from various dangers until marriage, or at least well into early adulthood. In this context, sexuality education has been and continues to be centered on preventing the negative consequences of sexual activity while upholding heterosexual purity (Fields, 2008; Lesko, 2010; Luker, 2006).

Sexuality education in the United States also has its roots in the social hygiene movement from the nineteenth century and first introduced into the public schools in the early twentieth century (Brandt, 1987). Fueled by religious, political and cultural ideologies, this pedagogy historically was utilized as a remedy to remove sexual deviancy; it has generated moral panics about masturbation, venereal disease and homosexuality, and was anchored within a heteronormative context (Elia & Eliason, 2010a). According to Michel Foucault, "when 'sex' comes to school, it is institutionalized, subject to strict monitoring, surveillance, regulation, and techniques of governance, thereby disciplining behavior, attitudes, and use of bodies" (as cited in Allen, Rasmussen, & Quinlivan, 2013, p. 106). The emphasis on risk and danger has long played a significant role in US sexu-ality education (Elia & Eliason, 2009; Fields, 2008; Herdt, 2009; Luker, 2006; Rubin, 1984; Tolman & Diamond, 2006), wherein some version of the "just say no" agenda has for decades impeded sexuality education, culminating in Abstinence Only sexuality edu-cation policy, which some have referred to as "ignorance only" (Schleifer, 2002).

Beginning with the Reagan (1980–88) administration in the early 1980s, the federal government has consistently funded curricula that have been exclusionary, ideologically driven and filled with fear, shame and stigma with the goal to control rather than educate youth about sex and sexuality. According to the *Sexuality Information and Education Council of the United States* (SIECUS), since the 1980s, over two billion dollars in federal and state funding has been spent on programs that are thought to prevent sex and information about sexuality (SIECUS, 2018). These abstinence-only programs are often founded on Christian religious ideology rather than medical accuracy and focus on the benefits of abstaining from sexual behaviors. Abstinence is not only argued to be the only certain way to avoid STIs and unwanted pregnancies but is also promoted as the most respectable and morally sound decision for youth (DiMauro & Joffe, 2009; Fields, 2008; Kohler, Manhart, & Lafferty, 2008; Luker, 2006). Sexuality is treated as a distraction and students are encouraged to resist sexual temptations and put off or "save" sex for adulthood and heterosexual marriage (Elia & Eliason, 2010a, 2010b). Critics of these policies were proved right that they would be ineffective (Kirby, 2008).

Abstinence-only programs gained particular popularity in the 1990s with increased federal funding as a part of the Welfare Reform Act that was passed in 1996. A year later, in 1997 new guidelines for abstinence-only education went into effect and imposed a number of restrictions on curricula known as the A–H Guidelines of Abstinence Education (Santelli et al., 2006). The A–H guidelines narrowly defined what curricula should entail and favored faith-based organizations and the abstinence-only movement. A plethora of abstinence-only programs were dispersed across the country, many referred to as abstinence-only-until-marriage (AOUM) programs. States experiencing financial hardship could apply for federal monies in exchange for implementing AOUM programs in their schools. When these grants, channeled under Title V as part of the Welfare Reform Act of 1996, first became available, all but one state, California, accepted these federal funds and committed to statewide abstinence-only education (Raymond et al., 2008; SIECUS, 2018).

The spread of abstinence-only education resulted in several unfortunate consequences. Curricula founded on religious ideologies provided inaccurate information regarding the effectiveness of contraception, false information about the risk associated with abortion and inaccurate information about the transmission of STIs including HIV. In 2004, representative Henry Waxman (CA-D) released a report containing a review of the 13 most popular abstinence-only programs funded with Title V grants during 2003. The report showed that over 80 percent, 11 out of the 13 programs, contained false, misleading or distorted information about reproductive health (Waxman, 2004). Several of the abstinence-only curricula reviewed provided false information about the effectiveness of condom use in preventing STIs and pregnancy. According to the report:

> One curriculum says that "the popular claim that 'condoms help prevent the spread of STDs,' is not supported by the data"; another states that "[i]n heterosexual sex, condoms fail to prevent HIV approximately 31% of the time"; and another teaches that a pregnancy occurs one out of every seven times that couples use condoms. (p. i)

In regard to abortion, one of the curriculums falsely claims that legal abortion is associated with a 5–10 percent risk of causing sterility (Waxman, 2004). In fact, legal abortion in the United States is one of the safest medical procedures performed and rarely associated with complications. A landmark study by the National Academies of Sciences, Engineering and Medicine found no long-term consequences on either physical or mental health as a result of a legal abortion (NASEM, 2018). Waxman's (2004) report ensued political debates over how abstinence-only policies violated human rights by misleading students and withholding information that could potentially improve the health and well-being of youth (Ott & Santelli, 2007). In response, Congress commissioned a study to determine the effectiveness of abstinence-only education. Researchers from Mathematica Policy Research (Trenholm et al., 2007) carried out an experimental study to estimate the effects of four well-funded abstinence-only programs under Title V. The study surveyed a total of 2,057 youth; 1,209 were randomly assigned to the program group, the remaining 848 served as the control group. The final data set included two scales, one measured sexual behavior (rates of sexual abstinence, rates of unprotected sex, number of sexual partners, expectations to abstain and reported rates of pregnancy, births and STIs). The second scale measured knowledge and perceptions of risk associated with teen sexuality. In 2007, Mathematica published the study, and their findings suggested that the abstinence-only programs evaluated had little to no beneficial impact on young people's sexual behavior (Santelli et al., 2006; SIECUS, 2018; Trenholm et al., 2007). Despite research challenging the accuracy and effectiveness of abstinence-only programs, funding for these programs continued up until 2010.

In 2009, President Obama's 2010 budget eliminated most of the federal funding for abstinence-only programs (Calterone, 2011). Money that previously had been reserved for abstinence-only or what today is often referred to as "sexual risk avoidance" education was no longer a guarantee. The Office of Adolescent Health (OAH) was established and federal resources—some of which were authorized under the *Affordable Care Act* colloquially known as Obamacare—began to fund comprehensive sexuality education with a focus on risk reduction (Fields, 2012). This shift in curricula contributed to a push for developing stronger evidence-based practices that had proven effective through "rigorous evaluation," to delay sexual activity, increase contraceptive use (without increasing sexual activity) or reduce teen pregnancy.

Under the administration of President Obama, there was a period of progressive thought and positive development for comprehensive sexuality education. However, since 2016, when President Donald Trump took office, we have experienced regression to the prior period of progress (Jones, 2018). The current Trump administration has largely shown hostility toward comprehensive sexuality education, favoring programs that promote abstinence for sexual risk reduction, despite the proven ineffectiveness and the many ethical controversies surrounding these programs. US sexuality education continues to be a politically charged issue subject to the shifting agenda of each new administration.

Teaching Sexuality Education

Owing to the political controversies surrounding sexuality education, attention has been focused on curricula and content and pedagogical practices have often been neglected (Sanjakdar et al., 2015). For nearly four decades, the main focus in both public and political debates has been about what constitutes appropriate content for sexuality education, abstinence-only or comprehensive sexuality education (Elia & Eliason, 2010a). Recent research, however, suggests that a majority of American parents support comprehensive sexuality education in public schools (Kantor & Levitz, 2017). Although most states (currently, 28 states and the District of Columbia) mandate sexuality education, decisions about how and when sexuality education should be taught are often left to school districts and individual principals (Guttmacher, 2019). Increasing awareness of interpersonal violence has prompted many states to mandate instruction on skills that promote healthy relationships and prevent sexual violence.

A central goal of most sexuality education programs, whether abstinence- or comprehensive-focused, is to prevent risky sexual practices that could result in STIs, unwanted pregnancies, sexual coercion and violence (Sanjakdar et al., 2015; Santelli et al., 2006). When sexuality education is driven by issues focused on risk, it is not uncommon for teaching to reflect a heteronormative agenda that serves to exclude rather than include diverse sexuality. It is therefore important that teachings about STIs, contraception and sexual violence and abuse include diverse stories and representation, so that learning has the opportunity to become an act of empowerment rather than an act of exclusion. Pedagogy is of paramount importance to bring comprehensive sexuality education to this next level of inclusive curricula. It is necessary to take a closer look at pedagogical practices to enhance not only teaching but also student learning. Students have the right to experience and participate in sexuality education that recognizes and affirms all sexualities (Sanjakdar et al., 2015). Critical pedagogy (Freire, 2014; hooks, 2014; McLaren, 2003) with an emphasis on love can serve as a useful source of inspiration when queering pedagogical approaches (Meyer, 2007) to better support the development of sexual literacy.

Queering Pedagogical Practices in Sexuality Education

Student voices are of central importance when learning about sexuality, and yet they are seldom present (Fine & McClelland, 2006). Students come to the classroom already filled with experiences, hopes and desires, as well as concerns, fears and anxieties. Because of the many injustices that surround sexuality, teaching about sexuality can be an act of empowerment by creating opportunities for change and transformation. Teachers' pedagogies play an important role in facilitating learning and critical pedagogy with an emphasis on love that may serve as a useful mode of teaching sexuality education (Sanjakdar et al., 2015).

Critical pedagogy fosters a learning environment where students learn to analyze, expose and challenge social, cultural and political agendas that are embedded in knowledge construction (Burbules, 2000; hooks, 2014; McLaren, 2003; Shor, 1999). As such, critical pedagogy plays a major role in shedding heteronormative beliefs and values that too often dominate curricula. "Critical pedagogy can be employed to help correct the social and educational injustices that have been perpetuated in school-based sexuality education since its inception nearly a century ago" (Elia & Eliason, 2010a, p. 29).

Learning about sexuality can be a vulnerable process and it is crucial that students feel valued and encouraged to be able to voice thoughts and negotiate new knowledge. Teaching with and about love can contribute to the creation of a supportive learning environment that welcomes diversity. Love is a uniquely human emotion and is what overcomes fear. Fear sometimes inhibits our ability to feel compassion, and to accept and respect diversity. Like critical pedagogy, teaching with love also implies fighting for social justice. "There can be no love without justice [...] Abuse and neglect negate love. Care and affirmation, the opposite of abuse and humiliation, are the foundation of love" (hooks, 2000, p. 22). Love acts as the glue that connects all and brings meaning to learning. We all share experiences with love—having been in love, been loved by others, desired love, failed love, hurt by love and so forth. By centering sexuality education as an act of love, the negative aspects, the risks and the dangers rather become secondary, treated as by-products instead of the main focus. This is what queering pedagogical practices is about—to offer teachings that include and connect students rather than separate and alienate them.

A challenge for comprehensive sexuality education is to become more representative of all sexualities in both content and pedagogy. Despite the broad range of topics addressed by comprehensive sexuality education, content too often lacks diverse representation of sexual bodies and lives (Snapp & Russell, 2017). When using curricula, it is vital that teachers are aware of discourse that excludes certain groups and exposes harmful social structures that both oppress and empower (Meyer, 2007). Students should have the opportunity to recognize themselves, have their stories represented and their questions answered in both content and pedagogical practices of sexuality education. When students have the ability to not only see themselves in curricula but also see others who may differ from them, understanding, acceptance and empathy of diverse sexuality increase (Baams, Dubas, & Aken, 2017; Haberland & Rogow, 2015). Inclusive sexuality education has also been shown to improve overall school climate by increasing feelings of safety and reducing bullying in the form of homophobic slurs and physical victimization (Baams et al., 2017; Goodenow, Szalacha, & Westheimer, 2006; Ingrey, 2018; Kosciw, Greytak, Zongrone, Clark, & Truong, 2018; Snapp, Mcguire, Sinclair, Gabrion, & Russell, 2015; Snapp & Russell, 2017).

Teaching inclusive comprehensive sexuality education and utilizing critical pedagogy focused on love all have the potential to advance sexual literacy through understanding and appreciation for all sexual lives. It can also move people into action to help further their own sexual well-being. This form of inclusive sexuality education also portrays sexuality in its truest form: as uniquely diverse. To live up to the promise of sexuality education as a human right, educators should be encouraged to continue teaching inclusive comprehensive sexuality education that supports sexual literacy and speaks to the lives of all students.

References

Allen, L., Rasmussen, M., & Quinlivan, K. (2013). *The politics of pleasure in sexuality education: Pleasure bound* (pp. 1–204). doi:10.4324/9780203069141

Baams, L., Dubas, J., & van Aken, M. (2017). Comprehensive sexuality education as a longitudinal predictor of LGBTQ name-calling and perceived willingness to intervene in school. *Journal of Youth and Adolescence, 46*(5), 931–942. doi:10.1007/s10964-017-0638-z

Brandt, A. (1987). *No magic bullet: A social history of venereal disease in the United States since 1880.* New York: Oxford University Press.

Brugman, M., Caron, S. L., & Rademakers, J. (2010). Emerging adolescent sexuality: A comparison of American and Dutch college women's experiences. *International Journal of Sexual Health, 22*(1), 32–46. doi:10.1080/19317610903403974

Burbules, N. C. (2000). The limits of dialogue as a critical pedagogy. In P. Trifonas (Ed.), *Revolutionary pedagogies: Cultural politics, education, and the discourse of theory* (pp. 251–273). https://doi.org/10.4324/9780203901557

Calterone Williams, J. (2011). Battling a "sex-saturated society": The abstinence movement and the politics of sex education. *Sexualities, 14*(4), 416–443. doi:10.1177/1363460711406460

Dereuddre, R., Van de Putte, B., & Bracke, P. (2016). Ready, willing, and able: Contraceptive use patterns across Europe. *European Journal of Population, 32*(4), 543–573. doi:10.1007/s10680-016-9378-0

Di Mauro, D., & Joffe, C. (2009). The religious right and the reshaping of sexual policy: reproductive rights and sexuality education during the Bush years. *Moral panics, sex panics: Fear and the fight over sexual rights* (pp. 47–103). New York: New York University Press.

Elia, J. P., & Eliason, M. J. (2009). Values-free sexuality education: Myth or reality? In E. Schroeder & J. Kuriansky (Eds.), *Sexuality education: Past, present, and future* (vol. 1) (pp. 174–198). Westport, CT: Praeger.

Elia, J. P., & Eliason, M. J. (2010a). Dangerous omissions: Abstinence-only-until-marriage school-based sexuality education and the betrayal of LGBTQ youth. *American Journal of Sexuality Education, 5*(1), 17–35. doi:0.1080/15546121003748848

Elia, J. P., & Eliason, M. J. (2010b). Discourses of exclusion: Sexuality education's silencing of sexual others. *Journal of LGBT Youth, 7*(1). doi:10.1080/19361650903507791

Fields, J. (2008). *Risky lessons: Sexuality education and social inequality.* New Brunswick, NJ: Rutgers University Press.

Fields, J. (2012). Sexuality education in the United States: Shared cultural ideas across a political divide. *Sociology Compass, 6*(1), 1–14. doi:10.1111/j.1751-9020.2011.00436.x

Fine, M., & McClelland, S. (2006). Sexuality education and desire: Still missing after all these years. *Harvard Educational Review, 76*(3), 297–338.

Freire, P. (2014). *Pedagogy of the oppressed.* 30th anniversary ed. New York: Bloomsbury Academic.

Goodenow, C., Szalacha, L., & Westheimer, K. (2006). School support groups, other school factors, and the safety of sexual minority adolescents. *Psychology in the Schools, 43*, 573–589. doi:10.1002/pits.20173

Guttmacher Institute (2019). *State policies in brief as of January 1, 2020: Sex and HIV education.* Retrieved from https://www.guttmacher.org/statepolicy/explore/sex-and-hiv-education

Haberland, N., & Rogow, D. (2015). Sexuality education: emerging trends in evidence and practice. *Journal of Adolescent Health, 56*(1), S15–S21. doi:10.1016/j.jadohealth.2014.08.013

Herdt, G. (Ed.). (2009). *Moral panics, sex panics: Fear and the fight over sexual rights* (vol. 8). New York: New York University Press.

Herdt, G., & Howe, C. (2007). What is sexual literacy, and why is it needed now? In G. Herdt & C. Howe (Eds.), In *21st Century Sexualities* (pp. 37–39). Florence: Routledge. https://doi.org/10.4324/9780203947470-8

Herdt, G., & Polen-Petit, N. (2013). *Human sexuality: Self, society, and culture.* New York: McGraw Hill.

hooks, b. (2000). *All about love: New visions.* New York: William Morrow.

hooks, b. (2014). *Teaching to transgress.* New York: Routledge.

Ingrey, J. (2018, May 24). Queer studies in education. Oxford Research Encyclopedia of Education. Retrieved April 2, 2021, from https://oxfordre.com/education/view/10.1093/acrefore/9780190264093.001.0001/acrefore-9780190264093-e-249

Jones, T. (2018). Trump, trans students and transnational progress. *Sex Education, 18*(4), 479–494. doi:0.1080/14681811.2017.1409620

Kantor, L., & Levitz, N. (2017). Parents' views on sexuality education in schools: How much do Democrats and Republicans agree? *PloS One, 12*(7), e0180250. doi:10.1371/journal. pone.0180250

Kirby, D. B. (2008). The impact of abstinence and comprehensive sex and STD/HIV education programs on adolescent sexual behavior. *Sexuality Research & Social Policy, 5*(3), 18. doi:10.1525/ srsp.2008.5.3.18

Kohler, P. K., Manhart, L. E., & Lafferty, W. E. (2008). Abstinence-only and comprehensive sexuality education and the initiation of sexual activity and teen pregnancy. *Journal of Adolescent Health, 42*(4), 344–351. doi:0.1016/j.jadohealth.2007.08.026

Kosciw, J. G., Greytak, E. A., Zongrone, A. D., Clark, C. M., & Truong, N. L. (2018). *The 2017 National School Climate Survey: The experiences of lesbian, gay, bisexual, transgender, and queer youth in our nation's schools.* Gay, Lesbian and Straight Education Network (GLSEN). 121 West 27th Street Suite 804, New York, NY 10001.

Lesko, N. (2010). Feeling abstinent? Feeling comprehensive? Touching the affects of sexuality curricula. *Sex Education, 10*(3), 281–297. doi:10.1080/14681811.2010.491633

Luker, K. (2006). *When sex goes to school: Warring views on sex and sexuality education since the sixties.* New York: W.W. Norton.

Magar, V. (2015). Gender, health and the sustainable development goals. *World Health Organization: Bulletin of the World Health Organization, 93*(11), 743. doi:10.2471/BLT.15.165027

Mcgee, M., & Mcgee, M. (1998). Comparing European and U.S. approaches to adolescent sexual health. *Educator's Update, 3*(3), 1–3. Retrieved from http://search.proquest.com/docview/ 79626905/

McLaren, P. (2003). Critical pedagogy: A look at the major concepts. In A. Darder, M. et al. (Eds.), The critical pedagogy reader (pp. 69–96). New York: Routlege/Falmer.

Meyer, E. (2007). "But I'm not gay": What straight teachers need to know about queer theory. In N. Rodriguez & W. Pinar (Eds.), *Queering straight teachers: Discourse and identity in education* (pp. 17–32). New York: Peter Lang.

National Academies of Sciences, E., Health and Medicine Division, Board on Health Care Services, Board on Population Health and Public Health Practice, & Committee on Reproductive Health Services: Assessing the Safety and Quality of Abortion Care in the U.S. (2018). *The safety and quality of abortion care in the United States.* https://doi.org/10.17226/24950

Ott, M. A., & Santelli, J. S. (2007). Abstinence and abstinence-only education. *Current Opinion in Obstetrics & Gynecology, 19*(5), 446–452. https://doi.org/10.1097/GCO.0b013e3282efdc0b

Raymond, M., Bogdanovich, L., Brahmi, D., Cardinal, L., Fager, G., Frattarelli, L., ... Santelli, J. (2008). State refusal of federal funding for abstinence-only programs. *Sexuality Research & Social Policy, 5*(3), 44–55. https://doi.org/10.1525/srsp.2008.5.3.44

Rubin, G. (1984). Thinking sex: Notes for a radical theory of the politics of sexuality. In P. M. Nardi & B. E. Schneider (Eds.), *Social perspectives in lesbian and gay studies: A reader* (pp. 100–133). New York: Routledge.

Sanjakdar, F., Allen, L., Rasmussen, M. L., Quinlivan, K., Brömdal, A., & Aspin, C. (2015). In search of critical pedagogy in sexuality education: Visions, imaginations, and paradoxes. *Review of Education, Pedagogy, and Cultural Studies, 37*(1), 53–70.

Santelli, J., Ott, M. A., Lyon, M., Rogers, J., Summers, D., & Schleifer, R. (2006). Abstinence and abstinence-only education: A review of US policies and programs. *Journal of Adolescent Health, 38*(1), 72–81. doi:0.1016/j.jadohealth.2005.10.006

Santelli, J. S., & Schalet, A. T. (2009). *A new vision for adolescent sexual and reproductive health.* Ithaca, NY: ACT for Youth Center of Excellence.

Schalet, A. (2000). Raging hormones, regulated love: Adolescent sexuality and the constitution of the modern individual in the United States and the Netherlands. *Body & Society, 6*(1), 75–105.

Schalet, A. (2004). Must we fear adolescent sexuality? *MedGenMed: Medscape General Medicine, 6*(4), 44–44. Retrieved from http://search.proquest.com/docview/67273624/

Schleifer, R. (2002). Ignorance only: HIV/AIDS, human rights, and federally funded abstinence-only programs in the United States. Texas: A case study. *Human Rights Watch, 14*(5), 1–47.

Sexuality Information and Education Council of the United States. (2018). A history of federal funding for abstinence-only-until-marriage programs. Retrieved October 28, 2019, from https://siecus.org/wp-content/uploads/2018/08/A-History-of-AOUM-Funding-Final-Draft.pdf.

Shor, I. (1999). What is critical literacy? *Journal for Pedagogy, Pluralism & Practice, 4*(1), 1–26. Retrieved from https://digitalcommons.lesley.edu/jppp/vol1/iss4/2

Snapp, S., Mcguire, J., Sinclair, K., Gabrion, K., & Russell, S. (2015). LGBTQ-inclusive curricula: why supportive curricula matter. *Sex Education, 15*(6), 580–596. https://doi.org/10.1080/14681811.2015.1042573

Snapp, S., & Russell, S. T. (2017). Inextricably linked: The shared story of ethnic studies and LGBTQ-inclusive curriculum, for sexual orientation. In S.T. Russell & S. Horn (Eds.), *Gender identity, and schooling: The nexus of research, practice, and policy* (pp. 143–162). New York: Oxford University Press.

Tolman, D., & Diamond, L. (2006). In a different position: Conceptualizing female adolescent sexuality development within compulsory heterosexuality. *New Directions for Child and Adolescent Development, 2006*(112), 71–89. https://doi.org/10.1002/cd.163

Trenholm, C., Devaney, B., Fortson, K., Quay, L., Wheeler, J., & Clark, M. (2007). *Impacts of Four Title V, Section 510 Abstinence Education Programs.* Retrieved from http://search.proquest.com/docview/2080928212/

Waxman, H. (2004). *The content of federally funded abstinence-only education programs.* Washington, DC: United States House of Representatives Committee on Government Reform—Minority Staff Special Investigations Division. http://oversight.house. gov/documents/20041201102153-50247.pdf

Chapter 3

SITUATIONAL ANALYSIS AND CRITICAL SEXUALITY STUDIES

Adele E. Clarke and Christoph Hanssmann

Situational Analysis (SA) is an excellent conceptual metaphor for thinking through and with critical sexuality studies. SA is also an especially appropriate *interpretive qualitative research method* for critically studying diverse sexuality issues across cultures, spaces, genders and geopolitics. This chapter first discusses why SA focuses on the situation per se. It is precisely the breadth of the situation as a focus of analysis that makes it eminently suitable for *glocal critical sexuality studies*: distinctive attributes from local to global lively in a specific situation can be specified and analyzed. We then turn to the theoretical foundations of SA.

Next, we introduce the four different kinds of mapping and analysis that constitute doing SA research: messy maps of all the elements lively in the situation; maps of relationships *among* elements made using messy maps; social worlds and arenas maps of collective actors; and positional maps analyzing discourses found in the situation. We conclude with distinctive SA "affordances" for doing critical sexuality studies.

Why "the Situation" and Not Just "Context"?

SA as a method of qualitative inquiry is an extension of grounded theory (GT), the most popular qualitative method both transnationally and transdisciplinarily (Charmaz, 2014; Glaser & Strauss, 1967). SA has similarly been taken up very widely (see exemplars in Clarke, Friese, & Washburn, 2018, pp. 374–84; https://study.sagepub.com/clarke2e). While GT research focuses on elucidating "basic social processes" or key actions in a situation, SA turns this on its head, focusing instead on the situation per se.

In GT, situational conditions were seen as "context" *surrounding* the acting humans, but not integral to the action. In SA, the conditions *of* the situation are understood to be *in* the situation itself. To clarify, in SA, a situation is not merely a moment in time, a narrow spatial or temporal unit or a brief encounter or event (or at least rarely so). Rather it usually involves a somewhat enduring *arrangement of relations among many different kinds and categories of elements that has its own ecology*. Clarke (2005, p. 73) therefore conceptualized a Situational Matrix showing the elements as explicitly integral (see Figure 3.1).

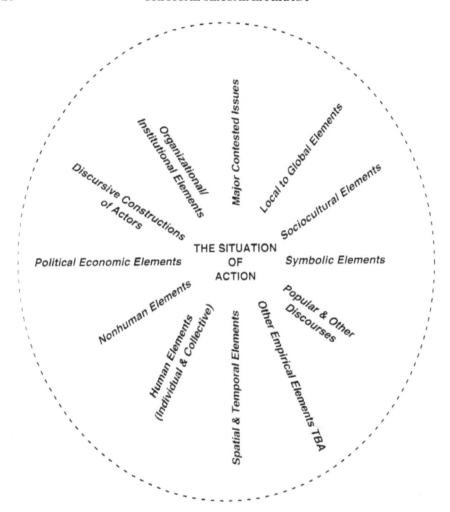

Figure 3.1 Clarke's (Revised) Situational Matrix (Clarke et al., 2018, p. 45). Used with permission, Sage.

Here you can see all the different kinds of elements that constitute a situation as studied in SA research through making the different kinds of maps. Notice that many of the elements are nonhuman. We turn next to why and how that is so important.

Theoretical Foundations of Situational Analysis

One profound insight of science and technology studies (STS) is that *everything that is in a scientific situation matters—human and nonhuman* (Latour & Woolgar, 1979). There is no such thing as "context." In science, nonhuman elements include such things as technologies, laboratory animals, slides, databases, journals and so on. In sexuality studies, nonhuman elements may include, for example, condoms, sexually transmitted infections and diseases, contraception, LGBT journals, newsletters and social media posts circulating the globe, sex toys, LGBT health, antidiscrimination laws and so forth.

In SA, explicit inclusion of the nonhuman in the situation was provoked first by pragmatist philosopher George Herbert Mead's (1938, 1972) ecological framework, carefully attending to *things* in the environment/situation as fully salient *relationally/ecologically* (Cefai, 2016, p. 165), and sustained in critical interactionism (Clarke, 2019).

Researchers in sexuality studies routinely confront widely varied situations of interest in which quite different things may matter most—and may matter *very differently* in different places and times. SA allows their detailed situated and comparative geopolitical study, for example, public health STD ads in Quebec analyzed by Gagnon and colleagues (2015), discourses about queer youth suicide analyzed by Grzanka and Mann (2014) and bisexual activism by Nutter-Pridgen (2015).

Another theoretical resource was Foucault whose centrality to sexuality studies we surely need not detail! Foucault's (1973) ideas about the tremendous import of discourses in the generation of selves and social worlds demanded the inclusion of discourses in SA as agentic nonhuman elements. A situation typically includes multiple and competing discourses, *all analyzed in SA*. Foucault's work contributes especially to positional maps in which positions taken and *not taken* in specific discourses found in the situation under study are analyzed, helping silences to speak.

Deleuze and Guattari (1987) contributed concepts of rhizomes and assemblages as modes of relationality: "The rhizome pertains to a map that must be produced, constructed, a map that is always detachable, connectable, reversible, modifiable, and has multiple entryways and exits and its own lines of flight" (p. 21). Their concept of assemblage similarly draws together heterogeneous entities in dynamic, fluid relations. These two concepts undergird the messy maps of the situation.

Anselm Strauss's (1978, 1993) social worlds and arenas theory inspired the inclusion of social worlds and arenas maps in SA to examine the collective actors in the situation and their interrelations. *Social worlds* are groups—collectivities—of various kinds through which people organize, becoming committed to act. *Arenas* of shared concern where multiple social worlds meet are commonly associated with conflict and contestation. Social worlds and arenas serve as units of conflict analysis in SA (Clarke et al., 2018, pp. 61–76).

Last but far from least, SA had feminist inspirations. Clarke's (e.g., 1998) work in reproductive rights and contraception provided insights. Donna Haraway's (1991) classic paper on "Situated Knowledges" offers a feminist analysis of how situations matter in the production of knowledge of *all* kinds, including the embodiment of the knower.

The late Susan Leigh Star's (1995) critical feminist and antiracist ecologies of knowledge draw on the pragmatist concept of "an ecosystem, and equally important all the components that constitute the system" (p. 2), examining interrelationships among them, and listening especially to those at the margins. Her key question was: "*Cui bono?*" (Who benefits?; Bowker et al., 2015). All these theoretical strands are braided together as foundational to doing SA research.

SA Strategies for Mapping the Situation

Doing SA involves making and analytically memoing four different kinds of maps. SA method is wide open to using all kinds of empirical materials to generate these maps: interviews, ethnographic notes and documents collected in the situation. Moreover, SA encourages including extant discourse materials found in the situation—narrative, visual and/or historical—from websites to archives. As more empirical materials are generated and gathered, all the maps are revisited, revised and reanalyzed across the life of the research project.

Messy maps focus *on empirically detailing precisely what elements are in the broader situation.* These may include humans, nonhuman things, animals, technologies, organizations, institutions, natural resources, political economic elements, social and cultural events and traditions, particular visuals, cultural phenomena, spatial and temporal issues, popular and other discourses pertinent to the situation, symbolic elements, contested elements, discursive constructions of actors in the situation and so forth. Preliminary situational maps are especially useful in *research design* (Clarke et al., 2018, pp. 110–23). Specifying precisely *how* specific elements matter, their relative power and so on happens downstream in the research process.

Messy maps are then used to make the second kind of map, relational maps. Here the analyst draws lines between one element and all the other elements, working one by one, and asking: *"What is the nature of the relationship between these two elements?"* Gradually, and very systematically, key relationships among elements are specified and analyzed in memos. Relationships in need of greater specificity are noted and further data are gathered about them, densifying the *relational analysis.* Exemplars in sexuality studies include Barcelos (2014, 2018) and Martin and colleagues (2016).

Third is the *social worlds/arenas map that frames the social worlds, organizational and institutional structures and their interrelations in the broader arenas of commitment in the situation. Collectivities in the situation are social worlds committed to social action in one or more arenas of concern. The analyst(s) usually generates one social worlds/arenas map for the project, refining it through analyzing new data. Most methods of qualitative inquiry simply do not attend to collective social, organizational and institutional aspects* of the situation, but they are fundamental to critical research and hence to SA. One example is the aforementioned work of Martin and colleagues (2016).

The fourth and last maps in SA are *positional maps of discourses.* In any situation, there are a number of contested or debated issues, and positional maps analyze them. Positional maps lay out the full range of *positions articulated in the data.* Moreover, positional maps also allow the analyst to specify *positions not taken* in the materials and to determine whether there are *implicated actors* in the situation (an analysis of power discussed below). SA researchers commonly do a number of positional maps addressing all the major contested issues (exemplars include Barcelos, 2014; Salazar-Torres and Öhman, 2015). Some SA sexuality studies also focus on discourse analysis (e.g., Barcelos, 2014, 2018; Gagnon Jacob & Holmes, 2015; Nutter-Pridgen, 2015).

In sum, SA extends Straussian and constructivist GT to take poststructural and interpretive turns into account, shifting the focus from action to the situation and mapping and analyzing relationalities of multiple kinds in that situation.

Distinctive Affordances of SA for Glocal Sexuality Studies

The useful concept of "affordances" (Gibson, 1986; Hammond, 2010) draws attention to the opportunities and resources offered and the constraints confronted by engaging with some phenomenon. The concept allows us to "focus on possibilities for action" (Hammond, 2010, p. 205) in ways similar to Foucault's (1973) concept of "conditions of possibility." Here we address a range of distinctive affordances of SA useful in critical sexuality studies.

Attentiveness to Differences, Marginalities and "Epistemic Diversity"

Most social science research relentlessly seeks "commonalities" and "simplifications" while evading and avoiding "differences" and "contradictions"—the "mess" of actual social life (Law, 2004). Variation is even called "noise" or "dirty data." In contrast, SA views grasping variation as fundamental.

The inclination of social science toward simplification also tends to produce "discrete" categories or objects of analysis. SA instead explores imbrications, complex power relations and partialities. This foregrounds SA's usefulness for varied engagements that trouble the binary of "global" and "local," including transnational feminist accounts of sexuality. As such, SA attunes to sexualities' inextricability from processes, histories and formations of race, gender, ability, nationality, indigeneity and other phenomena (e.g., Barcelos, 2018; Hanssmann, 2017).

SA emerged in part from feminisms, antiracisms and related commitments to social justice toward creating a more *explicitly critical approach* that not only does not erase or paper over differences but also actively seeks to engage, name and address them (e.g., Clarke & Keller, 2014). SA *actively* seeks to make differences legible, to help silences speak—silences of resistance, protection, co-optation and collusion.

To engage and specify differences in SA, we include the broadest range of variation within our data sources. Indeed, with Deleuze and Guattari (1983) we encourage beginning SA discourse analyses from the margins, pursuing "minor" discourses seeking to present a different voice, to affirm *alternative and critical* readings of "the situation" and to articulate *means of changing that situation* (Clarke et al., 2018, pp. 225–227).

SA mapping also enhances the visibility of *epistemic diversity* (Anderson, 2006) via explicit recognition that different "ways of knowing" or "local epistemologies" may well be lively in the situation. Careful representation of epistemic diversity is requisite for decolonizing, transnational feminist, indigenous and (post)colonial research. Diverse ways of knowing are also highly characteristic of communities centered around nonnormative sexualities.

Distinctive Power Analytics

SA offers distinctive tools for analyzing how subjugation, power and inequities differentially affect individuals, groups and categories of people. Analyzing power—forms of domination, subordination and injustice—is especially important. First, social worlds/ arenas maps of the broader situation facilitate analysis of the collective, organizational and institutional elements in the situation and their relative power, thereby providing a "big picture" of extant hierarchies and usually quite stratified "conditions of possibility." These maps detail *collective* conflict and contestation, the arenas in which it is occurring, linkages with other worlds and arenas and so on. Such rare structural portraits that limn social conflict and sites of potential social change are requisite in critical sexuality studies.

Second, SA analyses seek to specify whether there are *implicated actors* in the situation, actors who are *discursively* constructed by other actors with greater power in that situation for their (these *other* actors') own purposes (Clarke et al., 2018, pp. 76–77). Implicated actors may be human or nonhuman, physically present but silenced or solely discursively present. Regardless, they are *not* allowed self-representation. A classic example is constructions of women as users of contraception generated by developers of contraceptive technologies—for example, "one-size-fits-all" claims about the pill, IUDs, condoms, injectables such as Depo-Provera and so on (Clarke, 1998). Analyzing precisely *how and for what purposes* implicated actors are discursively constructed by others, and *the consequences of those constructions for the implicated actors* as well as for those who construct them, provide SA with distinctively critical tools for grasping subtle and blatant uses of power and their consequences.

Third, Star (2010) and Star and Griesemer (1989) developed the concept of *boundary objects* as entities that exist at junctures where varied social worlds meet in an arena of mutual concern. In sexuality studies, boundary objects might be the green scarf worn by activists supporting abortion in South America (Dicenta, 2019); laws about anti-LGBT discrimination in housing or employment; even concepts themselves as they travel across disciplines (Bal, 2009). The boundary object must be "translated" to address the specific demands placed upon it by the different worlds involved, while retaining sufficient identity to remain recognizable across those worlds. Boundary objects are often key issues for many worlds involved in an arena, often sites of intense controversy and competition for the power to define and use them. This makes them excellent sites for analytic entrée and critical power analysis (Bowker, Timmermans, Clarke, & Balka, 2015).

Collaborative Capacities for Participatory, Decolonizing and Related Research

Critical research, especially but not only when exploring or implementing sexuality policy change, increasingly draws upon more collaborative strategies of research participation to assure more useful outcomes in "the real world." Both constructivist GT and SA offer excellent capacities for feminist, participatory, decolonizing, Indigenous, (post) colonial and related research for two primary reasons.

First, both are *radically empirically* open, usable in heterogeneous research settings. Rather than preconfiguring what matters, both allow the foregrounding of elements and issues salient to the situation of inquiry *as identified by researchers and participants and in extant discourse materials* (Charmaz, Thornberg, & Keane, 2017). Both are fiercely *situated* (Haraway, 1991). In SA, the *situation* can be featured, allowing a distinctive *research setting* to take center stage.

Second, both GT coding and SA mapmaking and analysis can easily be undertaken collaboratively, demonstrated for many years in the "working group" format of doing GT research (Wiener, 2007), now extended to SA. Distinctively, SA maps and mapmaking provoke intense engagement. Maps operate as "incitements to discourse" (Foucault, 1973), pushy lift-off devices raising the level and intensity of interaction—urging people to question, discuss, clarify and keep on analyzing. Research teams note the usefulness of maps in organizing work sessions and deepening collaborative analysis (Clarke et al., 2015, pp. 234–40, 314–22, 285–91).

Conclusions: Sexualities and Relationalities

In sum, SA offers strong, flexible tools for critical, feminist, participatory, decolonizing, (post)colonial and related research on sexualities precisely because SA mapping *empirically specifies the situation*. The mess, differences and complexities that SA intentionally engages are everywhere with us glocally. Such knowledge can be crucial in creating effective democratizing interventions to promote social justice vis-à-vis access to sexual literacy and safety in varied sexual practices. SA not only tolerates the messy complexities and relationalities of life but also relishes and succeeds in describing, engaging and analyzing them (e.g., Clarke with Keller, 2014).

Each SA map focuses on analyzing different *relationalities* that may inhabit varied sexuality studies. Situational and relational maps portray relations among any and all of the elements in the situation. Social worlds/arenas maps portray relations within and between social worlds and within and between arenas. Positional maps portray relations among contested issues in the situation's discourses and positions taken and not taken on those issues. Thus, SA analyzes conflictful processes and contingencies by focusing on complexities and relationalities. Last, SA offers a range of affordances including analytics of power and capacities for collaboration. This is why we believe that SA is a distinctively powerful and useful research method for the highly important and highly heterogeneous field of endeavors collapsed into the shorthand critical sexuality studies.

References

Anderson, E. (2006). The epistemology of democracy. *Episteme: A Journal of Social Epistemology*, *3*(1–2), 8–22.

Bal, M. (2009). Working with concepts. *European Journal of English Studies*, *13*(1), 13–23.

Barcelos, C. (2014). Producing (potentially) pregnant teen bodies: Biopower and adolescent pregnancy in the USA. *Critical Public Health*, *24*(4), 476–488.

Barcelos, C. (2018). Culture, contraception, and colorblindness: Youth sexual health promotion as a gendered racial project. *Gender & Society*, *32*(2), 252–273.

Bowker, G., Timmermans, S., Clarke, A. E., & Balka, E. (Eds.). (2015). *Boundary objects and beyond: Working with Susan Leigh Star*. Cambridge, MA: MIT Press.

Cefaï, D. (2016). Social worlds: The legacy of Mead's social ecology in Chicago sociology. In H. Joas & D. Huebner (Eds.), *The timeliness of G. H. Mead* (pp. 164–184). Chicago: University of Chicago Press.

Charmaz, K. (2014). *Constructing grounded theory: A practical guide through qualitative analysis* (2nd ed.). London: Sage.

Charmaz, K., Thornberg, R., & Keane, E. (2017). Evolving grounded theory and social justice inquiry. In N. K. Denzin & Y. E. Lincoln (Eds.), *Handbook of qualitative research* (5th ed., pp. 411–443). Thousand Oaks, CA: Sage.

Clarke, A. E. (1998). *Disciplining reproduction: Modernity, American life sciences and the "problem of sex."* Berkeley: University of California Press.

Clarke, A. E. (2005). *Situational analysis: Grounded theory after the postmodern turn.* Thousand Oaks, CA: Sage.

Clarke, A. E. (2019). Situational analysis: A critical interactionist method. In M. H. Jacobsen (Ed.), *Critical and cultural interactionism* (pp. 189–209). London: Routledge.

Clarke, A. E., Friese, C., & Washburn, R. (Eds.). (2015). *Situational analysis in practice: Mapping with grounded theory.* London: Routledge.

Clarke, A. E., Friese, C., & Washburn, R. (2018). *Situational analysis: Grounded theory after the interpretive turn* (2nd ed.). Thousand Oaks, CA: Sage. Companion website: https://study.sagepub.com/clarke2e

Clarke, A. E., in conversation with Keller, R. (2014). Engaging complexities: Working against simplification as an agenda for qualitative research today. *FQS Forum: Qualitative Social Research, 15*(2) [online journal].

Deleuze, G., & Guattari, F. (1983). What is a minor literature? R. Brinkley (Ed.), *Mississippi Review, 11*(3), 13–33.

Deleuze, G., & Guattari, F. (1987). Introduction: Rhizome. In *A thousand plateaus: Capitalism and schizophrenia II* (B. Massumi, Trans., pp. 3–25). Minneapolis: University of Minnesota Press.

Dicenta, M. (2019, March 13). The abortion green scarf as a boundary object: Beyond the curse of the left. *Somatosphere.* Retrieved October 31, 2019, from http://somatosphere.net/2019/the-abortion-green-scarf-as-a-boundary-object-beyond-the-curse-of-the-left.html/

Foucault, M. (1973). *The order of things: An archeology of the human sciences.* New York: Vintage/Random House.

Gagnon, M., Jacob, J.-D., & Holmes, D. (2015). Governing through (in)security: A critical analysis of a fear-based public health campaign. In A. E. Clarke, C. Friese & R. Washburn (Eds.), *Situational analysis in practice: Mapping research with grounded theory* (pp. 270–284). London: Routledge.

Gibson, J. (1986). *The ecological approach to visual perception.* New York: Lawrence Erlbaum.

Glaser, B., & Strauss, A. (1967). *The discovery of grounded theory.* Chicago: Aldine.

Grzanka, P., & Mann, E. S. (2014). Queer youth suicide and the psychopolitics of "It gets better." *Sexualities, 17*(4), 369–393.

Hammond, M. (2010). What is an affordance and can it help us understand the use of ICT in education? *Education and Information Technologies, 15,* 205–217. https://doi.org/10.1007/s10639-009-9106-z

Hanssmann, C. (2017). *Care in transit: The political and clinical emergence of trans health* (Doctoral dissertation). University of California, San Francisco. Retrieved from https://escholarship.org/uc/item/4j2639zb

Haraway, D. (1991). Situated knowledges: The science question in feminism and the privilege of partial perspectives. In D. Haraway (Ed.), *Simians, cyborgs, and women: The reinvention of nature* (pp. 183–202). New York: Routledge.

Latour, B., & Woolgar, S. (1979). *Laboratory life: The social construction of scientific facts.* Beverley Hills, CA: Sage.

Law, J. (2004). *After method: Mess in social science research.* London: Routledge.

Martin, W., Pauly, B., & MacDonald, M. (2016). Situational analysis for complex systems: Methodological development in public health research. *AIMS Public Health, 3*(1), 94–109.

Mead, G. H. (1938). The philosophy of the act. In C. W. Morris (Ed.), *The philosophy of the act.* Chicago: University of Chicago Press.

Mead, G. H. (1972). The philosophy of the act. In C. W. Morris (Ed.), *The philosophy of the act* (2nd ed.). Chicago: University of Chicago Press.

Nutter-Pridgen, K. L. (2015). The old, the new, and the redefined: Identifying the discourses in contemporary bisexual activism. *Journal of Bisexuality, 15*(3), 383–413.

Salazar-Torres, V. M., & Öhman, A. (2015). Negotiating masculinity, violence, and responsibility: A situational analysis of young Nicaraguan men's discourses on intimate partner and sexual violence. *Journal of Aggression, Maltreatment & Trauma, 24*(2), 131–149.

Star, S. L. (Ed.) (1995). *Ecologies of knowledge: New directions in the sociology of science and technology.* Albany: State University of New York Press.

Star, S. L. (2010). This is not a boundary object: Reflections on the origin of a concept. *Science, Technology, & Human Values, 35*, 601–617.

Strauss, A. L. (1978). A social world's perspective. *Studies in Symbolic Interaction, 1*, 119–128.

Strauss, A. L. (1993). *Continual permutations of action.* New York: Aldine de Gruyter.

Wiener, C. (2007). Making teams work in conducting grounded theory. In A. Bryant & K. Charmaz (Eds.), *Handbook of grounded theory* (pp. 293–310). London: Sage.

Chapter 4

DISPELLING THE MYTHS ABOUT SEXUALITY EDUCATION

Hon. Helen Clark

All girls and boys—and all women and men, for that matter—can benefit from comprehensive knowledge about safe sexual behavior. Yet opposition to sexuality education is loud, persistent and widespread, often because critics lack an accurate understanding of what it entails.

NEW YORK—Sexuality education empowers people to make informed choices about their own bodies and sexuality—and to stay safe in the process. It is therefore an essential element of a quality education. Yet, far from promoting comprehensive sexuality education, many are fighting to limit it. The consequences—especially for young people—are serious, lasting and sometimes deadly.

As "Facing the Facts," a new policy paper by UNESCO's Global Education Monitoring Report, reminds us, each year some 16 million girls aged 15–19 (and two million under 15) give birth—a development that often marks the end of their formal education. Another three million girls aged 15–19 undergo unsafe abortions each year.

These numbers are linked to a lack of education about sex, sexuality and the human body. For example, in the Islamic Republic of Iran, according to WaterAid, around one-half of girls think that menstruation is a disease. In Afghanistan, 51 percent of girls know nothing about menstruation before experiencing it themselves. In Malawi, that figure jumps to 82 percent. If girls—let alone boys—do not know what menstruation is, how can they possibly be expected to protect themselves against unwanted pregnancy?

The same goes for sexually transmitted infections like HIV. Young people aged 15–24 account for one-third of new HIV infections among adults. This is partly because only one-third of young women in most low- and middle-income countries know how to prevent the transmission of the virus.

But, contrary to popular belief, sexuality education is not just about sex. As "Facing the Facts" highlights, it also includes lessons about families and social relationships. These can benefit children as young as 5, not least by enabling them to differentiate between appropriate physical contact and abuse.

Moreover, sexuality education offers important lessons about gender dynamics, including issues such as consent, coercion and violence. Some 120 million girls worldwide—slightly more than one in 10—have experienced forced intercourse, forced sexual acts or other forms of intimate partner violence at some point in their lives. This helps to explain why violence is the second leading cause of death among adolescent girls globally.

Comprehensive sexuality education can go some way toward countering the warped messages about masculinity that encourage male sexual dominance and so often lead to exploitation and violence. It can also assist in breaking the silence on such experiences among victims, potentially inspiring them to seek help.

All girls and boys—and all women and men, for that matter—can benefit from comprehensive knowledge about safe sexual behavior. Yet opposition to sexuality education is loud, persistent and widespread. Some call for it to be banned outright. Others insist that schools should teach only abstinence, despite evidence showing that such programs often provide medically inaccurate information.

Like critics of LGBTQI+ education, opponents of comprehensive sexuality education seek to justify their stance on cultural, religious, social or even political grounds. But, whatever the apparent motivation, their opposition often reflects a lack of knowledge about what such education entails. Improving the public's understanding of sexuality education could therefore help to neutralize the negative hype and open the way for more young people to benefit.

Leaders worldwide must stand up for comprehensive sexuality education, by touting its clear, evidence-based benefits and dispelling harmful myths. An informed news media and advocacy by civil-society groups must also contribute to this process. With accurate information, the public is far more likely to accept sexuality education.

But for such education to be meaningful, it must be of high quality. Teachers must therefore be given the knowledge, resources and, thus, confidence they need to teach these lessons effectively. Scripted lessons, like those introduced in Namibia and Chile, or online resources for teachers, as Tanzania provides, can go a long way toward fulfilling that need.

Furthermore, sexuality education should ideally be provided as a standalone program, rather than integrated into other subjects (a common practice that diminishes its impact). And it must be complemented by widely accessible, youth-friendly sexual and reproductive health services.

It is time to face the facts: humans have sex, often long before they reach adulthood. And it is immoral—perverse, even—to withhold potentially life-saving information from young people. After all, knowledge is power. By giving today's youth, and girls in particular, a better understanding of their bodies, we can give them the power to protect their health—and their futures.

Chapter 5

ADVOCATING BLACK SEXUAL LITERACY IN U.S. SEXUALITY EDUCATION EFFORTS

Jermisha J. Frazier

I talk about sex all the time. I'm a poet.

But in certain spaces I try not to show it.

It's so frowned upon to say, "I love to fuck."

I mention that sexuality is fluid, and everyone says "that's enough"

I open my mouth, and I'm immediately told hush!

"Here goes Misha on that white people shit, you know that's not for us"

"God made Adam and Eve, not Adam and Steve or Eve and Kesha"

I told my Grandma I think I like girls and she pointed me to the preacher

"Let's pray that gay away!

Don't you want to make it to heaven one day?!"

I'm over it. I'm pretty sure God loves me anyway

Can't continue to pass on the negative attitudes I was taught.

Dismantling systemic oppression is a place to start

Let me unlearn the things I was conditioned to believe

Do a little unpacking to reveal a few keys

To understanding the root of these negative views in my community

Other races can openly do "freak shit" why are we forced into immunity?

Because Black people have to be "so much better"

Got my girl embarrassed about asking strategies to get my pussy wetter.

Herpes running rapid, but we can't have a conversation

Because Lord knows if you admit you have it, you run the risk of isolation.

Ostracizing members of our nation

Causing so much suicidal ideation.

Continually misinforming generations.

How can we grow?

What comfortable spaces do we have to discuss what we think we know?

I grew up under the impression that if I wasn't getting wet then my pussy was broke

Sex education classes in grade school are a joke.

I remember mine was taught by my coach.

The old white man told me if I had sex, I was guaranteed to make a baby

Another white woman told me erectile dysfunction occurred because women are lazy.

The false information we pass down genuinely amazes me.

It's crazy the shit we choose to believe.

But I'll break the curse

Demonstrating that the pursuit of liberation is worth-

The headaches, uncomfortable conversations, and odd looks.

It's worth challenging what we read in history books.

I'm telling you, THIS IS OUR BATTLE.

Cultural representation matters.

And if I want to wave my freak flag proud,

I must not only encourage others, but also be an example of fearlessly living out loud.[1]

In 2006, my sex education teacher told me that I should not have sex until after I married my husband. This was particularly interesting to me especially since I was developing romantic attractions to women. This absence led me to believe lesbians were not considered valuable enough to be discussed. My gym coach and health teacher taught me that if I had sex, I would either get pregnant or a sexually transmitted infection (STI) because our curriculum demonized individuals with incurable STIs by declaring them dirty or unclean. I remember believing that the worst thing that could ever possibly happen as a result of sexual activity was contracting HIV or herpes. Both of the previously mentioned sex educators are White, and the content they shared was based on White cultural context that arguably dominates norms of the United States and many Western countries' approaches to secondary school sexuality education.

The problem with these one-sided approaches to sex education usually goes unseen until we examine collective attitudes toward sexuality depicted in particular communities. For example, the absence of discussions about single parenthood, same-sex attractions, or the historical hypersexualization of Black bodies leads one to believe that

---

1   SEXUALITY (a poem by Jermisha J. Frazier).

those populations are not worth mentioning or even educating. Spreading information grounded in research conducted by White researchers on predominately White subjects and claiming its relevance to the general public erases the experiences and relevance of non-White populations (Gillborn, 2006). We then go on to shape cultural scripts based on information that prioritizes Whiteness because it is all we were ever taught.

Since porn is often the first source adolescents use to learn about sex, let's explore it as an example. I have not stumbled upon the White tab on my favorite porn websites, yet people of color are fetishized and distributed into "exotic" categories such as Ebony, Latinx or Asian (Glover, 2017). Our Caucasian counterparts are not categorized because the viewer is assumed to be White and is therefore granted the privilege of perspective. People of color have been conditioned to expect White as the standard.

Black queer or questioning youth are often still not encouraged to explore, but instead forced to figure out how to navigate a world that views them as a sort of double entendre, that is, of being oversexed and uninteresting—all without much formal sex education. This lack on inclusion in formal sexuality education regarding representation and issues specific to the Black community while simultaneously bearing this conflicted interpretation as being oversexed and erased messages to Black people that our lives are not included in institutional supports via systemic racism. When will we cover the unit explaining why young Black girls are considered "too grown" [up] if they wear dresses that showcase their curves? None of my past sex educators discussed variations in contraceptive preferences between African American men and women (Thorburn, 2007). They also failed to describe the high maternal mortality rates for Black women or high postpartum mental health issues (Brinlee, 2017; Keefe, Brownstein-Evans, & Rouland Polmanteer, 2016). Is it not valuable to inform young people that Black women with certain pregnancy complications are more likely to die from those conditions than White women (Tucker, Berg, & Callaghan, 2007)? This has to change.

Professor David Takacs at the University of California, Hastings College of the Law, has described positionality as the multiple, unique experiences that situate each of us in our lived experience (2003). The opening poem situates my positionality and throughout I discuss the sex education I received as well as the sex educators I came in contact with. This is because context and positionality matter—especially in shaping what we as researchers, sexuality educators and individuals find valuable and how we progress with our own sexual literacy over our own lifetime—these are all related. As a reflexive Black scholar, I find it difficult to believe that my White teachers were intentional about sharing diverse, inclusive content, but not because they did not want to address our concerns. Rather, they were simply regurgitating what they were taught and what seemed important to them from their experience/s; the content was *normalized*. Nevertheless, critical race theory has shown us how blindly enforcing a White-centered norm in sexuality education can be a form of unintentionally upholding White supremacy (Gilborn, 2006). I join others in challenging academics and sex educators to consider evaluating how we determine what is *normal* in our formal sexuality education curricula.

The White norming of sexuality education curricula is a problem among Black people and Black sex educators alike. The questions I present above about specific sexual concerns of Black community members were inspired by actual conversations I have participated in with other Black people. By disidentifying with White-norm sexuality education efforts and considering contextual specifics when thinking through sexuality education norms as these shift from place to place, we hone our sexuality curricula. For example, we are used to speaking about methods to coach young Black girls through hypersexualized experiences they will inevitably face yet also understand that these situations differ based on geographic location in the United States and elsewhere. In my own lifetime and during my adolescence, I was forced to figure out when to be Black, when to be gay and when it was safe enough to be both in various contexts including contexts that were predominantly or totally Black—ways of being Black also shift between groups. These shifting glocal realities are often left out of curriculum because Black voices were not represented or valued. Revisiting my question about changing the course of sex education, I wonder if the answer comes in the form of culturally relevant curriculum through increased representation? Or from a fundamental reworking of how we think about constructing the topics that matter in sexuality education based on context?

A prime example of what I am talking about is found in the work of Dorothy Roberts, who in the late twentieth century highlighted Black sexuality with the release of her book *Killing the Black Body* (1997). She tackles the sterilization of poor Black women as well as the erasure of their reproductive needs from both civil rights and feminist agendas—showing sexuality educators the kinds of historical precedents that boys and girls in these communities still face (Roberts, 1997). Even decades later, her work continues to inspire advocacy for intersectional approaches to sex education.

Killing the Black Body (1997) shows the need for mirrors and windows as reflected in the form of Black sex educator representation in the classroom (Moss, 2016). Yet sexuality educators who are Black will still come into cultural differences in how the Black community discusses and avoids gender fluidity, the negative impacts of heteronormativity let alone strategies to improve sexual pleasure. The conversations on these issues in Black communities have progressed in fits-and-starts. Even the best laid curricula presented by the most informed Black sex educator may become stalled if an intersectional approach to holding both sexuality issues and racial issues are not dually prioritized. In my experience, when being Black becomes prioritized over sexuality issues in potentially productive sex ed courses conversations may turn to ridiculing nonnormative groups or be met with blatant silence. However, women such as Shamyra Howard, Shemeka Thorpe and Gabrielle Evans, of *The Minority Sex Report*, or Dr. Wendasha Jenkins Hall are creating platforms for traditionally unconventional conversations that do engage these contextual and intersectional issues with positive impact and sense of urgency toward positive future changes (Evans & Thorpe, 2020; Howard, 2020; Jenkins Hall, 2020). Shamyra Howard[2] (2020) has used her background in social work to catapult her career supporting a wide array of clients through sex and relationship therapy. She has developed a following of

---

2   Shamyra Howard is a sexologist, sex and relationship therapist, Amazon best-selling author and international speaker who was named one of the most Influential Dating Experts of 2019 by Datezie. https://www.onthegreencouch.com

almost 20,000 individuals on Instagram (Howard, 2020). *The Minority Sex Report*[3] (Evans & Thorpe, 2020) strives to provide representation in sexuality education by addressing barriers to achieving optimal sexual health as well as intersectional inequalities people of color face. Dr. Wendasha[4] (Jenkins Hall, 2020) prides herself on creating a space for honest conversations about sexuality that centers modern Black women and femmes. All consistently share information that promotes transformational thinking through a form of translational science writing that is accessible to laypersons as well as academic scholars. Their advocacy and presence ignite innovative approaches to sex education.

Academics have been exploring the impact of having diverse educators in the classroom, and it has been shown that such increased cultural representation has substantial, positive effects on all students (King, 1993, 2016). Representation is especially important when we consider supporting younger generations as they navigate an ever-changing sexual and gendered landscape. Educators interviewed by Dr. Ashley Griffin and University of Chicago doctoral candidate Hilary Tackie, in *Through Our Eyes: Perspectives and Reflections from Black Teachers* (2016), spoke highly of their role in encouraging students, especially those who look like them, and they commented:

> I think we bring history, a lot of history, and some of us have lived that history. We're not just reading it from the books. We have actually lived that history, and we're able to share that with our students, and I think help them to understand a little better that this is what it takes to be successful in this world. (p. 5)

Another educator shared, "So we can share the challenges [...] with students of color. This is what you're going to have to deal with but look at us. You can be successful. This is the focus you have to have" (Griffin & Tackie, 2016, p. 5). The lessons to sexuality education are as striking from this work as they are for teaching in Black communities in general.

In an ideal world, voices of as many communities as possible would be reflected across all areas of general curricula, and Black sex educators should contribute to/teach sex ed as standard bearers. Since sex is often viewed as a taboo topic in our everyday lives, the need for accurate and adequate information dissemination is pertinent especially in the few courses individuals are required to complete (Schnitzer & Richards, 2019). Unfortunately, ideal does not always equate to reality and, in this case, we still have some growing up to do—among sex educators generally.

Intentional cross-cultural collaboration promotes critical discourse which, in turn, may cause individuals to question the norm. Step one is initiating the conversation through advocacy. We move the needle forward by intentionally diversifying teacher

---

3 The Minority Sex Report is a space for people of color to have conversations about sexuality. It is their mission to provide representation and advocate for comprehensive sexuality education. https://theminoritysexreport.com

4 Dr. Wendasha Jenkins Hall presents engaging workshops that challenge participants to consider how the intersection of race, gender and sexuality directly influences the sexual livelihoods of women and girls of color. https://www.thesensibleexpert.co

representation *and* curriculum so that these reflect the diverse glocally informed Black communities we intend to serve. Organizations such as *The Black Teacher Project*[5] (https://www.blackteacherproject.org/), *Offor*[6] (https://www.offor.co/), *Prism*[7] (https://www.ourprism.org), *The Women of Color Sexual Health Network*[8] (http://www.wocshn.org) or *the Association of Black Sexologists and Clinicians*[9] (http://www.theabsc.com) are taking strides to help identify Black educators and share research conducted for and by Black people. It is my hope that I have moved the needle forward by reminding us that conversations on sexuality are distinctly different among Black communities in the United States and that curricula should contextualize the specific and distinct historical forces informing both our understanding of and teaching toward intentional Black sexual literacy. As a lifetime learner, I have witnessed the effects of absence of the Black experience from sexuality education curricula, and as a queer Black sexologist I will not only assist in shifting that as a representative who has lived these realities but also ask that those reading this today take up this call.

References

Brinlee, M. (2017, November 7). Race and mortality are linked and black mothers are paying the price. *Bustle*. https://www.bustle.com/p/race-maternal-mortality-are-linked-black-mothers-are-paying-the-price-3017625

Evans, G., & Thorpe, S. (2020, March 20). *The minority sex report—representation in sexuality education.* Retrieved from https://theminoritysexreport.com

Gillborn, D. (2006). Rethinking white supremacy: Who counts in "WhiteWorld." *Ethnicities, 6*(3), 318–340.

Glover, C. (2017). Sex education centers Whiteness—and it's a problem. *Wear Your Voice Magazine.* Retrieved from https://www.wearyourvoicemag.com/sex-education-centering-whiteness/

Griffin, A., & Tackie, H. (2016). Through our eyes: Perspectives and reflections from black teachers. *Education Trust,* 1–9. https://edtrust.org/resource/through-our-eyes/

Howard, S. (2020, March 20). *On the green couch with sexologist Shamyra.* Retrieved from https://www.onthegreencouch.com

Jenkins Hall, W. (2020, March 20). *The sensible sexpert.* Retrieved from https://www.thesensiblesexpert.com

---

5   The Black Teacher Project's mission is to develop and sustain Black teachers to lead and reimagine schools as communities of liberated learning. https://www.blackteacherproject.org

6   Offor is an organization that serves boards and c-suite leaders to build executive dream teams by designing culture summits for organizations to redefine talent rules. https://www.offor.co/about#services

7   Prism was established to challenge dominant and toxic national narratives by centering people closest to the problems and amplifying their ideas, experiences and solutions. https://www.ourprism.org/genderjustice

8   The Women of Color Sexual Health Network creates opportunities for inclusion and retention of people of color with a focus on women and gender-expansive people of color. http://www.wocshn.org/about/

9   The Association of Black Sexologists and Clinicians is an interdisciplinary professional organization dedicated to improving the sexual expression and lives of persons of African descent.

Keefe, R. H., Brownstein-Evans, C., & Rouland Polmanteer, R. S. (2016). Having our say: African-American and Latina mothers provide recommendations to health and mental health providers working with new mothers living with postpartum depression. *Social Work in Mental Health, 14*(5), 497–508. Retrieved from https://doi-org.ciis.idm.oclc.org/10.1080/15332985.2016.1140699

King, J. (2016). The invisible tax on teachers of color. *Washington Post.* Retrieved from https://www.washingtonpost.com/opinions/the-invisible-tax-on-black-teachers/2016/05/15/6b7bea06-16f7-11e6-aa55-670cabef46e0_story.html

King, S. (1993). The limited presence of African-American teachers. *Review of Educational Research, 63*(2), 115–149.

Moss, J. (2016, Summer). Where are all the teachers of color? *Harvard Graduate School of Education.* Retrieved from https://www.gse.harvard.edu/news/ed/16/05/where-are-all-teachers-color

Roberts, D. E. (1997). *Killing the black body: Race, reproduction, and the meaning of liberty.* New York: Vintage Books, a division of Penguin Random House LLC.

Schnitzer, P., & Richards, M. (2019, November 12). Scholar presents sex education research findings. The Justice. Retrieved from https://www.thejustice.org/article/2019/11/scholar-presents-sex-education-research-findings-brandeis

Takacs, D. (2003). How does your positionality bias your epistemology? *Thought & Action, 27,* 27–38. http://repository.uchastings.edu/faculty_scholarship/1264

Thorburn, S. (2007). Attitudes toward contraceptive methods among African-American men and women: Similarities and differences. *Women's Health Issues, 17*(1), 29–36.

Tucker, M. J., Berg, C. J., & Callaghan, W. M. (2007). The Black-White disparity in pregnancy-related mortality from 5 conditions: Differences in prevalence and case-fatality rates. *American Journal of Public Health, 97*(2), 247–251. Retrieved from https://doi-org.ciis.idm.oclc.org/10.2105/AJPH.2005.072975

Chapter 6

READING MACKINNON IN SAN FRANCISCO

Rita M. Melendez

Undergraduate students taking my "Sex, Power and Politics" class at San Francisco State University (SFSU) often sign up to hear about political sex scandals. SFSU was one of the first universities in the United States to teach courses on sexuality, starting in the early 1970s. Overall, the students at SFSU are politically engaged and aware of sexuality and gender power issues. Over the many years I have taught this class (15 plus years), I notice students love political scandals; news involving sexuality and a politician or politics is eagerly dissected and discussed. For example, students enjoyed discussing President Trump's various sexual scandals, especially the infamous Access Hollywood audio recording of him stating that he grabs women by their genitals without talking to them. While these scandals highlight important lessons regarding sexuality, I also notice that scandals remain removed from their personal sexual lives. The Trump scandal remains distant to their own lives—yet, sex, power and politics are also about interpersonal forms of power. Applying lessons regarding interpersonal and familiar aspects of sexuality is a challenging aspect of sexual literacy and often difficult for students to apply to their lives.

Interpersonal forms of power, the kind you see within relationships, are less visible but quite impactful in people's lives. Being in a relationship wherein there is unequal power, coercion or violence will have a tremendous, often very negative impact on an individual's life. For this reason, I discuss interpersonal forms of power in the first half of the semester—what interpersonal forms of power are, how to recognize them and the impact they have personally, professionally and politically. Raising awareness about personal relationships can have a huge impact on the well-being of my students' lives.

I assign Catharine MacKinnon in this first half of the class. Students read two chapters from her most recognized work, *Towards a Feminist Theory of the State* (1989). The readings consistently evoke strong reactions from students. The chapters review the ways socially constructed gender roles create a system of oppression that is inescapable. MacKinnon posits that women are socialized to sexually desire big, burly men who take control of sexual situations—make the first moves and initiate sex. She goes further to write how women are taught that being in control of sex and sexuality is unbecoming, unfeminine and unappealing to men who will like them more as sexually passive. MacKinnon is writing about a state-controlled system of oppression for women and her theory is on par with Marx's theory of class oppression. She moves from federal laws to the bedroom and she lays out a power system that is impossible to escape. She states that even when adult women consent to sex with men, they are unable to truly consent because of the system of power that invades their understanding of sex and relationships. Essentially, MacKinnon states that all heterosexual sex is akin to rape because of the unequal context in which it takes place.

MacKinnon theorizes many points that have since come to light in empirical research, for example, in Deborah Tolman's *Dilemmas of Desire* (2002), wherein she exposes how girls are left without a voice to talk about their own sexual desire. Pleasure for young girls is often not explored, leading to young girls not having control over their own sexuality. Likewise, the *#Me Too* movement has further concretized the ways that women are treated as sexual objects for the gratification of powerful men. Ronan Farrow's *Catch and Kill* (2019), for instance, documents a media system that protects men's sexual aggressions, harassments and rapes. Men in powerful positions are allowed to continue abusing women for their pleasure and without repercussion. Much like the child sexual abuse scandal in the Catholic Church, the American capitalist system covered up and deflected abuse allegations to protect those deemed worth protecting—those creating profits such as Matt Lauer and Harvey Weinstein. In Farrow's book, women act as MacKinnon predicted. Women felt their experiences were the norm. They felt they needed to succumb to abuse to protect their livelihood and their physical well-being. They felt that the men who had abused them were more powerful than them. And, they felt voiceless and alone.

Nonetheless, despite these connections between MacKinnon's classical text and today, MacKinnon's thesis is still a hard pill to swallow for students. The overwhelming sentiment I see in class discussions is anger. Some are angry *at* MacKinnon and some are angry *at what she is pointing out*.

Students who are angry *at* MacKinnon are in the minority. These students tend to be divided between men and women. Some men who read MacKinnon understand her as someone spreading vicious misinformation about men. One of the students[1] writes: "I didn't know this class focused so much on hating men." He went on:

> There might be a lack of respect for women, but not to the extent MacKinnon proposed in her book. She made it seem like all men are pigs, all women are victims, and everything is rape. This week's readings are ridiculously one-sided.

This student's sentiments on MacKinnon open up a lot of contemporary power issues. First is the emphasis on men's behaviors with regard to sex—but second and most important is the emphasis on rape. As MacKinnon theorizes, it is impossible for heterosexual couples to escape the dominance that men have over women, thereby making traditional gender norms part and parcel of rape and the system of rape in which heterosexual relationships take place.

---

1 I slightly alter the writings of the students to protect their anonymity. The meaning of what they wrote remains intact.

The anger expressed by some male students may come from several diverse sources. One is that their typical actions with regard to sexuality have been exposed as being part of an old gender system that promotes their sexual satisfaction over the satisfaction of their female partners. Their social norms have just been called out to them as rape. Another reason for anger at MacKinnon may stem from the unclear social/gender roles that young men engage with. Men are caught between two gender roles: old gendered expectations and new emerging roles. Traditional gender roles emphasize the importance of sex and how sex with women is a way of men gaining acceptance and status in their world. Emerging gender roles however emphasize being passive with regard to sexual encounters, letting women make the first move. Nevertheless, these emerging gender roles may not always be successful for men—they are caught between two shifting gender plates—that of waiting versus pursuing.

Women also express anger at MacKinnon. One student who was a victim of sexual violence wrote me an e-mail during the MacKinnon segment: "Rape, rape, rape, rape, when are we going to stop talking about rape?" I urged her to take steps to care for herself over completing the readings that made her remember past traumas. In speaking to her, we discussed the importance of discussing rape and sexual assault to other students who have little knowledge of it. Discussing aspects of rape can thus help highlight alternative ways of taking control over women's sexuality—of having a sexuality that belongs to women and not to the men they are having sex with. My students understood this and said that women often see forced sexual encounters as "normal." However, it was difficult for this student to read the pessimism in MacKinnon. In this reading, there is no way of escaping heterosexual power imbalances and finding agency in your body and relationships.

But, by contrast to these students, the great majority of the class expressed anger over *what* MacKinnon writes. Students' anger stems from their agreement with MacKinnon. One student who fits into this category states:

> This week's readings were very disturbing and frustrating. The dominance of a man raping a woman would definitely instill fear into the women and thus is the reason why women do not speak up. However, there are millions of rape victims in the world. It is shocking how common it is for none of them to speak up. Women deserve to speak their voice and address these issues without having the need of fearing for their life or fearing that something bad will come back to haunt them in the future.

Other students find ways of applying MacKinnon to their lives especially as it relates to issues of race and ethnicity. One student applies MacKinnon to Latino culture she comes from:

> It's very sad but this reading is the reality of what women go through. Women are displayed as weak and controlled by men. Being Latina, I see this in a lot of my culture. "Machismo" is what a man is "supposed" to have. I was raised by a single mother. She taught me the opposite of my culture and showed me how to stand up for myself and speak my mind. Growing up, I feel like shows or movies show how men had as the dominators taking charge while women would just try to please them.

The following student applying MacKinnon to her work at a fitness center, states:

> This week's material has been very heavy, but also I am glad that I did this reading because now I am able to use correct language with the things I come in to contact with. An example is: I work at a gym [...] these men and sometimes women think they can say any obscure remark that pops into their head to whoever they want. They think it should be met with gratitude, when the other person feels uncomfortable, they overcompensate and call the women names and harass her. It shows that they have been taught that women exist for them and they feed into it to a point that makes women feel unsafe. The article written by McKinnon gave me insight to what concept is really taking place here.

Some students seem to take MacKinnon and be angry by what she is saying but also find ways to take what she is saying and applying it to their future selves; one student states:

> It is frustrating navigating our lives when we are constantly belittled and talked down upon. You are "on point" when you reiterate what MacKinnon talks about with regard to how rape and sexuality is defined by men. It bugs me how much we [women] are unfairly treated and expected to "smile" and not fight back. I just want my life and sexuality to be mine and mine alone. Because at the end of the day, I am the one in this body and I am the only one who should be making decisions.

This final student's reaction to MacKinnon seems to bring up the anger that the *#Me Too* movement ignited—the anger at being expected to remain quiet—the incitement to speak out—and of demanding punishment for abusers. She takes with her, from this reading, the understanding that she has right over her body and her sexuality.

MacKinnon's theory and readings have been useful over the years. But I find it challenging to balance the message MacKinnon gives with the emotions she elicits. The following student, for example, offers this:

> This week's readings were sobering. Although, I found many of Mackinnon's claims to be unsupported generalizations, the underlying argument is still important. Today almost every woman has been the victim of some kind of sexual assault or harassment by the time they reach adulthood. This is our reality and it is extremely problematic. However, this problem will not be solved if we continue to rely on oversimplifications rather than proven fact. All men are not to be blamed for the actions of some. To do so only continues to magnify the issue and creates increasing polarization. I do believe that women are disproportionately affected by sexual offenses in comparison to men, however they are not the only ones affected. Although I do agree with the overall argument of this week's readings, I found there to be some difficult generalizations that tended to portray all women as victims and all men as the offenders.

As a teacher, I struggle with the range and depth of emotions raised by this reading. MacKinnon's work from 1989 is similar to what today is termed *rape culture*—norms that make women's sexual autonomy, choice and pleasure secondary to men's. While MacKinnon offers great insight into values surrounding sexuality and gender roles, her reading invokes strong reactions in students. The reading and my student's reactions to the reading highlight important issues about teaching sexual literacy. Sexual literacy is not only about political and social events but also relate to our most intimate relationships. These readings touch very vulnerable areas of how students relate to others and how they have been perceived by others in their everyday lives. The students' reactions to the reading often make me question myself, my teaching method and my class. I have thought about removing the reading and sticking to readings that do not bring up such reactions. However, I think for the majority of my students, MacKinnon's reading remains one that provides a new but often difficult viewpoint on their lives and sexuality. Sexual literacy is uncomfortable and difficult. It brings up issues that have been festering in students: sometimes a defensive reaction to current gender politics, sometimes anger over issues of sexual violence that are personal and sometimes harassments that occur daily. While I cannot control students' reactions, I can control the tone and the purpose of the class—the slow and steady movement toward personal awareness around issues of sexuality.

References

Farrow, R. (2019). *Catch and kill: Lies, spies, and a conspiracy to protect predators*. New York: Little, Brown.

MacKinnon, C. A. (1989). *Toward a feminist theory of the state*. Cambridge, MA: Harvard University Press.

Tolman, D. L. (2002). *Dilemmas of desire: Teenage girls talk about sexuality*. Cambridge, MA: Harvard University Press.

Chapter 7

ARGUING FOR SEXUAL LITERACY IN FIELDWORK PREPARATION

Jerika Loren Heinze

Sexual harassment, gendered violence and sexual assault are far-reaching challenges that impact researchers as well as professors in higher education, especially now in the MeToo era. Still largely in the peripheries are the more nuanced experiences of researchers working in the field. Fieldwork denotes hands-on data collection or research administered in a natural environment or real-world context rather than in a controlled setting like a lab or archive. It is an approach to empirical data collected originating in the discipline of anthropology but is now used across many disciplines and fields. Fieldwork often takes place in glocal settings in which a researcher strives to experience local context amidst larger global entanglements (Appadurai, 2008).

In 2018, I conceived and began the Fieldwork Initiative, a grassroots organization focusing specifically on trainings and research around sexual harassment and gendered violence during research fieldwork mainly in anthropology departments but also with other academic programs. Our Fieldwork Initiative to Stop Sexualized Trauma (FISST) training (Heinze, 2020) is a seminar that prepares students for the possibility of gendered violence during their research fieldwork. The training includes safety strategies and is substantiated by input from survivors of fieldwork violence—information that they wish they would have had before entering the field.

Drawing on my experiences and connected research in leading this institute, this essay explores some key insights on how sexual literacy training among fieldworkers may assist them and makes a broader argument for why explicit trainings on this issue are needed for researchers using fieldwork as a means for gathering data (Kloss, 2016; Richards & Hanson, 2019; Schneider, 2020). My position is that there is engrained institutional resistance to changing or responding to the trauma and sexual violence faced by non-White, nonmale, non-cisgender, nonheterosexual (non-WMCH) researchers. This is evidenced in the field by a general lack of mandatory pre-fieldwork trainings that educate people on how to protect themselves from sexually based harassments and traumas and an absence of trainings that center sexual literacy as a means of empowerment (Cai, 2019; Thambiah, Chakraborty, & Sarker, 2016). Even when presented with trainings created by victims of sexual harassment, such as the FISST training we conduct through the Fieldwork Initiative, most anthropology departments have shied away from engaging in such conversations. This serves as case that points to the ways in which anthropology as a discipline has consciously ignored (whether based on outright or unconscious bias) the traumatic situations researchers face in relation to gender, sexuality and violence. Thus, while anthropologists and social scientists more generally examine power structures as core pursuits (Britton, 2017; Wolf, 1993), a common and contradictory practice is that they erase the inherent power structures of gender within research protocols, while field-work privilege remains unaddressed and understudied. As such, sexual literacy has been willfully kept out of fieldwork preparation.

Maintaining Sexual Illiteracy in Fieldwork

While anthropology spends a great deal of energy on theoretical and methodo-logical pedagogy before deeming students ready to embark on fieldwork, the lack of standardized sexual harassment training for fieldwork is startling, given the fact that 72.4 percent of researchers have been directly privy to sexually inappropriate conduct in the field (Clancy, Nelson, Rutherford, & Hinde, 2014). Sexual violence in research field-work has been evidenced in the academic literature since the early twentieth century and has been common among non-WMCH researchers since their entry into the practice of fieldwork (Easterday, Papademas, Schorr, & Valentine, 1977; Green, Barbour, Barnard, & Kitzinger, 1993; Steffen, 2017). These experiences are most predominant among graduate students, early career and junior academics (Gifford & Hall-Clifford, 2008).

While secrecy or denial of this problem is encouraged through well-known examples of victim blaming, alienating or retaliation against those who come forward with reports of rape or sexual intimidation and harassment, seasoned professors and dissertation students alike are often aware of violent happenings that can take place during field-work (Armstrong, Gleckman-Krut, & Johnson, 2018). In my experience working in this area, gendered violence against non-WMCH researchers is frequently commented on in the form of jest. Some academics, advisors and principal investigators (PIs) who run grant-funded studies have been known to make jokes about researchers getting marriage proposals or being highly sought after in their field sites. Such "jokes" are often shared in public forums like conferences and departmental meetings and met with jovial laughter. More privately though, advisors might vaguely suggest that non-WMCH researchers should wear a wedding ring in the field to avoid unwanted advances or do other things like ensure they find a roommate in the field as to not be alone at night.

Further, wearing a "fake" wedding ring in the field has long been suggested as the sole safety measure researchers could take, so commonplace it now occupies the place of tradition in fieldwork (Daubenmier, 2008; Marti, 2016; Weston & Djohari, 2020). This is problematic because it assumes that if a woman presents herself symbolically belonging to another man, they will be considered "off-limits." It not also condones the reality that harassers are more likely to show respect to a hypothetical man than a woman doing fieldwork but also ignores the reality that cisgender men do experience rape and sexual harassment. Adding to this, the practice is inherently heterosexist in the sense that it asks queer researchers to engage in performative heteronormativity for the purpose of false safety, which can take a great personal toll on the individual's sense of self (La Pastina, 2006).

In "Field of Screams," Amy Pollard documents the many occurrences of violence and a spectrum of trauma among doctoral studies in anthropology, noting "PhD students should be prepared for a wide range of difficulties in the field [...] a significant number may face difficulties that they never anticipated, and which no academic examination will have tested their ability to cope with" (2009, pp. 1–2). These findings substantiated not only the extensive prevalence of gendered and sexual violence in fieldwork but also the need for adequate preparation and support. The notion that sexual literacy training leads to safer outcomes and increased individual agency is bolstered by a body of research that indicates such education not only promotes sexual health but is also an important tool against sexual violence since such knowledge elevates confidence in boundary setting (Braeken & Cardinal, 2008; Weinstein, Walsh, & Ward, 2008).

Indeed, anthropology remains benighted to the pervasive threat of sexual violence facing researchers in the field, yet great insight can be gained from understanding that these issues go beyond seeking just trainings as direct remedy (Cai, 2019; Hanson & Richards, 2017; Rinkus, Kelly, Wright, Medina, & Dobson, 2018; Ross, 2015). The implications of grappling with these issues in fieldwork and more broadly across research practices in academia are far reaching and stand as a potential threat to the domain itself. Institutional reluctance to accept the need for sexual literacy in pre-fieldwork education modules rests on admitting such a need affirms (1) fieldwork standards are based on historical outcomes that favored exclusively cis White male elites (Sundburg, 2003); (2) its processes are inherently flawed and inequitable for non-WMCH researchers; and (3) prioritizing safety has been made a low priority as it might slow down research efforts presenting a latent threat to the often cutthroat, competitive culture of acquiring data at all costs (Cai, 2019; Kaspar & Landolt, 2016). Especially in anthropology there exists an unspoken custom and expectation of "collecting war stories" in order to legitimize oneself as not only adequate but also competitive. This custom further erases the threats that non-WMCH people face during fieldwork and sets a double standard.

Traditionally then the dangers of sexual harassment and assault in the field have been cast as a personal concern, an individual not systemic problem that could be addressed by sexual literacy trainings (Kloss, 2016; Richards & Hanson, 2019; Schneider, 2020). As such, researchers are usually just expected to apply their own personal knowledge to fieldwork because the field is regarded to be the "real" world. Following this logic, any mention of sexual violence during fieldwork is often regarded as "unprofessional" (Huang, 2016), sidestepping realities out of loyalty for training customs that were developed when only White men were practicing fieldwork (Hanson & Richards, 2017). Further, this practice of rendering sexual violence as a personal not a systemic problem within the culture of anthropology requires that women, people of color, LGBTQIA and disabled scientists give up their freedom to speak out and receive support for their experiences. The irony of course is that those who stay silent often trade autonomy for the privilege of being among "the big boys"—a select few of seniors yielding power yet hiding their own and others' traumas (Hanson & Richards, 2019; Pollard, 2009).

The discussion above argues how and why sexual literacy training in fieldwork remains dangerously underdeveloped (Backe, 2015; Cai, 2019). The anthropological tradition I reviewed above that is used in place of sexual literacy training is a process that

I have coined the "roughcasting model," whereby researchers are encouraged toward stoicism and silence in the face of these struggles, which they should welcome in the form of "adventure" (Richards & Hanson, 2019). Difficulties in fieldwork are thus thought to be formative and when overcome prove that the researcher or student is worthy of the position or degree that they seek: roughcasted like pearls formed under abrasive environmental pressure. In fact, much of the initial pushback I experienced when pitching the Fieldwork Initiative and FISST Training echoed that such training threatened the laissez-faire ways in which anthropologists have been reared since the birth of the discipline. One professor even commented, "We're not supposed to hold students' hands; they need to go out there and figure it out for themselves." This not only reverberates the primitive ideologies of colonial anthropology, headed by elites who are cisgender men, but also egregiously overlooks the reality that the "it" is often sexual assault, unwanted advances from interlocutors and gendered violence in the field (Moreno, 1995; Mügge, 2013).

What Does Fieldwork Sexual Literacy Look Like? The FISST Module

Sexual literacy must be a concern of all programs or studies using fieldwork to collect data and should inform how it prepares its students and researchers for work in the field and within academia (Clark & Grant, 2015). Academia is an institution fraught with disbalanced power dynamics, many of which are reproduced in cases of fieldwork sexual harassment (Schmerler, 2017). Anthropology as a discipline then suffers not only from an absence of sexual literacy but more fundamentally an avoidance from reckoning with the fact that those practicing fieldwork are more diverse and enter into a world that is markedly more complex than it was at the fieldwork practice in the early 1900s.

Comprehensive sexual literacy that encompasses intersectionality asks that we take into consideration the whole person doing the fieldwork research and their social locations inclusive of plural sexualities and identities: this approach is paramount to their safety and well-being (Armstrong et al., 2018). In my experience, what this means is that we impart onto fieldworkers a corpus of various strategies on how to recognize and mitigate potentially dangerous sexual situations, stressing that no one should ever have to endure uncomfortable sexual advances or potentially threatening sexual situations in order to get their research data or as a rite of passage as a researcher (Berry, Argüelles, Cordis, Ihmoud, & Estrada, 2017; Pollard, 2009). It should also be made unequivocally clear to researchers that they will be supported in their decisions to leave or pause future fieldwork in the event that dangerous conditions arise regarding sexual harassment, rape or gender-based violence.

Yet, more than just that, fieldwork trainings must focus on active agency in the field, such as boundary setting, best safety practices and basic situational awareness. Such trainings on sexual harassment, gendered violence, consent and sexual assault are virtually nonexistent in preparatory curriculum in anthropology (Cai, 2019; Hanson & Richards, 2017; Rinkus et al., 2018; Ross, 2015). As such, we are presented with a paradox of ambiguity; though literate, most fieldworkers are ignorant when it comes to sexual literacy.

A direct solution to bring about the structural change necessary in anthropology departments and in other programs is to make pre-fieldwork safety trainings part of permanent curriculum (Cai, 2019). Using the FISST training as example (Heinze, 2020), pre-fieldwork training modules highlight the cultural change those practicing fieldwork must attend to. FISST trainings work with researchers, professors and student research advisors to understand how to report sexual and gendered violence, and are asked to consider commonly overlooked questions about the places and communities that they plan to work in. They are also connected with various resources and situational conversations about fieldwork sexual harassment and gendered violence in the area and more generally are connected to safety support networks for fieldwork researchers. Further, we encourage departments to create fieldwork emergency funds as well as offering free safety resources such as GPS devices that could allow researchers to be tracked while in the field. While this work could be done internally by respective anthropological departments, the best practices module encourages this work to be done by outsiders since, as I have argued above, academic departments are often places where sexual violence in fieldwork is not just overlooked but also lauded. Researchers and students should be aware of these power imbalances and discriminatory attitudes that might result in further ignoring of these problems or worse may result in silencing or driving out people who report such issues. As a remedy, external trainings and networks such as FISST would be used to encourage more responsibility by departments in the preparation of their fieldwork studies.

Conclusion

In affirming the need to expand conversations of inequality amidst glocal projects and research, sexual literacy among fieldwork researchers must be of paramount importance. Sexual harassment, sexual assault, gendered violence or "returning back to the closet" via imposed heterosexist norms of wearing a wedding ring in lieu of sexual literacy training should not be condoned. These are not and should not be simple, acceptable parts of the fieldwork experience in which "the ends justify the means." Pre-fieldwork sexual literacy trainings, like the FISST training, not only interrupt ignorance of the potential threats that fieldworkers face (and thus their need for an empowering preventative toolkit) but disrupts the reproduction of toxic milieu that foment harmful fieldwork experiences. Sexual literacy trainings vis-à-vis fieldwork lastly disrupt customary fieldwork practices that have kept conversations about inequality in fieldwork out of mainstream anthropological focus and academic pedagogy. Anthropologists and academics more generally have diversified, we are no longer only White, male, cisgender, heterosexual fieldworkers. Thus, we must no longer risk ignoring the social and sexual inequities within research practices that we are usually at pains to deconstruct and address in our research. We can and must do better.

References

Appadurai, A. (2008). Discussion: Fieldwork in the era of globalization. *Anthropology and Humanism*, *22*(1), 115–118.

Armstrong, E. A., Gleckman-Krut, M., & Johnson, L. (2018). Silence, power, and inequality: An intersectional approach to sexual violence. *Annual Review of Sociology*, *44*, 99–122.

Backe, E. (2015). Playing along: Fieldwork, emotional labor and self-care. Retrieved from https://thegeekanthropologist.com/2015/07/24/playing-along-fieldwork-emotional-labor-and-self-care/

Berry, M. J., Argüelles, C. C., Cordis, S., Ihmoud, S., & Estrada, E. V. (2017). Toward a fugitive anthropology: Gender, race, and violence in the field. *Cultural Anthropology*, *32*(4), 537–565.

Braeken, D., & Cardinal, M. (2008). Comprehensive sexuality education as a means of promoting sexual health. *International Journal of Sexual Health*, *20*(1–2), 50–62. doi:10.1080/19317610802157051

Britton, D. (2017). Beyond the chilly climate: The salience of gender in women's academic careers. *Gender & Society*, *31*(1), 5–27.

Cai, Y. (2019) Confronting sexual harassment in the field. *Made in China Journal*. Retrieved from https://madeinchinajournal.com/2019/10/25/confronting-sexual-harassment-in-the-field/

Clancy, K. B. H., Nelson, R. G., Rutherford, J. N., & Hinde, K. (2014). Survey of academic field experiences: Trainees report harassment and assault. *PLOS One*, *9*(7). Retrieved from https://doi.org/10.1371/journal.pone.0102172

Clark, I., & Grant, A. (2015). Sexuality and danger in the field: Starting an uncomfortable conversation. *Journal of the Anthropological Society of Oxford*, *7*(1), 1–14.

Daubenmier, J. M. (2008). *The Meskwaki and anthropologists*. Nebraska: University of Nebraska Press.

Easterday, L., Papademas, D., Schorr, L., & Valentine, C. (1977). The making of a female researcher: Role problems in field work. *Urban Life*, *6*(3), 333–348.

Gifford, L., & Hall-Clifford, R. (2008). From catcalls to kidnapping: Towards an open dialogue on the fieldwork experiences of graduate women. *Anthropology News*, *49*(6), 26–27. Wiley, doi:10.1111/an.2008.49.6.26

Green, G., Barbour, R. S., Barnard, M., & Kitzinger, J. (1993). "Who wears the trousers?": Sexual harassment in research settings. *Women's Studies International Forum*, *16*(6), 627–637.

Hanson, R., & Richards, P. (2017). Sexual harassment and the construction of ethnographic. *Sociological Forum*, *32*(3), 587–609.

Hanson, R., & Richards, P. (2019). *Harassed: Gender, bodies, and ethnographic research*. Berkeley: University of California Press.

Heinze, J. L. (2020). FISST training. *Fieldwork Initiative*. Retrieved from http://fieldworkinitiative.org/

Huang, M. (2016). Vulnerable observers: Notes on fieldwork and rape. What does it mean to produce knowledge through an experience that includes trauma? *Chronicle of Higher Education*. Retrieved from www.chronicle.com/article/Vulnerable-Observers-Notes-on/238042

Kaspar, H., & Landolt, S. (2016). Flirting in the Field: Shifting positionalities and power relations in innocuous sexualisations of research encounters. *Gender, Place & Culture*, *23*(1), 107–119.

Kloss, S. (2016). Sexual(ized) harassment and ethnographic fieldwork: A silenced aspect of social research. *Ethnography Journal*, *18*(3), 396–414.

La Pastina, A. (2006). The implications of an ethnographer's sexuality. *Qualitative Inquiry*, *12*, 724–735. doi:10.1177/1077800406288615

Marti, J. (2016). *Starting fieldwork: Methods and experiences*. Long Grove, IL: Waveland Press.

Moreno, E. (1995). Rape in the field: Reflections from a survivor. In D. Kulick & M. Willson (Eds.), *Taboo: Sex, identity, and erotic subjectivity in anthropological fieldwork* (pp. 219–250). New York: Routledge.

Mügge, L. M. (2013). Sexually harassed by gatekeepers: Reflections on fieldwork in Surinam and Turkey. *International Journal of Social Research Methodology*, *16*(6), 541–546.

Pollard, A. (2009). Field of screams: Difficulty and ethnographic fieldwork. *Anthropology Matters*, *11*(2). Retrieved from http://www.anthropologymatters.com/index.php/anth_matters/article/view/10/10

Rinkus, M., Kelly, J. R., Wright, W., Medina, L., & Dobson, T. (2018). Gendered considerations for safety in conservation fieldwork. *Society & Natural Resources*, *31*(12), 1419–1426.

Ross, K. (2015). "No sir, she was not a fool in the field": Gendered risks and sexual violence in immersed cross-cultural fieldwork. *Professional Geographer, 67*(2), 180–186.

Schmerler, G. (2017). *Henrietta Schmerler and the murder that put anthropology on trial.* Iowa: Scrivana Press.

Schneider, L. (2020). Sexual violence during research: How the unpredictability of fieldwork and the right to risk collide with academic bureaucracy and expectations. *Critique of Anthropology, 40*(2), 173–193. doi:10.1177/0308275x20917272

Steffen, M. (2017). Doing fieldwork after Henrietta Schmerler: On sexual violence and blame in anthropology. American Ethnologist. Retrieved from http://americanethnologist.org/features/reflections/doing-fieldwork-after-henrietta-schmerler

Sundberg, J. (2003). Masculinist epistemologies and the politics of fieldwork in Latin Americanist geography. *Professional Geographer, 55*(2), 180–190.

Thambiah, S., Chakraborty, K., & Sarker, R. (2016). Negotiating male gatekeeper violence in team-based research on Bangladeshi migrant women in Malaysia. *Gender, Place & Culture, 23*(8), 1150–1163.

Weinstein, R. B., Walsh, J. L., & Ward, L. M. (2008). Testing a new measure of sexual health knowledge and its connections to students' sex education, communication, confidence, and condom use. *International Journal of Sexual Health, 20*(3), 212–221. doi:10.1080/19317610802240279

Weston, G., & Djohari, N. (2020). *Anthropological controversies: The "crimes" and misdemeanors that shaped a discipline.* New York: Routledge.

Wolf, D. L. (1993). Feminist dilemmas in fieldwork. *Frontiers: A Journal of Women Studies, 13*(3), 1–8.

Chapter 8

CELEBRATING BLACK SEXUAL FREEDOM: PRIORITIZING ACCURATE RESEARCH OF BLACK SEXUALITY

Ericka Burns

The complexity of Black sexuality is beautiful, passionate and pleasurable and it deserves to be accurately represented by researchers and activists alike. This is especially true when researchers endeavor to explore the spectrum of fluid sexualities. The history of these issues begs greater sensitivity. For example, the history of being forced into inhumane scientific experiments (Collins, 2004; Rushton, 1995) and the lingering racism that impinges upon the free expression of sexuality among Black people make it important to be culturally sensitive to how Black sexuality is represented in research. I argue that Black sexuality should be about freedom—freedom of expression, desires and identity. Freedom-informed research as methodology means that Black sexuality needs to be investigated and described in ways that do not always center on negative impacts or the HIV/AIDS epidemic (Collins, 2004; Malebranche, 2003; Stockton, 2007). Black sexual freedom is sexuality that includes pleasure, which is "natural, safe, and liberated part of life" (brown, 2019, p. 13). Those leading a cultural shift to incorporate sexual pleasure and resilience are Black youth. Black youth in the United States are redefining themselves and creating more space for queer identities, which is reflected in media, social media and through activism (Aniobi & Allen, 2016; Biko, 2016; Johnson, 2018).

Sexual freedom is the basis of fluid sexuality research; however, when it pertains to Black sexuality, there is much that is absent from these studies as they relate to Black sexual experiences and identity (Diamond, 2008; Elizabeth, 2013; Kaufman and Powell, 2014; Savin-Williams, 2006). These hegemonic studies lack "contextual, environmental, historic, socio-cultural, socio-economic, political, and geographical differences [...] these differences, as well as other factors including age and ethnicity, [that] may result in variations in the process by which an individual identifies as a sexual minority" (McInroy & Craig, 2012, p. 139). Elevating the voices of Black queer and nonqueer identifying sexualities alike is one way to have a lasting social and cultural impact since it will combat the current narrative of Black sexuality as pornographic (Miller-Young, 2014) and animalistic (Collins, 2004; Rubin, 1999). These views of Black sexuality contribute to such inaccurate and dangerous portrayals of Black queer and nonqueer identifying people.

Black representation in fluidity research allows for more of an accurate understanding of the emergent concept of sexual fluidity that goes beyond White middle-class samples that have historically dominated the research in the United States.

Fluid sexualities include orientations and nonexclusive sexual attractions that are not limited to sexual desires, labels, attractions or behaviors with just one sex, sexuality or gender identity. Examples of such identities are labels such as sexual fluidity, bisexuality, pansexuality and mostly straight. I do agree that sexual fluidity is about having the "capacity for change in attractions" at any point in a person's lifetime (Diamond, Dickenson, & Blair, 2017, p. 194). Bisexuality is primarily focused on sexual attractions, desires and behaviors with two sexes. Gonzalez, Ramirez, and Galupo (2017) acknowledge that the term *bisexual* can be limiting and many "are starting to create new words to define their sexual identities" (p. 497). Pansexuality is "more inclusive of trans people" or other people outside the gender binary (Elizabeth, 2013, p. 333). Finally, the term *mostly straight* is an emergent label where youth report being comfortable with identifying as heterosexual but are "aware of their own potential to experience far more – sexual attraction, sexual desire, and, perhaps, romantic attraction for others of their biological sex" (Kaufman & Powell, 2014, p. 12). Research by Kaufman and Powell (2014) explores the various sexual orientation labels identified by youth that demonstrate fluidity in their sexuality such as homoflexible, pseudo-bisexual, tri-sexual or plainly stating that "I love who I love" as sufficient for youth in that study to determine their sexual identity (Kaufman & Powell, 2014, p. 12). These changes that continue to move over time make sexual identity labels and identities less straightforward and less constructed than understood in the recent past in the United States (Diamond, 2008).

My argument is that the foundations of this research are flawed. This is because the historic research on Black youth and their sexualities has failed to adequately define and describe the spectrum of Black youth sexual orientation expressions. Researchers such as Lisa Diamond (2008) and Ritch Savin-Williams (2006) have alluded to but have not carefully examined what it means for *all* youth to "identify" their sexual orientation, that is, their research has failed to specifically address sexual orientation, including fluid sexuality labels, used among Black youth. More broadly, such limiting research also does not account for the fact that such labels shift and condense over time, removing the certainty that past sexual and gender labels allude to a broad societal level but that are cogenerated via glocal processes.

Moreover, Anglo-Western sexual orientation labels such as homosexual, heterosexual and bisexual (Yon-Leau & Muñoz-Laboy, 2010) and other nonbinary labels or nonexclusive sexual attractions constructed by primarily White researchers such as sexual fluidity, pansexuality and mostly straight (Diamond, 2008, 2016; Elizabeth, 2013; Kaufman & Powell, 2014) often misrepresent Black sexuality (Diamond, 2008; Irvine, 2000; Lovelock, 2014; Reisman, Eichel, Muir, & Court, 1990; Savin-Williams, 2006). Historically, prominent researchers on the subject of fluid sexualities as represented by Alfred Kinsey, Fritz Klein, Lisa Diamond and Ritch Savin-Williams have not portrayed the realities of Black sexuality, given limited racial diversity in their empirical sampling.

Sexuality Research Studies

We need a paradigm shift in the academy, one that enables researchers now to discuss these operant, changeable terms and to figure out how to map them. This will in turn lead to truly understanding how Black sexual freedom and expression work in contemporary environments to represent sexual attractions, desires and behaviors among Black youth. My view is that this new approach will better enable us to be glocally informative of emergent identity formation and movement making among us all—these ideas move and not only among one race as implied when research only focuses on White people as the universal experience. Youth are creating their own spaces for Black queer-identifying and nonqueer-identifying youth to gather either locally in person or through social media and define themselves in their own globally informed contexts (Durham, 2015). Blackburn and McCready (2009) believe that school-aged youth "have served as the catalyst for several new social movements in America's cities" (p. 226).

One powerful example of this globally informed movement is the *Black Lives Matter* movement, commonly referred to as BLM, which started as a hashtag, by Alicia Garza, Patrisse Cullors and Opal Tometi (Black Lives Matter, n.d.). These Black millennial women, "two of whom identify as queer" (Johnson, 2018, p. 335), began the BLM movement in 2013 "in response to the acquittal of Trayvon Martin's murderer, George Zimmerman"—a local murder that happened to Travon, a Black youth, and that ignited a global movement (BLM, n.d., para. 1). BLM amplified anti-Black racism utilizing social media, eventually encouraging organizers across the country to plan various marches, boycotts, sit-ins, die-ins and other forms of activism and political organizing in order to protest the acquittal and other murders of Black men, women, trans folks and youth including Michael Brown, Sandra Bland, Philando Castile, Eric Garner, Stephon Clark, Willie McCoy, Mya Hall and Tamir Rice—and certainly more by the time you are reading this chapter. Researcher E. Patrick Johnson (2016) argues that to revitalize the queer movement, the new agenda should reach "across lines of race, ethnicity, gender, and gender expression, class, religion and nationality" (p. 36). BLM is doing just that, especially with youth.

Indeed, the BLM movement is mobilizing youth activist and community leaders in incredible ways. BLM contests anti-Blackness and heteronormative values, "the children are seizing the worldwide stage that the Internet provides; and they are turning civil rights songs and spirituals into a *vogue* [...] these children also specifically and particularly call out violence against trans and queer folks" (Johnson, 2016, pp. 37, 39). Cherno Biko, a Black trans activist and founder of "#BlackTransLivesMatter" movement, stated that after the murder of Michael Brown in Ferguson, "the power and resilience of queer and trans [B]lack women especially, gave me hope that this iteration of the movement for [B]lack lives would not fail to center our most vulnerable and precious members" (2016, para 4). Although much work has been accomplished inside such movements, there continue to be police executions, and Johnson goes on to argue that politically we are still only witnessing "'performative solidarity' of LGBTQ groups [which] actually belies complicity with the selfsame neoliberal policies that support the fact that, 'in fact, Black lives do not matter'" (Johnson, 2016, pp. 36–37).

To inspire change, Kiesling argues that "queer mainstream organizations, activism, and politics cannot ignore anti-Blackness" (2017, p. 10) and this includes those working in academia. Understanding, mapping and tracking language and labels specific to Black queer youth are imperative because it gives Black youth their own queer space to relate in academia, social justice movements and their own communities. Such youth identity movements are not new in the United States, but this fact underlines the necessity to frame Black queer youth into such cultural coming-of-age practices. There does exist research on Black men's sexuality for both heterosexual and homosexual desires (Malebranche, 2003; Mackenzie, 2013; Pettaway, Bryant, Keane, & Craig, 2014), and Black lesbians are beginning to have more representation in research (Greene, 2000, Hammonds, 1997; Johnson, 2018); however, it is difficult to find research on Black bisexuality that does not center itself in the HIV/AIDS epidemic and secrecy (Collins, 2004; Malebranche, 2003; Stockton, 2007). Love (2017) suggests that "Black queer youth need a methodological perspective that aims to understand how 'even in the face of the brutally imposed difficulties of [B]lack life, [life] is cause for celebration'" (Moten, 2013, p. 742, as cited in Love, 2017, p. 545). Black queer youth sexuality can be celebrated and understood via more intentional research approaches that conceptualize them accurately.

Researching Black fluid sexualities requires innovative methodologies that are intersectional and culturally sensitive to improve our understanding of race, gender and sexuality. Hegemonic sexual research historically was conducted on fluid sexualities by Alfred Kinsey and Fritz Klein who created two separate sexuality scales both of which have been uncritically included as representative of the spectrum of the general population, when this is obviously untrue (Irvine, 2000; Kinsey, Pomeroy, & Martin, 1948; Lovelock, 2014; Mereish, Katz-Wise, & Woulfe, 2017), and have inspired research about exclusively heterosexual or homosexual identities (Izazola-Licea, Gortmaker, de Gruttola, Tolbert, & Mann, 2003; Savin-Williams, 2018). Again, none of this hegemonic research considered race and cultural differences when examining sexual orientation. Exceptions to this practice of considering sexual orientation as always-already stable and somehow separable from other context-specific influences are rare, but the notable example of Gail Wyatt's excellent research (1997) comes to mind. She created her own sexuality scale to account for consensual and nonconsensual experiences connecting culture with sexuality among Black, White and Latina women. Also, Miguel Muñoz-Laboy's (2004) important study used sexual histories of Latino men to discuss the various sexual experiences throughout the lifetime, which could be used to capture Black men's (and other's) experiences. Bettina Love (2017) also provides a recent methodological critique on how to work with Black queer youth in order "to recognize Black queer youth's agency" (p. 541). Together, these methods should be used to discover and continually update accurate labels and language pertaining to Black sexuality, especially those with fluid sexual desires, attractions and behaviors.

Media Analysis

An additional approach to understanding Black sexuality is via media analysis as a way to track the trends in language via analyses on how Black queer experiences are portrayed in TV and film. This is not a new approach since renowned researchers Patricia Hill Collins (1990, 2004) and Kimberlé Crenshaw (1991) used media analysis to further understand how Black femininity, masculinity and sexuality were portrayed in media in their foundational research. Media, such as television, movies and music, often reflect cultural or political movements that are then reflected back through media-based social commentary. Stuart Hall (1973) first described this process in his now-famous 1973 essay "Encoding and Decoding in the Television Discourse" where he discusses how audiences play an active role in decoding media messages based on their own contexts and even changing those messages via collective action, which is now easier than ever via social media applications and digital connectivity. Not surprisingly, Hall was a Jamaican-born sociologist, cultural theorist and activist and one of the founders of the influential Birmingham School of Cultural Studies. Social scientists writ large should integrate methodologies that go beyond disciplinary boundaries toward the accurate and timely investigation of sociocultural phenomena. I argue that such methodological adjustments are the antidote to erroneous approaches of studying sexual fluidity vis-à-vis White sexuality as universal.

Indeed, analyzing current trends in media to understand how Black sexuality is currently depicted provides accessible data for testing these methods. For example, the term *sexual fluidity* was mentioned on HBO's *Insecure*, in an episode titled "Guilty as Fuck" (Aniobi & Allen, 2016). *Insecure*'s cast is predominately Black with topics that address race, masculinity and sexuality that resonate with many Black millennials. The "Guilty as Fuck" episode tackles the topic of whether cisgender heterosexual Black women would or should date a cisgender man who has had a sexual encounter with another cis-man in the past (Aniobi & Allen, 2016).

This episode provoked much online debate, which is a reflection of the current views held among Black men and women on the topic of sexuality in the United States. First, there are stereotypes of bisexual men that include being:

(1) confused and indecisive regarding their sexual and romantic preferences, (2) untrustworthy, (3) less inclined towards monogamous relationships, and therefore less likely to maintain long-term relationships and more likely to cheat on their partners, (4) sexually promiscuous, and (5) open minded and open to new experiences. (Zivony & Lobel, 2014, p. 1165)

Second, "Black women have been told both by popular media and by public health entities that Black [men who have sex with men and women] MSMW pose a major threat to their health and, in many cases, have been presented narrow, morally corrupt images of these men" (Harawa, Obregon, & McCuller, 2014, pp. 872–73; see also Muñoz-Laboy, 2004). Since sexual fluidity expresses the freedom of sexual expression and identity (Savin-Williams, 2006), Black people should likewise be accorded the dignity to have the same freedom without it being labeled deviant by the public and sexuality researchers alike. By continuing to allow sexual freedom for some while focusing on what seems to be a public health crisis for underrepresented communities (Mackenzie, 2013), Black sexualities continue to be oppressed thwarting dignity, liberation and celebration in the Black community.

In 2018, pansexuality was popularly introduced to the Black community by artists such as the hip-hop rapper Roes (formally known as Angel Haze), singer Kehlani, singer Janelle Monae (Hill, 2018) and also actress Amandla Stenberg (who played Rue in *Hunger Games*). Roes stated in an interview with *Out Magazine*, "people talking about me, like, 'I'm glad there's an actual woman of color representing queerness and pansexuality, someone who is like me in the spotlight'" (Symonds, 2014, para 9). Such artists in the music industry have historically had an impact on Black youth notions of themselves (Jones, 2018). Janelle Monae stated in her recent interview with Rolling Stone Magazine, "being a queer [B]lack woman in America, someone who has been in relationships with both men and women – I consider myself to be a free-ass motherfucker" (Spranos, 2018, para 2). The article discusses how Janelle Monae originally identified as bisexual but in the same interview she states, "but then later I read about pansexuality and was like, 'Oh, these are things that I identify with too. I'm open to learning more about who I am'" (Spranos, 2018, para 2). If researchers such as Kaufman and Powell accept "mostly straight" or "pseudo-bisexual" as a sufficient sexual identity created by youth, then should being a "free-ass motherfucker" be considered a label that is ideal for other Black queer youth if they pick this up from Monae?

Monae, Roes, Stenberg and Kehlani attract younger audiences, and this could be a reflection of how youth are starting to be more comfortable with their sexuality or a sign of increased curiosity to learn more about their sexuality options. Either way, the labels generated from within Black youth communities, the media stars who are influencing and reflecting them, and the ones to which these youth identify with from outside of their claimed communities demonstrate the glocal nature of sexual literacy. The heft and methodological creativity required in the research community to accurately describe current youth identity creation is certainly necessary to capture such complexities. More research is urgently necessary to determine the language and influence that pop and Internet culture has on Black queer youth identity formation. With the examples of Black musicians and actors identifying as pansexual or as a "free-ass motherfucker" there is a growing understanding of how sexuality transgresses binaries: Black/White, Gay/Straight, Man/Woman—to craft a place for Black youth into their own imagined, globally informed, locally lived futures that allow them to be as complexly sexual and free—and celebrated for it is the inspiration for my work.

Researchers should be held accountable for being accurate and for truly understanding the spectrum of Black sexual freedom. This is part of basic sexual literacy for all researchers today: the hegemonic, one-sided views of race, gender, class and sexuality—including exclusively conducting studies on only White populations to the negation of varied social locations (even for Whites). Conducting such exclusive studies as if they are universally applicable ignores the sociocultural impacts that reinforce sexual discrimination, such as homophobia and biphobia (Herek, 2000), as well as direct and structural violences against Blackness that movements like BLM are frontally addressing (Gaber & Wright, 2016). It is important to incorporate methodologies that are more intersectional and culturally informed to combat negative, damaging stereotypes and improve research efforts so that sexual literacy as it evolves across populations can be accurately identified. Although the works of fluid sexualities are influential (Diamond, 2008, 2016; Elizabeth,

2013; Irvine, 2000; Kaufman & Powell, 2014; Savin-Williams, 2006), researchers can no longer ignore the impact and possible expression of fluid sexualities in the Black community nor the larger implications of these expressions into broader discourses of sexual literacy in the United States and beyond.

References

Aniobi, A. (Writer), & Allen, D. (Director). (2016, November 13). Guilty as Fuck (Season 1, Episode 6) [Television series episode]. In P. Penny, M. Rotenberg, M. Matsoukas, D. Becky, J. Berry (Executive Producers), *Insecure*. HBO.

Biko, C. (2016). Black trans live matter, too. *Huffpost*. Retrieved from https://www.huffingtonpost.com/cherno-biko/black-trans-lives-matter-_b_9157514.html

Black Lives Matter. (n.d.). Herstory. Retrieved from www.blacklivesmatter.com/about/herstory.

Blackburn, M. V., & McCready, L. T. (2009). Voices of queer youth in urban schools: Possibilities and limitations. *Theory into Practice, 48*(3), 222–230. Retrieved from http://search.ebscohost.com.ciis.idm.oclc.org/login.aspx?direct=true&db=eric&AN=EJ857773&site=ehost-live&scope=site

brown, a. m. (2019). *Pleasure activism*. Chico: AK Press.

Collins, P. H. (1990). *Black feminist thought: Knowledge, consciousness, and the politics of empowerment.* New York: Routledge.

Collins, P. H. (2004). *Black sexual politics: African Americans, gender, and the new racism.* New York: Routledge.

Crenshaw, K. (1991). Mapping the margins: Intersectionality, identity politics, and violence against women of color. *Stanford Law Review, 43*, 1241–1299.

Diamond, L. M. (2008). *Sexual fluidity: Understanding women's love and desire.* Cambridge, MA: Harvard University Press.

Diamond, L. M. (2016). Sexual fluidity in male and females. *Current Sexual Health Reports, 8*(4), 249–256.

Diamond, L., Dickenson, J., & Blair, K. (2017). Stability of sexual attractions across different timescales: The roles of bisexuality and gender. *Archives of Sexual Behavior, 46*(1), 193–204. Retrieved from https://doi-org.ciis.idm.oclc.org/10.1007/s10508-016-0860-x

Durham, A. (2015). While Black: Millennial race play and the post-hip-hop generation. *Cultural Studies/Critical Methodologies, 15*(4), 253–259. Retrieved from https://doi-org.ciis.idm.oclc.org/10.1177/1532708615578414

Elizabeth, A. (2013). Challenging the binary: Sexual identity that is not duality. *Journal of Bisexuality, 13*(3), 329–337. Retrieved from https://doi-org.ciis.idm.oclc.org/10.1080/15299716.2013.813421

Gaber, N., & Wright, A. (2016). Protecting urban health and safety: Balancing care and harm in the era of mass incarceration. *Journal of Urban Health: Bulletin of the New York Academy of Medicine, 93*(Suppl. 1), 68–77. Retrieved from https://doi-org.ciis.idm.oclc.org/10.1007/s11524-015-0009-6

Gonzalez, K., Ramirez, J., & Galupo, M. (2017). "I was and still am": Narratives of bisexual marking in the #stillbisexual campaign. *Sexuality & Culture, 21*(2), 493–515. Retrieved from https://doi-org.ciis.idm.oclc.org/10.1007/s12119-016-9401-y

Greene, B. (2000). African American lesbian and bisexual women. *Journal of Social Issues, 56*(2), 239. Retrieved from http://search.ebscohost.com.ciis.idm.oclc.org/login.aspx?direct=true&db=pbh&AN=3632800&site=ehost-live&scope=site

Hall, S. (1973). *Encoding and decoding in the television discourse.* Centre for Contemporary Cultural Studies, University of Birmingham, Birmingham [West Midlands].

Hammonds, E. M. (1997). Toward a genealogy of Black female sexuality: The problematic of silence. In M. J. Alexander & C. T. Mohanty (Eds.), *Feminist genealogies, colonial legacies, democratic futures* (pp. 93–104). New York: Routledge.

Harawa, N., Obregon, N., & McCuller, W. (2014). Partnerships between Black women and behaviorally bisexual men: Implications for HIV risk and prevention. *Sexuality & Culture, 18*(4), 870–891. Retrieved from https://doi-org.ciis.idm.oclc.org/10.1007/s12119-014-9227-4

Herek, G. M. (2000). The psychology of sexual prejudice. *Current Directions in Psychological Science, 9*(1), 19–22. Retrieved from https://doi.org/10.1111/1467-8721.00051

Hill, Z. (2018). 5 things to know about pansexuals and the "free ass motherf**kers" who identify as such: Thanks, Janelle. Retrieved from https://blavity.com/5-things-to-know-about-pansexuals-and-the-free-ass-motherfkers-who-identify-as-such

Irvine, J. (2000). *Disorders of desire: Sex and gender in modern American sexology*. Philadelphia, PA: Temple University Press.

Izazola-Licea, J. A., Gortmaker, S. L., de Gruttola, V., Tolbert, K., & Mann, J. (2003). Sexual behavior patterns and HIV risks in bisexual men compared to exclusively heterosexual and homosexual men. *Salud Publica De Mexico, 45*(Supp. 5), S662–S671. Retrieved from http://search.ebscohost.com.ciis.idm.oclc.org/login.aspx?direct=true&db=mnh&AN=14974278&site=ehost-live&scope=site

Johnson, E. P. (2016). *No tea, no shade: New writings in black queer studies*. Durham, NC: Duke University Press.

Johnson, E. P. (2018). *Black. Queer. Southern. Women: An oral history*. Chapel Hill: University of North Carolina Press.

Jones, E. (2018). The kids are queer: The rise of post-millennial American queer identification. In C. Stewart (Ed.), *Lesbian, gay, bisexual, and transgender Americans at risk: Problems and solutions*. Santa Barbara, CA: Praeger.

Kaufman, J., & Powell, D. (2014). *The meaning of sexual identity in the twenty-first century*. Newcastle-upon-Tyne, United Kingdom: Cambridge Scholars.

Kiesling, E. (2017). The missing colors of the rainbow: Black queer resistance. *European Journal of American Studies*. Retrieved from http://journals.openedition.org/ejas/11830; DOI: 10.4000/ejas.11830

Kinsey, A. C., Pomeroy, W. B., & Martin, C. E. (1948). *Sexual behavior in the human male*. Philadelphia, PA: Saunders.

Love, B. L. (2017). A ratchet lens: Black queer youth, agency, hip hop, and the Black ratchet imagination. *Educational Researcher, 46*(9), 539–547.

Lovelock, J. M. (2014). Using the Klein sexual orientation grid in sociological studies. *Journal of Bisexuality, 14*(3/4), 457–467. doi:10.1080/15299716.2014.946197

Mackenzie, S. (2013). *Structural intimacies: Sexual stories in the Black AIDS epidemic*. New Brunswick, NJ: Rutgers University Press.

Malebranche, D. (2003). Black men who have sex with men and the HIV epidemic: Next steps for public health. *American Journal of Public Health, 93*(6), 862–864.

McInroy, L., & Craig, S. L. (2012). Articulating identities: Language and practice with multiethnic sexual minority youth. *Counselling Psychology Quarterly, 25*(2), 137–149.

Mereish, E. H., Katz-Wise, S. L., & Woulfe, J. (2017). We're here and we're queer: Sexual orientation and sexual fluidity differences between bisexual and queer women. *Journal of Bisexuality, 17*(1), 125–139. Retrieved from https://doi-org.ciis.idm.oclc.org/10.1080/15299716.2016.1217448

Miller-Young, M. (2014). *A taste for brown sugar: Black women in pornography*. Durham, NC: Duke University Press.

Moten, F. (2013). Blackness and nothingness (mysticism in the flesh). *South Atlantic Quarterly, 112*(4), 737–780.

Muñoz-Laboy, M. A. (2004). Beyond "MSM": Sexual desire among bisexually-active Latino men in New York City. *Sexualities, 7*(1), 55–80.

Pettaway, L., Bryant, L., Keane, F., & Craig, S. (2014). Becoming down low: A review of the literature on black men who have sex with men and women. *Journal of Bisexuality, 14*(2), 209–221. doi:10.1080/15299716.2014.902346

Reisman, J. A., Eichel, E. W., Muir, J. G., & Court, J. H. (1990). *Kinsey, sex and fraud: The indoctrination of a people: An investigation into the human sexuality research of Alfred C. Kinsey, Wardell B. Pomery, Clyde E. Martin, and Paul H. Gebhard.* Lafayette, LA: Lochinvar-Huntington House.

Rubin, G. S. (1999). Thinking sex: Notes for a radical theory of the politics of sexuality. In R. Parker & P. Aggleton (Eds.), *Culture, society and sexuality: A reader* (pp. 143–178). London: UCL Press.

Rushton, J. P. (1995). *Race, evolution, and behavior: A life history perspective.* Piscataway, NJ: Transaction.

Savin-Williams, R. (2006). *The new gay teenager.* Cambridge, MA: Harvard University Press.

Savin-Williams, R. C. (2018). An exploratory study of exclusively heterosexual, primarily heterosexual, and mostly heterosexual young men. *Sexualities, 21*(1/2), 16–29. Retrieved from https://doi-org.ciis.idm.oclc.org/10.1177/1363460716678559

Spranos, B. (2018). Janelle Monáe frees herself. *RollingStone.* Retrieved from https://www.rollingstone.com/music/music-features/janelle-monae-frees-herself-629204/

Stockton, K. B. (2007). *Beautiful bottom, beautiful shame: Where "Black" meets "queer".* Durham, NC: Duke University Press.

Symonds, A. (2014). The emancipation of Angel Haze. Retrieved from https://www.out.com/entertainment/music/2014/02/04/emancipation-angel-haze

Wyatt, G. E. (1997). *Stolen women: Reclaiming our sexuality, taking back our lives.* New York: Wiley.

Yon-Leau, C., & Muñoz-Laboy, M. (2010). "I don't like to say that I'm anything": Sexuality Politics and cultural critique among sexual-minority Latino youth. *Sexuality Research & Social Policy: Journal of NSRC, 7*(2), 105–117. doi:10.1007/s13178-010-0009-y

Zivony, A., & Lobel, T. (2014). The invisible stereotypes of bisexual men. *Archives of Sexual Behavior, 43*(6), 1165–1176. Retrieved from https://doi-org.ciis.idm.oclc.org/10.1007/s10508-014-0263-9

Chapter 9

VNOKECETV: TWO-SPIRIT LOVE AT THE BAAITS POWWOW

Roger Kuhn

Acknowledgment

This chapter was conceptualized and written in unceded Ramaytush Ohlone territory, now known as San Francisco, California, and Pomo territory, now known as Guerneville, California. Acknowledging the land and the violently displaced or murdered inhabitants of that land is the first step in any decolonial process. It is important to acknowledge the peoples of any colonized location because people have bodies, and bodies have stories. Please read this as a story about love. Not the kind of love you may be used to seeing in films or reading about in romance novels. This is a story about *vnokeckv* (pronounced—aw-no-geh-che-kuh), the Muscogee word for community love. More directly, this is a story about vnokeckv and Two-Spirit community. This chapter also positions Indigenous knowledge and storytelling as valid forms of discourse. Positioning oneself within the context of one's work is central to acknowledging Indigenous scholarship as an integral aspect of critical sexuality studies (Driskill, Finley, Morgensen, & Gilley, 2011; Driskill, Kenney, & Lara, 2011; Justice, Rifkin, & Schneider, 2010; Tallbear, 2019). It is important that I situate myself in the community of Two-Spirit people, because I also identify as Two-Spirit. I am an enrolled member of the Poarch Band of Creek Indians, a federally recognized sovereign nation in what is now known as Alabama. I have served as a board member of the Bay Area American Indian Two-Spirit Society (BAAITS) for seven years and was the powwow Chair in 2020. This chapter is not written on behalf of or for BAAITS.

In this chapter, I use the terms *sexual sovereignty* and *erotic survivance* to describe aspects of decolonizing sexuality. These terms are not exclusive to this chapter, nor is the author claiming any ownership of the phrases. Decolonization and decolonizing sexuality impact colonized people across the globe and include issues such as land, water, agriculture, food, sex, gender and sovereignty. The inclusion of these terms is intentional as they are meant to evoke an understanding that the narratives of decolonization, sovereignty and eroticism (love) are not exclusive of one another, rather they inform gaps in the literature from both Western and Indigenous perspectives. Sexual sovereignty is a direct challenge to White settler colonialism and heterocentric idealism, which fail at understanding how Indigenous communities experience gender and sexuality. Sexual sovereignty is also a claim that Two-Spirit bodies have a right to identify with gender and sexual orientation fluidity and the physical acts of intimacy, pleasure and sex as an extension of decolonization and a return to Indigenous roles, identities and practices that existed prior to first contact. Erotic survivance is an extension of Vizenor's (2008) work and creates space for Two-Spirit people to share and express how their sexuality (gender, orientation, practice) has been an important aspect to their story of survival. Vizenor (2008) refers to survivance as:

> an active sense of presence over absence, deracination, and oblivion; survivance is the con-tinuance of stories, not a mere reaction, action, however pertinent" [and] "survivance stories are renunciations of dominance, detractions, obtrusions, the unbearable sentiments of tra-gedy, and the legacy of victimry. (p. 36)

Further, erotic survivance is the stories, poetry, prose, songs, dances, medicine, art, activism and gatherings Two-Spirit people and communities engage in to celebrate their resiliency, survival, sexual expression and sexual sovereignty.

With the inclusion of the terms *sexual sovereignty* and *erotic survivance*, I hope to invoke in the reader an immediate connection to Indigeneity and narratives of decolonization. I seek to inform the reader that even though these terms are being used in conjunc-tion with Two-Spirit people, sexual sovereignty and erotic survivance can be applied to all marginalized and oppressed people who continue to heal from what Jolivette (2016) terms *post traumatic invasion syndrome*, the continued settler and colonial ideology of dom-ination over aspects of a person's or group's identity.

My inclusion of these terms is also inspired by Crenshaw's (1989, 1991) theory of intersectionality. Crenshaw (1989) recognizes the importance of analyzing the intersections of race, class and ethnicity in regard to daily lived experiences because, "otherwise-privileged group members creates a distorted analysis of racism and sexism because the operative conceptions of race and sex become grounded in experiences that actually represent only a subset of a much more complex phenomenon" (p. 140). Sexual sovereignty and erotic survivance examine the intersectionality of Two-Spirit people alongside discourses of colonization (Simpson, 2017), HIV/AIDS (Jolivette, 2016) and what I hope to examine further: love.

Vnokeckv

At 6 a.m., before the crowd of spectators, vendors, dancers and drummers arrives, the large 50,000 ft.² warehouse known as the Festival Pavilion at Ft. Mason Center in San Francisco, California, can seem both daunting and exhilarating. Volunteers have arrived and are busy setting up chairs, loading in sound equipment, making last-minute changes to the schedule and sharing their excitement about what lies ahead. Around 8 a.m. the first of the vendors arrive and begin to set up their booths selling a variety of beaded jewelry, Native American arts and crafts, powwow regalia and Native American food. By 10 a.m. the drums are beginning to be set up, followed shortly by the arrival of the dancers. The doors open to the public at 11 a.m. and by 12 p.m. the Festival Pavilion has transformed into a powwow arena with approximately 1,000 spectators eager for the Grand Entry, where all the dancers gather and welcome one another to the circle. Like this chapter, the powwow also acknowledges the land we gather upon and an opening blessing led by members of the Ohlone nation reminds everyone that Native culture is alive and thriving.

Now in its ninth year, the BAAITS powwow was the first public Two-Spirit powwow in the world. It is now the largest and longest running public Two-Spirit powwow, with the BAAITS powwow committee making plans for their 10-year anniversary. The BAAITS powwow is similar to other powwows and also unique in its own way by openly welcoming the multiple identities of a Native person, which might include Two-Spirit, Indigequeer, LGBTQIA, traditional and/or urban and so on. Also unique to the BAAITS powwow, the dance categories are not gendered. Any registered dancer who is interested in dancing a particular style is welcome to perform. The BAAITS powwow is modeled after an Oklahoma style powwow and includes dance categories such as Tiny Tots, Fancy Shawl, Northern/Southern Buckskin and Golden Age. Each of these dances plays a significant role within the powwow and the community. Tiny tots creates a space for Two-Spirit children, or children of Two-Spirit parents and allies, to be seen and welcomed into the circle. Similarly, Golden Age creates a space to honor and acknowledge Two-Spirit elders and allies. At the BAAITS Two-Spirit Powwow, categories such as Fancy shawl and Norther/Southern Buckskin have been de-gendered. These dances are traditionally based upon strict gender ideas of male/female and/or man/woman. With gender identity and expression no longer an issue at the BAAITS powwow, these dance categories become an additional space where gender-variant Two-Spirit people can express themselves and feel supported by their community. Having been a member of the BAAITS board as well as a powwow committee member, I have first-hand knowledge of the intense feelings of vnokeckv that can be experienced at the BAAITS powwow. It is at the BAAITS powwow that I came to understand the true meaning of the word "vnokeckv."

Decolonize Sexuality

Decolonizing sexuality is a multitiered process of challenging dominant narratives of sexuality to advocate for sexual sovereignty and erotic survivance. To decolonize sexuality is not just an academic exercise; rather, it is an engaged process that includes the geographic, emotional, somatic, spiritual and sexual experiences that all the colonized, oppressed and marginalized people have a right to explore and claim as part of their sovereignty and lived experiences. As I have begun the process of considering what it means to decolonize sexuality, I have become interested in how colonized people, communities and bodies have survived despite the deleterious impacts of colonization—a colonization that seeks to in many cases erase those whom it colonizes. I am interested in what role (if any) the idea of love, whether it be erotic, romantic or platonic, or love of community or an idea, has played in the resiliency narrative, or what I call erotic survivance in the face of the histories my people endure and continue to survive.

Two-Spirit as a cultural and personal identity is rich and varied, with its meaning and usage shifting over the years (Gilley, 2006). It is first and foremost situated within

Indigeneity and though the term has been culturally appropriated by other people and groups who are not Indigenous, in this chapter, I use it exclusively to understand the term *Two-Spirit*. This is of course a political process because claiming Indigenous blood, land and tribal enrollment is a political act in and of itself due to the Bureau of Indian Affairs (United States) and Indigenous and Northern Affairs North's (Canada) blood quotient requirements that force members of sovereign nations to prove they are Indigenous. No other racial group in the United States or Canada is required to prove membership in a racial or ethnic group (Dunbar-Ortiz, 2015). The term *Two-Spirit* is often used as an umbrella term for Native American/American Indian/Indian/First Nations/Aboriginal people who experience gender and sexual orientation variance. It is not meant as a replacement for Indigenous languages that already have a word to describe Two-Spirit people. Examples include wintke (Dakota), nadleeh (Navajo) and lhamana (Zuni) (Roscoe, 1987). The term was coined in 1990 (Balsam, Huang, Fieland, Simoni, & Walters, 2004; Morgensen, 2011) challenging years of problematic language perpetuated by anthropologists (Mead, 1949; Williams, 1986; see also Weston & Djohari, 2020).

Two-Spirit love can be thought of as erotic, in the way we think of eros (Plato, 326 BCE as cited in Soble, 1989)—the way to spirit (spirit is used as an umbrella term and not in a monolithic or dogmatic way) and as survivance because Two-Spirit stories and traditions have survived over 500 years of colonization (Roscoe & Burns, 1988). Finally, to decolonize sexuality is to claim sexual sovereignty and erotic survivance in Two-People's stories and expressions of love, intimacy, sex and pleasure.

Vnokeckv at the BAAITS Powwow

By the time grand entry has finished, there is a swell of energy in the air. The once empty 50,000 ft.[2] warehouse has been filled with prayers, drums, feet connecting with the ground and voices singing lulu in a high-pitched vocalization where the tongue clicks the back of the top teeth, in a call and response fashion. There is a look of joy across people's expressions and a sense of pride in the way they hold their bodies. Here, they feel welcome. Here, they feel seen. Here, all parts of their identity are welcome. Here, they feel community. When they feel community, they feel love. One of the founders of the BAAITS powwow, Miko Thomas (Chickasaw), states, "we wanted a powwow that accepted everybody and was welcoming to all people. We stress that everyone in our community is welcome. It's not just about Two-Spirit people or LGBT people. It's something we can give back to our community" (Thomas, 2018). This sense of giving back to community is a traditional Indigenous value. It is in the value of community that vnokeckv lies. This sense of community love is what drives the BAAITS powwow committee to provide a space where Two-Spirit people and their allies can come together and work toward healing colonial trauma and use their sexual sovereignty and erotic survivance as tools for liberation. Powwow participants and attendees experience a sense of community love and witness the transformative experience.

Once the powwow is well under way, I always take a moment to go up into a loft area and look at what was created. It is in this moment that I understand vnokeckv because I feel and see the community and connections that are being made. This view has helped me understand vnokeckv is a dynamic moving practice. Vnokeckv at the BAAITS powwow is a bidirectional process wherein participants and attendees create a community of support, nonjudgment and healing. There is an overwhelming sense of visibility. Two-Spirit people are thriving, creating and giving back to each other and the broader community of Indigenous people and allies in and around the Bay Area. The BAAITS powwow has also served as the model for other Two-Spirit powwows that are now taking place across the United States and Canada.

At the end of the night, after the attendees, vendors, dancers, drums and volunteers have made their way out of the pavilion, my attention is once again drawn to the daunting and exhilarating space that only moments before was, to many people, a kind of return to the circle and a reclamation of Indigeneity and Two-Spirit pride. I wonder what will happen for the participants and the attendees between now and the next powwow. Will this sense of vnokeckv last?

Buscaglia (1972) writes, "real love creates it never destroys" (p. 88). I am reminded of a Lakota mother I met at the BAAITS Powwow a few years ago. She shared that her teenage son had attempted suicide because he felt shame for being gay. When she learned about Two-Spirit people she shared the information with her son who found out about the BAAITS powwow on Facebook. Together they traveled to San Francisco to attend the powwow. The mother shared how loved and accepted they both felt at the powwow. She wanted to share how much love she and her son were feeling. Their story evokes Buscaglia's (1972) idea about love as a force of creation. The powwow and sense of acceptance they felt helped to create the love they experienced. My hope is this feeling has lasted for this family and for all the attendees of the previous BAAITS powwows. I also hope that those that have yet to attend, though feeling uplifted knowing the powwow exists, will continue to feel excited and inspired. Let us advocate for the inclusion of vnokeckv and Two-Sprit love as aspects of Indigenous knowledge that should be included as part of sexuality studies. Vnokeckv and Two-Spirit love are about creation, the creation of a community of people who share a similar idea of what it means to have your sexuality be an integral part of your sexual sovereignty and erotic survivance and aid in decolonizing sexuality.

References

Balsam, K., Huang, B., Fieland, K. C., Simoni, J. M., & Walters, K. L. (2004). Culture, trauma, and wellness: A comparison of heterosexual and lesbian, gay, bisexual, and two-spirit Native Americans. *Cultural Diversity and Ethnic Minority Psychology*, *10*(3), 287–301. https://doi.org/10.1037/1099-9809.10.3.287

Buscaglia, L. (1972). *LOVE*. New York: Prelude.

Crenshaw, K. (1989). Demarginalizing the intersection of race and sex: A Black feminist critique of antidiscrimination doctrine, feminist theory and antiracist politics. *University of Chicago Legal Forum*, *1989*(1), 8th ser., 139–167.

Crenshaw, K. (1991). Mapping the margins: Intersectionality, identity politics, and violence against women of color. *Stanford Law Review*, *43*(6), 1241. doi:10.2307/1229039

Driskill, Q., Finley, C., Morgensen, S., & Gilley, B. (Eds.). (2011). *Queer indigenous studies critical interventions in theory, politics, and literature*. Tucson: University of Arizona Press.

Driskill, Q., Kenney, M., & Lara, J. (2011). *Sovereign erotics: A collection of two-spirit literature* (Q. Driskill, D. Justice, L. Tatonetti, & D. Miranda, Eds.). Tucson: University of Arizona Press.

Dunbar-Ortiz, R. (2015). *An indigenous peoples history of the United States for young people*. Boston, MA: Beacon Press.

Gilley, B. J. (2006). *Becoming two-spirit gay identity and social acceptance in Indian country*. Lincoln: University of Nebraska Press.

Jolivétte, A. (2016). *Indian blood: HIV and colonial trauma in San Francisco's two-spirit community*. Seattle: University of Washington Press.

Justice, D., Rifkin, M., & Schneider, B. (Eds.). (2010). Sexuality, nationality, indigeneity. *A Journal of Lesbian and Gay Studies, 16*. Plato. (360 B.C.E.). *Symposium* (B. J., Trans., n.d.). Retrieved from http://classics.mit.edu/Plato/symposium.html

Mead, M. (1949). *Male and female*. New York: Perennial.

Roscoe, W. (1987). Bibliography of Berdache and alternative gender roles among North American Indians. *Journal of Homosexuality, 14*(1/2), 81–171.

Roscoe, W., & Burns, R. (Eds.). (1988). *Living the spirit: A gay American Indian anthology*. New York: St. Martin's Press.

Simpson, L. B. (2017). *As we have always done*. Minneapolis: University of Minnesota Press.

Soble, A. (Ed.). (1989). *Eros, agape, and philia: Readings in the philosophy of Love*. New York: Paragon House.

TallBear, K. (2019). Polyamory, indigeneity, and cultural politics in the US and Canada. Retrieved from http://www.criticalpolyamorist.com/

Thomas, M. (2018). *Largest two spirit pow wow in the nation*. Retrieved from https://youtu.be/gjZAb01U3Ac

Vizenor, G. (Ed.). (2008). *Survivance: Narratives of native presence*. Lincoln: University of Nebraska Press.

Weston, G., & Djohari, N. (2020). *Anthropological controversies: The "crimes" and misdemeanors that shaped a discipline*. New York: Routledge.

Williams, W. L. (1986). *The spirit and the flesh: Sexual diversity in American Indian culture*. New York: Beacon Press.

Chapter 10

WHITE FRAGILITY AND DECOLONIZING SEXUALITY RESEARCH

Satori Madrone and Carole Clements

According to DiAngelo (2018a), White fragility is composed of six predominant pillars that support and perpetuate its invisible structure: a good/bad binary, implicit bias, individualism, universalism, internalized superiority, White supremacy and segregation. While the scope of this chapter precludes a thorough examination of the pillars, naming them highlights the complexity and insidiousness of White fragility and its complicit role in maintaining interpersonal biases and the racialized social order within sexuality research.

To succinctly frame our discussion for this brief examination, we will first show how sexuality continues to be shaped by the invisibility of a historically nonreflexive, nonembodied Whiteness that permeates research by continuing to anchor investigations into sexuality to heteropatriarchal, hegemonic and colonizing ideologies. Second, we will highlight key issues and explore how effective decolonizing sexuality research must explicitly interrogate White fragility to address the dilemma of institutional and interpersonal biases of Whiteness. This interrupts the default for Western-based social order and epistemologies that saturate, assimilate and organize bodies, time and space, including research on sexualities. Finally, we will unpack how the valuable methods provided by a reflexive, embodied inquiry not only can reshape critical sexuality studies but also can reconfigure the approach of sexuality research to contextualize its glocal impacts.

Constructing Sexuality

First, it is vital to illuminate that sexuality research and scholarly production largely continue to be affected and shaped through the lens of Whiteness. Sociologically, *Whiteness* is the operating system of race and racial hierarchy that situates itself as the central reference point of racial identity through the naming of difference. As such, Whiteness and the White body have become an invisible or *default* identity, which has influenced how sexuality has been conceptualized, investigated and understood. It is also important to recognize that *Whiteness* is not solely a racial category. Rather, Whiteness is constructed alongside heteropatriarchy, androcentrism and biological essentialism, thereby conceiving sexuality in a very particular way. This has resulted in a production of science across various fields that names difference from the White (male) body as a motivator for study, including homosexuality, women's sexuality and Black sexuality.

Importantly, sexuality research has made vital strides in challenging and locating epistemologies and their construction, including feminism and decolonization as two ways to disrupt the systemic practice of engaging science through a White-biased lens and within the White space of research and academia. Applying feminist geography to the occupation of space, for example, considers that "to think geography[ically] […] is to occupy a [white] masculine subject position" (Rose, 1993, p. 4). When the very space in which reality is conceptualized, described and engaged is influenced by one dominant perspective, such as that of Whiteness or maleness, then the existence of all other ways of understanding reality is ignored, suppressed or viewed as "alternative." In this way, Whiteness remains largely unaddressed in sexuality research, although it occupies the background on which the research is conducted and data interpreted. This is evident in the lack of discourse around the existence of *White sexuality*, even though sexuality has been racialized and predicated on Whiteness since the scientific study of sex and race arose in the same historic time–space of the eighteenth century (Laqueur, 1990).

Decolonizing Sexuality Research Interrogates White Fragility

While *colonization* is often thought of in historical terms, it describes the strategic system of appropriation and dominance, including the formation and consumption of assets such as property and territorialization, as practiced through the subjugation of one group over another (Moreton-Robinson, 2015). We argue that colonization can function within sexuality research as a method of stabilizing and solidifying Whiteness as the origin of producing legitimate bodies, including bodies of knowledge, segregating sexuality according to a White understanding of difference and sameness, which may account for the invisibility of the concept and study of White sexuality.

As a legal status, the law's construction of Whiteness defined and affirmed critical aspects of identity (i.e., by answering "who is White?"); of privilege (i.e., defining which benefits accrue to that status); and of property (i.e., by creating a framework of which legal entitlements arise from that status; Harris, 1993). Whiteness at various times signifies and is deployed as identity, status and property, sometimes singularly, sometimes in tandem (Harris, 1993, p. 1744). Consequently, the bodies, sexualities and (re)production of women, People of Color, children and the fertility of the land have been historically institutionalized and legalized as an extension of White patriarchal property and its legacy.

The continued fight for social equanimity and equality among groups of nonheteronormative and non-White identities and their allies amplifies the dilemma of how to disrupt hegemonic systems and logics that have been conceptualized and organized by patriarchal White space. Sexuality research is both a location for potentially reproducing unexamined institutional bias as well as an emergent platform to explore and apply the praxis of decolonization that interrogates Whiteness and its fragility, particularly for White sexuality researchers. Decolonization is often considered to be in binary and oppositional relationship with colonization as a means to "undo" and/or rectify racialized superiority and wrongdoing, although it is often approached as more theoretical or metaphorical, than the actual (Tuck & Yang, 2012). To be effective, decolonizing sexuality research must explicitly interrogate Whiteness and the fragility that accompanies it, or it remains a largely conceptual endeavor instead of a potential research program informed by visceral, glocal and lived experience impacting the materiality of being.

White fragility describes the condition of psychological and emotional distress and state of overwhelm that White people (including researchers) often report experiencing when interrogating Whiteness (DiAngelo, 2011, 2018b). As White researchers (including the authors) examine our unearned privilege, the reflex of White guilt that is endemic to White fragility can lead to overwhelm and immobility that creates a barrier to moving forward. Becoming aware of the impacts of White privilege and colonization in society at large and within sexuality research in particular can feel like a task too formidable to approach. However, once we understand that this common response is how White fragility operates to recenter Whiteness, we can pause and redirect our focus. In taking action, we will inevitably bring our Whiteness (and White fragility) with us, yet by developing compassionate awareness we can simultaneously attune to our feelings of discomfort and the task at hand, which is to interrogate and disrupt the perpetuation and effects of Whiteness and White fragility in sexuality research.

Embodied Reflexivity as a Decolonizing Method

Sexuality is manifested through the body, which is a complex amalgamation of biology and culture, subjectivity and objectivity, the individual and collective, traumatic suffering and joyful celebration as well as uncertainties and new discoveries. With the body as a site of sexuality research, the idea of *embodiment* challenges us to approach the body as fluid rather than fixed and multimodal in its expression. To be effective as a decolonizing method, embodied reflexivity moves researchers and their questions beyond the limitations of individuals and their "internal cogitations" toward queries that involve embodied (not just linguistic) communication and collective experience (Nellhaus, 2017, p. 44).

As a method, decolonization begins to transform research when Whiteness-producing biases about sexuality are made explicit and mindfully interrogated through reflexive embodiment in research that moves beyond the limitations of linguistics. Whereas discursive reflexivity orients toward questioning and cognitive understanding, embodied reflexivity "engages all three aspects of agency: embodiment, efficacy and intentionality" (Nellhaus, 2017, p. 55). Performing research involves intentional and unintentional activities that create experiential, emotive and social meaning (Nellhaus, 2017). Conceiving and performing methodology through embodied reflexivity is a paradigmatic shift critical to examining how Whiteness is enacted within sexuality research programs. Bringing self-awareness and embodiment into the research process illuminates "not only speech acts, but also acts that speak" (Nellhaus, 2017, p. 46).

If we conceptualize Whiteness as an "act that speaks," embodied reflexivity begins to interrupt the default for a Western-based social order and epistemologies that saturate and organize bodies, time and space in response to White supremacy. White-*body* supremacy locates the visceral, bodily trauma of White supremacy *in the body* (Menakem, 2017), foregrounding the invisibility and impact of White supremacy's omniscience and power to annihilate. According to Menakem (2017), "The cultural operating system of white-body supremacy influences or determines many of the decisions we make, the options we select, the choices open to us, and *how* we make those decisions and choices" (p. xix). This is true regardless of skin color.

Given advances in neurobiology, we now know that our emotions operate in con-cert with our body, manifesting physiologically through the vagus nerve in a conditioned autonomic pattern of survival that causes our nervous system to react in a fight, flight or freeze response when under real or imagined threat (Menakem, 2017). We argue that White supremacy *is* a state of near-constant threat that causes habituated trauma-like responses: fight, flight or freeze. An embodied reflexivity is the antidote to interrupt a trauma response that is White fragility, even in sexuality research.

Impacts of Decolonizing Sexuality Research

Decolonizing sexuality research through the method of embodied reflexivity is a prac-tice in intentionally increasing the capacity for dissonance or discomfort at the somatic and cognitive levels that reconfigure Whiteness. Interrogating Whiteness through the lens of White fragility and engaging embodied reflexivity to move beyond the limits of language *is* the work of decolonizing sexuality research that advances the possibilities of glocal transformation. In this way, new frameworks such as "White sexuality" appear among the many vibrant social locations from which to apply critical sexuality research, rather than as the unexamined point of inquiry through which deviating experience is interpreted as "Other." An embodied reflection on the positionality of Whiteness and its fragility among (especially White) sexuality researchers has the potential to develop necessary praxis within critical sexuality research that incorporates context, reduces reli-ance on implicit assumptions and bias, and allows for an examination of the influences of global and local as differentially impactful. Finally, as White researchers examine and mine our biases with curiosity, rather than shame, self-judgment and/or guilt, the more empowered we can become to create and implement new possibilities for transformative sexuality research.

References

DiAngelo, R. (2011). White fragility. *International Journal of Critical Pedagogy, 3*, 54–70.

DiAngelo, R. (2018a). Deconstructing white privilege [Video file]. Retrieved from https://robindiangelo.com/media/

DiAngelo, R. (2018b). *White fragility: Why it's so hard for white people to talk about racism.* Boston, MA: Beacon Press.

Harris, C. I. (1993). Whiteness as property. *Harvard Law Review, 106*(8), 1710–1791.

Laqueur, T. (1990). *Making sex: Body and gender from the Greeks to Freud.* Cambridge, MA: Harvard University Press.

Menakem, R. (2017). *My grandmother's hands*. Las Vegas, NV: Central Recovery Press.

Moreton-Robinson, A. (2015). *The white possessive: Property, power and indigenous sovereignty*. Minneapolis: University of Minnesota Press.

Nellhaus, T. (2017). Embodied collective reflexivity: Peircean performativities. *Journal of Critical Realism, 16*(1), 43–69. http://dx.doi.org/10.1080/14767430.2016.1257198

Rose, G. (1993). *Feminism and geography: The limits of geographical knowledge*. Cambridge, MA: Polity Press.

Tuck, E., & Yang, K. W. (2012). Decolonization is not a metaphor. *Decolonization: Indigeneity, Education & Society, 1*(1), 1–40.

Chapter 11

DOING CRITICAL SEXUALITY STUDIES

Michelle Marzullo

Sexuality is not reducible to a body part or a drive; it must be understood as integral to an entire matrix of social, economic, cultural, and relational forces; it is constructed rather than given. (Petchesky, 2004, p. 13)

My work in the field of critical sexuality studies is situated across my biography of the last 20 years as activist, applied researcher, mentor and professor. Currently, I help shape one of the only dedicated sexuality doctoral programs in the United States at the California Institute of Integral Studies (CIIS). I began my career working in what is now generally referred to as "the field of sexuality studies." One degree was pursued via the first master's degree in human sexuality in the United States offered at San Francisco State University in the early 2000s, and my doctoral work was pursued at American University in Washington, DC, in the discipline of anthropology with a concentration in race, gender and social justice.

In both programs, I found one common comment that most professors of mine working on issues of sexuality would share, which went something like this:

> When I started my career I wanted to study sexuality but since there were no programs on this at the time and also doing research on sexuality was risky for one's career, I needed to do work on studies that had little if anything to do with sexuality and then wait until I had tenure to pursue a research agenda that focuses directly on sexuality. Otherwise, I would not have been offered a job in higher education or would not have been taken seriously, or worse—been considered a threat by my colleagues.

Such comments would sometimes be made in class lectures and others in advising sessions; yet always these feelings were shared earnestly with a hopeful subtext behind their words. In each interaction, the subtext was: I must understand the particular responsibility that I had building on their efforts. These were efforts born of struggle and heartbreak, of deferred dreams and actions, and of an audacity to *do*.

In this way, I understood that the work that I had chosen was always-already laden with power—as dangerous, taboo, scintillating, necessary and impactful as is the subject of sexuality itself. The main lesson remains that the subtext of power and the importance of the "social" (or sociality) in sexuality and sexuality studies are always there;

ignoring these issues is detrimental to our scholarship. Critical sexuality studies thus broadly articulates sexuality as irreducible from and yet fundamental to power matrices in glocally informed sociocultural contexts (Herdt & Marzullo, this volume; Fahs & McClelland, 2016; Plummer, 2012; Sigusch, 1998). It is one reason that I open this essay with a definition of sexuality as matrixed with power (Petchesky, 2004).

This essay discusses how we are doing critical sexuality studies work at this moment in the program that I am leading at CIIS. I temper this writing with two caveats. First, what I talk about here is not the only way to do or think *critical sexuality studies*, nor am I proposing that the approach articulated here is complete or final. In fact, the articles that I cite, which explicitly discuss critical sexuality studies as a field of inquiry, are written by sociologists (Erel, Haritaworn, Gutiérrez Rodríguez, & Klesse, 2010; Plummer, 2012), two psychologists (Fahs & McClelland, 2016) and a sexologist/physician (Sigusch, 1998)—all provide partial views of critical sexuality studies from their disciplinary vantage points (though they are not in conversation with each other as far as I know). This lack of inter-disciplinary coordination or agreement is one limitation of talking about critical sexuality studies now as it is emergent. Different scholars will draw on and point to the sources they are most engaged with. Yet as I look across these perspectives from a field-based vantage point that is not limited by a specific disciplinary or topical boundary, there emerges a way of doing this work as I present here. My second caveat is practical as with any praxis (the place where theory meets practice): the doing of critical sexuality studies that I write about here will change as I will change.

Hence, I offer this essay as a work in progress and as a call to learning and teaching critical sexuality studies together with other scholars across fields and disciplines—as an exemplar of expanding sexual literacy via research training programs and pedagogy. Our approach in the field of critical sexuality studies takes as a given that we never work alone in the academy or in research but rather in concert with those who came before—scholarly and ancestrally—as well as with faculty, students, staff, community and colleagues who are all glocally situated—reciprocally we always-already deeply influence, inspire, wrangle and keep each other moving forward. It is in this spirit that I offer this essay.

Thinking Criticality in Critical Sexuality Studies

So how do we think critical sexuality studies and how is this approach different from other ways of doing sexuality studies? What was left out of conventional sex/sexuality research? What did researchers ignore that has moved us to engage so centrally with the questions of power in critical sexuality studies? An answer may most simply be proposed by looking at two central epistemological definitions of "sex" via (1) *essentialism* and (2) *constructivism* to examine the underlying assumptions that shape/d both layperson and scholarly engagements with the topic. Epistemology is a concept that refers to knowledge creation and ways that we come up with what we know and how we know it.

Examining these two contrary epistemologies entails critical interrogation of their definitions and perspectives; this allows us to find ways to think about popular and community discussions on sex and sexuality that have shaped past works and through critique explicitly shape current works in critical sexuality studies. In my discussion below, I am not suggesting that we are past these definitions or that these have been replaced—this is not a progress narrative of sex or sexuality "facts" as now somehow agreed on among researchers, academics, advocates or in people's personal lives. Instead, I offer this section as a sketch that helps us orient critical sexuality studies as a distinct, emergent approach for thinking and doing.

The first epistemology I offer is called *essentialism* and is the one that is probably most familiar to the average person. Sexual essentialism is "the belief that sexuality is purely a natural phenomenon, outside of culture and society, made up of fixed and inherent drives, and that nature and these drives dictate our sexual identities" (Harding, [1998] 2003, p. 7). In this definition of essentialism, sex is only found in the body (e.g., in sex only involving penis–vagina penetration, in the genes through XX and XY sex chromosomes, in our ability to reproduce, etc.). In this rendering, sex is "natural" or "instinctual" so should be the same to everyone, everywhere. This way of examining sex and producing knowledge from this vantage is an essentialist epistemology.

The second epistemology of sex is the *constructivist* approach, also called *social constructionism*, which is just a way of saying that what we understand about sex and sexuality is actually based on cultural, social and historical discourses and learnings about these topics (Barad, 1996). Sexuality can be thought of as changing/changeable: identities that people use at a given time and place, ways that we have sex and ways that we think about conceiving children. To constructivists, these practices and ideas connected to sexuality are formed and kept alive in our social imaginary directly from how we think of our social relations, such as between race, ethnicity, gender, class, geographic context and historical time period through messages we receive from cultural, media, legal, biomedical, religious, technological and economic institutions and practices.

What distinguishes the "critical" component of critical sexuality studies is a commitment to ongoing interrogation of any epistemological frames used for understanding the way we talk about, think about, do and investigate sexuality. Although we may be critical of naturalizing all things sex, critical sexuality studies does not reject biological knowledge but instead treats that information as one source—not always the best source—and thinks closely about sociality as also a central source for understanding sex and sexuality-related issues.

Gayle Rubin's 1984 work, *Thinking Sex: Notes for a Radical Theory of the Politics of Sexuality*, is foundational to critical sexuality studies today. Through a nuanced review of historical Western society that is attendant to power structures, Rubin articulated a hegemonic sex hierarchy that she defined as "the charmed circle vs. the outer limits" ([1984] 1999, pp. 152–53). There she argued that the people most valued and protected are those within what she called "the charmed circle" considered to have "good, normal, natural blessed sexuality," which, at that time in the 1980s, included "heterosexual, married, monogamous, procreative, non-commercial people, in pairs, in a relationship, of the same generation in private, not pornography, bodies only and vanilla" (Rubin, [1984] 1999, pp. 152–53). Within this historically specific example we witness various essentialist assumptions of "normal" or "natural" sexuality linked to marriage and monogamy that are actually cultural and social practices that vary widely from place to place and throughout time.

Yet, "the charmed circle" is not only past practice. I use it as an example to make the point of characterizing what critical sexuality studies does in avoiding the naturalization of sex and sexuality; and I call for us to instead think critically about what we take for granted in the way that we do our research, think our advocacy and activism, and approach our intimate lives—What is "the charmed circle" of sexuality today? How is it different from place to place? and How has this changed since the time that Rubin wrote her groundbreaking essay?

" 'Constructionism' entails the belief that sexuality has no inherent essence but must be understood as a configuration of cultural meanings which are themselves generated within matrices of social (power) relations" (Harding, [1998] 2003, p. 7, citing Gagnon & Parker, 1995; Segal, 1994; Weeks, 1985). Studies using constructivism to form what we know about sex and sexuality often focus on such norms, practices, relations and institutions as highlighted in the Rubin essay. As Moore and Reynolds wrote in 2018, the example of the "charmed circle" was so effective because it embeds a critical pedagogical approach to sexual literacy that used Rubin's cultural insights to reflexively relay important sexuality information and unearth implicit assumptions (pp. 203, 215).

Central to the constructivist epistemology on sexuality is the notion that we must examine how those in power retain power as well as reexamine the ways that social structures are maintained, including where we personally fall in this power matrix. A constructivist approach to sexuality studies asks researchers to question the assumptions and power structures we often take for granted as merely "common sense," as "natural" or as "the way it's always been."

But what happens when there is not a hegemonic epistemology that is foundational to construct the problems of our research—nor an agreed-upon person or group practicing the only "good, normal, natural blessed sexuality?" How do those studying sexuality advance knowledge in those circumstances? The way that we approach an answer in our program is to understand the impact of essentialist thinking on constructions of history, such that we do not approach "tradition" or history as a sovereign past or as a kind of universal fantasy of omniscience, neutrality and sameness that denies difference (Felski, 2000, pp. 10–11). We do not "naturally" assume that all humans have a sexuality/sexual identity or participate (or not) in certain kinds of sex acts over others. Instead, we think of the contexts in which we are trying to understand a problematic in our research by rendering possible the coexistence of "multiple and mutually exclusive narrative possibilities without a point of abstraction from which we might survey them" (Felski, 2000, p. 14 quoting Elam).

If we are interested in explicitly forming an approach to critical sexuality studies, then our concern with sexuality and gender must be attendant to situational contexts as simultaneous to glocal power "locations." Examples of these locations from a U.S. perspective might include race and ethnicity; class; geographic location such as rural, suburban, rural, immigrant, citizen; age; religious affiliation; a sexed body; dis/ability; or various other salient sociocultural glocal identities and ascriptions that mean very different things in different parts of the globe. In other words, we must understand critical sexuality studies as always-already concerned with the complexities of power relations in sociocultural context, even as we understand the operation of power differently across situations.

The two contrary epistemologies that I reviewed above are often literally used to show what sexualities should be and should do. These are, however, just two different ways of constructing knowledge around sexuality. There are many epistemologies, or ways of constructing knowledge on and around sexuality and the ones that gain the most traction are those that are hegemonic, meaning not only mainstream but those that contribute to maintaining power for certain people and groups over others.

The term *epistemic violence* (Spivak, [1965] 1988) is often used in critical sexuality studies to reveal how and where certain ways of constructing knowledge around sexuality actually show us a battle that persists between who is in power versus who is controlled. Epistemic violence is a term created by Gayatri Spivak ([1965] 1988) to attend to the ways that non-elite people are not only kept from power but—via social or language practices backed by repressive actions such as arrest or criminalization—are also kept from being allowed to express themselves on their own terms. They are instead cajoled into using the words, concepts and ways of thinking about sexuality and gender like those who hold power do. A shorthand for discussing the impact of epistemic violence is to say that such non-elites are kept from being able to speak even if they have the physical ability to—or put more directly that they are silenced and their voices not heard even if they are literally speaking.

Understanding epistemic violence in sexuality studies is critical to our work, since identifying operant epistemological logics around a problematic is how scholars and activists open avenues for accurately articulating how people negotiate and construct ideas of sexuality themselves within power structures (see Erel et al., 2010 for various examples of critical sexuality studies doing this work). For non-elites or those who find themselves in "the outer limits," this is especially important as the point is to examine what people are saying about their sexuality or sex practices in the words and action of the people themselves—so as researchers we must be aware of the epistemologies that we are using and reflect on these to not allow our ways of constructing knowledge of the world to influence our interpretation of others.

For example, the term *sex trafficking* has been argued as holding within the concept an epistemology of sexuality that is implicitly informed by an essentialist frame assuming that people are only ever "naturally" interested in having sex with those that they know and never with strangers. Sex trafficking *is* exploitative and uses people against their will and without their consent, children and adults inclusive, to profit off of sexual violence and imprisonment. Yet the very term is often equated with sex work and then the two constructs are often spoken about interchangeably such that both are rendered with the same exploitative essentialist inferences even for people who are consensually engaging in sex work (Chapman-Schmidt, 2019). As Rubin ([1984] 1999) noted in her now classic work, the term *sex worker* encompasses

> the many jobs of the sex industry. Sex worker includes erotic dancers, strippers, porn models, nude women who will talk to a customer via telephone hook-up and can be seen but not touched, phone partners, and the various other employees of sex businesses such as receptionists, janitors and barkers. Obviously, it also includes prostitutes, hustlers, and "male models." (p. 172)

A collapsing of "sex worker" with "sex trafficking" means that two ideas begin to be treated as one—with the same judgments placed on both. This conflation is arguably epistemic violence in a pure form as it leverages the strong, emotional, social and legal responses against the sexually exploited and trafficked people versus those engaging in any form of consensual sex work (see Chapman-Schmidt, 2019 for this argument).

Such epistemic violence has practical, real-world impacts. For example, a federal law in the United States was passed in 2018 that purportedly aimed to abolish online sex trafficking (known as FOSTA/SESTA composed of two combined legislative efforts as the US House of Representatives H.R. 1865 Allow States and Victims to Fight Online Sex Trafficking Act of 2017 [FOSTA] and the US Senate S.1693 Stop Enabling Sex Traffickers Act of 2017 [SESTA]). The point of this package of laws seemed quite laudable as helping to stop online sex trafficking, especially focusing on stopping children from being trafficked, by making it illegal for online platforms and services to knowingly facilitate, assist or in any way support sex trafficking. Further, the law holds these online services legally liable if their users were found to be doing such things. These bills sailed through both houses of the US Congress finding bipartisan support among even the most progressive lawmakers (Soderberg-Rivkin, 2020). But the effect of FOSTA/SESTA, drawing as it did on the conflations of sex work with sex trafficking, was to shut down any sex work website or app and enable broad censorship of sex online driven by the idea that removing any online platforms for sex work would simultaneously remove sex trafficking. The impact has not only failed to stop online sex trafficking (Kessler, 2018; Tung, 2020) but has been tragic for sex workers who would use various online platforms to "protect their health, safety, and independence by building communities, distributing harm-reduction information and techniques, and identifying and screening potential clients" (Soderberg-Rivkin, 2020). In the two years after the law was passed, major cities in the United States saw a marked increase in street-based (rather than Internet-based) sex work crimes with many more sex workers missing or murdered than in the years directly preceding (Tung, 2020). The law also has far-reaching international implications for online services and platforms (Goldman, 2018; Jackman, 2017, 2018; Romano, 2018).

The total impact of FOSTA/SESTA has been to push sex workers into the streets using older forms of control such as exploitative pimps as middlemen, decreased financial independence through limiting their ability to advertise and decreased safety information sharing between sex workers who now are no longer able to share information about things like which clients are known to rape, kidnap and drug them, or which intentionally expose them to sexually transmitted infections (McCombs, 2018; Shakti, 2018; Soderberg-Rivkin, 2020; Tung, 2020). Working to critically think about epistemological differences and violences that influence how we talk about sexuality ideas in our everyday glocal contexts and how researchers and advocates go about constructing knowledge (remember the disciplinary differences between sociology, psychology and sexology discussed above) is critical sexuality studies at work.

In our sexuality program, we frame the "critical" in critical sexuality studies as based on the field of critical theory (see Easthope & McGowan, 2004; Parker, 2012). Critical theory is an orientation to critiquing the standard "disciplines" of the nineteenth century (for examples of critical sexuality approaches to these disciplines see: for the discipline of psychology: Fahs & McClelland, 2016; for biology: Fasto-Sterling, 2012; for sociology: Plummer, 2012; for anthropology: Vance, [1991] 1999). This notion of critique most famously emerged from the Frankfurt School (Easthope & McGowan, 2004) and within later currents of critical theory and philosophy emerging out of the humanities, converging notably in the field of cultural theory (see Baker & Jane, 2016).

Current forms of critical theory include feminist theory and critique, queer theory, critical race theory, postcolonial theory, decolonial studies, gender studies, and theories and approaches that arose with poststructuralist contributions—we introduce students to this theoretical array to allow them to understand the breadth of a "critical approach" in sexuality studies. By thinking critically about the ways that different disciplines have constructed knowledges around sexualities as well as the ways that we are investigating sexuality from our field-based perspective, we are opening a way of doing sexuality research that builds on the strengths of such different approaches and stays open to sexuality as an ever-evolving, glocally informed area of investigation.

Most importantly, we also teach our students to consider the moral and ethical dimensions of valuing certain people over others by charting glocally informed knowledge systems about sexualities and associated gender/s to accurately get a handle on why people behave as they do. For example, anthropologist Hector Carrillo's (2017) book examining the impact of the process of migration on gay men's ideas of their sexuality discusses the impact on sexual desire through the movement of a person from one part of the world through multiple other geographies to a particular destination. He argues that moving one's body across such glocally informed, ever-shifting geographies invokes various epistemological renderings with contextually specific historically bound meanings of sexuality (see Jolly; Long, this volume for similar examples). In effect, this contextualism means that the ways in which bodies are rendered sexually in terms of who is attracted to whom, and who the migrating person feels attracted to as they move, changes via geohistorical contexts in surprising ways through the migration process.

This section has reviewed how we think about the "critical" in critical sexualities studies. It reviews a way of engaging our works on sexuality driven by intricate understandings of people living in power relations to centrally examine contextual influences from one place to another that change not only how we do, identify with (or not) and think about sex and sexuality but also how our bodies actually are differently considered or impacted relationally across social and geographic contexts (see Clarke & Hanssmann, this volume; Coole & Frost, 2010; Fox & Allred, 2017).

Doing Critical Sexuality Studies

Even as critical sexuality studies does not yet coalesce around an agreed-upon definition or specific set of methodological approaches, our program draws upon the following useful conceptual and analytic anchors for training doctoral researchers (Broad, 2011; Browne & Nash, 2010; McCall, 2005; Valocchi, 2005):

1. Queering the relationship between sex, gender and sexuality so that taken-for-granted concepts and histories considered normative are closely examined in contexts of power, known as the Foucauldian genealogical approach (Foucault, 1977);

2. Taking seriously the nonnormative alignments, or "the outer limits," as areas to be investigated outside of epistemological ideals to understand people on their own terms (Rubin, [1984] 1999);

3. Resisting the tendency to essentialized identity or conflate it with a broad range of common sexual and gendered practices;

4. Broadening an understanding of power to include identity formation as well as other discursive formations and sexual acts; and

5. Treating the construction of intersectional subjectivities (e.g., thinking about a person or a group by taking seriously different social locations such as religion, age, class, race, gender and geographical location) as possibly performative (Butler, [1990] 2006) as well as intentionally performed.

The contextual specificity and focus on power underlined by this approach coupled with an assumption that sexualities are always-already relational, uneven and in constant flux means that it is a challenge to locate an object of study that is manageable within a world of locations, identities and practices related to sexuality and outside of epistemological/disciplinary restraints and debates.

In a broad-ranging review article, Fahs and McClelland (2016) lay out an approach for how we might identify an object of study in critical sexuality studies that takes power seriously. The works that inform this approach are drawn from a glocal register as "feminist hybrid scholar/activist groups that stretch across several countries and continents" (Fahs & McClelland, 2016, p. 393). The critical sexuality studies research epistemologies useful for doing such studies are (Fahs & McClelland, 2016, pp. 393–94):

1. analysis of specific concepts (such as homonormative, sex trafficking, consent);

2. analysis of abject bodies (or those that are often ignored because they are considered disgusting, repulsive, disposable, killable or somehow break boundaries; see Kristeva's 1982 work developing the concept of abjection); and

3. a critical assessment of heterosexual privilege.

Apparent in this framework for doing critical sexuality studies are the analytical and conceptual anchors reviewed above that focus inquiry on: queering (or genealogically analyzing) normative meanings of sex, gender and sexuality to avoid merely naturalizing cultural concepts; understanding manifestations of the nexus between culture and the body; and broadening our lenses across interlocking power systems by considering how and why we value certain people over others—this is critical sexuality studies.

Conceptual analysis in critical sexuality studies is a means for both epistemologically focusing our work and examining how scholars and activists, or scholar-activists, use these concepts in research and practice. Thus, critical sexuality studies must highlight "the conceptual slippages and blind spots that remain within these concepts and the research they produce" (Fahs & McClelland, 2016, p. 395). The approach is resonant

with the concerns and commitments of the critical and cultural theoretics and method-
ologies informing critical sexuality studies laid out thus far (see, e.g., Barker & Jane, 2016;
Broad, 2011; Browne & Nash, 2010; Erel et al., 2010; McCall, 2005; Plummer, 2012;
Sigusch, 1998; Valocchi, 2005; Vance, [1991] 1999).

Thus, when we think of doing our work in critical sexuality studies, we construct
problematics that are irreducible to only genes, to only individual decisions, to only one
single historical event, to some timeless identity. Critical sexuality studies pays attention
to how we value certain people over others in connected and traceable historical
accounts across vast global information flows to community-based activism to intimate
encounters. In our practice of it, then, critical sexuality studies engages the branch of
Western philosophy known as axiology to examine questions of what and who we value
and why (Bahm, 1993; Handoyo, 2011; Hartman, Ellis, & Edwards, 2002). Axiology is
concerned with ethics as well as aesthetics (i.e., what we consider beautiful or worthy on
our adulation and valuation) and political philosophy (including politics)—these themes
that are well known in the fields of advertising that use sex to sell things via aesthetics
and in politics around sex, sexuality and gender. Such a commitment to thinking about
value is meant to produce works that are "centered on the life chances and life situations
of people who should be cared about" (Crenshaw, 1989, p. 166). The key here is "should
be" or "oughtness" (Bahm, 1993; Hartman et al., 2002), which are the aims driving
axiological inquiries that also fuel so many studies on sexuality.

To continue with the example of Rubin's charmed circle ([1984] 1999), future critical
sexuality studies might ask others which people "ought to be" in the "charmed circle"
(these are studies of sexual normativities) and examine why they think this, or our studies
might ask how people conceive of and treat those who are in the "outer limits" (these
are studies on abjection that focus on aspects of sexuality and gender that are often
used to justify harming or surveilling certain groups over others), or ways to queer the
circle altogether? Upon which or whose epistemologies do we draw conclusions from
and upon whose values do we rely in such specific examinations of sexualities? There
are not black and white, right or wrong answers to every question that these examples
generate. Instead, an approach that is contextually situated, glocally informed and takes
questions of epistemology and axiology as central is key to doing critical sexuality studies
that advance accurate knowledge contributing to the sexual literacy efforts discussed in
various ways across the world (as examined in this volume). Practiced in this way, critical
sexuality studies is well positioned to continue exploring and advocating a florescence of
emergent sexuality-related identities, practices and topics.

Doing critical sexuality studies in the ways articulated in this essay means that our
works must necessarily include: an ethical commitment attendant to the influences of
glocal networks; an awareness of researcher positionality and self-reflexivity; being critical of received knowledge, including taken-for-granted concepts from our own culture/
s and training; and being attendant to "relational, uneven, and in constant flux of [...] a
continuum of materiality" as it impacts the body and sociality (Fox & Alldred, 2017, p. 4).

Therefore as scholars in critical sexuality studies we must: (1) be trained broadly and
keep up with social theory applied to produce more accurate, timely works on sexuality;
(2) take a stand in our work to engage the philosophical field of axiology, which means we

engage value across the fields of ethics, aesthetics and politics; (3) deploy self-reflexivity to clearly interrogate our approaches on sexuality issues; and (4) use the Foucauldian genealogical approach to accurately frame the people and concepts at the center of our inquiries as these/we operate within power structures that condition agency, behavior, meaning and opportunity for the people and issues at the center of our work.

References

Bahm, A. J. (1993). *Axiology: The science of values.* Amsterdam: Brill.

Barad, K. (1996). Meeting the universe halfway: Realism and social constructivism without contradiction. In L. H. Nelson & J. Nelson, J. (Eds.), *Feminism, science and the philosophy of science* (pp. 161–194). Amsterdam: Kluwer Academic.

Barker, C., & Jane, E. A. (2016). *Cultural studies: Theory and practice* (5th ed.). London: Sage.

Broad, K. (2011). Sexualities sociologies and the intersectional potential of two qualitative methodologies. In Y. Taylor, S. Hines, & M. E. Casey (Eds.), *Theorizing intersectionality and sexuality* (pp. 193–211). Houndmills: Palgrave Macmillan.

Browne, K., & Nash, C. J. (Eds.). (2010). *Queer methods and methodologies: Intersecting queer theories and social science research.* New York: Routledge.

Butler, J. ([1990] 2006). *Gender trouble: Feminism and the subversion of identity.* New York: Routledge.

Carrillo, H. (2017). *Pathways of desire: The sexual migration of Mexican Gay Men.* Chicago: University of Chicago Press.

Chapman-Schmidt, B. (2019). "Sex trafficking" as epistemic violence. *Anti-trafficking Review, 12,* 172–187.

Coole, D. H., & Frost, S. (2010). Introducing the new materialisms. In D. H. Coole & S. Frost (Eds.), *New materialisms: Ontology, agency, and politics* (pp. 1–43). Durham, NC: Duke University Press.

Crenshaw, K. K. (1989). Demarginalizing the intersection of race and sex: A black feminist critique of anti-discrimination doctrine, feminist theory and antiracist politics. *University of Chicago Legal Forum, 1*(8), 139–167.

Easthope, A., & McGowan, K. (2004). *A critical and cultural theory reader* (2nd ed). Toronto: University of Toronto Press.

Erel, U., Haritaworn, J., Gutiérrez Rodríguez, E., & Klesse, C. (2010). On the depoliticization of intersectionality talk: Conceptualizing multiple oppressions in critical sexuality studies. In Y. Taylor, S. Hines, & M. E. Casey (Eds.), *Theorizing intersectionality and sexuality* (pp. 56–77). Houndmills: Palgrave Macmillan.

Fahs, B., & McClelland, S. I. (2016). When sex and power collide: An argument for critical sexuality studies. *Journal of Sex Research, 53*(4–5), 392–416.

Fasto-Sterling, A. (2012). *Sex/gender: Biology in a social world.* New York: Routledge.

Felski, R. (2000). *Doing time: Feminist theory and postmodern culture.* New York: New York University Press.

Foucault, M. (1977). *Discipline and punish [Surveiller et punir].* (A. Sheridan, Trans.). New York: Pantheon. (Original work published 1975.)

Fox, N. J., & Allred, P. (2017). *Sociology and the new materialism: Theory, research, action.* London: Sage.

Goldman, E. (2018, February 26). Congress probably will ruin section 230 this week (SESTA/ FOSTA Updates). *Technology & Marketing Law BLOG.* Retrieved from https://blog.ericgoldman. org/archives/2018/02/congress-probably-will-ruin-section-230-this-week-sestafosta-updates. htm

Handoyo, P. E. (2011). *Exploring values: An analytic study of the philosophy of value (Axiology).* VDM Verlag Dr. Müller/Omniscriptum.

Harding, J. (2003). Investigating sex: Essentialism and constructionism. In Suzanne LaFont (Ed.), *Constructing sexualities: Readings in sexuality, gender and culture* (pp. 6–17). Upper Saddle River, NJ: Prentice Hall. (Original work published in 1998.)

Hartman, R. S., Ellis, A. R., & Edwards, R. B. (2002). *The knowledge of good: A critique of axiological reason*. Amsterdam: Brill.

Jackman, T. (2017, August 1). Senate launches bill to remove immunity for websites hosting illegal content, spurred by Backpage.com. *Washington Post*. Retrieved from https://www.washingtonpost.com/news/true-crime/wp/2017/08/01/senate-launches-bill-to-remove-immunity-for-websites-hosting-illegal-content-spurred-by-backpage-com/?utm_term=.537d3826da0c

Jackman, T. (2018, February 27). House passes anti-online sex trafficking bill, allows targeting of websites like Backpage.com. *Washington Post*. Retrieved from https://www.washingtonpost.com/news/true-crime/wp/2018/02/27/house-passes-anti-online-sex-trafficking-bill-allows-targeting-of-websites-like-backpage-com/?utm_term=.c66b4db8cdee

Kessler, G. (2018, August 20). Has the sex-trafficking law eliminated 90 percent of sex-trafficking ads? *Washington Post*. Retrieved from https://www.washingtonpost.com/politics/2018/08/20/has-sex-trafficking-law-eliminated-percent-sex-trafficking-ads/

Kristeva, J. (1982). *Powers of horror*. New York: Columbia University Press.

McCall, L. (2005). The complexity of intersectionality. *Signs*, *30*(3), 1771–1800.

McCombs, E. (2018, May 17). "This bill is killing us": 9 Sex workers on their lives in the wake of FOSTA. *Huffington Post*. Retrieved from https://www.huffingtonpost.com/entry/sex-workers-sesta-fosta_us_5ad0d7d0e4b0edca2cb964d9

Moore, A., & Reynolds, P. (2018). *Childhood and sexuality: Contemporary issues and debates*. London: Palgrave Macmillan.

Parker, R. D. (2012). Critical theory: A reader for literary and cultural studies. Oxford: Oxford University Press.

Parker, R. G., & Gagnon, J. H. (Eds.). (1995). *Conceiving sexuality: Approaches to sex research in a postmodern world*. New York: Routledge..

Petchesky, R. (2004). Introduction: Sexual rights across countries and cultures: Conceptual frameworks and minefields (policy brief). *Sexuality policy watch*. Retrieved from http://www.sxpolitics.org/wp-content/uploads/2009/03/sexual-minorities1.pdf

Plummer, K. (2012). Critical sexuality studies. In G. Ritze (Ed.), *The Wiley-Blackwell companion to sociology* (pp. 243–268). West Sussex: Wiley-Blackwell.

Romano, A. (2018, April 18). A new law intended to curb sex trafficking threatens the future of the internet as we know it. *Vox*. Retrieved from https://www.vox.com/culture/2018/4/13/17172762/fosta-sesta-backpage-230-internet-freedom

Rubin, G. S. (1999). Thinking sex: Notes for a radical theory of the politics of sexuality. In R. Parker & P. Aggleton (Eds.), *Culture, society and sexuality: A reader* (pp. 143–178). UCL Press. (Original work published in 1984.)

Segal, L. (1994). *Straight sex: The politics of pleasure*. London: Virago.

Shakti, A. (2018, April 10). SESTA-FOSTA proves lawmakers don't see sex workers like me as human. *THEM*. Retrieved from https://www.them.us/story/sesta-fosta-backpage-sex-workers

Sigusch, V. (1998). The neosexual revolution (J. S. Southard, Trans.). *Archives of Sexual Behavior*, *27*(4), 331–359.

Soderberg-Rivkin, D. (2020, April 8). The lessons of FOSTA/SESTA from a former content moderator. *Medium*. Retrieved from https://medium.com/@Daisy_Soderberg_Rivkin/the-lessons-of-fosta-sesta-from-a-former-content-moderator-24ab256dc9e5

Spivak, G. C. (1988). Can the subaltern speak? In C. Nelson & L. Grossberg (Eds.), *Marxism and the interpretation of culture* (pp. 271–316). Urbana: University of Illinois Press. (Original work published in 1965.)

Tung, L. (2020, July 10). FOSTA-SESTA was supposed to thwart sex trafficking. Instead, it's sparked a movement. *The Pulse (WHYY/PBS)*. Retrieved from https://whyy.org/segments/fosta-sesta-was-supposed-to-thwart-sex-trafficking-instead-its-sparked-a-movement/

Valocchi, S. (2005). Not yet queer enough: The lessons of queer theory for the sociology of gender and sexuality. *Gender & Society*, *19*(6), 750.

Vance, C. S. (1999). Anthropology rediscovers sexuality: A theoretical comment. In R. Parker & P. Aggleton (Eds.), *Culture, society and sexuality: A reader* (pp. 39–54). UCL Press. (Original work published in 1991).

Weeks, J. (1985). *Sexuality and its discontents*. New York: Routledge.

PART TWO

SEXUAL LITERACY IN POLICY
AND SOCIAL DISCOURSE

Chapter 12

MORAL AND SEX PANICS: BARRIERS TO SEXUAL LITERACY

Gilbert Herdt

Moral panics are the local tsunamis of society; they upend notions of good and bad and play havoc with the foundations of trust and respect in human relations. The history of moral and sex panics reveals a strange oscillation between the global and local, as panics that derive from distant places intrude into local awareness; and sometimes the reverse happens, with the eruption in a local community of a panic that seeks to strike a chord of anxiety and fear in a larger society. The combination of imported rhetoric and local community meanings is frequently operationalized in emotions run riot with fear, accusation and aggression that seem characteristic of moral panics. Moral panics are hence a liminal phenomenon, that is, the existential panic is located neither completely in the global nor in the local situations. The "glocal" construct is a helpful advance in thinking about how to situate and ameliorate the moral and sex panics of our times. Here I argue that the moment a moral panic breaks into local awareness, that moment provides the greatest challenge and opportunity for doing glocal sexual literacy.

A critical sexuality studies that neglects these openings for analysis and understanding is in danger of bypassing some of the most significant ways to build and increase human awareness and sexual literacy in society. The first aim of this chapter is to describe and illustrate just how moral panics undermine sexual literacy; while the second goal is to provide us with the knowledge, skill sets and practical aim of countering moral panic moments wherever possible with tactics to increase sexual literacy to sustain well-being, human rights and happiness.

A moral panic is a seemingly spontaneous and often emotional eruption of collective anxiety and fear that targets one or more scapegoats. Originally coined by the British sociologist Stanley Cohen ([1972] 2002, p. vii), "moral panic" was created in social deviancy analysis of British punk culture but was soon extended into a more general image of the "folk devil," that is, a condition, episode, person or group thought responsible for societal ills and evil. In this chapter, I will study the production of moral panics that victimize social and sexual scapegoats, such as LGBTQ people. Cohen's work was critical in initiating the sociological examination of the construct and then expanding upon it to study how different agents had contributed to it, especially the mass media, moral entrepreneurs, a vague notion of "control culture" and the public at large. Critcher (2008) has provided a lucid historical and sociological analysis of the functions and efficacy of the model. Here I will concentrate on some key earlier historical examples of moral panics that turn into sex panics that have been incited by the threat and fear of folk devils in many times and places forming an historical and cultural pattern across societies. In general, I will provide analysis of what I call cultural anger, that is, deep-seated episodes of emotions such as rage triggered by social conditions, and placed into the service of homophobia and used as a weapon of social oppression against marginal people and groups.

Since early modern times the moral panic has served as a connective tissue for inciting violence and destabilizing humane relationships in society. As I have written elsewhere (Herdt, 2009, p. 7), we might think of Socrates as the first victim of a pure moral panic in the era of Ancient Greece. He was accused of moral pollution by teaching the young to be critical thinkers, thus potentially fermenting subversion against the City State. Socrates famously committed suicide with dignity rather than compromise himself to the moral violence of the enemies of democracy (Stone, 1988).

Moral and sex panics evoke events and episodes of deep emotional reaction. Where the moral panic stirs up deep negative emotions to target scapegoats in society, the sex panic focuses on sexual issues as the means to marginalize and vilify people. These conflicts stir up communities into fear and hate, evoking episodes of hysterical mass rage that channel cultural anger vis-à-vis scapegoats so violently that the eruption of the moral panic forever alters the community's identity, its sense of dignity, trust and the meaning of its boundaries. Historically it becomes apparent that moral panics compress fears and anxieties, overwhelming individual freedom, dignity and rights.

Moral panics expose ideologies, hierarchies and social fissures or weaknesses in the social fabric. As I have observed before (Herdt, 2009), there is an increasing trend for the moral panic to be sexualized and weaponized. As Gayle Rubin (1984) and later Roger Lancaster (2011, p. 12) suggest, moral panics have victimized sexual minorities and in general incited emotional reaction to sex in the United States, creating a "parade of panic [...] [that] provides an important model [...] for the pervasive politics of fear." With lesson in hand, I argue that it is precisely the analysis of this use of fear and anger in social politics, particularly in glocal contexts, that must occupy the work of critical sexuality studies. When the rumors and fears get started, and the scapegoats targeted, truly dreadful things can happen, such as direct and terrible violence like victimizing young people because of their age and then changing definition of statutory rape in the 1970s and 1980s (Lancaster, 2011, pp. 64–65). Understanding the social and political manipulation of mass public emotions such as guilt, shame, fear, xenophobia and collective panic is vital to preventing these panics from disrupting sexual and gender expression (Ahmed, 2014).

Moral panics are thus very significant in shaping mainstream glocal sexual discourse through social sanctions, oppression, mass communications and political manipulation of individuals and groups, especially people living on the margins of society. Glocal analysis involves an understanding of how agents and networks permeate the boundaries of local communities, sometimes massaged by media (Critcher, 2008), and in our time, social media, which uses local panics as a way to interrupt and expand upon controversies occurring at the national or even global levels. Glocal analysis enables us to see this bidirectionality of influence from local to global, from global to local, creating a glocal zone that may be original in virtual space but become actualized into real-world events, movements and performances.

To sharpen this understanding of the intersectionality of local, glocal and global contexts it will be helpful to review several classic examples of moral panics in the history of sexuality. Time and again moral panics have been mobilized historically to sanction and scapegoat people who step outside of a temporalized norm: sexual progressives, misfits, outlaws and deviants, such as LGB people and transgender people, as well as women and children. These examples are not always thought of as "sexual panics," and yet, upon closer examination, the contents seem to help us understand the sexualization of panics. When people veer away from traditional sexual codes, as for example, children who engage in same-age peer sexual play, teens who engage in premarital sex and adults who engage in bisexual behavior, they have been labeled and stigmatized as morally "bad" yet as we know these so-called norms change over time. Yesterday's moral panic is not today's and today's will not be tomorrow's. Such judgments and stereotyping not only expose the fault lines in social cohesion and sexual inequality but also display the geohistorical mutability of such panics—moral and sex alike.

Consider first the historical epidemic of witch hunts during the Middle Ages in the Old World and the New World: perhaps you have never considered them in the context of moral and sex panics? The witch hunts spread through Europe (England, Germany, France, Holland, Spain and so on) and into North and South America (Colonial America and the Spanish and Portuguese colonies in the New World). They were especially horrific in communities that straddled ethnic borders wherein economic and religious competition between Catholics and Protestants was intense, as was exemplary in Germany where leaders created intense pressure and vulnerability, questioning: who was a member of the group and who was an outsider (Leeson & Russ, 2017)? In general, accusations and confessions of witchcraft were part of the political, social and psychological apparatus employed by the Roman Catholic Church to suppress, control, regulate, humiliate, punish and extinguish opposition in Catholic Church control and authority. The accusation of witchcraft could trigger a moral panic, which were usually whipped up to account for all sorts of misfortunes, plague, natural disasters or human death, insinuating the presence of cults and cabals within the community. Widows seem to have been a special scapegoat. Older widows, who begged alms, and who were very vulnerable due to the absence of economic and social support, were easily targeted. They were accused of cavorting with Satan or engaging in ritualistic sexual and evil activities such as blood sacrifices, cursing crops and causing sterility (Levine, 1973, p. 17). Perhaps these accusations of witchcraft were triggered unconsciously by how the denial of helping the widows may have led to guilt, shame and the projection of paranoid fantasies that imagined them as enemies of the patriarchal church and state (Levine, 1973). As these great fears of devil worship and anxieties about sex spread through rumor, gossip and accusations of witchcraft to villages and regional towns or institutional centers such as monasteries, the moral panic of witch-craft accusations wrought terrible havoc.

Indeed, this sort of rising great fear found its most horrific climax in the torture process known as the formal Inquisition of the Roman Catholic Church. Known from medieval Southern France, Northern Italy, Spain, Portugal, Germany and then the colonies of these great powers, the Inquisition was a kind of ethnic cleansing and ideological purity movement that for a time united the Roman Catholic Church and the patriarchal state. Men, women and children were tortured and executed through the Inquisition, sometimes as a result of nothing more than superstition, rumor, jealousy, misunderstanding and competition over resources. These moral panics locally created terrible spectacles of people being tortured, quartered or physically abused, including burning people alive in public settings to serve as a moral warning to others. There is no doubt that many of these victims were entirely innocent of any of the charges leveled; widows and children, men and women were charged with being in collusion with Satan or practicing black magic and blood sacrifices and sexual orgies, frolicking in dark forests and mysterious places (Phillips & Reay, 2011). Today we understand that a combination of dark unconscious projections to ward off feelings of guilt, as well as ethnic and religious rivalry in borderlands that created divided loyalties were among the salient causes of these panics (Herdt, 2009).

There can be little doubt that these waves of emotional and religious witch hunts were for centuries effective in the social control and oppression of sexuality and gender roles (Schiff, 2016), as a means of punishment of role violations or deviations from norms. No doubt the pilgrims' stiff attitudes toward sexuality in general and nudity and vice in particular fueled many a moral panic in the centuries that followed in the young United States. One of these latter-day pilgrims, Anthony Comstock, sexual conservative-moralist (Robinson, 1976), minister, postal inspector and crusader against women and their sexual and reproductive rights, became a household name in America in the 1870s. Right up until his death in 1915, Comstock played a major role in the demonization of nudity, obscenity and antiwomen moralizing. In fact, the moral panics stirred up by his sermons, followers and actions created a cultural anger that was effective in pushing through punitive laws (Werbel, 2018). There seems little doubt that Comstock's strident, antisexual literacy views directed toward women and children were strongly fueled by his religious and spiritual condemnation of lust, Eros, sexual expression and reproductive freedom. He famously used the Comstock Laws of the United States, which were a set of laws regulating what could be sent through the US mail system to primarily stop pornography and contraception from being mailed. Such persecuted important champions of sexual literacy and freedom were Victoria Woodhall, Emma Goldman (who called him a "moral eunuch," perhaps because he never married or because he seemed to hate women) and of course Margaret Sanger, renowned founder of Planned Parenthood. Sanger, a nurse who assisted in thousands of abortions, had to flee America and go to Holland for a time to escape arrest under Comstock's campaigns, and she luckily discovered the remarkably more open attitudes of the Dutch, which convinced her of the need for a new reproductive movement in the United States (Levine, 2000).

Through the centuries following the Inquisition, homosexuality remained a suspect practice, often associated with evil and madness. In such places as Holland in the
Golden Age, adulterers and homosexuals were targeted as part of this accusatory, toxic
discourse, that associated the moral panic of sodomy ("unnatural sex") with Satanism
(Van der Meer, 1994). The sodomites were sometimes thought of as corrupting and
making degenerate "normal" people. This was possible because there has been a tendency in the modern period to evoke the argument of the moral slippery slope, whereby
if one deviates from the norm just once, it leads down the primrose path to much more
deviancy, breeding sin, degeneracy, disease, destruction and death (Van der Meer, 1994).
To keep this kind of particular moral populism going, great barriers had to be erected
to control people and ensure that sexual deviants were punished or killed. Sodomites in
the eighteenth-century Golden Age of the Netherlands became the new evil, the new
"witch," for a new secret Inquisition. Rumors and accusations built up moral panics that
effectively extended persecution and even a sort of Inquisition in secret of these victims.
The Dutch authorities oversaw the execution of more than a hundred people in secret
trials of boys as young as 11 years old (Van der Meer, 1994) during this rash of moral
panics. Such capital punishments were largely stopped in Europe after 1811 but the
anti-homosexual laws and policies including incarceration continued well into the 1950s
and 1960s.

Now reconsider the facts surrounding the Holocaust during the Second World War: the
horrific offspring of moral panics created by Hitler in nationalist Germany. The monu-
mental anti-Semitism and hatred of the Jews by the Nazis, which was institutionalized
as National Socialism and reinforced by eugenics, was a most horrifying ethnic cleansing
and scapegoating. The moral panics that were central to Nazi ideology initiated an epic
tragedy beginning in the 1920s and right up to the day the Allied Forces seized control of
the gas camps. Their nationalistic, "pure" Aryan racial and tribal ideology whipped up
toxic emotions in ordinary Germans, including fear, shame, envy, greed and the impulse
to destroy. The Nazis effectively manipulated a variety of glocal situations throughout
Germany and indeed border areas, inciting moral panics that swept up whole regions and
created mayhem, looting, vandalism, random aggression, destruction of property and
murder. Additionally, the Nazi regime perverted medicine and science to render some
of the most unspeakable crimes that were sanctioned as medical experiments involving
extreme cold and heat, malaria, jaundice, mustard gas, horrible kinds of medical torture,
sterilization, castration and cruel experimentation on the genitals (Barenbaum, 1993).
Using lies, made up stories and false accusations in public rallies, about the Jews "controlling the banks" and "hoarding all the money," Hitler effectively produced an ongoing
tsunami of panic that made demons of Jewish people. Additionally, he scapegoated
homosexuals, mixed race people, non-Christians, the Roma, people with disabilities
and heroic intellectuals who dared to speak out against these deadly Nazi emotional
manipulations, accusing professors and artists of promoting godless communism (Mosse,
2003). In a practical way, of course, it was the Nazis who were the greedy capitalists,
because the moral panics enabled them to confiscate homes, wealth, art and intellectual property of some of Germany's leading citizens. It was inevitable that this moral

campaign would lead to catastrophe: the intentional mass murder of more than six million innocent people in what has become known as the holocaust.

Notice that in these two examples of prior historically tragic instances, extremely powerful state-like institutions (the Roman Catholic Church of the Inquisition and the Nazi Germany regime led by Hitler, respectively) used their awesome, structural power to squash, oppress and eliminate enemies real and imagined, imposing illiteracy wherever possible, to strengthen their grip on authority. This hegemony extended not only to who got to have sex with whom, and who got to reproduce, but who got to live, have dignity and freedom, or die. This is a power that Achille Mbembe terms *necropolitics*, or the politics of death (2003).

Sexual abuse of children is a theme of moral and sex panic in twentieth-century America. The classic and tragic example is the accusation of sexual abuse of very young children at the McMartin daycare center in Kern County, California, which eventually proved to be bogus and false. This involved bizarre and elaborate accusations of kidnapping, satanic rituals, group sex with very young children and so on in the 1980s. Whatever the reasons for accepting such fantastic rumors and accusations, the source was later identified as beginning with a schizophrenic parent, incited by overzealous prosecutors. Eventually all charges were dropped and the investigation essentially disclosed that this was the result of a moral and sex panic (Jenkins, 2004). But terrible damage was already done to the lives of the children and families; remarkably these same kinds of accusations of sexual orgies in day care centers spread to other communities, even Europe. Obviously, traditional print media coincided with emergent social media to play a role in implicit promotion of this transatlantic sex panic, inciting and in some ways irresponsibly reporting as factoids what was inuendo or worse (De Young, 2009). Perhaps even the very old Western notion of the "innocent child" has been destabilized by these incendiary rhetorical discourses (Jenkins, 2004).

IV. The later twentieth-century decolonization in the Global South is also associated with moral panics and sex panics as a general discourse of social life. Historically, of course, the issues previously mentioned, such as the witch hunts of the Middle Ages, were certainly carried into the colonial spaces of the Western colonizers through ideological systems codified into folkways, mores and state-based policies and laws.

In the twentieth century, however, we began to observe how the same kinds of moral and sex panics could be fanned into even the most remote and previously unknown social locales. For example, Christine Stewart (2015) reveals incisive examples of how, after the state of Papua New Guinea became independent in 1975, a series of moral and sex panics involving homosexuality and prostitution were spread by gossip and the traditional media of the times. Homosexuality, previously unknown to the social discourse of Papua New Guinea, was being weaponized to control and impugn its victims, perhaps motivated in part by the rising Evangelical church in Papua New Guinea (Herdt, 2019). One observer writes of how homophobia in Ghana was (and continues to be) manipulated by sexual conservatives and then further mishandled by the media, creating a moral panic that eroded the rights of sexual minorities (Tettey, 2016). These examples of state-sponsored homophobia arise from traditionalists who accuse homosexuals of being an import from the West, and Christian evangelists who have imported anti-homosexual discourse from the West.

Here is where the critical lens of literally seeing in the "glocal" example a larger lens of examining cultural patterns keeping in mind the contextual influences of local and global discourses can be useful. For example, in Indonesia at the end of the second decade of the 2000s, we can see numerous examples of how moral panics begin with the accusation of corrupting youth and children The accusations include making children into "homosexuals," and perceiving transgender people who work in hair salons as devilish or destructive (Ulung, 2019). These sorts of moral and sex panics destabilize sexual and social knowledge and agency, creating a new threat to full sexual and gender citizenship and democracy (Correa, Petchetsky, & Parker, 2008). As we know, sex workers and people in the gay and transgender communities enjoy freedom and protection in various locales around the globe. Studying these events and understanding these moral panics as processes that regulate certain people at certain times informed by specific time-bound logics is part of the work of critical sexuality that aims to enable full sexual agency and citizenship for everyone as part of normative sexual literacy.

Moral and sex panics seem to galvanize public outrage at one or another level of the population, and regional or even global levels, generally triggering a cascade of consequential collective panics (Herdt, 2009). In the Global South, it is interesting to note that the construct "moral panic" appears more widely in print, rather than online, media, which may relate to a generational difference in literacy and media (Altheid, 2009).

By contrast, there is a growing sense of expanding moral and sexual abuse that has transformed itself into a moral campaign known as the #MeToo Movement. While this has many characteristics of a moral panic its effect seems to expose rather than cover up. The sudden revelation that the Hollywood producer Harvey Weinstein sexually abused many stars and starlets in the industry, and corporations and bosses and lawyers systematically covered this up was a huge bombshell. Others argued that this had long been rumored but kept a screaming secret. Finally, after decades a flood of accusations, and what we may appropriately call deep cultural anger, spilled out, and culminated by propelling the #MeToo Movement into the national spotlight. We have witnessed many other stars, including those such as Kevin Stacey, accused of abusing male stars and underlings, and politicians and corporate titans all encompassed by this spreading pattern of hegemonic abuse of sexual power by cisgender men, and sometimes women. Secrecy and sexual shame were pivotal to these events. In the history of moral and sex panics, sexual illiteracy that is built up from secrecy and sexual shame plays a huge role not only in getting to the base of the original controversies but also in the public reactions and cover-ups that are part of the production of social, economic, political, gender and sexual inequalities (Teunis & Herdt, 2006).

Moral and sex panics in Western countries appear to originate in several distinctive structural processes in society that play out politically and emotionally quite differently in glocal contexts. To understand this intersectionality, I outline six key forms of moral and sex panics that vary by scale, history and force of expression, as follows (Herdt, 2009, pp. 2–3):

1. *Moral shocks* may instigate a panic (Bill Clinton's sexual abuse of his White House aide, Monica Lewinski, that provoked an effort at Impeachment).
2. *Great fears* may generalize these shocks and generate moral panics in diverse places (masturbation as a disease in the nineteenth century, the communist "witch hunts" of the 1950s Cold War in the United States).
3. *Moral campaigns* that may occur within a community but spread to a whole society, and scapegoat specific victims leading into sanctions and moral havoc (anti-abortion campaigns that criminalized women in the nineteenth, twentieth and twenty-first centuries, anti-homosexual campaigns in the 1980s that blamed gays for spreading HIV/AIDS, and today's anti-immigrant xenophobic rallies in America and Europe).
4. *Moral panics* then result, at first confined to particular contexts but then fanned by media spontaneously erupt across the society (fears that preschoolers were being sexually abused in schools in America and Europe, and today's widespread gun violence associated with mass shootings in public places such as malls, schools and churches driven by political, racist and homophobic fears of social degradation).
5. *Sex panics* may grow out of the moral campaigns and moral panics, leading to precise accusations about vice and the moral slippery slope that center sexual acts of some sort (sexual abuse scandals in the Catholic Church, for example, can erupt in a particular parish, school or community that fears widespread abuse, especially of children).
6. *Mass cultural anger* that dominates institutions and whole nations. These are collective historical processes that sometimes erupt into mass crowd panics with sexualized targets exemplified by figures in the early Roman Catholic Church, and later twentieth-century Hitler and the Nazis mobilizing antisemitism, feeding the Holocaust. Mass cultural anger can be fueled by fear, rage, guilt and shame that instigates action against perceived folk demons as scapegoats, and may unite glocal actors regionally against a perceived, common imaginary enemy.

For the better part of a century, moral panics have grown increasingly obsessed with sexual ideas and anxieties, such as masturbation as a "disease," homosexuals spreading vice or women enjoying pleasure that was believed to make them into prostitutes, lesbians, nymphomaniacs and mental deviants in the nineteenth century. In the twentieth century, homosexuals have been strongly identified with pedophilia—the rape and sexual abuse of children, despite the fact that most pedophilia is perpetrated by heterosexual men, often with someone who is socially close or intimate with a family (Seto, 2008). Likewise, in the later twentieth century, the HIV epidemic created extraordinary conditions for moral and sex panics (Watney, 1987). In the 1980s, for example, gay men and bisexuals, prostitutes and hemophiliacs, both White and people of color, were strongly feared due to the moral panic surrounding the HIV virus spreading into the blood supply, spreading into the water, the food chain and even into the air. The resulting panics involved the closing down of bath houses, restrictions on who could give blood, children being taken out of schools who had inadvertently contracted HIV and the temporary closing down of the schools in Atlanta, Georgia, from the fear of mosquitoes carrying the HIV virus, and other severe social reactions (Herdt, 2009).

In general, these kinds of moral panics not only passively support but also breed prejudice, and societal inequality, fueling the attacks by sexual conservatives to control minority and marginal people as scapegoats, that is, as the new demons. Of course, historically, such moral and sex panics have always provided a broad framework for what historian and philosopher Michel Foucault (1980) would call a technology for social and racial oppression, and for the sexual repression of the entire society. In this sense, we need a new critical sexuality studies that can empower sexual literacy for all people and shine a light on the continued demonization of the oppressed in the United States.

Some experts believe that the incidence and frequency of moral panics has been increasing over the past century, perhaps promoted intentionally or unintentionally by social media (Altheide, 2009; Herdt, 2009). It is not clear why; could it be that sex has become so common and suspect via social media that it is a means to an end, whether virtual or online? Certainly, critical sexual studies must deal with the profound role that the social media plays in the production of moral panics today; whereas in the past, word of mouth, rumor and gossip, pulpit preaching, lynch mobs and newspapers drummed up cultural anger, today the 24/7 relentless stream of social media in real time enables a whipping up of cultural anger at lighting speed. Or taking a thread of classical sexual theory, is it possible that the pleasure inherent in sexuality is suspect to society, and especially to its control agents such as church, family and school, and now social media companies, such as Facebook, who have legions of people working around the clock to free its pages of anything that remotely looks like sex online.

These collective outbursts of mass cultural anger, hatred, fear, anxiety and paranoia are especially illustrative of the dialectic between global, national, regional and local meanings and practices. Indeed, this is a long-term theme of the discourse of some of our greatest thinkers—from Sigmund Freud, to Alfred Kinsey, Michele Foucault, John Money, Robert J. Stoller, Eve Sedgewick and Judith Levine, among others.

In the moral panic we see contained the seeds of how global and regional meanings get inserted into local community processes, including resource competition, communication, household security and related "glocal" spaces. Here we can observe more acutely how mass cultural anger and toxic emotions intersect with mainstream and peripheral controversies, values, attitudes, beliefs and social practices to destabilize collective well-being, and impugn sexual literacy for individuals.

To summarize, moral panics may spawn sex panics and in turn precipitate mass collective violence of various kinds, sometimes leading to great catastrophes in human society. Historically, I have reviewed a range of key examples of how moral panics may transform the imagined community and state into a hotbed of danger and peril to marginal peoples. The political and social uses of moral panics by institutions and states to control, intimidate, confiscate, appropriate, scapegoat and even engage in ethnic cleansing is a powerful, indeed, almost a pervasive narrative embedded within the construct of moral panic. The emotionality of the panics is a key to analyzing these events (Ahmed, 2014). Focus on the emotions generated and how they can rally the collective shadow or unconscious in society—but also remember that these moral and sex panics have characteristics as outlined above that can be used in critical sexuality studies to analyze what a certain socioemotional moment is about.

Wherever and whenever they occur, however, moral and sex panics are a basic challenge to all human rights, to dignity, to freedom and to the most elemental of all rights, the right to live. They challenge sexual, gender and reproductive literacy at every turn. The moment a moral panic breaks out is the moment to advocate teaching sexual literacy, to clarify and engage with people to understand the context of the often glocal discourse fueling the moment, and to teach about empathy for and compassion in support of those being cajoled, persecuted and killed. This is an especially important calling for critical scholars to think beyond our own emotions to what we know about moral and sex panics, not get caught up into them ourselves, and try to remember our humanity in these moments of great strife. Indeed, a key reason to reconsider the meaning, patterning, location in time and space and impact on communities of moral and sex panics from the perspective of sexual literacy, emotional literacy and social interventions is that we can mitigate the tragic impact of these caustic episodes in human society. The world would be a much better place without moral panics. But in lieu of that, let us at least endeavor to create a universal moral campaign for human rights and sexual literacy that embraces critical thinking, social difference and cultural inclusion.

References

Ahmed, S. (2014). *The cultural politics of emotion*. Edinburgh: Edinburgh University Press.

Altheid, D. L. (2009). Moral panic: From sociological concept to public discourse. *Crime, Media, Culture, 5*, 79–99.

Barenbaum, M. (1993). *The world must know: The history of the Holocaust as told in the United States Holocaust Memorial Museum*. Boston, MA: Little, Brown.

Cohen, S. (2002). Introduction. *Folk devils and moral panics* (3rd ed.). New York: St. Martin's Press. (Original work published in 1972.)

Correa, S., Petchetsky, R., & Parker, R. (2008). *Sexuality, health and human rights*. New York: Routledge.

Critcher, C. (2008). Moral panic analysis: Past, present and future. *Sociology Compass, 2*(4), 1127–1144.

De Young, M. (2009). *The day care ritual abuse moral panic*. London: McFarland.

Foucault, M. (1980). *The history of sexuality*. New York: Pantheon.

Herdt, G. (2009). Introduction: Moral panics, sexual rights, and cultural anger. In G. Herdt (ed.), *Moral panics, sex panics* (pp. 1–46), New York: New York University Press.

Herdt, G. (2019). Intimate consumption and new sexual subjects among the Sambia of Papua New Guinea. *Oceania, 89*(1), 36–67.

Jenkins, P. (2004). *Moral panic: Changing concept of the child molester in modern America*. New Haven, CT: Yale University Press.

Lancaster, R. (2011). *Sex panic and the punitive state*. Berkeley: University of California Press.

Leeson, P. T., & Russ, J. (2017). Witch trials. *Economic Journal, 128*, 2066–2105.

Levine, J. (2000). *Disorders of desire*. Philadelphia, PA: Temple University Press.

Levine, R. A. (1973). *Culture, behavior, and personality*. Chicago: Aldine.

Mbembe, A. (2003). Necropolitics. *Public Culture, 15*, 11–40.

Mosse, G. (2003). *Nazi culture*. Madison: University of Wisconsin Press.

Phillips, K., & Reay, B. (2011). *Sex before sexuality: A premodern history*. Cambridge, MA: Polity Press.

Robinson, P. (1976). *The modernization of sex*. New York: Harper and Row.

Rubin, G. (1984). Thinking sex: Notes for a radical theory of the politics of sexuality. In C. S. Vance (Ed.), *Pleasure and danger: Exploring female sexuality* (pp. 267–319). New York: Routledge and Kegan Paul.

Schiff, S. (2016). *The witches: Salem, 1692*. Boston, MA: Little, Brown.

Seto, M. C. (2008). *Pedophilia and sexual offending against children*. Washington, DC: American Psychological Association.

Stewart, C. (2015). *Name, shame, and blame*. Canberra: ANU Press.

Stone, I. F. (1988). *The trial of Socrates*. New York: Anchor Press.

Tettey, W. J. (2016). Homosexuality, moral panic, and politicized homophobia in Ghana: Interrogating discourses of moral entrepreneurship in Ghanaian media. *Communication Culture and Critique, 1*, 85–106.

Teunis, N., & Herdt, G. (Eds.). (2006). *Sexual inequalities and social justice*. Berkeley: University of California Press.

Ulung, A. K. (2019, October 1). Shinta Ratri strives to give transgender youth a better future. *Jakarta Post*. Retrieved April 1, 2021, from https://www.thejakartapost.com/news/2019/10/01/shinta-ratri-strives-to-give-transgender-youth-a-better-future.html.

Van der Meer, T. (1994). Sodomy and the pursuit of a third sex in the early modern period. In G. Herdt (Ed.), *Third sex, third gender: Beyond sexual dimorphism in culture and history* (pp. 137–212). New York: Zone Books.

Watney, S. (1987). *Policing desire: Pornography, AIDS and the media*. Minneapolis: University of Minnesota Press.

Werbel, A. (2018). *Lust on trial: Censorship and the rise of American obscenity in the age of Anthony Comstock*. New York: Columbia University Press.

Chapter 13

SEXUAL LITERACY BARRIERS FOR INTERSEX PEOPLE

Angela Towne

Sexual literacy involves building skills for critically receiving (hearing), contemplating and communicating about sex and sexuality (Kruse, 2017). Sexual literacy programs often seek to engage learners in outcomes such as empowered health decision-making, sexual wellness and respect for bodily autonomy. Curricula also have great capacity to expand on these individual and interpersonal outcomes to include goals that impact greater ecological systems. For example, programs could potentially encourage critical reflection on taken-for-granted assumptions to create environments more inclusive of marginalized bodies while examining power hierarchies that have spread globally through colonization and imperialism (e.g., gender essentialism, heteronormativity; Fahs & McClelland, 2016; Jones, 2016; Kruse, 2017). One such assumption that regularly goes unquestioned in sexual literacy education, and in larger society, is the idea that only two biological sexes naturally exist, an implicit ideology called *binary sex* that often justifies hierarchical ideas about sex, gender and heteronormativity (Oyěwùmi, 1997). Naturalizing binary sex (i.e., female/male) results in *intersex* exclusion or pathologization, and this in turn creates numerous barriers to sexual literacy for *intersex* and non*intersex* people. Global movements to end this form of oppression are currently making strides to gain official recognition for *intersex* people's existence including burgeoning advocacy for *intersex* sexual literacy inclusion (Jones et al., 2016). Educators will want to consider these barriers in developing inclusive sexuality pedagogy.

What Does the Term *Intersex* Mean?

The umbrella term *intersex* refers to variations in genital anatomy, sex hormone configuration and/or genotypic sex where an individual cannot be easily categorized into a binary sex classification (i.e., female/male; Fausto-Sterling, 2000; Koyama & Weasel, 2002; Reis, 2009). Intersex variations often result in differences in secondary sex characteristics as well (e.g., facial hair, breast tissue). Although much information can be found using the search term *Disorders of Sex Development* (DSD), which came out of the 2005 International Consensus Conference with little input from intersex activists, the claim that intersex is always a "disorder" reinforces a false sex binary and acts as a barrier to social justice activism[1] (Merrick, 2019; Viloria, 2016). Although DSD has since been reinterpreted to stand for "Differences in Sex Development" (Advocates for Intersex Youth, 2016), my ontological praxis suggests reshaping the nomenclature by endorsing the terms *intersex*, *sex variation*, *sex diversity* and *nonbinary sex*.

Positionality

I am not an intersex person myself; I come to this work both as a gender and sexuality educator and as an ally who has loved people with intersex variations. I earned an MEd (Master of Education) and PhD in Human Sexuality Studies. I began teaching social justice-oriented sexuality in the nonprofit sector in 2001 and have served as faculty in collegiate Gender and Sexuality Studies since 2013. Although I often hear that intersex diversity is supposedly rare, I have had two long-term, intimate relationships with intersex partners. While acknowledging that I do not personally embody the subject, I believe that sexual literacy barriers have lifetime impacts that not only affect intersex people but also those who have sexual and love relationships with intersex people.

Considerations in Intersex Sexual Literacy

It is difficult to estimate the number of intersex learners that may be accessing sexual literacy information, whether in a classroom, online or through another modality. Reported frequencies vary anywhere from one in 2000 infants born visibly intersex, to one in 100 people with biological sex diversity in the general population (Fausto-Sterling, 2000; Koyama & Weasel, 2002; LaHood & Keir, 2012; Migeon, Berkovitz, & Brown, 1994). Because intersex constitutes a wide constellation of sex variations, criteria for intersex inclusion is debatable (Intersex Society of North America, 2008; Koyama & Weasel, 2002). For example, sports governing bodies, including the International Association of Athletics Federations, revise and update sex eligibility requirements for athletes dictating the point at which sex hormone levels (e.g., testosterone) and genital anatomies (e.g., clitoral size) become an intersex variation (Karkazis & Jordan-Young, 2016). Further, secrecy surrounds sex diversity (LaHood & Keir, 2012). Parents may keep a child's intersex status a secret, even from the child, or medical intervention may take place without parental knowledge under the ethical frame that nonbinary sex constitutes a medical emergency, even when physical health is not at risk (Anonymous OBGYN, personal communication, March 8, 2008; Chase, 1998; Koyama & Weasel, 2002; LaHood & Keir, 2012; Latham & Morgan Holmes, 2017; Reis, 2009). In addition, intersex variation may not be discovered until puberty because a person has "typical" external genitalia (Reis, 2009). Because of all these considerations, learners may discover their intersex status during educational experiences, perhaps right in the classroom. Educators must be sensitive to this possibility

---

1   Some intersex individuals may embrace the term *disorder* when they experience intersex variation as gender incongruent and/or as needing medical intervention.

and should thus assume that they have intersex learners in their audiences and classes (Koyama & Weasel, 2002).

Erasure, the denial that intersex people exist, is a primary barrier to sexual literacy for intersex people (Jones, 2016; Koyama & Weasel, 2002). In an Australian study with 272 intersex people, 92 percent indicated that they had received no education about congenital sex variation in an inclusive and positive manner (Jones, 2016). Instead, their education stressed "abstinence, notions of body normativity, binary sex and gender constructions, and an exclusive focus on reproductive penetrative 'penis-in-vagina' sex" (Jones, 2016, p. 611). This insistence on reinforcing a false sex binary in the service of heteronormativity makes intersex people incomprehensible to others, in effect, not only denying intersex sexuality but also their very existence (Butler, 1993; Chase, 2006). Intersex people (and nonintersex people) may compare their genitals and bodies to oversimplified diagrams, labels and messages without a way to understand difference (Brömdal, Rasmussen, Sanjakdar, Allen, & Quinlivan, 2018). This lack of representation and acknowledgment may result in a student taking a defensive stance against learning, and a student may close their mind even against information that may be useful to them (Dweck & Elliott-Moskwa, 2010). This type of erasure can also (unintentionally) contribute to learning environments supportive of hostility against intersex people, social isolation and discrimination (CECHR, 2015; Jones, 2016; Latham & Morgan Holmes, 2017). It is important for educators to understand that erasing intersex people can lead to both overt hostility and can be perceived as a kind of hostility in and of itself. One study participant offered, "I always knew I had a penis and a vagina, but I didn't find out that it was abnormal until I saw a diagram of the penis at school when I was eight […] I knew I'd have to hide it from the other kids to avoid being bullied" (Jones, 2016, p. 612). Sexual literacy education then becomes a milieu for devaluation wherein strict sex binaries are presented as natural fact.

If intersexuality is acknowledged, another sexual literacy barrier can occur when educators label intersex as a "condition" or "disorder" in need of fixing (Chase, 1998; Jones, 2016). Although intersex anatomy may occasionally indicate an underlying health concern, such as adrenal malfunction, "ambiguous genitals are in and of themselves neither painful nor harmful to health" (Chase, 1998, p. 192). Instead, a variety of harms may stem from the ideological denial of sex diversity and assumption that intersex bodies are disordered (Latham & Morgan Holmes, 2017; Reis, 2009). This ideology is based in hierarchical thinking and supports body norming regimens that are also implicated in ableism, ageism, sizeism, racism and transphobia. For example, where anatomy and physiology lessons define "healthy" or "normal" bodies inflexibly by stereotypical sex binaries, educators have responded to student questions about male breasts (e.g., "man boobs") or female facial hair as if the sex assignment were incorrect (Brömdal et al., 2018). Not only are people's understandings of one another diminished, intersex learners may internalize strict binary sex ideologies that devalue physiognomies that, for them, may be profound characteristics of their personhood (Alexander, 2010; Reis, 2009). Strict genital and body norming thus hinder all learners as norming does not demonstrate that diverse bodies, including intersex bodies, could be healthy (Bacon, 2010; Morland, 2009; Weil, 2007). Furthermore, this aspect of sexual literacy contributes to lifelong systematic oppression. The Council of Europe Commissioner of Human Rights (CECHR) noted:

> Visible physical differences such as androgyneity or sex characteristics usually attributed to the sex considered opposite to the one assigned at birth (e.g., breast development on [sex-assigned] males) may serve as a pretext for bullying and exclusion in schools, as well as under-employment or dismissal later in life. (2015, p. 43)

While defining intersex more positively helps advance human rights, sexual literacy educators can contemplate intersex sexuality more deeply. For example, body norming by medical intervention comes with its own set of sexual consequences. Surgery and hormones commonly prescribed (Jones, 2016) may cause shame, tactile desensitization, an association of genital touching with pain and bodily dissociation (Breu, 2009; Haines, 2019; Latham & Morgan Holmes, 2017; Morland, 2009). Overwhelmingly, medical interventions privilege normative aesthetics and selective functionality (e.g., urinating "correctly" or developing the capacity for penile–vaginal intercourse), which displace intersex sexual potential, especially that of pleasure (Chase, 2006; Latham & Morgan Holmes, 2017). Many intersex scholars have shared their experiences about these issues. Morgan Holmes stated, "All the things my body might have grown to do, all the possi-bilities, went down the hall with my amputated clitoris to the pathology department" (Chase, 1998, p. 195). Reflecting on medical procedural impacts on his sexuality, Breu (2009, p. 102) stated, "Sex and pain, desire and violence were complexly intertwined in my adolescent mind. Like most teenage boys, I wanted to have sex; unlike most, I was also terrified by the possibility." Morland too writes:

> When the nerves in one's genitalia have been damaged by surgery, the time of the touch changes. For example, one sees a lover's hand touching one's genitalia, but one does not feel it […] I know from direct personal experience that this is profoundly disorienting. (2009, p. 285)

Social stigma interrelated with medical intervention may influence a person's ability to develop intimate relationships in ways educators may also want to consider (Morland, 2009). The *Intersex Stories and Statistics from Australia* study found that intersex people who have experienced medical intervention were significantly less likely to experience orgasm, masturbation, petting and other types of sexual activity, and more likely to experience sexual pain or fear of sexual pain (Jones et al., 2016). In the documentary *Intersexion*, Mitchell explained, "For me, I haven't had a loving relationship. After all, I was a child being told my body was so horrendous, and so not okay, it had to have pieces cut off it" (LaHood & Keir, 2012).

Educators can plan proactively in a way that the early sex educators did not, for how to improve consent and sexual touch messages for intersex learners. Educators can become aware that (unnecessary) shame and secrecy in response to intersexuality, along with frequent nonconsensual genital touching and viewing under the paradigm of med-ical care, may actually groom intersex children for sexual assault (LaHood & Keir, 2012; Latham & Morgan Holmes, 2017). While that seems like a harsh statement, Mani in the documentary *Intersexion* explained, "Our genitals are touched right from when we are little. We've been taught never to talk about our different bodies, and so, sexual predators are very good at picking out children that would make good victims" (LaHood & Keir, 2012). Thus, educators will want to unpack learners' understanding of the "right to autonomy and bodily integrity" as an important aspect of intersex activism (Latham & Morgan Holmes, 2017, p. 86). A study participant with two intersex variations commented, "If this were more widely talked about, I may have had a chance of knowing what was happening to me" (Jones, 2016, p. 612). Intersex shaming and secrecy may also predispose learners to dissociate from sexual literacy material as an adaptive coping mechanism learned during genital procedures (Haines, 2019); educators may want to take precautions not to reinforce shame through unintentional victim blaming.

Intersex stigma is dependent on the prejudices of heteronormativity. Jacquet (2008) suggested that a body that is not clearly male or female suggests to some people a lack of masculinity or femininity and is, by extension, a heterosexual failure because "the division of sexual roles between penetrated/penetrating is at the heart of the heteropatriarchal sexual system" (p. 55). Indeed, health professionals often justify surgeries and hormonal interventions to allow for penile–vaginal intercourse (Cornwall, 2010; LaHood & Keir, 2012). Vaginas capable of penile insertion may be constructed in very young children "which often require extensive and sometimes painful dilation with a series of dildos to stop them closing up again," and penises "deemed too small to penetrate a vagina" may be amputated (Cornwall, 2010, p. 81). While keeping in mind that intersex people may identify as heterosexual, we might consider how sex norming and genital standardizations taking place in both medical and sexual literacy venues limit multiplicities of sexuality, sexual practice and freedom in love choices for everyone (Jacquet, 2008).

Rather than seeing intersex information as an additional section only relevant to intersex people, this contemporary inclusion is relevant and necessary to all students seeking comprehensive sexual literacy. Many learners have concerns about being "normal" when it comes to sexuality (Breu, 2009). Framing sexual anatomy and physiology in terms of diversity not only creates an inclusive environment, but it may also assist all learners in alleviating anxieties about body variations in appearance, physiology and sensation. We could upgrade sexuality curricula in ways that do not begin and end with binary sex and penile–vaginal intercourse. One example appropriate for older learners is to begin anatomical lessons with nondifferentiated embryo anatomy. Most embryos have gonads (Francavilla et al., 1990). Gonads will typically develop to produce reproductive cells (i.e., sperm or ova) and a combination of the sex hormones testosterone, estrogen and progesterone. Under the influence of the SRY gene some gonads develop into testicles, whereas others develop into ovaries, and some people have both (Foster & Graves, 1994). Beginning anatomical lessons on common ground with nonsex differentiated, nongendered sites before further differentiating anatomical potentials allows for more accurate understanding of sexual anatomy and physiology and aligns with a social justice orientation. It leaves room for understanding an intersex range of sex differentiation, creates space for transgender experiences and permits genital diversity in cultures under increasing pressure to norm genitals (e.g., in cultures influenced by pornography).

Global intersex movements have made progress toward official recognition that intersex people exist, and intersex sexual rights are coming to the forefront (Latham & Morgan Holmes, 2017). South Africa was the first country to explicitly include intersex in its equality legislation in 2005, followed the same year by Germany, whereas Australia adopted the first law including intersex status as a stand-alone prohibited discrimination in 2013 (CECHR, 2015; United Nations Born Free & Equal, 2018). Australia's Sex Discrimination Amendment Act "requires all schools to make education environments non-discriminatory on the basis of intersex status" and lays down positive provisions for puberty and sex education (Jones, 2016, p. 602). Indeed, sexual justice organizations around the world indicate emerging advocacy for sexual literacy programming that includes intersex people (e.g., New Zealand's Rainbow Youth (2018) and Planned Parenthood Federation of America (2020)).

Although intersex rights are advancing globally, more work has yet to be done. For example, the US *National Sexuality Education Standards Core Content and Skills K-12* recommends core competencies related to sexual anatomy in terms of binary sex (i.e., female/male). The glossary provides the sole mention of intersex, an incomplete definition: "Those whose chromosomes are different from XX or XY at birth are referred to as 'intersex'" (2012, p. 39). Educators, working together with activists, have the capacity to improve and to develop more inclusive, positive and accurate conceptual frameworks supporting intersex sexual literacy.

Sexual literacy programs have the potential to act as profound interventions against intersex injustices, eliminating barriers that keep people uninformed about their bodies. Attention to the excluded other has the capacity to open people up to loving relationships, creative eroticism and sexual health empowerment (Jacquet, 2008; Kruse, 2017). "If we stop thinking about sexuality in binary terms, a whole unexplored range of sexual practices, ways of thinking about these practices, sexuality itself or the parts of the body, open up to us" (Jacquet, 2008, p. 59). Pathologizing or erasing intersex sexuality, on the other hand, encourages a collective denial of lived experiences and supports greater systems of exploitative power. These characteristics diminish the capacity for public action advocating acceptance, value for and celebration of intersex and multiply diverse bodies (Alexander, 2010; Jones, 2016), whereas intersex inclusion calls into question biological determinism at the heart of hierarchical sex and gender relations and thus has transformative potential for all of us (Fahs & McClelland, 2016; Jones, 2016; Kruse, 2017).

References

Advocates for Intersex Youth. (2016). What is intersex? Retrieved from https://interactadvocates. org/our-advocacy/intersex-youth/youth-faq/

Alexander, M. (2010). *The new Jim Crow: Mass incarceration in the age of colorblindness.* New York: New Press.

Bacon, L. (2010). *Health at every size: The surprising truth about your weight.* Dallas, TX: BenBella Books.

Breu, C. (2009). Middlesex meditations: Understanding and teaching intersex. *English Journal, 98*(4), 102–108. Retrieved from https://www.jstor.org/stable/40503274

Brömdal, A., Rasmussen, M. L., Sanjakdar, F., Allen, L., & Quinlivan, K. (2018). Intersex bodies in sexuality education: On the edge of cultural difference. In L. Allen & M. L. Rasmussen (Eds.), *The Palgrave handbook of sexuality education* (pp. 369–390). London: Springer Nature.

Butler, J. (1993). *Bodies that matter: On the discursive limits of "sex."* New York: Routledge.

Chase, C. (1998). Hermaphrodites with attitude: Mapping the emergence of intersex political activism. *Gay and Lesbian Quarterly, 4*(2), 189–211.

Chase, C. (2006). *Hermaphrodites speak!* [documentary]. Ann Arbor, MI: Intersex Society of North America. Retrieved from https://www.youtube.com/watch?v=9HwnxbQ57DY&list=PL1Cfx60VSHRIK1NbCsA04Fc9pRXZq-4u3&index=3

Cornwall, S. (2010). Ratum et consummatum: Refiguring non-penetrative sexual activity theologically, in light of intersex conditions 1. *Theology & Sexuality, 16*(1), 77–93. doi:10.1558/tse.v16i1.77

Council of Europe Commissioner of Human Rights (CECHR). (2015). *Human rights and intersex people* (2nd ed.). Strasbourg: Council of Europe.

Dweck, C. S., & Elliott-Moskwa, E. S. (2010). Self-theories: The roots of defensiveness. In J. E. Maddux & J. P. Tangney (Eds.), *Social psychological foundations of clinical psychology* (pp. 136–153). New York: Guilford Press.

Fahs, B., & McClelland, S. I. (2016). When sex and power collide: An argument for critical sexuality studies. *Journal of Sex Research, 54*(4–5), 392–416. doi:10.1080/00224499.2016.1152454

Fausto-Sterling, A. (2000). The five sexes, revisited. *Sciences, 40*(4), 18–23.

Foster, J. W., & Graves, J. A. (1994). An SRY-related sequence on the marsupial X chromosome: Implications for the evolution of the mammalian testis-determining gene. *Proceedings of the National Academy of Sciences of the United States of America, 91*(5), 1927–1931. Retrieved from https://doi.org/10.1073/pnas.91.5.1927

Francavilla, S., Cordeschi, G., Properzi, G., Concordia, N., Cappa, F., & Pozzi, V. (1990). Ultrastructure of fetal human gonad before sexual-differentiation and during early testicular and ovarian development. *Journal of Submicroscopic Cytology and Pathology, 22*(3), 389–400.

Future of Sex Education Initiative. (2012). *National sexuality education standards: Core content and skills, K-12* [a special publication of the Journal of School Health]. Retrieved from http://www.futureofsexeducation.org/documents/josh-fose-standards-web.pdf

Haines, S. (2019). *The politics of trauma: Somatics, healing, and social justice*. Berkeley, CA: North Atlantic Books.

Intersex Society of North America. (2008). Intersex conditions. Retrieved from https://isna.org/faq/conditions/

Jacquet, L. (2008). La reinvention de la sexualité chez les intersexes (google Trans.). *Nouvelles Questions Féinistes, 27*(1), 49–60. https://www.jstor.org/stable/40620392

Jones, T. (2016). The needs of students with intersex variations. *Sex Education, 16*(6), 602–618. doi:http://dx.doi.org/10.1080/14681811.2016.1149808

Jones, T., Hart, B., Carpenter, M., Ansara, G., Leonard, W., & Lucke, J. (2016). *Intersex stories and statistics from Australia*. Cambridge: Open Book.

Karkazis, K., & Jordan-Young, R. (2016). The trouble with too much T. In J. Schneiderman (Ed.), *Queer: A reader for writers* (pp. 221–225). Oxford: Oxford University Press.

Koyama, E., & Weasel, L. (2002). From social construction to social justice: Transforming how we teach about intersexuality. *Women's Studies Quarterly, 30*(3–4), 169–178. https://www.jstor.org/stable/40003252

Kruse, M. (2017). Rethinking sexual literacy in the comp classroom: Huffer, Alexander, Foucault. *Feminist Formations, 29*(3), 186–192. doi: https://doi.org/10.1353/ff.2017.0040

LaHood, G. (Director), & Keir, J. (Producer) (2012). *Intersexion: Gender ambiguity unveiled* [Video file]. Ponsonby Productions: New Zealand.

Latham, J. R., & Holmes, M. M. (2017). Intersex ageing and (sexual) rights. In C. Barrett & S. Hinchliff (Eds.), *Addressing the sexual rights of older people: Theory, policy, and practice* (pp. 104–116). Abingdon: Routledge.

Merrick, T. (2019). From "intersex" to "DSD": A case of epistemic injustice. *Synthese, 196*, 4429–4447. doi: https://doi.org/10.1007/s11229-017-1327-x

Migeon, C. J., Berkovitz, G. D., & Brown, T. R. (1994). Sexual differentiation and ambiguity. In M. S. Kappy, R. M. Blizzard, & C. J. Migeon (Eds.), *Wilkins: The diagnosis and treatment of endocrine disorders in childhood and adolescence* (pp. 573–715). Springfield, IL: Charles C. Thomas.

Morland, I. (2009). What can queer theory do for intersex? *Gay and Lesbian Quarterly, 15*(2), 285–312. doi:10.1215/10642684-2008-139

Oyěwùmi, O. (1997). *The invention of women: Making an African sense of western gender discourses.* Minneapolis: University of Minnesota Press.

Planned Parenthood Federation of America. (2020). What happens during puberty if I'm intersex? Retrieved from https://www.plannedparenthood.org/learn/teens/puberty/what-happens-during-puberty-if-im-intersex

Rainbow Youth. (2018). Rainbow youth's statement on the findings from the education review office: "Promoting wellbeing through sexuality education support report." Retrieved from https://www.ry.org.nz/who-we-are/news/rainbowyouths-statement-on-the-findings-from-the-education-review-office-promoting-wellbeing-through-sexuality-education-support-report

Reis, E. (2009). *Bodies in doubt: An American history of intersex.* Baltimore, MD: Johns Hopkins University Press.

United Nations Born Free & Equal. (2018). *Intersex* [PDF file]. Retrieved from https://www.unfe.org/wp-content/uploads/2018/10/Intersex-English.pdf

Viloria, H. (2016). What's in a name: Intersex and identity. In J. Schneiderman (Ed.), *Queer: A reader for writers* (pp. 213–217). New York: Oxford University Press.

Weil, A. (2007). *Healthy aging: A lifelong guide to your well-being.* New York: First Anchor Books.

Chapter 14

CHILDHOOD AND SEXUAL LITERACY

Allison Moore and Paul Reynolds

Childhood is a particularly acute focus for sexual literacy.[1] It is in childhood sexual learning that children are assumed to become cognizant of their sexual needs and desires and are educated in legitimate and illegitimate responses to them. Yet the category of the child is contested, both in its identification and the developmental assumptions about children. Depending on the age of the child, the literature uses "early childhood," "child," "youth" and "young people." For consistency, in this essay we will use the term "child," "childhood" or "children" as referenced by the *United Nations Convention on the Rights of the Child* (1989), which describes the status of the child as applying to all those under 18. This is distinct from the ages of majority or consent to sex, which are often culturally influenced in national law-making (https://www.ageofconsent.net/world, 2020; Moore & Reynolds, 2018, pp. 79–98; Waites, 2005). The terminology has political ramifications—in exploring issues of children and sexuality, the language and rhetoric of child and children, as opposed to young people or youth, inevitably has an impact on perceptions of sex education. In this short essay, we will briefly outline the dominant approaches to childhood and sexuality, summarize how they are reflected in the development of sex education as a critical example and underline the main obstacles and problems that beset childhood sexual literacy.

Child maturation is understood as a developmental process that can be conceived in stages, though the boundaries and meanings of these developmental stages are contested on the basis of disciplinary focus (biology, medicine and psychology) or adherence to or criticality toward common child development staging used by professionals (Doherty & Hughes, 2013; Porter, 1999, 2005; Smith, Cowie, & Blades, 2015). The notion of developmental maturation is predicated on natural and normal physiological, emotional, cognitive and intellectual markers of how children grow and behave. The terms "natural" and "normal" suggest maturation is a common, staged and functional process, which is contested by radical thinkers who suggest developmentalism is less a descriptive aid and more a disciplinary imposition (Moore & Reynolds, 2018, pp. 23–44). In addition to being a homogenization of development that establishes a normal/abnormal-deviance

---

1 The authors would like to thank the editors for their comments on a previous draft. Much of this essay is informed by, and therefore elaborated in, Moore and Reynolds (2018). We acknowledge the publisher, Palgrave, in permitting us to cite, quote and draw from that text.

model of how children develop, intersections with class, race, gender, sexuality and disability among other identity categories have an impact on the sociocultural construction of childhood and its stages (Moore & Reynolds, 2018, pp. 44–50, 143–65). Any discussion of childhood invariably discusses a category used to describe or distinguish children, rather than the rich heterogeneity of children.

Underpinning the problems of discussing childhood and sexuality is how child development is conceived and what is "age appropriate" knowledge for children to know at what "stage" of development. As we elaborate elsewhere (Moore & Reynolds, 2018, pp. 22–28), the discourse of child development is governed by a naturalistic and development fallacy that a staged model of "normal/natural" development can be discerned and should guide the social and cultural development of the child.

> Historically, these understandings have been naturalistic, assuming that human growth and development is a physiological process from birth to death. As such, it is framed by scientific and medical approaches that map stages and characteristics of development. Specifically, the disciplines of medicine, biology and psychology have grown to underpin not simply understandings of the body as a biological organism, but as a subject whose physical, mental and emotional health and growth is a primary consideration in understanding and optimising the life course.
>
> What is assumed to be "normal" child development is not simply informed by bio-medical and psychological criteria of functionality, but children's functional capacity to enter into social relationships and grow and mature to be able to enter adult society. Hence what is "normal" extends from the physical and mental attributes of the child to normal expectations of conduct and inter-relationships. This natural/normal order governs what is appropriate for children to be responsible for and to be asked to do during their development, and what adults should ask, compel or prohibit them to do. This naturalised and developmental approach to both childhood and sexuality established a natural and normal order and pattern of growth, development and behaviour that was considered healthy, morally correct and socially functional. (pp. 24–26)

While any biological, physiological or scientific model will generalize to a natural or normal statistical distribution, there are two problems with this approach. The first is that the statistical norm becomes a moral and cultural norm, legally and politically enforced. Second, departures from the norm, which can and should be understood as differences, are often framed as deviances or abnormalities, where norm recognition becomes hierarchical. This means that children who do not follow age-appropriate developmental "signposts," and whose interest in or early experimentation with sex "signposts" are the subject of pathologies, rather than the developmental model itself. Plummer (1991, pp. 233–35) neatly frames this in a matrix where danger and pleasure are juxtaposed with the sexual and nonsexual child. Children who show an interest in sex are either precocious or being corrupted, where precociousness is not regarded as advanced. The sexual child, ironically, ceases to be seen as a child and therefore loses the protections and rights afforded to other children (Kitzinger, 1997). Children's sexuality needs to be repressed, and a model that relates to learning and understanding sensual pleasures is largely regarded as something speculated upon by intellectuals but in practice too much a danger to give space to.

This naturalistic developmental model provides the basis for a dominant understanding of the nature of sexual risk and danger to children and overlays the protection of children over the development of their sexual understandings. In doing so, it provides an impetus toward conservative judgments about what "age appropriateness" is, treats childhood as a homogenous category and assumes that sexual behavior and relationships conform to mainstream moral and sexual values (Moore, 2018). These include a bias toward heteronormativity monogamy and "settled relationships," a bias toward genitocentric and penetrative sexuality, a bias for "commonsense" knowledge to be infected by heteronormativity (and more recently homonormativity).

The groundwork for children to enter the adult world is *formally* the domain of sex education, which assists in their becoming sexually knowledgeable agents, with an understanding of their opportunities for intimate and sexual relationships and respect for others' sexual choices. Informally, it is the interplay of parental and peer communications and media representations presented during childhood experiences. Because these informal mechanisms are variable in quality of knowledge and ethical import, there is a reliance on states or provider institutions to ensure a basic standard (Moore & Reynolds, 2018, pp. 172–83). Sex education and learning *should* provide a developmental structure and curriculum that gives confidence to and enables children to develop with a sense of moral, cultural and interpersonal preparedness to engage in mutually respecting sexual relationships, and to self-identify sexually in a way that expresses their desires. It should enable them to have clear understandings of sexual difference, of the conditionality of sexual norms and of an openness and confidence to adopt a lifelong learning approach to sex and sexuality. That it fails to do so, and that such an approach is itself regarded as controversial, shows how childhood sex education and sexual literacy are significantly different projects.

Public discourses of childhood sexuality have often been subject to three forms of characterization: romanticized innocence, exploitation or perceived risk and danger. As Foucault (1978, p. 104) observed in outlining the causes and strategies by which children's sexuality was conceived and produced:

> A *pedagogization of children's sex:* a double assertion that practically all children indulge or are prone to indulge in sexual activity; and that, being unwarranted, at the same time "natural" and "contrary to nature," this sexual activity posed physical and moral, individual and collective dangers; children were defined as "preliminary" sexual beings, on this side of sex, yet within it, astride a dangerous dividing line. Parents, families, educators, doctors, and eventually psychologists would have to take charge, in a continuous way, of this precious and perilous, dangerous and endangered sexual potential: this pedagogization was especially evident in the war against onanism, which in the West lasted nearly two centuries.

Children's learning about sexuality has been influenced by perceived fears and dangers: the sexual exploitation by adults; the encouragement of sexual precociousness and the loss of innocence; risky sexual behavior that may produce unwanted pregnancies or the spread of STI (sexually transmitted infections); the association of sexual knowledge with the moral degradation of children and youth (Moore & Reynolds, 2018, pp. 23–44). Yet education as "age-appropriate" knowledge and understandings has no direct relationship with these prejudices and pathologies. For example, it is important to recognize children's sexual feelings and children's tentative sexual experimentation, such as with masturbation or sexual questioning, as a healthy feature of their sexual development. In no way, however, does that recognition suggest that adults have the right to consume or use children sexually (Moore & Reynolds, 2018, pp. 247–54).

Sexual precociousness is a value-laden judgment on the observation that childhood, as a category, are not homogenous, and their differences might include such factors as physical and emotional maturity or sexual desires, which should be a subject of enquiry and understanding rather than pathology. Innocence, as we observe elsewhere, is a value-loaded means by which adults impose an idealized ignorance on children as part of parental possession and (often rose tinted) nostalgia and, like all ignorance, is dangerous and problematic (Moore & Reynolds, 2018, pp. 89–90). As to risky sexual behavior, the assertion that risk is present as children learn about sex and sexuality could be countered by the argument that learning about sex mediates these risks (e.g., Ott & Santelli, 2007; Santelli et al., 2006, on the limits of abstinence sex education, Collins, Alagiri, & Summers, 2002, on arguments around abstinence against comprehensive sexuality education programs and McKay, 1998, on competing sexual ideologies of sex education in the United States, and Williams, 2003, for the UK contrast).

Yet the notion of educating children about sex, and the characterization of age appropriateness, are both contested grounds. In the United States, sexual conservatives use moral arguments for abstinence as the basis for "educating" the young, which has been a key battleground in the "sex wars" around permissive and diverse sexualities (Duggan & Hunter, 2006; Luker, 2007). In much of Europe, sex education has been driven by concerns around fertility and reproduction, sexual health, child protection and risk aversion (Mckay, 1998, pp. 13–60; Moore, 2013). These are clearly important factors as *part* of sexual education, but there has always been greater controversy as to what is legitimate sex education beyond issues of reproduction and risk. The political struggle to establish a curriculum that develops these public health issues within a context of legal protections, such as consent and sexual violence, has often meant that issues such as sexual difference and diversity, and sexual experimentation and pleasure, have been neglected, overlooked or deferred (Allen, Rasmussen, & Quinlivan, 2016; Epstein & Sears, 1999).

Globally, organizations such as UNESCO and WHO have championed Compulsory Sex Education (CSE), which seeks to promote sex positivity (Bonjour & van der Vlugt, 2018; Montgomery & Knerr, 2018; UNESCO, 2015). CSE is bound to principles of enabling people to know and exercise their sexual and reproductive rights, beyond a purely heteronormative focus and moving from immediate health and reproductive terms to wider issues of ethical intimacy. Nevertheless, it is not without its critics. It is primarily programmed as a development initiative, exported from advanced postindustrial western societies to the global south, with concerns that it imposes western moral and cultural judgments on indigenous practices and understandings (Bonjour & van der Vlugt, 2018; Roodsaz, 2018). While the principles are progressive, the level of resourcing and the scale of problems of sexual violence and exploitation, disease and traditional gendered inequalities results in limits to its programs.

The naturalized and normalized underpinning of conceptions of childhood and sexuality can be illustrated by the example of new guidance consolidating legislative and regulatory change in sex education in the UK since 1993 (Department of Education, 2019). This sets central themes in the relationship and sex education curriculum for primary education (7–11-year-olds) as:

- Understanding families and people who care for the child, including the privileging of marriage and the importance of safeguarding children
- Understanding caring friendships and respectful relationships (including online relationships), both recognizing worthwhile friendships and recognizing signs of distress/discomfort
- Being safe
- Health and changes in the body through to puberty, especially reproduction and emotional well-being (Department of Education, 2019, pp. 20–22)

Guidance sets the equivalent curriculum themes for secondary education (11–16-year-olds) as:

- Families (with an orientation toward long-term relationships and protection and safety issues)
- Respectful relationships including friendships (recognizing the problems of stereotypes and prejudice)
- Being safe with a separate focus on online and media representations and risks
- Intimate and sexual relationships, with specific reference to health (including reproduction and pregnancy), intimacy without sex, pressure/peer pressure; contraception; STIs; the law in relation to sexual violence, consent, using sexual representations. (Department of Education, 2019, pp. 27–29)

The (globally relatively progressive) guidance focuses primarily on health, safeguarding and protection of the child. While these are important features of preparing children for sexual relationships and activities, the emphasis on risk, danger and protection and a biomedical, naturalized logic precludes a more sex-positive agenda. The guidance is explicit in its onus:

> Effective RSE does not encourage early sexual experimentation. It should teach young people to understand human sexuality and to respect themselves and others. It enables young people to mature, build their confidence and self-esteem and understand the reasons for delaying sexual activity. Effective RSE also supports people, throughout life, to develop safe, fulfilling and healthy sexual relationships, at the appropriate time. (Department of Education, 2019, p. 25)

What the guidance assumes is that all forms of sexual experimentation, discussions of sexual diversity and explicit questioning of sexual norms, values and activities are oriented toward risk rather than pleasure. While guidelines and law inevitably focus on what requires prohibition or regulation, the lack of balance is telling, and the UK is not excessively prohibitive when measured with legal frameworks across the globe.

Discourses of discipline, control, correction, risk, danger, repression, corruption, exploitation, innocence, normal/abnormal and natural/unnatural have become the vocabulary of the discursive field of childhood sexuality. (Moore & Reynolds, 2018, p. 43)

The limited space for sexual diversity is still controversial. In the UK, community protests against teaching about LGBT issues have demonstrated the power of conservative heteronormativity (indicatively, Ferguson, 2019). Sex education (within relationships and education) remains the only curriculum subject where parents religious (or faith) beliefs for their children are taken into account. The ability of parents to withdraw their children from sex education has only been recently curtailed in this guidance and legislation, and from developmental norms. There is still considerable discretion as to how the curriculum is enacted by schools, particularly those who have private ownership (not being maintained directly by state funding) or faith schools (Moore & Reynolds, 2018, pp. 177–83). The sketch here shows that both the underlying foundations of a developmental and naturalistic model and the overlay of curriculum provide relatively little in the way of the tools for children and young people to learn about sexual identities, orientation, relationships, behaviors and acts in an enabling and open fashion.

This is not to discount that there are schools where teachers engage positively with educating children on sex and sexuality (sometimes at risk to their livelihood), nor that there are not child-based initiatives that have a more constructive approach to sex education (e.g., Elley, 2013) or intellectuals who aim to advance sexual knowledge and understandings (see Barker, 2013; Barker & Hancock, 2017). There is also some evidence that parental- and peer-based learning can have some positive effects, though its piecemeal and partially informed nature often results in the propagation of fear and prejudiced folklore (Moore & Reynolds, 2018, pp. 172–77). These initiatives may be advancing sexual literacy, but they have a relatively limited impact on mainstream relationship and sex education.

The implications of the naturalized and "normal" developmental model are that this cultural lens impedes enabling literate young people with the tools to engage in clear sexual decision making with a focus on both pleasure and learning. It actively instils prohibitions and disincentives upon questioning sexual norms, prioritizing sexual learning or unlearning prejudices and pathologies. Effectively, it occupies the space for creativity and learning with fear.

The developmental "age-appropriate" model produces sexual learning focused on adolescence (post 11–12-year-olds). This involves a failure to address the importance of educating younger children (5–11-year-olds—kindergarten/elementary stages) about sex, rather than bodily development, reproduction and "normal" families, which dominates early education initiatives. This reinforces prejudices as to what children should understand, when and how to interpret their experimentation and is a limited base from which sex can be addressed at a later age when it begins to be addressed. The prevalence of rape, sexual violence, tolerance of unwanted sex, sex marred by lack of knowledge and understanding, and sexual exploitation in adult life suggests that the current orthodoxy of sexual education is a significant failure (see indicatively Bruess & Greenberg, 2004, 149–62).

Finally, the natural-developmental model underpinning sex education programs reinforces a web of orthodox concepts into a norm-based network—patriarchal heteronormativity—that reinforces the status quo rather than questioning it. This includes (selectively): monogamy; reproduction–sex linkage; love–sex linkage; the risks and dangers of "disease"—both physical and moral—as debilitating; hetero- (and more recently homo-)normativity and sexual conformity around sexual hierarchy based on the "normal" and "natural"; gendered sex roles; cultural stereotypes as to what is sexy and not (which desexualize the old, the disabled, the queer, the child); decency and innocence and sex as corrupting and obscene/indecent; sex as private. Concepts such as monogamy and love in themselves are not problematic. Their meshing into dominant discourse, however, constitute a cultural hegemony in which the dominant "mainstream" is continually reinforced, and forms of emergent or historical forms that oppose or differ from the dominant are restricted, oppressed or diminished (using Williams model of cultural hegemony, see Williams, 1980, pp. 31–49).

A critical discussion of childhood sexual literacy recognizes the severe and counterproductive impact of the natural/normal developmental model of childhood. The current educational orthodoxy implies that strategies for enabling children to become sexual agents should focus on presenting a limited set of choices and limiting—in a passive pedagogic voice—the space for children to think for themselves. Sexual literacy, in contrast, advocates that there should be *more* space for children to articulate their own knowledge and understandings of sensual feelings and experiences that are not readily subsumed into an adult framing of sexuality. Adult articulations of childhood experience and understandings are very different to the child's, and only begin to have correspondence and convergence as the child develops through puberty and is inducted in adult sexuality. There is a virtue to listening to and taking seriously children's learning from a position where such knowledge and understanding is acquired and shared, rather than prescribed. This would certainly suggest that children's learning should be guided less by adults and pedagogy should be about promoting learning as a creative activity—such as in play—rather than or alongside elements of programmed knowledge. In that respect, a more circulatory model of sexual pedagogy that focuses on sharing learning and appreciating different voices would be more inclusive for children (here critical pedagogy approaches might provide a better model, selectively Freire, 1996; hooks, 1994; Illich, 1995). Any introduction of adult knowledge and understandings should be in creative dialogue rather than focused on an adult developmental schema.

One example of a creative approach toward sexual literacy might be to reconsider the relationship between learning and play, where play allows creativity, expression of feelings and experiments with meaning making (Andrews, 2012; Brown, 2012). This reflects Buck-Morss (1991, p. 264), quoting Paul Valery:

If they are fit and well, all children are absolute *monsters* of activity [...] tearing up, breaking up, building, they're always at it! And they'll cry if you can't give them something better to do [...]. You might say they are conscious of all things around them insofar as they can *act* on them, or through them, in no matter what way: the action, in fact, is all.

The logical conclusion to draw from this question is that children require spaces to explore and experience, cognitively and emotionally, to practice and develop their literacy. These spaces might have different degrees of adult guidance and regulation, but these spaces need to allow children to feel they can tentatively experience and then reflect and discuss with other children and with adults. It implies that children's touching, seeing and feeling should be given space, and is controversial in respect to protection from sexual harm and exploitation. Nevertheless, sexual literacy should take sexual meaning-making, including pleasure and its understanding seriously, and of necessity this involves some sense of allowing children sexual play and the space to explore, question and to practice. How this is organized—and to what extent it is permissive or regulated—is an open question that implies that there should be negotiation with the individual child. At present, such forms of debate are limited or constrained by naturalized development model.

This new cultural lens calls for a more inclusive, progressive, praxeological and dialogical understanding of children's development as sexual (and heterogeneous) agents is useful and raises important questions as to how we understand and relate to children and their wants, desires and pleasures. The focus on the importance of space and practice, material resources and the need to give children the tools to question for themselves dominant orthodoxies and engage in meaningful dialogue with other children and adults, without directing how they use these tools seems an important place to begin thinking about a more enabled children's engagement with sexuality.

References

Allen, L., Rasmussen, M. L., & Quinlivan, K. (Eds.). (2016). *The politics of pleasure in sexuality education: Pleasure bound.* London: Routledge.

Andrews, M. (2012). *Exploring play for early childhood studies.* London: Sage (Learning Matters).

Barker, M. (2013). *Rewriting the rules: An integrative guide to love, sex and relationships.* London: Routledge.

Barker, M. J., & Hancock, J. (2017). *Enjoy sex: How, when and if you want to.* London: Icon Books.

Bonjour, M., & van der Vlugt, I. (2018). *Comprehensive sexuality education: Knowledge file.* Utrecht: Rutgers.

Brown, F. (2012). *Rethinking children's play.* London: Bloomsbury Academic.

Bruess, C. E., & Greenberg, J. S. (2004). *Sexuality education: Theory and practice* (4th ed.). Sudbury: Jones and Bartlett.

Buck-Morss, S. (1991). *The dialectic of seeing: Walter Benjamin and the Arcades project.* Cambridge, MA: MIT Press.

Collins, C., Alagiri, P., & Summers, T. (2002). *Abstinence only vs comprehensive sexuality education: What are the arguments/what is the evidence?* San Francisco, CA: University of California, AIDS Policy Research Center/Center for AIDS Prevention Studies Policy Monograph Series.

Department of Education. (2019). *Relationships education, relationships and sex education (RSE) and health education—draft statutory guidance for governing bodies, proprietors, head teachers, principals, senior leadership teams, teachers.* London: Crown Copyright. Retrieved from https://assets.publishing. service.gov.uk/government/uploads/system/uploads/attachment_data/file/781150/Draft_ guidance_Relationships_Education__Relationships_and_Sex_Education__RSE__and_ Health_Education2.pdf

Doherty, J., & Hughes, M. (2013). *Child development: Theory and practice 0-11*. London: Longman.

Duggan, L., & Hunter, N. D. (2006). *Sex wars: Sexual dissent and political culture*. London: Taylor and Francis.

Elley, S. (2013). *Understanding sex and relationship education, youth and class: A youth work based approach*. Houndsmill: Palgrave Macmillan.

Epstein, D., & Sears, J. T. (Eds.). (1999). *A dangerous knowing: Sexuality, pedagogy and popular culture*. London: Cassell.

Ferguson, D. (2019, May 26). "We can't give in": The Birmingham school on the frontline of anti-LGBT protests. *The Observer*. Retrieved from https://www.theguardian.com/uk-news/2019/may/26/birmingham-anderton-park-primary-muslim-protests-lgbt-teaching-rights

Foucault, M. (1978). *The history of sexuality volume 1: An introduction*. London: Penguin.

Freire, P. (1996). *Pedagogy of the oppressed*. Harmondsworth: Penguin.

hooks, b. (1994). *Teaching to transgress—education as the practice of freedom*. London: Routledge.

Illich, I. (1995). *Deschooling society* (new ed.). London: Marion Boyars.

Kitzinger, J. (1997). Who are you kidding? Children, power and the struggle against sexual abuse. In A. James & A. Prout (Eds.), *Constructing and reconstructing childhood: Contemporary issues in the sociological study of childhood* (pp. 165–189). London: Falmer Press.

Luker, K. (2007). *When sex goes to school: Warring views on sex—and sex education—since the sixties*. New York: W.W. Norton.

McKay, A. (1998). *Sexual ideology and schooling: Towards democratic sexuality education*. New York: State University of New York Press.

Montgomery, P., & Knerr, W. (2018). *Review of the evidence on sexuality education: Report to inform the update of the UNESCO international technical guidance on sexuality education*. Paris: UNESCO.

Moore, A. (2013). For adults only? Young people and (non)participation in sexual decision making. *Global Studies of Childhood*, *3*(2), 163–172.

Moore, A. (2018). Toward a central theory of childhood sexuality: A relational approach. In S. Lamb & J. Gilbert (Eds.), *The Cambridge Handbook of sexual development childhood and adolescence* (pp. 35–53). Cambridge: Cambridge University Press.

Moore, A., & Reynolds, P. (2018). *Childhood and sexuality: Contemporary issues and debates*. London: Palgrave Macmillan.

Ott, M., & Santelli, J. (2007). Abstinence and abstinence-only education. *Current Opinion in Obstetrics & Gynecology*, *19*(5), 446–452.

Plummer, K. (1991). Understanding childhood sexualities. In T. Sandfort, E. Brongersma & A. van Naerssen (Eds.), *Male intergenerational intimacy: Historical, socio-psychological, and legal perspectives* (pp. 231–249). New York: Harrington Park Press.

Porter, R. (1999). *The greatest benefit to mankind: A medical history of humanity*. London: Fontana.

Porter, R. (2005). *Flesh in the age of reason*. London: Penguin.

Roodsaz, R. (2018). Probing the politics of comprehensive sexuality education: "Universality" versus "cultural sensitivity": A Dutch–Bangladeshi collaboration on adolescent sexuality education. *Sex Education*, *18*(1), 107–121.

Santelli, J., Ott, M. A., Lyon, M., Rogers, J., Summers, D., & Schleifer, R. (2006). Abstinence and abstinence-only education: A review of U.S. policies and programs. *Journal of Adolescent Health*, *38*(1), 72–81.

Smith, P. K., Cowie, H., & Blades, M. (2015). *Understanding child development*. Chichester: John Wiley.

UNESCO. (2015). *Emerging evidence and practice in comprehensive sexuality education: A global review*. Paris: UNESCO. Retrieved from https://www.icmec.org/wp-content/uploads/2017/03/CSE_Global_Review_2015.pdf

United Nations. (1989). *United Nations convention on the rights of the child*. London: UNICEF. Retrieved from https://downloads.unicef.org.uk/wp--ontent/uploads/2010/05/UNCRC_united_nations_convention_on_the_rights_of_the_child.pdf?_ga=2.24740349.698794129.1590099500-2054779189.1590099500

Waites, M. (2005). *The age of consent: Young people, sexuality and citizenship*. Houndsmill: Palgrave Macmillan.

Williams, E. S. (2003). *Lessons in depravity: Sex education and the sexual revolution*. London: Belmont House.

Williams, R. (1980). Base and superstructure in Marxist cultural theory. In *Culture and materialism: Selected essays* (pp. 31–49). London: Verso.

Chapter 15

LET'S CANCEL THE CIRCULAR FIRING SQUAD: ARGUING AGAINST CANCEL CULTURE IN THE CLASSROOM TOWARD THE SEXUAL LITERACY JOURNEY

Nicole C. Polen-Petit

If I am being honest, I am relieved that both my undergraduate and graduate education took place before social media exploded onto the world's landscape. My road to scholarship in sexuality studies, and particularly LGBTQIA+ scholarship and advocacy, was not a path easily forged. The reality is that if I embarked on that journey just one decade later, I don't know that I would be in the same place now. I entered undergraduate education largely ignorant of the complexity of sexual identity and certainly cloaked in my own privilege as a white, cis-gender, heterosexual young person from a relatively conservative, evangelical community. Both college and graduate school became places where my educational and intellectual journey collided with my faith, my inexperience and relative ignorance to the lived experiences and realities of people different from me. Over a period of 11 years (and continuously still), I leaned into my own discomfort and actively confronted and dismantled much of what I initially brought to the table intellectually, spiritually and emotionally. And at times, it was not pretty. I am not immune to the multiple ways in which growth can be impacted by white fragility, privilege, or heteronormativity. These are all issues that I needed to engage with, be called on and actively confront in the midst of discomfort. In all honesty and being completely transparent, I am so thankful that social media was not as prominent an institution as it is today as I worked through my own growth and change because I believe I would have been stifled by an overwhelming fear of being publicly "called out" or "cancelled" given the absolute likelihood I would unintentionally insult or emotionally injure the very people I was trying to better understand. It is from this space that I immerse in this discussion. Here I consider the environment, both real and virtual, that myself as a professor, my students and others currently engage towards the transformative learning implicit in sexual literacy journeys.

Inherent in the notion of sexual literacy is the concept of a "journey." This journey toward sexual literacy encompasses all of what we consider to be classically central to sexual education, such as sexual health and well-being. As time marches on, however, this journey toward sexual literacy has grown exponentially to include identifying privilege, ignorance and prejudice as it relates to humans' interactions with one another and the major systems and social institutions that intersect with our sexuality (Herdt & Polen-Petit, 2021). As understanding of sexual literacy expands, so have the platforms used to communicate. Where once a student or individual could engage in transformative change by privately leaning into discomfort to pursue unlearning and seeing the world through a new lens maybe with the help of a trusted friend, teacher, classroom cohort or community, this educational experience has expanded today to include multiple contexts of public exhibition and display of the journey, whether through discussion boards in online courses or private thoughts documented in numerous social media applications. In recent years, this phenomenon known as cancel culture and conducted by "calling out" someone has threatened and thwarted powerful transformative change in spaces of activism and higher education activism, directly impacting university courses on sexuality and gender.

Cancel culture is a relatively recent phenomenon of public shaming, largely carried out via social media as well as taking a prominent place within institutions of higher education. "Calling out" is the act of publicly shaming another person for behavior considered unacceptable. Call outs are loud and particularly vicious, often fueled by the anonymity provided by online spaces (Ross, 2019). This kind of calling out is considered to be a precursor to cancelation (Bennett, 2020; Ross, 2019). Unfortunately, cancel and call out culture have also become a political football of sorts and has taken hold in more than one context of social discourse and engagement. Generally, this kind of public punishment does not allow for redemption (Holman, 2020). Being called out or "canceled" in a public space on social media typically involves very public withdrawal of support (i.e., followers, "likes") for those who have been judged to have said or done something deemed unacceptable. Cancel culture has also been responsible for a significant increase in the anxiety of academics who reveal a culture of fear among faculty, less protected nontenured faculty and others who dissent, even slightly with the "woke left" (McWhorter, 2020). Typically, people are canceled from a social justice perspective, that is due to their perceived sexism, heterosexism, racism and/or homophobia (Ng, 2020). In addition to the withdrawal of support, many commenters or followers actively call out—publicly and mercilessly—the wrongdoing and often the character of the person who has committed the offense in question.

In the era of *#MeToo*, calling out someone like this has been praised as finally bringing the necessary public justice upon those who have inflicted sexual violence against others privately. Today, in response to the centuries' old pain that people of color have experienced who have died violently at the hands of police persons who are supposed to protect and serve, *#BLM (the Black Lives Matter movement hashtag)* has exploded into a national and international reckoning unlike anything seen in history. This movement in society-at-large has reactivated critical discussions of how racism is at its core an institution and was started as an intersectional movement that included issues of race, sexuality and gender. This calling out occurs in a variety of contexts and can be a useful and powerful tool for activists to deploy to raise awareness of their issues via social media as the most prominent vehicle for cancel culture. Yet more and more, the classroom and online coursework areas and related networked areas are places where such judgments and shaming are also practiced—making the subject of sexuality, which is already fraught with shame and misunderstandings for so many, all the more difficult to teach and learn.

We know that learning plus growth often means confronting mistakes and misunderstanding. As Maya Angelou so pointedly stated, "When you know better, you do better." But what if we are contributing to a social and educational environment that no longer allows for mistakes and reparation? If making a mistake immediately leads to being called out, or more critically blocked or canceled in public settings, will a stunting of personal growth result or will people just sign on to the viewpoint du jour unaware of what it all really means because they think it makes them look enlightened? The same holds for processes of learning, reparation and growth in these times.

As a psychology professor who teaches lower division human sexuality courses, I see students from multiple racial, ethnic and ideological backgrounds approach the course from vastly differing levels of knowledge and exposure to the continuum of sexuality knowledge. A student's sexual literacy journey becomes glaringly apparent when approaching subjects where students' deeply held beliefs and assumptions are revealed in response to the topic we are discussing. When I approach the discussion of gender, for example, I am aware of my own perspective that gender is far more complex than the binary framework (male/female or woman/man) often presented as in the media. Do I want my students to just adopt this perspective? Sure, it is more inclusive. Yes, it accounts for a greater breadth of human expressiveness and identity. But while I believe widening our understanding of gender beyond the binary is critical to create more supportive spaces for people, I also want students to actually go through the personal exercise of wrestling with their own assumptions. I don't want them to blindly adopt my view. I want them to think critically about how they understand gender and why. I want them to see and occupy a space of discomfort wherein they can hear from those whose identity and experience are not reflected in a binary conceptualization. For example, I want them to learn about and feel the gut-wrenching sorrow of a mother whose transgender child died by suicide as a direct result of the violence they were a victim of because they tried to live authentically in their high school community. I want students to ask questions and lean into the discomfort of questioning everyday assumptions and be active in expanding their view. Ultimately this serves the larger sexual literacy aim of increasing the number of people articulating and advocating a more progressive and inclusive understanding of gender identity and expression and all the linkages to sexuality that are implicit. This expanded view of human nature and advocacy is critical to any movement toward sexual literacy.

The effect of cancel and call out culture appears to be deeply influenced by the ideological rigidity of social discourse within social media platforms that has taken on a binary mentality wherein people are actually depersonalized and reduced to labels of "good versus evil" (Brooks, 2019). This results in a kind of vigilante justice that brutally punishes people who break social norms. There are countless stories in the press of faculty and scholars who have been subject to intense public punishment and even loss of employment because they assigned reading or engaged in a discussion where students felt injured in some way by the content (McWhorter, 2020).

What is intriguing about some of these instances is that these faculty are typically not espousing any beliefs supporting racism, sexism, heterosexism or conservative political orientation. On the contrary, many who have experienced this kind of punishment are left-aligning—but are considered to be not as left as they should be. "Thus the issue is not the age-old one of left against right, but what one [individual] calls the 'circular firing squad' of the left: It is now no longer 'Why aren't you on the left?' but 'How dare you not be as left as we are'" (McWhorter, 2020, p. 6). In such a higher educational environment, there is no room for mistakes, there is no opportunity to repair or even engage in a discussion where individuals can express their perspective and gather constructive feedback from others. The existing possibilities include perfection on one end based on movable social rules and social media influenced preferences versus an expectation that if one does not meet that bar sufficiently and immediately then they are righteously subject to call-out and cancel culture.

Thus, returning to the classroom situation example, students in that same sexuality course examining gender are hesitant to truthfully engage in self-learning and growth and afraid to ask questions in their social media spaces because if they ask in the "wrong way," and then offend someone unintentionally or not, they are subjected to brutal public punishment. So instead of engaging in the exercise of growth and learning, they are tempted to adopt the perspective that they interpret as being the "right one" or they may double down on a perspective they hold because the vulnerability and insecurity of the idea of exploration of novel insights is too fraught with fear and uncertainty of not doing it the "right way"—whatever that might mean in the moment.

As indicated previously, students are not the only ones subjected to this binary categorization of good or evil seen flourishing in social media spaces. Faculty, researchers and activists are also starting to document the damage being done as a result of call-out or cancel culture. In 2017, a blog post written by Frances Lee, a cultural studies scholar titled *Excommunicate Me from the Church of Social Justice,* brought to light some of the discontent felt by many activists and scholars in recent years. Lee stated:

> There is an underlying current of fear in my activist communities, and it is separate from the daily fear of police brutality, eviction, discrimination, and street harassment. It is the fear of appearing impure. Social death follows when being labeled a "bad" activist or simply "problematic" enough times. I've had countless hushed conversations with friends about this anxiety and how it has led us to refrain from participation in activist events, conversations, and spaces because we feel inadequately radical […] .I self-police what I say in activist spaces. I stopped commenting on social media with questions or pushback on leftist opinions for fear of being called out. (2017)

Frances Lee is not the only scholar who has written about the connection between the fear of public punishment for not being perfect in their activism. Faculty, researchers and other members of communities in higher education have begun documenting a shift on college campuses, and even within academic societies, trending toward ideological uniformity (Lukianoff & Haidt, 2018; McWhorter, 2020), shown clearly in this example.

Extremists have proliferated on the far right and the far left, provoking one another to even deeper levels of hatred. Social media has channeled partisan passions into the creation of a "call out culture"; anyone can be publicly shamed for saying something well-intentioned that someone else interprets uncharitably. New-media platforms and outlets allow citizens to retreat into self-confirmatory bubbles, where their worst fears about the evils of the other side can be confirmed and amplified by extremists and cyber trolls intent on sowing discord and division (Lukianoff & Haidt, 2018, p. 5).

It is critical to engage in understanding the connection between what people witness on social media when others make mistakes and are publicly punished. The subsequent willingness to immerse oneself in a highly vulnerable place of self-examination of one's own privilege, racism, sexism, heterosexism, ableism, classism and so on, and owning responsibility for this is vital to active participation in learning, social and community groups as well as for reflexively understanding where we are complicit in supporting and furthering these same systems and ideologies. This is a crucial practice for citizens, students and academic alike and absolutely essential praxis for advancing sexual literacy.

One example of helpful reflexive training is from Staley and Leonardi (2016), who looked at the effort to prepare literacy teachers for gender and sexual diversity in their teaching. Their findings demonstrated that when people willingly engaged and moved toward examining their own discomfort on social justice issues, the end result was that they were better positioned to become strong advocates (Staley & Leonardi, 2016). It is arguable then, to conclude that *leaning into personal discomfort is a productive tension* when grappling with critical dynamics of homophobia, heterosexism, racism and broader oppression (Staley & Leonardi, 2016). Yet in order for this to happen there must be a space provided for such leaning to support for the process of questioning, wrestling with novel perspectives and confronting existing biases and prejudices to actively work through and unlearn them in favor of new perspectives that elevate diversity, inclusivity and social justice. Those spaces, for those who are dedicated to leaning into discomfort and doing this work also, must allow for misunderstandings and mistakes—not to excuse but to confront them and repair in order to pursue the discovery of new ideals and practices that march us toward healing, reconciliation, growth and sexual literacy as lifelong process.

Unfortunately, many intentional spaces on social media and even within academic societies have not yet perfected this kind of environment and injury occurs to Black, Indigenous and people of color (BIPOC) and/or LGBTQ+ people as White, straight, cis-gendered individuals react, post and engage in discourse. One Facebook group is working to minimize the kinds of injury that can occur when people are engaged in such critical and difficult work. Be the Bridge, a nonprofit organization and community of people who share the goal of creating healthy dialogue about race and furthering understanding of racial injustice and disparity, requires its new members to sit silently and observe for three months. New members are not allowed to react, post or comment on any thread in the space. Additionally, they are required to engage with required units—reading articles and watching videos to listen and learn. This group acknowledges that mistakes will be made, but it actively works to mitigate harm to BIPOC members by requiring new members to be silent observers for three months. In this quiet space, the intention is for white people to listen and learn while refraining from reacting out of white fragility and engaging in tone policing or causing harm as they do the work of confronting their own racism and biases. When someone does make a mistake and cause harm they are confronted and given an opportunity to apologize, not explain or defend, and move on.

Additionally, there are advocacy groups and academic programs that are seeing the impact of call-out culture and its potential to squash this kind of transformative growth.

Loretta Ross, a Black feminist and expert on women's issues, racism and human rights, discussed changing this culture by "calling-in" rather than "calling out" (Ross, 2019). In simplest terms, *calling-in* is a *calling-out* that is done with love and care. Some corrections can be public but done with respect and others can be done privately. Calling-in is not, "tone policing, protecting white fragility or covering up abuse. It helps avoid the weaponization of suffering that prevents constructive healing" (Ross, 2019). This practice of calling-in has made a prominent place in syllabi in some institutions. For example, at the California Institute of Integral Studies, the master syllabi for courses in the Human Sexuality doctoral program include *Classroom Ground Rules* where calling-in is an encouraged practice as a part of their description of *Professionalism*.

> If disagreements arise during the course (with the instructor or other students), please first attempt to understand the other person's point of view and then express your own view in a way that facilitates understanding rather than forecloses it or attempts to argue your own personal moral or ethical high ground. This balance of remaining open and understanding ourselves enough to not impinge negatively upon others is an art, not a science […] Allow others to speak, limit side conversations, and respect the views of others, even those you disagree with […] We may hold each other accountable but do it in a way that can be received well and push the work/leaning forward, even if that means waiting to speak to someone in private, an approach that has been named "calling in" as opposed to "calling out." (California Institute of Integral Studies, n.d., p. 6)

This kind of syllabi language creates an environment that not only respects individuals and perspectives but also allows space for wrestling with and growing toward and puts at a premium care for one another in the learning space.

Those of us who serve as sex educators know (backed by volumes of evidence) that a curriculum whose foundation is built upon the perpetration of fear is woefully inadequate in its effectiveness to encourage young people to make healthy and wise sexual decisions (Rabbitte & Enriquez, 2018; Society for Adolescent Health and Medicine, 2017). It is critical that we not allow a culture of fear to continue preventing true transformative learning in the classroom. At the same time, it is not appropriate for our BIPOC, LGBTQ+ and other marginalized community members to be held responsible for or further injured by the social shifting that must occur to awaken folks to the work that needs to be done both personally and within communities to pursue equality, equity and human rights. We need to once again embrace the fundamental right of academic freedom and discourse, so that intentional spaces of learning and transformation can be maintained to highlight our humanity and the reality that none of us is perfect and all of us need grace as we lean forward, learn and grow—student, professor and activists alike. The alternative to this is disconcerting. I can't help but wonder if ideological alignment brought about by fear of being called out or "canceled" will not leave us with a society that espouses beliefs that seem to demonstrate sexual literacy, but all the while not really understanding why. That is not the sexual literacy we urge us toward in this volume and is one that I am urging us against here. It is my hope that we cancel the circular firing squad to allow a flourishing of our sexual literacy journey and open discourses of reconciliation and transformative learning.

References

Bennett, J. (2020, November 19). "What if instead of calling people out, we called them in?" *New York Times*. Retrieved from https://www.nytimes.com/2020/11/19/style/loretta-ross-smith-college-cancel-culture.html

Brooks, D. (2019, January 14). "The cruelty of call-out culture." *New York Times*. Retrieved from https://www.nytimes.com/2019/01/14/opinion/call-out-social-justice.html

California Institute of Integral Studies. (n.d.). Master syllabus for doctoral courses.

Herdt, G., & Polen-Petit, N. C. (2021). *Human sexuality: Self, society and culture*, 2nd ed. New York: McGraw Hill.

Holman, K. J. (2020). *Can you come back from being cancelled? A case study of podcasting, cancel culture, and comedians during #METOO* (Publication No. 27955107) [Doctoral dissertation, University Of Nebraska at Omaha]. ProQuest Dissertations and Theses Global.

Lee, F. (2017, July 13). Excommunicate me from the church of social justice [Blog Post]. Retrieved from https://www.autostraddle.com/kin-aesthetics-excommunicate-me-from-the-church-of-social-justice-386640/

Lukianoff, G., & Haidt, J. (2018). *The coddling of the American mind: How good intentions and bad ideas are setting up a generation for failure.* New York: Penguin Books.

McWhorter, J. (2020, September 1). Academics are really, really worried about their freedom. *The Atlantic*. Retrieved from https://www.theatlantic.com/ideas/archive/2020/09/academics-are-really-really-worried-about-their-freedom/615724/?ocid=uxbndlbing

Ng, E. (2020). No grand pronouncements here ...: Reflections on cancel culture and digital media participation. *Television & News Media*, *21*(6), 621–627.

Rabbitte, M., & Enriquez, M. (2018). The role of policy on sexual health education in schools: Review. *Journal of School Nursing*, *35*(1), 27–38.

Ross, L. (2019, August 17). I'm a black feminist. I think call-out culture is toxic. There are better ways of doing social justice work. *New York Times*. Retrieved from https://www.nytimes.com/2019/08/17/opinion/sunday/cancel-culture-call-out.html

Society for Adolescent Health and Medicine. (2017). Abstinence only-until-marriage policies and programs: An updated position paper of the society for adolescent health and medicine. *Journal of Adolescent Health*, *61*, 400–403. doi:10.1016/j.jadohealth. 2017.0-6.001

Staley, S., & Leonardi, B. (2016). Leaning in to discomfort: Preparing literacy teachers for gender and sexual diversity. *Research in the Teaching of English*, *51*(2), 209–229.

Chapter 16

SEXUAL LITERACY AND SPORTS: MOVING BEYOND THE BINARY IN FAVOR OF EVIDENCE-BASED POLICIES

Lisa Rapalyea

The concepts of biological sex and gender identity have been shifting to a more complex framework in recent years. Recent scientific evidence indicates that both *gender identity* (GI) and *natal* (i.e., birth) *biological sex* (NBS) encompass a spectrum between male and female that is challenging the binary perspective embraced by many cultures (Pielke & Pape, 2019). Nonbinary classifications refer to variations of NBS (i.e., intersex) and GIs other than male/man or female/woman. Ainsworth (2015), via a limited but significant review of biological research, labels societal perception of just two sexes as "simplistic" (p. 288), which also refutes the socially constructed argument for GIs (Carter, 2014), given growing scientific evidence of biological influences (Saraswat, Weinand, & Safer, 2015).

With evolving scientific understanding, societies need ongoing education of the developmental processes underpinning NBS and GI. This aspect of sexual literacy is especially crucial in sports. Eitzen and Sage (2003) describe the sports environment as a "microcosm of society." Thus, it mirrors the larger culture, including the lack of sexual literacy regarding NBS and GI development. In addition, there are distinct cultures by type of sport, coaches and organizations (McPherson, Curtis, & Loy, 1989). If sports are a microcosm of society, it is critical to have an interdisciplinary, evidence-based approach to evaluating the performance of nonbinary athletes, who are subjected to sports policies affecting inclusion and fairness that are based on limited biological evidence. While some sports policies attempt to be inclusive of nonbinary athletes, they still emphasize the binary view of *natal biological male* (NBM) and *natal biological female* (NBF). Applying valid scientific evidence to NBS variations and GI is vital to creating more equitable opportunities for, and increasing understanding of, the performance of nonbinary athletes. The goal of this chapter is to explore how the intersection of sports cultures, NBS, GI and lack of sexual literacy influences sports policies regulating competition by nonbinary athletes.

Sports as a Male Heterosexual Domain: A Brief Historical Overview

Early eras of sports history reflect the binary male–female system, with NBS and GI assigned based on physical sex characteristics perceived at birth and influencing the gendering of sports as an NBM warrior domain. Research on sports' influences on society and individuals started in the mid-twentieth century with the field of sports history (Costa & Guthrie, 1994), primarily focused on male athletes over millennia. More recently, sports studies have examined gender and sexuality in sports. Hargreaves and Anderson (2014) compiled a comprehensive introduction into this latter area to encourage evidence-based interdisciplinary research. It seems imperative to examine how filtering attitudes through a male lens has influenced: (1) perceptions of NBF and nonbinary athletes; (2) the construction of binary-gender-based sports divisions; and (3) sports policies, all of which now need to be challenged with new evidence-based approaches.

Male sports have been interwoven with military skills from the ancient Greeks to modern times (Hargreaves, 1994). The ancient Olympic games were designed to maintain male warrior skills during peacetime (Segrave & Chu, 1988; Sherman, 2005). Both the ancient pentathlon (Olympic Museum, 2002) and the modern pentathlon (c.1900) reflect the evolution of military skills (CISM, 2019). This connection with sports (Lines, 2001) also illuminates gender segregation and the exclusion of sexual minorities in the military.

The exclusion of female participants (Reeser, 2005) or even spectators (Case, 2017) was tied to the feminine *arete*, or collection of qualities comprising character (e.g., beauty, modesty and obedience; Case, 2017; Spears, 1988) that many thought sports involvement would compromise. Nevertheless, some unmarried Greek females (called *parthenoi*) participated in the secret *Heraean* games, though these were limited to foot races (Dillon, 2000; Perrottet, 2004). Still, this early female competition was nonaggressive, recreational and playlike, conforming to *arete* expectations (Park & Hult, 1993; Vertinsky, 1994). This view was not universal, though. Spartan females trained in warrior skills like Spartan males, but this was not about gender equality or developing female warriors. Instead, Spartan culture: (1) valued physically fit females as being more attractive to males (Case, 2017), reinforcing heterosexual norms; and (2) trained females to pass on "masculine" qualities to their future warrior sons (Case, 2017; Perrottet, 2004; Spears, 1988).

Title IX, the 1972 civil rights law for gender equity (United States Department of Education, 2015), ironically reinforced gender segregation in sports, by significantly eroding female control over female sports (Park & Hult, 1993). Female coaches and administrators were replaced by male peers (Acosta & Carpenter, 2008; Gill, 2002; Videon, 2002), reasserting male dominion over policies and expectations for female athletes to be traditionally "feminine," in part to remain heterosexually attractive (Case, 2017), reinforced by contemporary media's sexualizing of female athletes (Lim, 2018).

The stereotypes of binary NBS and GI continued and contributed to the exclusion and stigmatization of nonbinary athletes. Female athletes interested in contact, or "aggressive" (i.e., masculine), sports such as soccer and lacrosse have frequently been disparaged as "masculine" or lesbian, while male athletes who took part in traditionally "feminine" sports such as figure skating were perceived as "feminine" or gay (Ladda, 2017; Plaza, Boiché, Brunel, & Ruchaud, 2017). These characterizations highlight the dearth of sexual literacy about NBS and GI. Improving knowledge and understanding of nonbinary athletes is crucial to combatting stereotypes that influence nonevidence-based policies governing sports participation.

Nonbinary Athletes

Although *nonbinary* includes both female and male transgenders, plus intersex individuals, sports restrictions have disproportionally targeted male-to-female (MtF) transgender and intersex athletes, on the unproven assumption that they have a physiological advantage over NBF athletes in competition.

A lack of sexual literacy about these issues in the 1930s led to cases where nonbinary athletes were labeled "gender frauds" (Heggie, 2010; Padawer, 2016), such as Dora Ratjen (Berg, 2009), for competing in female sports while presumed to be NBM. With increased understanding of biological sex variations that occur during fetal development, Ratjen (Berg, 2009; Heggie, 2010), along with many other of these early athletes, were later identified as transgender and/or intersex (Rogol & Pieper, 2018).

Historically, biological sex assigned at birth was based on clear presence or absence of a penis. If external genitalia did not appear "normal," they might be deemed "ambiguous." Today that is recognized as an intersex condition. Ratjen was identified with ambiguous genitalia and was raised as female, but during puberty she did not develop the expected degree of secondary female sex characteristics, or feminine "attractiveness," thus was accused of being male (Berg, 2009). In reality, the range of female phenotypes does not always fit societal expectations. No uniform standards exist, nor is it realistic to think such standards can be created. Nevertheless, NBF athletes have been harmed by being judged "not developed enough" during *gender/sex verification testing* (GSVT; Heggie, 2010).

Unlike in the 1930s, contemporary research supports the existence of biological variations in sex development, described as intersex conditions, or *differences (*formerly called *disorders) of sex development* (DSDs; Ainsworth, 2015). It is important to understand that these individuals are born with a biological and generally benign phenotype (Pielke & Pape, 2019) rather than an abnormality. However, the athletic community continues to stress the binary view of biological sex, and the lack of scientific understanding of DSD fuels ongoing controversy over nonbinary athletes in female sports. This debate postulates an "unfair" competitive advantage of female athletes: (1) who are hormonally intersex (i.e., with hyperandrogenism) or (2) who are MtF transgender previously assigned NBS as male.

Do Intersex and Transgender Athletes Have an "Unfair" Advantage?

Is this even the right question to ask? The idea of unfair advantage is based on assumptions about androgens' (i.e., male hormones) influence on performance in both natal and non-natal female athletes. However, both "male" and "female" biological sex hormones (i.e., androgens and estrogens, respectively) are endogenous in *all* human beings to varying degrees (Gillies & McArthur, 2010), and the effects of female hormones on NBF athletes' physiology is also not well understood (Sims & Heather, 2018), so it is difficult to identify clear NBS differences. This idea also assumes that there is a "dominant" effect of male hormones on athletic performance (Knox, Anderson, & Heather, 2019), but this conclusion is based mostly on research on NBMs. Last but not insignificant is whether there is a biological advantage (elite) athletes have compared to the general population aside from androgen levels.

There is so much yet to be understood about athletic performance. First, what biological advantages impact athletic performance? Second, why does this debate focus on MtF transgender and intersex athletes competing in female sports, and not all athletes with some form of biological advantage? Both involve the reality that athletes, especially at elite levels, are biologically privileged in some way (Reeser, 2005).

Biological Advantages

Very few become elite athletes without some biological phenotypes that may impart a competitive edge such as, for basketball, being taller or having bigger hands (Jones, Arcelus, Bouman, & Haycraft, 2017; Newbould, 2015), or having greater lung vital capacity, or possessing other polygenic factors (Ahmetov, Egorova, Gabdrakhmanova, & Fedotovskaya, 2016). These characteristics may give athletes a performance edge, yet are not discussed in making sports more equitable for athletes lacking these phenotypes. Another consideration is the possible physical and physiological overlap between NBMs and NBFs, in that there are NBFs who are more skilled, taller, stronger and faster than some NBMs. Yet these females are not scrutinized as having "unfair" advantage even if competing against males. The "biological advantage" for intersex athletes involves their natal phenotypes just like athletes born to be taller, faster and stronger. This leads to another issue: A distinction needs to be made between MtF transgender and DSD athletes with high androgen levels, because androgen has not been sufficiently linked to athletic performance. Many DSD individuals have high androgen levels but are androgen insensitive: Their bodies are not able to utilize the androgen (Knox et al., 2019), so it's unknown how their athletic performance might be affected. Knox and colleagues (2019) argued that male hormones play a role in developing other forms of biological advantages, but they did not consider athletes with androgen insensitivity, focusing only on MtF transgenders without *gender confirmation surgery* (GCS). GCS is the removal of male genitalia and reproductive structures, thus eliminating the main source of androgens (Pan & Honig, 2018).

MtF Transgender Athletes

These athletes therapeutically change their sex hormone levels and/or physical body to be congruent with gender identity (Klein, Krane, & Paule-Koba, 2018). However, there is an assumption that being born biologically male imparts *irreversible* male-hormone-influenced physiological characteristics that are unaffected by taking female hormones (Reeser, 2005), although this is not strongly supported by research (Krane, 2015). Nevertheless, these athletes are perceived as: (1) possessing an "unfair" athletic advantage over NBFs; and (2) actually "male" (aka "gender frauds") competing against females.

Therapeutically transitioning using *hormone therapy* (HT; i.e., natal male hormone suppression/female hormones supplementation) effects changes to the body's structural composition and physiology, resulting in loss of original musculature and function (Jones et al., 2017; Reeser, 2005), in effect losing their "biological advantage."

Not all MtF transitioning involves GCS, so exploring the differences between MtF with and without GCS is crucial to the debate about unfair advantage in athletics, and to clearly understand how natal androgen levels affect athletic ability after GCS (Knox et al., 2019). Although acknowledging the lack of research, Knox and colleagues (2019) concluded, through review of the science on *typical* NBM physiology, that MtF athletes with HT but not GCS would retain some advantages of natal male physiology. This is simply not established by research. It remains an open question.

At the same time that there is a clear bias against MtF transgender athletes, whereas female-to-male (FtM) transgender athletes in male sports are not subjected to the same scrutiny and suspicion. FtM transgender athletes are perceived to be less of a competitive threat (Reeser, 2005) because it is believed that HT does not make them competitive against NBMs (Jones et al., 2017). Even so, taking male hormones, per sports policies, means FtM transgender athletes are no longer eligible to compete in female sports (Klein et al., 2018).

Intersex / DSD Athletes

DSD female athletes who are hormonally intersex but not transgenders are also viewed with suspicion. The main controversy centers on these intersex athletes having *hyperandrogenism* (i.e., high levels of androgen production; Handelsman, Hirschberg, & Bermon, 2018; Hirschberg, 2019; Karkazis, Jordan-Young, Davis, & Camporesi, 2011) compared to "typical" NBF athletes. Hyperandrogenism is a medical condition with a range of complications, belying the view of it as an advantage. However, there are higher numbers of females with DSD conditions in sports than other activities (Bermon et al., 2014). The majority of hyperandrogenic female athletes are born with *polycystic ovary syndrome* (PCOS; Handelsman et al., 2018). Other conditions producing high androgen levels include *congenital adrenal hyperplasia* (CAH), undescended testes producing androgens (Handelsman et al., 2018) and *androgen insensitivity syndrome* (AIS; Bostwick & Joyner, 2012).

Misunderstandings by sports officials concerning DSDs have led to restricting intersex athletes' participation, and also MtF transgender athletes if their androgen levels exceed standards established for female sports. Yet biological advantage is not the sole factor for sports achievement. It also depends on environmental factors such as commitment, training methods and nutritional intake (Georgiades, Klissouras, Baulch, Wang, & Pitsiladis, 2017; Newbould, 2015). Even a gendered expectation may modulate hormone levels, particularly testosterone, regardless of NBS (Hyde, Bigler, Joel, Tate, & van Anders, 2019). Not taking these factors into account has led to wrongfully labeling athletes as "gender frauds" and to misinformed sports policies.

GSVT Policy in Sports

Mirroring societal beliefs about biological sex and gender as binary constructs, sports organizations have established policies for gender segregation and competition rules. The idea of "gender frauds" led to sports organizations implementing GSVT, which from inception both lacked evidence-based criteria and restricted nonbinary athletes for female, but not male, sports.

Initially, GSVT involved a visual inspection of female athletes, aka "naked parades" (Pielke & Pape, 2019; Reeser, 2005), to identify NBMs supposedly "hiding" their biological sex (i.e., a penis) or lacking "feminine" characteristics (Heggie, 2010), to prevent them from taking "unfair" advantage in female sports. An athlete's gender identity did not matter to early sports authorities. From these visual inspections, GSVT moved to genetic and hormonal assessments (Heggie, 2010). This led to some NBFs and intersex athletes being wrongfully disqualified from competition (Rogol & Pieper, 2018) because of misunderstandings about biological sex development (Klein et al., 2018).

Genetic GSVT illustrates how policy makers got the science wrong, by erroneously identifying the biological sex of individuals with certain DSD conditions (Reeser, 2005; Rogol & Pieper, 2018), such as a NBF athlete with only one X chromosome (i.e., Turner Syndrome; Heggie, 2010), as not female. Other DSD conditions could lead to similar errors involving male athletes (Reeser, 2005; Rogol & Pieper, 2018), so genetic testing to identify "gender frauds" is problematic when policy makers lack knowledge of the range of DSD or intersex conditions that can affect testing outcomes.

Hormone GSVT is also affected by incomplete science on hormonal variations. Both binary NBSs have endogenous androgens, but in different amounts (Handelsman et al., 2018). Hormone GSVT looks for atypically high levels of androgens, but that overlaps with detection of athletes possibly abusing steroids (i.e., androgens) as a performance enhancer. As a result, athletes transitioning with HT or who may be hormonally intersex can be misidentified as steroid abusers.

Controversial Case of Caster Semenya

Violation of medical privacy is also an issue with GSVT for athletes who may be intersex and/or undergoing HT. Such ethical violations are alleged in the case of South African runner Caster Semenya. Semenya has long been suspected by elite international and national sports organizations of having hyperandrogenism, in part influenced by perceptions that her features are not "feminine" (Karkazis et al., 2011; Levy, 2009; Pielke & Pape, 2019). As a result, she was accused of being male or a "gender fraud." By all accounts, Semenya consistently identified as female yet was forced to undergo GSVT (Levy, 2009). She was not protected by medical privacy, and the apparent findings of high androgens and undescended testicles were leaked to the press (Levy, 2009). If true (Semenya has not responded to the leaks), both these characteristics would indicate congenital DSDs.

Regardless of DSDs as congenital, the International Association of Athletics Federation (IAAF), which governs track and field, passed regulations for specific middle-distance events restricting participation of hyperandrogenic female athletes (Hirschberg, 2019; Pielke & Pape, 2019), an action viewed as targeting Semenya's specific competitive events. To continue competing, Semenya would have to use HT to lower her alleged naturally high levels of androgens (Pielke & Pape, 2019). Initially, the androgen limit was set at 10 nmol/L, the baseline of typical male androgen levels (Handelsman et al., 2018;

Karkazis et al., 2011) but then was lowered to 5 nmol/L (Hirschberg, 2019) as being closer to typical NBFs (Knox et al., 2019). This policy reinforces the view that being male is based solely on androgen levels. As discussed earlier, other polygenic factors influence the physiology of various biological sexes in a far more complex process. Efforts to restrict Semenya and other hyperandrogenic athletes by imposing androgen level limits is, as pointed out by Bostwick and Joyner (2012), ironic since these female athletes are not "unbeatable," as they do not reach male times in similar events. The IAAF policy restricting some, but not all, track and field events is categorically inequitable and lacking scientific evidence regarding effects of hormones on athletic performance.

Current Policies Governing Sports

Resistance to creating more inclusive sports policies continues because of the persistent misconception that MtF transgender and female intersex athletes possess unfair biological advantages. Continuing to use male androgen levels as a basis for restrictions in female sports reinforces the view of the NBM as athletically superior to females. A methodical literature review of sports policies concludes that limiting participation of transgender (and intersex) athletes on the basis of "biological advantages" is not evidence based (Jones et al., 2017).

Sports Policy per Competitive Level

Across the various competitive sports levels of youth, college and elite/professional, there are considerable inconsistencies in governance of sports participation by nonbinary athletes.

Youth and college sports policies in the United States are becoming more inclusive of nonbinary athletes. Transathlete.com ("Policies," 2019) categorizes sports policies by level as well as by organization. Not all policies are listed, and they vary by state and sport organization. Currently, only 17 US states follow inclusive youth sports policies that do not require GSVT or treatments (hormonal or surgical) to join sport teams reflective of the athlete's gender identity. The remaining states' policies have some restrictions or have no policies ("Policies," 2019).

At the college level, the National Collegiate Athletic Association (NCAA) establishes policies for the majority of college sports. NCAA policies restrict transgender athletes, but rules for intersex athletes lack specificity. The NCAA (2011) policy on transgender athletes (both MtF and FtM) requires a *diagnosed* gender dysphoria or having undergone GCS to allow medical exemption for HT. NCAA policy lets FtM transgender athletes taking HT compete on male or coed teams, but not female teams. MtoF transgender athletes can also compete on coed teams, but not female teams until a full year of HT has been completed (NCAA, 2011).

At elite sport levels, national and international sports policies vary greatly regarding transgender and intersex athletes. Similar to the NCAA, the International Olympic Committee (IOC) policy stipulates that FtM transgender athletes can compete in male sports without restrictions (IOC, 2015). However, for female sports, before first competition and during the desired period of eligibility: (1) MtF transgender athletes must avow a female gender identity for a minimum of four years (IOC, 2015), a stipulation viewed as excessive (Jones et al., 2017); and (2) MtF transgender and intersex athletes must have androgen levels below 10 nmol/L for at least a year (IOC, 2015). Failure to comply with monitoring/testing will result in loss of eligibility in female sports for one year (IOC, 2015). While the IAAF lowered hormone levels for specific female track events, as discussed earlier, the IOC has delayed making similar changes to hormone level guidelines because of disagreement within the IOC scientific panel (Ingle, 2019).

Transforming Sports for the Future: Inclusive and Equitable Policies

While youth sports are more inclusive, the NCAA and the IOC continue gender segregation of sports based on NBS (i.e., hormonal), not GI. Requirements involving medical diagnosis, HT, and a waiting period for athletes undergoing HT and/or transitioning perpetuate the bias of regarding NBMs as physiologically advantaged because of androgens. This goes to the argument about fairness of gender divisions in sports.

The growing number of states with inclusive youth sports policies is a movement that college and elite sports organizations should heed, given the number of transgender youths transitioning at younger ages and blocking puberty. Earlier transitioning with HT may have different effects on the body than later transitioning, an aspect of hormonal influence on athletic performance for which empirical data is lacking, and current sports policies may not be equitable regarding the timing of transitioning. It is vital that increased research on variations of biological sex physiology and hormones, and effects of timing of HT on athletic performance, be undertaken. Sports organizations need to advocate for research in order to develop sports policies using empirical evidence.

It is vital to this mission to move away from the persistent NBM lens and include diverse perspectives. Many young athletes, having experienced inclusive youth sports policies, will expect similar inclusion at higher levels of athletics, so exploring options to be both inclusive and fair should be undertaken with urgency, utilizing contemporary interdisciplinary evidence. Sports organizations can transform views of stakeholders with educational programs designed to improve both scientific and sexual literacy on NBS and GI development. Deeper scientific research inclusive of the full range of human physiology can affect an educational revolution in the sports world to achieve inclusivity and fairness in both organizations and policies that is necessary and long overdue.

References

Acosta, R. V., & Carpenter, J. C. (2008). *Women in intercollegiate sport: A longitudinal study thirty-one year update 1977–2008.* Retrieved from http://acostacarpenter.org

Ahmetov, I. I., Egorova, E. S., Gabdrakhmanova, L. J., & Fedotovskaya, O. N. (2016). Genes and athletic performance: An update. *Genetics and Sports, 61,* 41–54. https://doi.org/10.1159/000445240

Ainsworth, C. (2015). Sex redefined. *Nature, 518,* 288–291.

Berg, S. (2009). How Dora the man competed in the woman's high jump, *Der Spiegel International Online*. Retrieved from http://www.spiegel.de/international/germany/0,1518,649104,00.html

Bermon, S., Garnier, P. Y., Hirschberg, A. L., Robinson, N., Giraud, S., Baume, N., … Ritzen, M. (2014). Serum androgen levels in elite female athletes. *Journal of Clinical Endocrinology & Metabolism, 99*(11), 4328–4335.

Bostwick, J. M., & Joyner, M. J. (2012). The limits of acceptable biological variations in elite athletes: Should sex ambiguity be treated differently from other advantageous genetic traits? *Mayo Clinic Proceedings, 82*(6), 508–512.

Carter, M. J. (2014). Gender socialization and identity theory. *Social Sciences, 3*, 242–261.

Case, M. (2017). Heterosexuality as a factor in the long history of women's sports. *Law and Contemporary Problems, 80*(4), 25–46.

CISM (International Military Sports Council). (2019). *History.* Retrieved from http://www.milsport.one/cism/cism-history

Costa, D. M., & Guthrie, S. R. (1994). *Women and sport: Interdisciplinary perspectives.* Champaign, IL: Human Kinetics.

Dillon, M. (2000). Did Parthenoi attend the Olympic games? Girls and women competing, spectating, and carrying out cult roles at Greek religious festivals. *Hermes, 128*, 457–480. Retrieved from https://www.jstor.org/stable/4477389. Accessed August 2, 2019 02:35 UTC

Eitzen, D. S., & Sage, G. H. (2003). *Sociology of North American sports* (7th ed.). Boston, MA: McGraw Hill.

Georgiades, E., Klissouras, V., Baulch, J., Wang, G., & Pitsiladis, Y. (2017). Why nature prevails over nurture in the making of the elite athlete. *BMC Genomics, 18*(Suppl. 8), 835. https://doi.org/10.1186/s12864-017-4190-8

Gill, D. L. (2002). Gender and sport behavior. In T. S. Horn (Ed.), *Advances in sport psychology* (2nd ed., pp. 355–376). Champaign, IL: Human Kinetics.

Gillies, G. E., & McArthur, S. (2010). Estrogen actions in the brain and the basis for differential action in men and women: A case for sex-specific medicines. *Pharmacological Reviews, 62*, 155–198.

Handelsman, D. J., Hirschberg, A. L., & Bermon, S. (2018). Circulating testosterone as the hormonal basis of sex differences in athletic performance. *Endocrine Reviews, 39*(5), 803–829. https://doi.org/10.1210/er.2018-00020

Hargreaves, J. (1994). *Sporting females: Critical issues in the history and sociology of women's sports.* New York: Routledge.

Hargreaves, J., & Anderson, E. (2014). *Routledge handbook of sport, gender, and sexuality.* New York: Routledge.

Heggie V. (2010). Testing sex and gender in sports; reinventing, reimagining and reconstructing histories. *Endeavour, 34*(4), 157–163. doi:10.1016/j.endeavour.2010.09.005

Hirschberg, A. L. (2019). Hyperandrogenism in female athletes. *Journal of Clinical Endocrinology & Metabolism, 104*(2), 503–505. https://doi.org/10.1210/jc.2018-01676

Hyde, J. S., Bigler, R. S., Joel, D., Tate, C. C., & van Anders, S. M. (2019). The future of sex and gender in psychology: Five challenges to the gender binary. *American Psychologist, 74*(2), 171–193.

Ingle, S. (2019). IOC delays new transgender guidelines after scientists fail to agree. *The Guardian*, Retrieved September 24, 2019, from https://www.theguardian.com/sport/2019/sep/24/ioc-delays-new-transgender-guidelines-2020-olympics

International Olympic Committee (IOC). (2015). *IOC consensus meeting on sex reassignment and hyperandrogenism.* Retrieved from https://www.olympic.org/medical-and-scientific-commission#ancre14

Jones, B. A., Arcelus, J., Bouman, W. P., & Haycraft, E. (2017). Sport and transgender people: A systematic review of the literature relating to sport participation and competitive sport policies. *Sports Medicine, 47*(4), 701–716. https://doi.org/10.1007/s40279-016-0621-y

Karkazis, K., Jordan-Young, R., Davis, G., & Camporesi, S. (2011). Out of bounds? A critique of the new policies on hyperandrogenism in elite female athletes. *American Journal of Bioethics, 12*(7), 3–16. https://doi.org/10.1080/15265161.2012.680533.

Klein, A., Krane, V., & Paule-Koba, A. L. (2018). Bodily changes and performance effects in a transitioning transgender college athlete. *Qualitative Research in Sport, Exercise, and Health, 10*(5), 555–569.

Knox, T., Anderson, L. C., & Heather, A. (2019). Transwomen in elite sport: Scientific and ethical considerations. *Journal of Medical Ethics, 45*, 395–403.

Krane, V. (2015). *Gender non-conformity, sex variation, and sport.* In R. Schinke & K. McGannon (Eds.), *The psychology of sub-culture in sport and physical activity: A critical approach. Exercise, and health* (pp. 48–63). New York: Routledge.

Ladda, S. (2017). Homophobia in sport. In G. Sobiech & S. Günter (Eds.), *Sport & Gender—(inter) nationale sportsoziologische Geschlechterforschung. Geschlecht und Gesellschaft,* vol. 59. Springer VS, Wiesbaden. https://doi.org/10.1007/978-3-658-13098-5_11

Levy, A. (2009, November 30). Either/or: Sport, sex, and the case of Caster Semenya. *New Yorker.* https://www.newyorker.com/magazine/2009/11/30/eitheror

Lim, H. Z. (2018). Media coverage for female sports: A review of literature. *Kinesiology, Sport Studies, and Physical Education Synthesis Projects, 60.* https://digitalcommons.brockport.edu/pes_synthesis/60

Lines, G. (2001). Villains, fools or heroes? Sport stars as role models for young people. *Leisure Studies, 20*, 285–303.

McPherson, B. D., Curtis, J. E., & Loy, J. W. (1989). *The social significance of sport: An introduction to the sociology of sport.* Champaign, IL: Human Kinetics.

National Collegiate Athletic Association (NCAA). (2011). *NCAA inclusion of transgender athletes handbook.* Retrieved from https://www.ncaapublications.com/p-4335-ncaa-inclusion-of-transgender-student-athletes.aspx

Newbould, M. J. (2015). What do we do about women athletes with testes? *Journal of Medical Ethics, 42*(4), 256–259. https://doi.org/10.1136/medethics-2015-102948.

Olympic Museum. (2002). *The Olympic games in ancient Greece.* International Olympic Committee. Retrieved from http://multimedia.olympic.org/pdf/en_report_65 8.pdf

Padawer, R. (2016). The humiliating practice of sex-testing female athletes. *New York Times.*

Pan, S., & Honig, S. C. (2018). Gender-affirming surgery: Current concepts. *Current Urology Reports, 19*(8), 62. https://doi.org/10.1007/s11934-018-0809-9

Park, R. J., & Hult, J. S. (1993). Women as leaders in physical education and school-based sports, 1865 to the 1930s. *Journal of Physical Education, Recreation and Dance, 64*(3), 35–40.

Perrottet, T. (2004). *The naked Olympics: The true story of the ancient games.* New York: Random House.

Pielke, R., & Pape, M. (2019). Science, sport, sex, and the case of Caster Semenya. *Issues in Science and Technology.* https://issues.org/science-sport-sex/

Plaza, M., Boiché, J., Brunel, L., & Ruchaud, F. (2017). Sport = male ... But not all sports: Investigating the gender stereotypes of sport activities at the explicit and implicit levels. *Sex Roles, 76*(3–4), 202–217. http://dx.doi.org/10.1007/s11199-016-0650-x.

Policies. (2019). Retrieved from https://www.transathlete.com/policies

Reeser, J. (2005). Gender identity and sport: Is the playing field level? *British Journal of Sports Medicine, 39*(10), 695–699. https://doi.org/10.1136/bjsm.2005.018119

Rogol, A. D., & Pieper, L. P. (2018). The interconnected histories of endocrinology and eligibility in women's sport. *Hormone Research in Paediatrics, 90*(4), 213–220. https://doi.org/10.1159/000493646

Saraswat, A., Weinand, J. D., & Safer, J. D. (2015). Evidence supporting the biological nature of gender identity. *Endocrine Practice, 21*(2), 199–202.

Segrave, J. O., & Chu, D. (1988). *The Olympic games in transition.* Champaign, IL: Human Kinetics.

Sherman, N. (2005). *Stoic warriors: The ancient philosophy behind the military mind.* New York: Oxford University Press.

Sims, S. T., & Heather, A. K. (2018). Myths and methodologies: Reducing scientific design ambiguity in studies comparing sexes and/or menstrual cycle phases. *Experimental Physiology, 103,* 1309–1317.

Spears, B. (1988). Tryphosa, Melpomene, Nadia, and Joan: The IOC and women's sports. In J.O. Segrave & D. Chu (Eds.), *The Olympic Games in transition* (pp. 365–373). Champaign, IL: Human Kinetics.

United States Department of Education. (2015). *Title IX and sex discrimination.* Retrieved from https://www2.ed.gov/about/offices/list/ocr/docs/tix_dis.html

Vertinsky, P. (1994). Women, sport, and exercise in the 19th century (Chapter 5). In D. Costa & S. Guthrie (Eds.), *Women and sport: Interdisciplinary perspectives* (pp. 63–82). Champaign, IL: Human Kinetics.

Videon, T. M. (2002). Who plays and who benefits: Gender, interscholastic athletics and academic outcomes. *Sociological Perspectives, 45,* 415–444.

Chapter 17

NAVIGATING SURROGACY AS A GAY MAN: A PERSONAL AND PROFESSIONAL SEXUAL LITERACY JOURNEY

Elliott Kronenfeld

Growing up as a gay boy in the 1970s had its fair share of social challenges. Being easily identified due to my effeminate nature, participation in dance classes and drama, and having a high lilting voice ensured that everyone around me keyed into the putative inappropriateness of me. One of the joys of being so easily identified is that I did not have to work hard to cover, but spent my energy trying to stay out of the limelight and direct line of assault. Because I did not pass as straight, learning how to survive with a minimal cover was critical. Goffman (1963) wrote a seminal work that differentiated passing, the ability to manage discrediting information about one's self from being discovered from others, from covering, the ability to minimalize and diminish what is known for a reduced effect. For most of the time, covering and diminishing worked efficiently enough but the damage took its toll. I was withdrawn, avoided peers whenever possible and began to develop depressive symptoms and terrible eating, often drowning loneliness in junk food. I grew up knowing that I was not going to have the same future opportunities as my peers and began to think about what was available to me.

In the 1980s, it was assumed that I would have a future of loneliness, that I was at constant risk of being a social pariah, and of course that I could not have the family I dreamed of creating. These messages were confirmed not only by my local community but the core messages that were delivered on the daily from talk shows that were addressing the AIDS crisis, soap operas that crafted storylines showing gay and lesbian characters negatively, and movies such as *Deliverance*, *Cruising*, and *The Boys in the Band* contributed to spreading this limited and biased picture of bleakness for anyone not living up to heteronormative expectations.

By the time I got into college, and subsequently the Army, the case of Baby M was making major headlines around the world (Annas, 1987; Rust, 1987). Baby M is the pseudonym for a child at the center of a legal battle between a man and traditional surrogate that was hired to help him and his wife have a family. The case of Baby M became the center of my world, leading me to ask: How is it possible for a man to work with a woman who he is not married to or in a relationship with carry a child for him? This case became an obsession. There were so many interpersonal aspects to be considered. For example, was this "prostitution" as so many claimed? Was anyone being taken advantage of? Who was entitled to what? Why would she even do this? Why would he? I came to learn that a traditional surrogate was a woman who is clinically inseminated with the intention of surrendering the child to the sperm donor.

Before I move forward, I would like to clarify how I am using "traditional" surrogacy versus "gestational" surrogacy practices that are more common today. Traditional surrogacy is the process of creating a contract between a woman and an intended parent (the person who is expected to take custody of the child upon birth). The surrogate is then inseminated with donor sperm from the intended parent or from a sperm bank in the hope that her own egg (ova) will become fertilized so that she can gestate and deliver a child that will be surrendered to the intended parent(s). Gestational surrogacy is the process of separating the genetic function (ova production) from the biological function (gestation) so that the surrogate does not have any genetic link to the child. The ova come from the intended parent or from a third-party egg donor. Because the surrogate does not have a genetic tie to the child, the case of Baby M becomes moot. The Baby M case was centered on the surrogate's genetic tie to the child.

Ultimately, the foundational case of Baby M began to set the world of human reproduction on the edge (Kornegay, 1990; May, 1997; Merrick, 1990; Sandor, 2002; Spivak, 2010). I began researching and studying this new thing—surrogacy—that was in the shadows as are so many things that focus on the most challenging of human experiences. As early as I can remember, I never had a professional ambition. I never wanted to be a policeman or an astronaut, although there was that short period of time that I wanted to be Liza Minnelli. However, the one consistent dream I had was always to be a father. I loved children and wanted to raise one where I could give and receive love in ways that I did not always get in the other parts of my life. It felt like the part of my life that might also make me *normal* and help me find the place to fit in with the rest of the world. Seeing that straight people did not always "just have kids" was eye opening and informed me that if they could do it, I could do it too. These straight men were having children with women they were not married to and being allowed to keep their children. These messages ran counter to all of the previous messages I had received about what my options were. What I really began to believe was that even as a gay man, I could have a family! My commitment was sealed.

Not 10 years later in 1993, another court case caught my attention. *Calvert v Johnson* in the Fourth Circuit Court of the United States (Hansen, 1993; Rose, 1996; Rosenberg, 2011; Scott, 2009). This case was between a heterosexual couple and a surrogate who entered into an in vitro (IVF) fertilization. The surrogate was not inseminated, but rather was carrying an embryo that was not genetically hers—she had no biological tie to the child. The surrogate was gestating a child that was the result of another woman's egg. This case focused on who has legal rights to such a child. It was this case that determined that gestational surrogacy is significantly safer than traditional surrogacy (where the surrogate has a biological connection to the child) and that the legal contracts, when appropriately written and executed prior to any transfer of biological material (sperm, ova and/or embryo), could determine parentage, which secured the rights of those who entered the contract to have a child that they could not have on their own (intended parents; Snyder & Byrn, 2005). Now I knew I had a clear path to a family of my own.

As the Calvert case began to make news as the second such case to capture the public imaginary on the topic of surrogacy, the social media images of gay men began to improve. The 1990s was the decade when, for instance, the gay community began strongly organizing around marriage equality and family security. Likewise, because of advances in reproductive technology, the puzzle for how to create biological families for gay and lesbian couples began to come together in a way that was legal and medically safe albeit terribly expensive. Unlike those who can biologically reproduce through coitus, those who need medical intervention must rely on the privilege of health insurance in case it will cover some expenses and/or the ability to pay out of pocket for the extraordinary expenses where insurance has exclusions. Currently for gay men, the majority of expenses related to surrogacy are exclusionary in most insurance plans, leaving intended fathers with the cost of upward of $200,000, especially in the case where a surrogate or egg donor might need to be replaced, there is a medical complication, and/or more than one transfer is needed to achieve a successful birth added to other often hidden costs such as travel and other compensation (Men Having Babies [MHB], 2020). There is a new movement in trying to coordinate package plans with surrogacy agencies and IVF clinics to help reduce the possible expenditures, and financial supports such as the Gay Parenting Assistance Program offered by Men Having Babies (MHB, 2020).

It is clear that with the cost of surrogacy alone being extraordinary, being able to use this option to build one's family is a position of privilege. This often means that should intended parents want to pursue surrogacy as their family building option, they must be able to have a strong and stable income, be able to access financial resources from family or other sources or try to take loans and incur debt. For this reason alone, I work with many intended parents to help them choose between the adoption option and the surrogacy option. In my parenting journey, I have completed my surrogacy journey, and I have adopted a child. Because I have completed both journeys, clients often ask me if one path was *better* than the other. It has been my experience that parenthood is not about biology but how we engage our children and build meaningful relationships, help them to unpack who they are, and become witnesses to their lives. However, this is not how all clients look at the decision. For some men, the choice between having a biological child may be rooted in several factors: wanting to carry on a genetic line, wanting to parent from birth on and fearful that a newborn through adoption may not be possible, concerns over control/fear of loss after investing in an adoption situation and other concerns. When men have committed to the surrogacy option, the journey begins to focus decisions and resources to move ahead.

As a professional sex therapist and licensed mental health clinician, I have come to focus my work on counseling gay men in their fertility journey and the arduous tasks of identifying all of the important players: surrogacy agencies, lawyers, mental health professionals, reproductive endocrinologists/IVF clinics, donors, surrogates and so on. Learning hard lessons from my own journey and working in the expanding field of assisted reproductive technology (ART), it is apparent to me how uninformed the public is in regard to such services. Knowing the struggle of wanting a family of my own and having no one to guide me through the available options and how to base decisions, I made a conscientious decision to use my therapeutic training to help others discover their own vision of what they hope to accomplish. I am sure that had these services been available to me, I would have had children earlier, made different choices in how I chose providers such as lawyers and clinics, and would have brought my family and other significant people into my story with different approaches. My greatest lesson from my own journey is that you never do this alone, and you need to understand the long-term implications of how every decision you make crafts such a journey. As such, it has become a personal mission to assist other gay men to make informed decisions about how they build their family.

In the nearly 20 years that I have been counseling gay men in their journey to becoming fathers, I have learned a few key lessons. It is the rare situation when someone, regardless of orientation or identity, is given a solid education on how to build a family. Like basic sex education, this information often assumed, or learned by absorbing messages from the social environment. As a certified sex therapist, one of the key services I provide is to, not only provide quality sex education and support but also to help clients think through how sex and the functions of sex—to include reproduction—fit into their life vision. All too often, fertility and growing a family is based on assumptions about what is expected not what is possible. With that in mind, here are my guidelines for when I work clients who are struggling with fertility or need ART. First, it is important to help them keep perspective on the bigger picture. One of the most important aspects that I ask them to consider is how to leave every option on the table for as long as they can and to remember to have a long-term focus. Second, it is important not just to consider how to have a baby, but also to think through what their family will look like when it is complete. How many children will they have? How old do they want to be when their youngest child is born? Are they open to twins? If they are part of a couple, does biology matter to them and if so/not, how will they make decisions regarding who will be a biological father when and how? Lastly, I also remind them that the decisions they are making now are about them and how they want to fulfill their identity as gay men and fathers. It is, in many ways, a very self-fulfilling journey. However, the decisions they make will have a lifetime of implications for their children and how they see themselves in the world.

Beyond the cost of surrogacy, gay men face tremendous relationship dynamics that they must cope with due to the impact of these dynamics across the lifetime. What is to be the relationship with the egg donor? What is to be the relationship with the surrogate? How will I talk to my child about these dynamics? These unique relationships bring special emotional and practical challenges that heteronormative parents rarely must consider. Let's break down each separately.

In the case of the egg donor, there are several options that can be utilized. The first consideration is understanding what makes for a good egg donor. The *American Society of Reproductive Medicine* (ASRM) is the governing body for reproductive endocrinology and sets the standard for who can be an egg donor (ASRM, 2017a). At the time of this writing, egg donors must be between the ages of 21 and 34, must undergo psychological and medical screening, must be free of sexually transmitted infections, must not be carriers of cystic fibrosis and any other genetic disorders that intended parents may choose to test for, and other genetic tests may be run based on the donor's personal history and ethnic background.

If a woman is healthy enough and willing to donate her eggs, the relationship with the intended parents must be considered. There are several relationship choices that must be mutually agreed upon by all parties. Intended parents can purchase frozen eggs from their IVF clinic or egg donor agency. These eggs will come with a full battery of medical test results. A full history of the eggs from this donor will also be provided including whether any eggs have previously resulted in a live birth during a different donation cycle, which *can* be an indicator of future success. In such a situation, no personally identifying information regarding the donor is available.

The next option is an anonymous donor. This is a fresh cycle donation where the intended parents will receive all information about medical and psychological screenings but will not meet nor speak with the donor. There are cases where an agreement can be struck that contact can be made through the third-party agency if a medical emergency occurs and additional biological information is required by either side. Alternatively, a knowable donor can be selected. This is where some basic contact can be shared between the donor and the intended parents prior to and during the retrieval, but no ongoing relationship is expected. In some cases, when the child turns 18, donors may indicate that they are open to being contacted, with limits on how and for specific reasons for contact. All parties agree that once the donation is complete, the relationship is over and no other contact, with the exception of emergencies handled by a third party will occur. While it is possible to have an ongoing relationship with an egg donor, for most people this is not common practice.

The remaining option for surrogacy egg donation is having a friend or family member donate. This is a challenging factor as the preexisting relationship must be considered and the risks of how the relationship may change once a child is born or if the donation is not successful. For example, if a donor is a family member, it is critical to identify what the ongoing relationship between the donor and her family/children will be to the child in question. This can be a wonderful gift from someone who supports gay parenting and can hold healthy boundaries, but those agreements must be made clearly up front to ensure that no parties are confused about the healthy boundaries that are expected. These healthy boundaries can include clearly defining what the relationship between the donor and the child will be and how those connections will be explained to the child and other family members. For example, if an aunt is the donor, being clear about how the relationship dynamics will be explained to the child and any cousins they have from the aunt. Are the children cousins? Are they half-siblings? Where and when is the donation explained? Who needs to know the details of the donation? What role does the aunt play in the raising of the child? While there is no one *right* answer, family members must have a clear and shred vision of such issues before going forward.

Along with finding an egg donor, gay fathers must find a surrogate. Once again, the qualifications are set by ASRM (2017b). The surrogate must be between the ages of 21 and 45 who has already delivered a healthy child and has a network of support as she progresses through the pregnancy journey. There is a limit on how many successful deliveries a potential surrogate can have with a limit of not more than five previous vaginal deliveries or two cesarean deliveries. The surrogate will also undergo extensive medical and psychological testing. Her intimate partner/spouse will also undergo a psychological screening. Once a woman is cleared to be a surrogate, she and her partner along with the intended parent(s) have to begin to navigate a complex relationship that is deeply intimate.

In the rare situations where a friend or family member will gestate the child, the boundaries of such relationship, how it will affect others in the family network, and how safety for each party will determined must be negotiated and contracted. If a surrogate is found using an agency, the relationship must be formed quickly but in a deeply boundaried manner.

It can be challenging to have such an intimate relationship with someone you do not know, who literally is holding your future generation, while you have little control. The relationship between intended parent and surrogate can run a wide gamut. Some intended parents have a lifelong relationship with their surrogate who, along with her family, plays an extended family role. In other situations, parents usually deeply thank the surrogate but do not maintain the relationship after the birth. Each intended parent and surrogate team must navigate and decide in the context what is best for all involved.

Legally, surrogacy is banned in most countries around the world. The surrogacy laws are changing so rapidly it is critical to have lawyers who specialize in reproductive law involved in the process. In the United States, each state has its own unique and nuanced surrogacy laws, and surrogacy is not legal in all states. It is critical to understand the uniqueness of each state's laws when the intended parents, the surrogate and the egg donor might live in different states. US laws and guidelines are specific for how surrogacy journeys should be crafted for the protection of each role in the journey. For the case of transnational surrogacy (where the surrogate and/or donor live in another country than the intended parents), the issues are not only legal but involve navigating different social challenges and cultural dynamics that have the potential to take advantage of low income or socially lower caste women (Deomampo, 2013; Lustenberger, 2017; Pyrce, 2016; Rudrappa & Collins, 2015). Agencies working in transnational surrogacy do not always prepare intended parents for the difference in sociocultural realities that surrogates/donors may face in their home country and the extremely limited contact they will have with these women. Attorneys must know the laws of the country of the intended parents and the country where the surrogate resides as laws are often not compatible in terms of gaining legal citizenship and parental rights. Therapists who help intended parents navigate a transnational surrogacy journey must be aware of the significant cultural, social and legal challenges in such a journey.

In the US context, it is not an uncommon experience for me as a therapist to counsel gay intended fathers about how to engage with their surrogate. Having no sense of control over day-to-day life during pregnancy, and often having a surrogate that lives states away, can leave an intended father seeking some sort of control or involvement that results in awkwardness or damage to the relationship. Intended fathers can not only be deeply supportive and develop a lifelong friendship with the surrogate but can also become demanding, controlling and anxious, which can drive a wedge in this relationship.

In the counseling process as these challenges develop, I ask the intended fathers to consider some important perspectives on their relationship with the surrogate and the team supporting the process. The donor, the surrogate and the extended families of these women are giving unquantifiable gifts, so that a child can be born. It is critical to consider all they are doing—even though it is also a business transaction—and to recalibrate responses and behaviors accordingly. More importantly, I ask fathers to consider what options they want for their children. For example, how will they respond when their children want to know if they can meet the woman who donated the egg or who carried them? It is this concept that often will make intended parents stop to realize that this journey, which begins with their need for self-fulfillment necessarily ends with their crafting a path for their child.

Because the journey is so personal and expensive, many gay men in this situation would want to drive results and hold the process close. I remind them that there is a priority of decision that they must use as a guideline for behaviors and choice making. The first priority is to consider any child that is already in the world. For example, how will the surrogate's children be affected? Do you already have children from a previous similar journey or relationship? These children must be nurtured, included and protected in anticipation of the shift in family dynamic and before any other child joins. The second priority are the donor and surrogate, whose health and well-being must be protected at all costs. The third priority, though of course not the least, is the child that will be created from this journey. This child must be able to understand their world, their kinship network, and the journey that brought them into it. And, finally, the intended parents' desires are considered. This prioritization is often shocking to intended parents at first as they have often fought to get to the point of being able to consider and have children. To be told that they are the bottom of the prioritization list can be disheartening but when thoughtfully examined, especially under expert therapeutic guidance, most are able to use it to make well-informed decisions that guide their actions within this emotion-dense process.

Clearly, the journey is fraught with difficulty, expense and a deep need for self-reflection. One might think that when a gay father holds his baby for the first time that the journey has reached its natural conclusion. But, it hasn't.

I will close with one of my favorite personal memories of being a gay father. After having two children (a son and a daughter), I felt my family was complete. I relished in being able to provide the love and nurturance to these two amazing beings. Because there were not a lot of gay men who had children that were not a result of a previous heterosexual union, I was often nervous about how my children would face their reality without a mother in their life. And, then it happened. At the time, I was at the playground with my son, 7, and my daughter, 2. We were having a wonderful day getting dirty, eating snacks and seeing how fast we could spin the tire swing. A little boy asked my son "Where is your Mom?" My heart stopped and I felt a visceral need to intervene, protect him and teach this child that his heteronormative expectations did not work in our family. But my son answered first. He said, "They aren't here today." The other boy said "They? What do you mean?" To which my son responded, "I have lots of Moms. Grandmothers, godmothers, birth mothers, aunts that act like they are my mother [...] but these are my parents." And with that, he went down the slide.

In summary, sexual literacy means learning about and supporting gay men through their fertility options. This began with my own personal need and desire to have children.

Simply learning that I had options to have children expanded my thinking and world view and this has ultimately impacted my professional practice. First, it became apparent to me early in the process that my privilege of being a White, educated, resourced man enabled me to make greater choices and avail myself of greater opportunity with the world of ART. The awareness gained through the decision making heightened this sense of privilege unavailable to others. Second, gaining the awareness of how the journey of building my family changed my world view and what was important to me, I began to share my story. It was not long before I was sought out by other gay men asking me for advice. It was this interest in my experience that suggested I was not alone and there was a real need for sexual literacy. Finding a community of gay men who wanted to be parents without giving up their out and proud identity became the foundation for building my fertility practice. It is the unique quality of having the knowledge of assisted reproduction that has brought people to me: how to access the clinics, agencies, lawyers and other providers, as well as how to develop and navigate the nuanced relationships that must be built with surrogates/donors and their families. But it is the personal story of having walked the path and made the choices that has allowed other men to trust and believe they can have a future they want. Because I have been able to position myself as an insider, I have been able to help other intended parents, whether single or couples, regardless of their sexual identity, create opportunities that align with their resources, personal situations and desires.

Since my journey began, surrogacy has become a more open topic. It shows up as story lines in popular television and movies, celebrities are sharing their surrogacy journeys and the overall secrecy is being lifted. There are now so many new resources to help intended parents achieve their goals. To support family building, clinics and agencies are creating new programs such as donation sharing and discount programs to assist with social and financial challenges, professional organizations are looking at how to regulate and support all of the partners in the process to ensure fair treatment and men are more open about asking for help on their journey.

References

American Society for Reproductive Medicine (ASRM). (2017a). Egg donation fact sheet. Retrieved from https://www.reproductivefacts.org/news-and-publications/patient-fact-sheets-and-booklets/documents/fact-sheets-and-info-booklets/egg-donation/ (February 29, 2020).

American Society for Reproductive Medicine (ASRM). (2017b). Gestational surrogate fact sheet. Retrieved from https://www.reproductivefacts.org/news-and-publications/patient-fact-sheets-and-booklets/documents/fact-sheets-and-info-booklets/gestational-carrier-surrogate/ (February 29, 2020).

Annas. G. J. (1987). At law: Baby M: Babies (and justice) for sale. *Hastings Center Report, 17*(3), 13–15.

Deomampo, D. (2013). Transnational surrogacy in India: Interrogating power and women's agency. *Frontiers: A Journal of Women's Studies, 34*(3), 167–188.

Goffman, E. (1963). *Stigma: Notes on the management of spoiled identity*. London: Penguin Group.

Hansen, M. (1993). Surrogacy contract upheld: California Supreme Court says such agreements don't violate public policy. *ABA Journal, 79*(8), 34.

Kornegay, R. J. (1990). Is commercial surrogacy baby-selling? *Journal of Applied Philosophy, 7*(1), 45–50.

Lustenberger, S. (2017). "We are citizens"—Vulnerability and privilege in the experiences of Israeli gay men with surrogacy in India. *Journal of Comparative Family studies, 48*(3), 393–403.

May, E. T. (1997). The politics of reproduction. *Irish Journal of American Studies, 6,* 1–37.

Men Having Babies (MHB). (2020). Surrogacy directory. Retrieved from http://menhavingbabies. org/surrogacy-directory/directory/ (April 18, 2020).

Merrick, J. C. (1990). Selling reproductive rights: Policy issues in surrogate motherhood. *Politics and Life Sciences,* 8(2), 161–172.

Pyrce, C. (2016). Surrogacy and citizenship: A conjunctive solution to a global problem. *Indiana Journal of Global Legal Studies, 23*(2), 925–952.

Rose, M. (1996). Mothers and authors: Johnson v. Calvert and the new children of our imaginations. *Critical Inquiry, 22*(4), 613–633.

Rosenberg, M. B. (2011). Critical legal considerations for all parties to surrogacy arrangements. *Family Advocate, 34*(2), 23–27.

Rudrappa, S., & Collins, C. (2015). Altruistic agencies and compassionate consumers: Moral framing of transnational surrogacy. *Gender and Society, 29*(6), 937–959.

Rust, M. (1987). Family law: Whose baby is it? Surrogate motherhood after Baby M. *ABA Journal, 73*(8), 52–56.

Sandor, J. (2002). Reproduction, self, and state. *Social Research, 69*(1), 115–141.

Scott, E. S. (2009). Surrogacy and the politics of commodification. *Law and Contemporary Problems, 72*(3), 109–146.

Snyder, S. H., & Byrn, M. P. (2005). The use of prebirth parentage orders in surrogacy proceedings. *Family Law Quarterly, 39*(3), 633–662.

Spivak, C. (2010). The law of surrogate motherhood in the United States. *American Journal of Comparative Law, 58,* 97–114.

Chapter 18

SEXUALLY FLUID AND STRAIGHT PEOPLE IN THE THERAPEUTIC CONTEXT

Caroline Paltin

It was as a feeling of being completely me, instead of partially me. I would still say I am heterosexual, but that doesn't have the power to define my feelings desires and choices. I'm free to be who I have always been but couldn't always express.

—Eva, a client who identifies as heterosexual, female and sexually fluid, describes the experience of self following a same-sex sexual relationship

There are a multitude of nuanced expressions of sexuality not previously recognized in historically traditional Kinsey-based conceptualizations of sexuality. Sexual fluidity as identified by Diamond (2009) has given rise to a sociocultural sexual self-awareness revolution. Affirming advances in the theory and practice of psychotherapy have given queer individuals and couples opportunities for growth, resilience and repair in their relationships with families and loved ones. Sex and relationship author and therapist Esther Perel (2006) notes that we are no longer bound by rules dictating sexuality and relationships and refers to the current playing field as an "existential smorgasbord" offering infinite choices. Couples in therapy are faced with increasingly complex relational desires, needs and negotiations as well as greater opportunity to explore sexuality, sexual identity and relationships in general. Progressive theories rooted in an allied and affirming approach can assist the client in increasing awareness and freedom of expression of gender identity and sexual fluidity. These approaches reach beyond the restrictive sociopolitical frames of prior historically limiting theories and treatment. For Eva, therapy offered a holding space for safe exploration of her emerging self well before she was ready to step into relational explorations. She described her sessions as opportunities to "lay it all out and see what's inside of me," without the pressures to please friends or family, or engage in black and white notions of her sexual self.

Historical Overview

Early approaches to the study and treatment of nonheteronormative individuals were based in the psychoanalytic tradition. This model of psychotherapy held that homosexuality and all forms of sexual expression other than opposite sex relations were a form of perversion and highly pathological (Freud, 1905). The reverberations of these heteronormative approaches still manifest in the form of social constructs, and political positions that seek to oppress, limit and control nonheteronormative experiences of sexual identity gender fluidity and relationships. In response to microaggressions and pathologizing perspectives inherent in these older models, theories and treatment have evolved and expanded to focus on resiliency and mental health rather than pathology and inadequacies. In challenging existing norms, they affirm the lived life experience of the sexually fluid client.

As Lisa Diamond's ground-breaking research asserts, fluidity in sexuality can be conceptualized as a dimensional component of sexuality operating alongside one's sexual orientation, which influences desire, attraction, fantasies and behavioral expression throughout the lifespan (Diamond, 2009). Specifically, sexual fluidity can be viewed as "a capacity for situation-dependent flexibility in sexual responsiveness, which allows individuals to experience changes in same-sex or other-sex desire across both short-term and long-term time periods" (Diamond, 2016, p. 249). Further research has identified four types of fluidity, including a sexual responsivity to one's less-preferred gender; situationally variable fluidity in response to one's less-preferred gender; discrepancy between gender patterns of attraction and gender patterns of partnering, and instability in attractions over time (Diamond, Alley, Dickenson, & Blair, 2019).

While Diamond's body of work identifying sexual fluidity has led to sweeping changes in our understanding of sexual identity, gender and relationships, it has also been harnessed by religious and political groups to strengthen an agenda focused on oppression and stigmatization of individuals identifying as queer and sexually fluid. These groups claim that such individuals are "choosing" their sexuality, and should therefore be denied protections and legitimacy in their status. Diamond refuted this, arguing that sexual orientation is relatively stable across the lifespan, while sexual fluidity can manifest in fluctuations in desire, fantasy and expression of sexuality in tandem with one's orientation (Diamond, 2013). Religious and political organizations opposed to sexual and gender identity diversity (Pew Research Group, 2014) promote various forms of "conversion" or "reparative therapy" seeking to suppress or extinguish the sexual orientations of clients. In response to these efforts, the American Psychiatric Association's 2009 statement concludes that efforts to change a client's sexual orientation have not been demonstrated to be successful and may in fact pose risk of harm. The APA further recommends that therapy for individuals who seek to change sexual orientation should be based in support and empowerment, identity exploration, free of biased presumptions about sexual identity or goals about the specific outcomes (Glassburn, 2017). Similarly, the American Association of Sex Educators, Counselors and Therapists ("AASECT Position," 2017) asserts that sexual orientation is not a selected preference, and that feelings can shift over time. The notion of forcing such change for political or religious reasons is not only unlikely to work but can cause lasting harm and is currently illegal in 20 US states, Puerto Rico and several other countries. AASECT (2017) notes that conversion therapy is considered a form of psychological abuse by most medical and psychological organizations including the APA, and that the practice has been banned in several states (O'Neal & Connors, 2018). Specifically, the AASECT (2017) has issued the statement that they join with other organizations in banning any reparative or conversion therapy that attempts to change a person's orientation, identity or expression, and that they do not believe that sexual expression or gender nonconformity are something to be fixed. Our client Eva relayed an experience of how her aunt had offered to pay for a form of conversion therapy when she had confided in her. This resulted in a wounding rupture and strong feelings of betrayal, which were lasting. Eva spent a considerable amount of her initial therapy processing this betrayal, and developing resiliency to further encounters. Those who are coerced into such treatment suffer greatly.

The Well-Trained Therapist

The dynamic quality of both gender and sexual expression can lead clients to seek treatment as a safe affirming space to explore identity and sexuality in the context of a developing and creatively adapting self-concept and relationships. Progressive contemporary psychotherapies for the sexually fluid client draw on the postmodern approaches that seek to deconstruct assumptions and beliefs while examining the value they hold in the client's life (Corey, 2013). Postmodern therapies challenge assumptions about mental health and mental illness. Society's more predominant heteronormative models are abandoned in favor of examination of the diversity and fluidity of gender, sexuality and relationships. In addition, the relationship between patient and therapist is highly collaborative; change is the result of co-creation of dialogue and an allied partnership in exploring mental health resiliency and empowerment. This dialogue is rooted in development of sexual fluency for the client, who is then empowered with the language and conceptual framework necessary to navigate both internal and interpersonal sexual experiences. Sexual literacy can potentially improve confidence and communication allowing for greater sexual health and safer sexual encounters (Weinstein, Walsh, & Ward, 2008). While many psychotherapy training programs offer minimal sexual literacy training, it is incumbent upon the competent therapist to develop fluency in order to better assist their clients. The ethical and competent postmodern therapist must be capable of radically adjusting perspective on sexuality and gender, understanding the client's experience of sexual self and sexual interrelatedness. This understanding must include awareness of nonbinary gender identity, gender fluidity and sexually fluid experience. Eva entered into therapy dissatisfied with elements of her heterosexual relationship of many years, and uncertain of the way she felt about her attachments and intimate connections. By remaining open to examining her sexuality from an affirming and nonjudgmental perspective, Eva was able to shed many of the ideas about sexuality and relationships thrown upon her by family, society and religion. She grew to understand that her relationship was important to her, and that an open marriage was also important. Along with this came the awareness that much of her feelings toward women were sexual in nature, and her anxieties about relationships were now more easily understood as intimate erotic responses she had kept hidden and unexplored. Our therapy deconstructed her previous assumptions about herself and created space for her to construct her own meaning.

The Association for Lesbian, Gay, Bisexual and Transgender Issues in Counseling Task force (ALGBTIC LGBQQIA Competencies Task Force, 2013) provides detailed guidance on core competencies in therapy, which emphasizes wellness and resiliency.

A competent therapist is one who views the queer person in their own context and lived experience, and supports the client's strengths and diversity. Core competencies also include appropriate use of preferred pronouns and language reflective of the client's self-definitions. A fundamental awareness and affirmation of the marginalized, often oppressed status of the queer client must inform treatment. Similarly, awareness and attention must be given to the client's own self-limiting perceptions that may exist, while cocreating with the client opportunities to transcend limitations and strive to become self-affirming and flexible in their self-expression.

Common Issues in Therapy Today

Many clients inadvertently enter into therapy with dissatisfaction with their lives as a result of unacknowledged emerging sexual fluidity. Some report marital or relationship difficulties, later becoming aware of changes in desired sexual partner. Similarly, some clients struggle with never finding the right person to date, only to discover that they were focusing on opposite sex partners and defaulting to socially expected choices, rather than exploring sexual interest irrespective of societies' traditional norms. As client Eva describes, "I thought that I had lost interest in sex when in reality I had developed a stronger interest in exploring sexuality in ways I had not before imagined." Yet another client who had grown in awareness of gender fluidity found that many of the limitations they had experienced in not fitting into societal cisgender norms were not limitations at all, but instead variations in sense of gender, which became interesting and exciting to explore.

For some, therapy may provide support for coping with experiences of internal and external oppression, discrimination, stigmatization and marginalization. It may provide the opportunity to explore and negotiate how fluid gender identity and sexual fluidity will change or enhance an existing relationship. Therapy can also assist clients with integration of sexual identity and religious identity (Sherry, Adelman, Whilde, & Quick, 2010). Research suggests that mental illness occurring in LGBTQA+ and gender fluid individuals is typically rooted in the discrimination, stigmatization and stress due to lack of familial support (Barbara, Chaim, & Doctor, 2007). Other precipitating factors include internalized or externalized homophobia and workplace rejection. Similarly, a person's level of religiosity is positively correlated with mental health difficulties (Moleiro & Pinto, 2015). Therapy with sexually fluid clients should therefore proceed with awareness of the potential contexts existing, which give rise to stress and complicate the process.

An ethically conscious therapeutic experience is rooted in an environment that signals safety and affirmation. This begins with respect for personal pronouns and development of forms and interview questions that demonstrate knowledge and respect for diversity. The American Psychological Association Division 44 Society for the Psychology of Sexual Orientation and Gender Diversity (APA, 2015) recommends that culturally competent therapists taking a gender nonbinary stance, and adopt an empathic curious attunement to the client, practice use of singular pronouns such as they/them and zie/hir. They advocate for the development of inclusive intake forms with options other than "male/female" including a variety of options such as genderqueer and dual spirit. Many clients are anxious or distrusting of therapists, having experienced discrimination, homo-phobia, micro aggression stigmatization or pathologizing of their preferences, orienta-tion and sexual expression. Even the most well-intentioned therapists have demonstrated gross insensitivity unknowingly. The tendency to assume that sexual fluidity is a "phase" or the result of an existing co-occurring mental condition is all too common and unfor-tunate in the therapeutic setting. Untrained therapists may assume heteronormative values, and consider sexual diversity as a result of prior abuse or trauma. Moreover, many therapists avoid the topic entirely, and never create an opportunity for the client to discuss issues of sexual identity or fluidity. For the client coping with societal oppression and marginalization, this can serve to replicate the experience and result in limited or ineffective therapy and a rupture of trust. Intake forms prominently including questions about sexual experience, gender identity and preferred pronouns convey an affirming stance. Eva remarked that this put her at ease about my ability to relate to her in a non-judgmental informed manner.

Therapy with sexually fluid adolescents often involves maintaining the role of a strong ally and assisting parents in becoming affirming and supportive of the adoles-cent. Suicidality is a crucial issue to remain vigilant to in working with teens navigating gender identity development, as LGBTQA+ youth have considerably higher rates of suicide than their straight counterparts. Research indicates that this is heavily based in the stigmatization and duress created by a hostile or rejecting family experience (Ryan, 2010; Ryan, Huebner, Diaz, & Sanchez, 2009). New research demonstrates that the risk of suicide is greatly reduced in these teens when a parent is affirming and supportive. Thus, developing strong familial support should be a primary treatment focus (Barbara et al., 2007; Bouris et al., 2010).

With regard to the experience of transitioning for clients with gender identity, which does not align with their sex assigned at birth, the APA urges therapists to work within the client's timeframe, desires and preferences, and to avoid prescribing a definitive process or timeframe for when or if they may choose to transition medically or socially or at all (APA, 2015). An overly enthusiastic therapist may press a client to transition in an effort to demonstrate affirming stance. A comprehensive assessment of the client's presenting problems, key therapeutic issues and needs in the context of sexual, social, developmental and cultural functioning will assist the therapist in understanding the contextual variables impacting the client in order to effectively focus the therapeutic experience. Most therapists are not well trained in sexuality, and are taught primarily to consider sexual pathologies and addictions, but not sexual health per se. Some graduate training programs do not even offer a course in sexuality, and when they do, rarely is healthy diverse sexual exploration addressed. Therapists do not receive much training in how to overcome their own anxieties and biases surrounding sexuality (Miller & Byers, 2010).

It is not uncommon for practitioners to completely avoid the topic of a client's sex life. Making it a standard element in intake forms and discussion in the first visit can provide the client with a clearly affirming experience engaging in all aspects of their lives and relationships. Inquiring about preferred pronouns signals an affirming and respectful therapeutic relationship, as demonstrated with Eva, and when the therapist is comfortable with straightforward discussion about sexual interests, preferences and practices, the client is at ease and able to have open and honest conversation.

Therapists should also balance the tendency to overfocus attention and assume that all treatment issues are the result of the person's sexual or gender identity or conversely to ignore sexual fluidity and gender identity altogether. One example occurs in the tendency of the untrained therapist to fail to understand the possible implications of extramarital sexual encounters. Formerly, it was traditional to view such encounters as a symptom of a troubled marriage. While this is possible, it is also important to consider the possibility that the individual may not be interested in the traditional definition of marriage and monogamy. Emergence of sexual fluidity may precipitate extramarital sexual relations, and such experiences may require re-negotiation of the marital relationship to accommodate a fluid partner. It is thus important to consider that a client engaging in extramarital relations may signal an experimentation with sexual fluidity or preference for nonmonogamy that is not typically considered an option in a culture largely focused on monogamous marriage. Heteronormative approaches favoring monogamy have held that extramarital affairs were a sign of "the beginning of the end," were highly destructive, and were even the result of various mental illnesses. These were extremely limiting view of the client, and prescribed a pathologizing and moralizing stance in treatment. Modern approaches consider the client's choice in consensual nonmonogamy and open relationships, and allow the therapist to meet each client and couple where they are at, engaging in co-creating of a meaningful view of their sexuality, rather than disaffirming it.

Useful Modalities

The affirming allied therapist must be capable of perceiving and providing alternatives to treatments that were based in heteronormative, gender biased and outdated theoretical modalities. Moreover, the therapist must help the client to locate the therapeutic process within the awareness of the client's personal and unique sexual identity trajectory. Effective supportive treatment must be client-centered, affirming collaborative and rooted in attention to potential inherent bias, with an emphasis on consideration of the stigmatization, discrimination and marginalization, currently impacting sexually fluid individuals and their partners and families. Relational rupture and repairs in the client's interpersonal life are considered to be situational issues and patterns in the postmodern view, rather than pathologized expressions of inherent illness. Narrative and other postmodern approaches focus on honoring and respecting the client's creative adaptations in the context of sexual fluidity, sexual relations and nonbinary gender identity. Such a process takes into account the cultural and social context in which the client is embedded as well as their unique view of themselves. Eva's therapy often involved discussion of how to integrate both her emerging sexually fluid experience and her continued desire for a "typical" family life. While she walked into therapy believing she was about to end her marriage, she left realizing she wanted to expand it, and had developed the capacity to have fruitful dialogue to bring about that expansion. She and her husband agreed to an open relationship and her sexual transformation felt "finally no longer hidden and unfulfilled."

Meaningful therapy focuses on the outcome of a positive sense of self personal empowerment and fulfillment. Therapists can be effective in encouraging exploration and integration of sexuality facilitating the client's own curiosity and honoring one's fluid and fluctuating nature without the need to come to a "conclusion." To this end, art and expressive therapies can offer a powerful modality for exploration of sexual identity, sexual desire and sexual expression in both imagined fantasy and processing of the personal meaning of experiences, largely because symbolic art lends itself to a broader expression of experience beyond the constraining boundaries of societal definitions of expression (Pelton-Sweet, 2008). Art therapy allows for exploration of polarized views of the self to be expressed in visual, nonverbal form, which can be a freeing and useful experience for clients. Clients in the coming out experience can feel disenfranchised from their known life experience, and art creates fertile space to explore, integrate and identify the emerging self (Brody, 1994). In my work with LGBTQ+ clients, I have found mask making useful to help illustrate the internal self and the self society sees, and create dialogue for the process of integrating the two. Similarly, sand tray therapy offers a literal physical space to deconstruct and reconstruct one's world. Clients I have worked with have found this to be a very useful and transformative experience in their efforts to work with the dynamics of their changing self and relationships (Luke & Peters, 2019). Eva enjoyed art and was eager to engage in this modality in her therapy. We worked in many sessions using sand tray therapy in which life issues and experience are illustrated with a variety of miniature objects placed by the client in a box of sand. Eva's sand trays allowed her to create scenes of her internal conflicts around sexual identity and sexual expression and external issues with how social norms were limiting her functioning. These progressed into transformative experiences, as each movement she made in therapy was reflected in a movement within herself and in her relationships. One sand tray was filled with figurines she had labeled as "feminine" and buried under the sand beneath them were various objects. She explained that the objects were the other facets and qualities of these feminine aspects that were nontraditional, not accepted by society and not safe to bring out. This led to an impulse to change the story, and she began outward movements to feel more authentic in her sexuality experiences. Art making offers an infinite range of expression, and art therapy broadens the sexually fluid client's range of awareness by not being limited to the realm of language and dialogue, which is rooted in heteronormative culture. In art, language is limitless and the most authentic form of client-centered therapeutic work.

Modalities that encourage empowerment and heal the effects of societal oppression are key. Barbara et al. (2007) note that there are several factors that increase the likelihood of client self-disclosure regarding sexual fluidity, including a nonjudgmental and nonheterosexist/environment conveying affirmation and safety. Narrative therapy is one postmodern approach that holds promise in this regard, offering client-centered, relational therapy rooted in affirming and empowering the client. Tilsen's (2013) concept of "Queer theory" encourages a challenging of normative values and ideas in the therapeutic process of sexual identity transformation. Such approaches have given rise to a paradigm shift in not only LGBTQ+ therapies but also the broader notion of sexual relationships and sexual identity in general (Killian, Farago, & Peters, 2019). This was a strong element of the work with Eva.

Additionally, use of inclusive language and demonstration of knowledge of LGBTQA+ cultural issues are essential. Barbara, Chaim, and Doctor (2007) also note that therapists should be aware of both internalized oppression and homophobia and legitimate societal hatred and oppression the client may be experiencing. Therapists also need to assess for maladaptive coping strategies in clients who are experiencing considerable stigmatization, as many may resort to use of substances, overeating, overspending or self-harm in an effort to deflect overwhelming feelings resulting from discrimination, rejection and conflict surrounding sexual identity.

Social justice matters in psychotherapy today. While the buffet offerings Perel notes are indeed ever expanding, and researchers and clinicians are engaged in a constant process to better educate themselves and understand the existing evolving sexual experiences of their clients, it should also be noted that at the time of this writing, we are equally charged with the formidable political, legal and social climate that seeks to oppress many expressions of cultural diversity, sexual expression and gender identity (Schwartz, 2018). Many psychological organizations have mobilized in recent years to promote advocacy for social justice campaigns promoting equity and human rights in addressing injustice and discrimination on the basis of sexual orientation and gender identity (Desmond, 2010; Dworkin & Yi, 2003).

As society continues to grapple with the nature of sexual autonomy and empowerment of diversity, therapy that is affirming, empowerment based, compassionate and culturally informed remains crucial in the support of the sexually healthy client. As the client Eva explains: "Having a therapist who doesn't explain to me who I am, but who is willing to have curiosity about my changing experience, allows me to gain the clarity I need to live my best life."

References

ALGBTIC LGBQQIA Competencies Taskforce (2013). Competencies for counseling with lesbian, gay, bisexual, queer, questioning, intersex and ally individuals association for lesbian, gay, bisexual, and transgender: issues in counseling competencies for counseling with lesbian, gay, bisexual, queer, questioning, intersex, and ally individuals. *Journal of LGBT Issues in Counseling, 7*(1), 2–43.

American Association of Sexuality Educators, Counselors and Therapists (AASECT). (2017). AASECT position on reparative therapy. American Association of Sexuality Educators, Counselors and Therapists. Retrieved from https://www.aasect.org/position-reparative-therapy

American Psychological Association. (2009). *Resolution on appropriate therapeutic response to sexual orientation distress and change efforts*. Retrieved from http://www.apa.org/about/policy/sexual-orientation.aspx

American Psychological Association (APA) (2015). Guidelines for psychological practice with transgender and gender nonconforming people. *American Psychologist, 70*(9), 832–864.

Barbara, A., Chaim, G., & Doctor, F. (2007). *Asking the right questions, 2: Talking about sexual Orientation and Gender Identity in Mental Health, Counselling, and Addiction Settings*. Center for Addiction and Mental Health.

Bouris, A., Guilamo-Ramos, V., Pickard, A., Shiu, C., Loosier, P. S., Dittus, P., … Waldmiller, J. M. (2010). A systematic review of parental influences on the health and well-being of lesbian, gay, and bisexual youth: Time for new public health research and practice. *External Journal of Primary Prevention, 3*, 273–309.

Brody, R. (1994). Ambiguity and integration: A meeting ground for art therapy and lesbian and gay identity development. *Pratt Institute Creative Therapy Review*, *15*, 35–43.

Corey, G. (2013). *Theory and practice of counseling and psychotherapy* (9th ed.). Belmont, CA: Brooks/Cole.

Desmond, B. (2010). *A trainee supervisor's perspective; liberating the 'imprisoning' self of coach in becoming a supervisor.* Paper presented at the Annual Conference on Supervision, British Association for Supervision Practice and Research: "Competent Supervisors: Imprisonment or Liberation?"

Diamond, L. (2009). *Sexual fluidity: Understanding women's love and desire.* Cambridge, MA: Harvard University Press.

Diamond, L. (2013). *Just how different are female and male sexual orientation?* The Department of Human Development, Social and Personality Program Faculty, Cornell University.

Diamond, L. (2016). Sexual fluidity in males and females. *Current sexual health reports*, doi:10.1007/s11930-016-0092-z. Current Sexual Health Reports. Retrieved from https://www.researchgate.net/publication/309694747_Sexual_Fluidity_in_Male_and_Females

Diamond, L. M., Alley, J., Dickinson, J., & Blair, K. L. (2019). Who counts as sexually fluid? Comparing four different types of sexual fluidity in women. *Archives of Sexual Behavior*, *10*, 1007.

Dworkin, S., & Yi, H. (2003). LGBT identity, violence, and social justice: The psychological is political. *International Journal for the Advancement of Counseling*, *25*(4), 269–279.

Freud, S. (1905). Three essays on the theory of sexuality (1905). *The standard edition of the complete psychological works of Sigmund Freud, Volume VII (1901–1905): A case of hysteria, three essays on sexuality and other works* (pp. 123–246). London: Hogarth.

Glassburn, S. (2017). *Narrative therapy tactics to affirm gender identity and expression.* Good Therapy. Retrieved from https://www.goodtherapy.org/blog/narrative-therapy-tactics-to-affirm-gender-identity-expression-0822174

Killian, T., Farago, R., & Peters, H. C. (2019). Promoting queer competency through an experiential framework. *Journal of Counselor Preparation and Supervision*, *12*(4). Retrieved from https://repository.wcsu.edu/jcps/vol12/iss4/10

Luke, M., & Peters, H. C. (2019). LGBTQ+ responsive sand tray; creative arts and counseling. *Journal of Counseling Sexology & Sexual Wellness: Research Practice and Education*, *1*(1). https://doi.org/10.34296/01011002

Miller, S. A., & Byers, E. S. (2010). Psychologists' sexual education and training in graduate school. *Canadian Journal of Behavioral Sciences*, *42*(2), 93–100.

Moleiro, C., & Pinto, N. (2015). Sexual orientation and gender identity: Review of concepts, controversies and their relation to psychopathology classification systems. *Frontiers in Psychology*, *6*, 1511.

O'Neal, G., & Connors, E. (2018). *American Psychiatric Association, APA reiterates strong opposition to conversion therapy.* Retrieved from https://www.psychiatry.org/newsroom/news-releases/apa-reiterates-strong-opposition-to-conversion –therapy

Pelton-Sweet, L. (2008). Coming out through art: A review of art therapy with LGBT clients. *Journal of the American Art Therapy Association*, *25*(4), 170–176.

Perel, E. (2006). *Mating in captivity: Reconciling the erotic + the domestic.* New York: HarperCollins.

Pew Research Center. (2014). *The global divide on homosexuality: Greater acceptance in more secular and affluent countries* [Pdf file]. Retrieved from Pew Research Center: Pew-Global-Attitudes-Homosexuality-Report-REVISED-MAY-27-2014.pdf.

Ryan, C. (2010). Family acceptance in adolescence and the health of LBGT young adults. *Journal of Child and Adolescent Psychiatric Nursing*, *23*(4), 205–213.

Ryan, C., Huebner, D., Diaz, R. M., & Sanchez, J. (2009). Family rejection as a predictor of negative health outcomes in white and Latino lesbian, gay and bisexual young adults. *Pediatrics*, *123*(1), 346–352. Schwartz, A. (2018, December). Love is not a permanent state of enthusiasm, an interview with Esther Perel. *New Yorker*. Retrieved from https://www.newyorker.com/culture/the-new-yorker-interview/love-is-not-a-permanent-state-of-enthusiasm-an-interview-with-esther-perel

Sherry, A., Adelman, A., Whilde, M., & Quick, D. (2010). Competing selves: Negotiating the intersection of spiritual and sexual identities. *Professional psychology: Research and Practice*, *41*(2), 112–119.

Tilsen, J. (2013). *Therapeutic conversations with queer youth: Transcending homonormativity and constructing preferred identities*. New York: Jason Aronson.

Weinstein, R. B., Walsh, J. L., & Ward, L. M. (2008). Testing a new measure of sexual health knowledge and its connections to students' sex education, communication, confidence, and condom use. *International Journal of Sexuality and Health*, *20*(3), 212–221.

Chapter 19

RECONSIDERING THE SEXUAL CONTEXT OF NON-CONSENSUAL SEXUAL INTERACTIONS

Janna Dickenson and Rebecca K. Blais

Human rights include the ability to engage in sexual activity by choice, free of coercion or force (World Health Organization [WHO], 2020a). Sexual interactions that occur without consent are a serious human rights problem with short- and long-term psychological and public health consequences (WHO, 2020b). Terms that describe nonconsensual sexual events, including rape and sexual assault/coercion/violence, conflate lack of consent with exploitation, physical force, anatomy and penetrative sexual activity. Here, we adopt the term *nonconsensual sexual interactions*, or NCSI, to emphasize the lack of consent irrespective of specific sexual behavior, anatomy, exploitation or physical force. Sexual literacy policies, psychological interventions and public health prevention strategies aim to mitigate the incidence and impact of NCSI. Yet, such strategies disregard the complex social and sexual context in which lack of consent arises and presumes a heterosexual dynamic in which men are perpetrators and women are victims. In turn, policies, interventions and prevention strategies that lack relevance for men, LGBTQ individuals and marginalized populations who have endured NCSI. Thus, we argue for an approach that enhances population sexual literacy, by framing NCSI in the context of sexual well-being.

Sexual Illiteracy: Where Is the Sex in Nonconsensual Sexual Interactions?

Policies, campaigns, interventions and preventions ignore the social and sexual complexity of NCSI (Beres, 2007; O'byrne, Rapley, & Hansen, 2006). Various contextual and relational factors influence the ways in which people navigate sexual consent (Beres, 2010; Jozkowski & Ekbia, 2015; Jozkowski, Peterson, Sanders, Dennis, & Reece, 2014). Social rules for negotiating sexual activity differ based on an individuals' gender or gender role, sexual orientation, relationship structure, relationship duration and specific type of sexual activity. Disregarding these varied sexual contexts limits intervention and prevention strategists' ability to understand what, why and how people navigate consent effectively.

Research indicates that consent becomes obscured in practice by confusing sexual desire and willingness (only the latter indicates consent) and from the social consequences of rejecting sexual activity. In a video game simulation, college men interacted with a female avatar as if they would on an actual date (Woerner, Abbey, Pegram, & Helmers, 2018). The avatar was programmed to engage in low-level sexual activities (kissing, fondling) but refused requests for penile–vaginal intercourse, which became more intense if participants persisted their requests for intercourse. As college men's sexual desire increased, they pursued more low-level sexual activities, which in turn increased requests to engage in penile–vaginal intercourse, despite strong refusals. Men who received more refusals expressed more hostile comments, threats to end the relationship and nagging for sex (Woerner et al., 2018). The social consequences that arise from refusing sexual activity demonstrate the social complexity of navigating consent and explains prior findings indicating that people soften their refusals and engage in *consensual but unwanted* sexual activity (Muehlenhard & Peterson, 2005).

Although sexual desire can obscure the consent process, NCSI policies, interventions and prevention strategies focus on power and control as a primary contributor to NCSI (Miner, 2007). Indeed, individuals convicted of initiating NCSI are more likely to adhere to traditional masculine gender roles, hold sexist attitudes, show greater hostility toward women and endorse beliefs that corroborate rape (DeGue et al., 2014). The object of power and control in NCSI is the pursuit of sexual pleasure, and a wealth of research indicates that the pursuit of sexual activity contributes to NCSI (Baer, Kohut, & Fisher, 2015). In fact, gender bias interacts with sexual desire to predict risk for initiating NCSI; cisgender men who desire more impersonal sex *and* hold hostile attitudes toward women have much greater risk of initiating NCSI than men who display high levels of one but not the other (Berkowitz, 1992; Malamuth, Sockloskie, Koss, & Tanaka, 1991; Mann & Hollin, 2007; Zinzow & Thompson, 2015). During college, men's risk for initiating NCSI (Thompson, Swartout, & Koss, 2013) decreases as college men become less hostile toward women and feel less pressure to engage in high levels of sexual activity, college increases (Thompson, Kingree, Zinzow, & Swartout, 2015). Clearly, gender bias and sexuality work together to predict NCSI. Yet, public health strategies fail to recognize that one of the primary factors at the root of decisions to initiate NCSI relate to sexual desire, representing a systematic failure to use sexual literacy to adequately intervene and prevent NCSI.

The Mental Health Impact of NCSI

People who have endured NCSI are at risk for posttraumatic stress disorder (PTSD), depression, sexual dysfunction and lower sexual satisfaction (see review by Ba & Bhopal, 2017; Blais, 2019; Blais, Brignone, Fargo, Livingston, & Andresen, 2019; Blais et al., 2018; DeSilva, 2001; Maltz, 2002; Najman, Dunne, Purdie, Boyle, & Coxeter, 2005). Unfortunately, there are few, if any, trauma-informed protocols specifically designed to enhance sexual well-being following NCSIs. Extant psychological treatments indirectly improve sexual function and maladaptive sexual schemas among sexual trauma survivors (e.g., Pulverman, Boyd, Stanton, & Meston, 2017; Wells et al., 2019). However, such treatments do not alleviate the sexual concerns directly caused by NCSI, and many individuals incur permanent negative impacts on their sexuality (Lutfey, Link, Litman, Rosen, & McKinlay, 2008; O'Driscoll & Flanagan, 2016). Moreover, research demonstrates that most clients do not initiate conversations regarding sexuality (Reissing & Giulio, 2010), and mental health professionals are reluctant to discuss gender and sexuality with clients (Miller & Byers, 2008, 2009). Indeed, over 60 percent of mental health professionals have never asked clients about sexuality in the course of their entire careers (Apantaku-Olajide, Gibbons, & Higgins, 2011). Because treatment largely ignores the sexual nature and sequelae of NCSI, recovery from the deleterious impact of NCSI is limited.

Problems with Current Prevention Approaches

The (Binary) Gender Bias: Men as Perpetrators, Women as Victims

American society offers limited resources to explicitly acquire knowledge on sexuality and gender that is scientifically valid, resulting in a dearth of sexual literacy across the population. In the absence of acquiring scientifically valid sexual information, individuals must rely on knowledge they learned implicitly about gender and sexuality to inform laws, policies, intervention and prevention efforts. American depictions of male sexuality as driven and dominant implies that men are usually willing to engage in sexual activity and positions men as recipients and women as providers of consent. Resulting beliefs, such as "men cannot be sexually assaulted," are common across the public and within our social institutions, including medicine, law and the media (Todahl, Linville, Bustin, Wheeler, & Gau, 2009; Turchik, 2012; Turchik, Hebenstreit, & Judson, 2016). Yet, such beliefs run contrary to evidence indicating that one in every 8 to 10 cisgender men has endured a sexual interaction that occurred without their consent (Mellins et al., 2017).

Changes to federal law prompted a gendered approach to prevention and fundamentally altered the public discourse from women as victims to men as perpetrators. Before 2011, prevention efforts largely aimed to teach women to mitigate their own risk for NCSI (e.g., violence against women) and gendered attitudes were rarely addressed (DeGue et al., 2014), although cisgender men perpetuate the majority of *convicted* cases[1] of NCSI (Berkowitz & Schewe, 2002; Gidycz, Orchowski, & Berkowitz, 2011; Miller et al., 2012). Changes to the Office of Civil Rights in 2011 and 2014 spurred a national strategy to assess campus climate, develop prevention strategies that engage bystanders and men and improve reporting of NCSI (Harris, Terry, & Ackerman, 2019). These efforts critiqued and intervened on social norms that enable NCSI perpetration. Bystander interventions aimed to disrupt the social acceptability of gender bias and discrimination known to contribute to the widespread rates of NCSI in American culture by teaching bystanders to intervene when they hear a discriminatory remark regarding gender, race, ethnicity and sexual orientation (e.g., "*She*'s a mathematician?" "The sooner

---

1 Owing to legal differences of NCSI based on physical anatomy, there are no valid estimates regarding which genders commit majority of *all* NCSIs.

I get her drunk, the sooner I'll get laid," "You're gay"). Although such approaches are demonstrably effective, their benefits attenuate over time (DeGue et al., 2014).

Despite short-term benefit of prevention efforts, laws and policies continue to reinforce assumptions about the gendered and heterosexual context of consent. Legal definitions emphasize penetration of an orifice, and thus, the same terminology and degree of offense of NCSI differs drastically by physical anatomy. People who lack vaginal orifices may not be acknowledged, legally, as a prosecutable form of NCSI (see Turchik & Edwards, 2012). The consequences of this approach are pervasive, such that cisgender men are less likely to disclose NCSI (Banyard, Moynihan, & Plante, 2007; Turchik & Edwards, 2012), seek services (Turchik et al., 2016) and less frequently report NCSI to police or medical personnel (Isely & Gehrenbeck-Shim, 1997; King & Woollett, 1997). Laws that permit certain nonconsensual behaviors prevent populations from their basic right to achieve sexual health and ultimately deters prevention strategies related to NCSI. Ignoring the diversity of sexual contexts of NCSI has limited the advocacy for political and legal reform for NCSI that occurs outside of the presumed context of male "perpetrator" and female "victim."

Invisibility of LGBTQ Issues in NCSI Prevention

According to recent national estimates, 28 percent of cisgender women and 12 percent of cisgender men report enduring NCSI during college, whereas 38 percent of transgender and nonbinary people report enduring NCSI (Mellins et al., 2017). Moreover, people who identify as gay/lesbian, bisexual or other are more likely to endure NCSI than those who identify as heterosexual (Mellins et al., 2017). LGBTQ individuals face much higher rates of NCSI on college campuses; yet they are less likely to report NCSI (Eisenberg, Lust, Mathiason, & Porta, 2017). Additionally, LGBTQ individuals may not benefit from current prevention efforts, because prevention strategies target cultural norms that guide sexual behaviors for heterosexual contexts, which may have little to no relevance for LGBTQ relationships.

LGBTQ individuals state that NCSI is not addressed in their community and face many barriers to receiving treatment and services related to NCSI, including minority stress (Potter, Fountain, & Stapleton, 2012; Todahl et al., 2009). When forming romantic and sexual relationships, LGBTQ individuals face additional obstacles due to fear of discrimination or social rejection (Bauermeister, Ventuneac, Pingel, & Parsons, 2012; Buzzella, Whitton, & Tompson, 2012; Mustanski, Birkett, Greene, Hatzenbuehler, & Newcomb, 2014). The unique relational pressures due to minority stress contribute to higher rates of intimate partner violence, which involves physical, psychological or sexual violence by a partner, among LGBTQ relative to heterosexual populations (Dank, Lachman, Zweig, & Yahner, 2014).

Multiple minority stresses may further exacerbate risk for NCSI among the LGBTQ population. Research has demonstrated that transgender women of color have the highest rates of victimization across various forms of violence, including NCSI (Dinno, 2017; Graham, 2014). Moreover, college students who have limited access to material resources and those who come from marginalized racial and ethnic groups are more likely to endure NCSI than individuals who can easily access material resources and White Americans (Mellins et al., 2017). The inequities of American college culture exacerbate power imbalances of marginalized populations, relative to White, affluent heterosexual counterparts and these inequities lead to higher rates of NCSI among LGBTQ populations, people of color and LGBTQ people of color (Armstrong, Hamilton, & Sweeney, 2006; Bay-Cheng & Eliseo-Arras, 2008; Jozkowski, 2015). Strategies to change social norms on campus may be limited in their long-term effectiveness because people continue to encounter impressions from the media, peers and our network that directly conflict with the social norms that NCSI prevention strategies aim to counter. Thus, moving toward sexual literacy necessitates an approach that emphasizes intersectionality.

Sexual Well-Being as an Antidote to NCSI

Fortenberry (2016) proposed that sexual well-being may be a powerful lever to apply to gender and sexuality-based injustices. Sexual well-being includes sexual self-esteem, sexual self-efficacy that involves the ability to consent to or refuse sexual activity, desire and pleasure that can generate feelings of elation and satisfaction, and the absence of pain, danger, STIs, unwanted pregnancy and NCSI (Fortenberry, 2019). From a sexual literacy perspective, shifting the conversation of NCSI toward one of sexual well-being would enable the population to ask fundamentally different questions about their sexual experiences, such as "Is this relationship good for me and what I want?" "How satisfied am I with this interaction?" and "What would make this interaction better?" These questions drive conversations about willingness, desire and optimizing sexual pleasure via the consent process. Indeed, NCSI is best conceptualized as a failure to ensure safety, which impedes sexual pleasure and infringes on human rights of at least one party. A sexual well-being approach can augment the congruence between safety and pleasure by highlighting ways in which ensuring safety optimizes sexual pleasure. This approach has the potential to shift gender and sexual attitudes away from fear and shame and toward satisfaction, happiness and fulfillment.

Efficacy of the Sexual Well-Being Approach

Sexual well-being approaches have been adopted to solve other public health and sexual literacy problems. Historically, efforts to increase safer sex have utilized an epidemiological perspective, which focuses on certain activity as risky behavior. Yet, interventions designed to increase safer sex are more effective when they incorporate sexual pleasure. For example, sexual literacy strategies augment the efficacy of prevention efforts related to STIs, HIV reduction and unwanted pregnancy by integrating discussions about sexual satisfaction, sexual pleasure in partnered and solitary contexts, relationship health and proactive family planning augments (Cahill, Valadéz, & Ibarrola, 2013; Robinson, Bockting, Simon Rosser, Miner, & Coleman, 2002; Rosser et al., 2002; Sun, Anderson, Mayer, Kuhn, & Klein, 2019).

The sexual well-being approach may directly augment current prevention efforts by enhancing bystander intentions. Bystander interventions implicitly promote egalitarian gender norms by critiquing the norms associated with masculinity that permit NCSI. Research demonstrates that these interventions enhances bystanders' intent to intervene in social situations by increasing empathy (Abbott & Cameron, 2014; Foubert & Newberry, 2006). Empathy in sexual situations is associated with young people's enjoyment of sexual activity (Galinksy & Sonenstein, 2011), and young people enjoy their sexual relationships more when they feel that their sexual relationship embodies egalitarian gender norms (Galinsky & Sonenstein, 2013; Schick, Zucker, & Bay-Cheng, 2008). Research has also demonstrated that a lack of empathic responses in sexual situations has been tied to NCSI (Seto, 2019). Thus, increasing empathic responses has the potential to enhance both bystander interventions and sexual enjoyment, both of which directly counter NCSI.

Centering NCSI in sexual well-being carries potential for widespread dissemination to college students. Research indicates that young people are primarily engaged with topics that address their interests and concerns (van Clief & Anemaat, 2020). Specifically, integrating sexual pleasure with sexual health information attracts young people to seek out sex education (Bay-Cheng, 2001) and intentionally search for content related to reducing risk for STIs and unwanted pregnancy (van Clief & Anemaat, 2020). Thus, a sexual well-being approach could enhance the existing risk reduction approach to NCSI.

Sexual Literacy Implications

Reclaim Sexual Well-Being in Treatment for NCSI

Although gender and sexuality are fundamental aspects of psychology, discussing gender and sexuality can feel uncomfortable, challenge personal and professional values and activate biases (Eubanks-Carter & Goldfried, 2006; Ford & Hendrick, 2003; Gower, Rider, McMorris, & Eisenberg, 2018). Research indicates that mental health professionals at all stages of their career report a lack of training in sexuality science and that their discomfort to talk to clients about sexuality is largely due to their lack of scientific knowledge about gender and sexuality (Harris & Hays, 2008; Miller & Byers, 2008, 2010). Hence, an important avenue for improving policy related to intervening on NCSI is to enhance scientific training of gender and sexuality so that mental health professionals are adequately prepared to address the sequalae of issues that follow from NCSI. Moreover, clinicians would benefit from additional training with gender and sexually marginalized communities, given that these groups are at highest risk for enduring NCSI but are more likely to be stigmatized (Mizock & Lundquist, 2016) and experience microaggressions (Spengler, Miller, & Spengler, 2016) within therapy.

Prevent NCSI: Beyond Bias and Toward Sexual Well-Being as a Human Right

Research, policy, interventions and prevention strategies have often been hindered by misconceptions surrounding gender and sexuality. The problems associated with gendered laws and policies warrant substantial legal reform, as the current definitions of

NCSI are based on physical anatomy and therefore perpetuate the assumption of male perpetration and female victims. Such statues limit the ability for men and LGBTQ individuals to pursue legal action for NCSI and limit legal ramification against women who have initiated NCSI. Thus, campus policies should be critically examined to assess the scope of existing institutional initiatives and expand their focus to responding to and preventing NCSI endured by men, LGBTQ individuals and people of color. Situating NCSI in the context of sexual well-being complements existing strategies that aim to increase gender parity and promote awareness of power and privilege.

Prevention efforts make little effort with respect to enhancing consent and increasing sexual communication. Yet, a sexual well-being approach carries strong potential to increase ability to provide and receive consent to ensure safety and optimize sexual pleasure. Research should focus on identifying how individuals negotiate consent (i.e., verbal cues, nonverbal cues) and the differences and similarities of consent processes across various sexual activities, relationship dynamics, cultural values surrounding sexuality and access to material resources. Such work carries the potential to inform culturally relevant intervention and prevention efforts.

Include Sexual Well-Being Messaging in Sexual Literacy Campaigns

Policy and research should promote the development, testing and evaluation of novel initiatives and approaches that respond to the *sexual context* of NCSI. Although campaign messaging has gained sexual literacy by shifting from "no means no" to "yes means yes," the shift to affirmative consent policies oversimplify the social and sexual complexity of consent through campaign messaging such as "get an enthusiastic yes" (Beres, 2007). Specifically, this approach presumes that an internal desire (enthusiasm) is consistent with one's sexual goals and values (willingness to engage in sexual activity). Yet, sexual activity often involves ambivalence between wanting and willingness (Muehlenhard & Peterson, 2005). An enthusiastic yes assumes willingness and desire from the outset, but many individuals do not experience sexual desire prior to pursuing sexual activity (Basson, 2000). Rather, some individuals require the experience of sexual sensations within a sexual context to cognitively want to engage in sexual activity. Campaign messaging would benefit from acknowledging the complexities of sexual relationships while maintaining a simplistic message that NCSI is about willingness and consent.

Conclusion

Although prevention and intervention efforts neglect sexual well-being, there have been numerous beneficial changes to policies and prevention efforts aimed to reduce NCSI in recent years, particularly on college campuses. Current policy debates and public discourse surrounding NCSI provide us with a critical moment to provide high-quality empirical research that can advance effective interventions and preventions. Colleges should be at the forefront of developing collaborative, evidence-based innovations (Harris et al., 2019) that can address issues of nonconsent and helping students cultivate sexual well-being. If we wish to prevent NCSI, we need to situate NCSI education in the context of providing young people with information and guidance on how to have healthy and fulfilling sexual relationships.

Laws and policies provide the framework for the implementation of NCSI policies, prevention strategies and intervention services. Using a sexual well-being approach suggests a means to employ sexual health rights and principles that can aid in separating complex legal issues relevant to NCSI, particularly regarding the distinction between consent and exploitation. Ensuring our laws and policies complement the sexual well-being approach will facilitate the promotion of sexual well-being, which includes prevention of NCSI, across and within various populations. Just as the prevention of STIs and unwanted pregnancy are more successful when conceptualized as a corollary of sexual pleasure, NCSI should be conceptualized as a withdrawal of sexual pleasure that thwarts physical, emotional, sexual safety and sexual well-being.

In summary, NCSI occurs within a sexual context and involves a socially complex negotiation process. Current prevention efforts focus on the gendered social norms that influence NCSI. Yet, these norms ultimately exist outside of the sexual context in which NCSI occurs. Disregarding the diverse sexual contexts in which NCSI occurs, NCSI intervention and prevention evidence a failure in sexual literacy with widespread consequences for cisgender men, women and LGBTQ populations. We propose that closing the gap in sexual literacy can be achieved by facilitating population sexual well-being. The sexual well-being approach argues that NCSI must be positioned in the broader scope of sexual interactions and a sexual literacy approach that aims to increase pleasurable, consensual sexual experiences, if we wish to optimize prevention of NCSI.

References

Abbott, N., & Cameron, L. (2014). What makes a young assertive bystander? The effect of intergroup contact, empathy, cultural openness, and in-group bias on assertive bystander intervention intentions. *Journal of Social Issues*, *70*(1), 167–182.

Apantaku-Olajide, T., Gibbons, P., & Higgins, A. (2011). Drug-induced sexual dysfunction and mental health patients' attitude to psychotropic medications. *Sexual and Relationship Therapy*, *26*(2), 145–155.

Armstrong, E. A., Hamilton, L., & Sweeney, B. (2006). Sexual assault on campus: A multilevel, integrative approach to party rape. *Social Problems*, *53*(4), 483–499.

Ba, I., & Bhopal, R. S. (2017). Physical, mental and social consequences in civilians who have experienced war-related sexual violence: A systematic review (1981–2014). *Public Health*, *100*(142), 121–135.

Baer, J. L., Kohut, T., & Fisher, W. A. (2015). Is pornography use associated with anti-woman sexual aggression? Re-examining the confluence model with third variable considerations. *Canadian Journal of Human Sexuality*, *24*(2), 160–173.

Banyard, V. L., Moynihan, M. M., & Plante, E. G. (2007). Sexual violence prevention through bystander education: An experimental evaluation. *Journal of Community Psychology*, *35*(4), 463–481.

Basson, R. (2000). The female sexual response: A different model. *Journal of Sex &Marital Therapy*, *26*(1), 51–65.

Bauermeister, J. A., Ventuneac, A., Pingel, E., & Parsons, J. T. (2012). Spectrums of love: Examining the relationship between romantic motivations and sexual risk among young gay and bisexual men. *AIDS and Behavior*, *16*(6), 1549–1559.

Bay-Cheng, L. Y. (2001). SexEd.com: Values and norms in web-based sexuality education. *Journal of Sex Research, 38*(3), 241–251. doi:10.1080/00224490109552093

Bay-Cheng, L. Y., & Eliseo-Arras, R. K. (2008). The making of unwanted sex: Gendered and neo-liberal norms in college women's unwanted sexual experiences. *Journal of Sex Research, 45*(4), 386–397.

Beres, M. (2010). Sexual miscommunication? Untangling assumptions about sexual communica-tion between casual sex partners. *Culture, Health & Sexuality, 12*(1), 1–14.

Beres, M. A. (2007). "Spontaneous" sexual consent: An analysis of sexual consent literature. *Feminism & Psychology, 17*(1), 93–108.

Berkowitz, A. (1992). College men as perpetrators of acquaintance rape and sexual assault: A review of recent research. *Journal of American College Health, 40*(4), 175–181.

Berkowitz, A. D. (2002). Fostering men's responsibility for preventing sexual assault. In P. A. Schewe (Ed.), *Preventing violence in relationships: Interventions across the life span* (pp. 163–196). Washington, DC: American Psychological Association.

Blais, R. K. (2019, epub ahead of print). Lower sexual satisfaction and function mediate the associ-ation of assault military sexual trauma and relationship satisfaction in partnered female service members/veterans. *Family Process.* https://doi.org/10.1111/famp.12449

Blais, R. K., Brignone, E., Fargo, J. D., Andresen, F. J., & Livingston, W. S. (2019). The importance of distinguishing between harassment and assault military sexual trauma during screening. *Military Psychology, 31*(3), 227–232.

Blais, R. K., Geiser, C., & Cruz, R. A. (2018). Specific PTSD symptom clusters mediate the asso-ciation of military sexual trauma severity and sexual function and satisfaction in female service members/veterans. *Journal of Affective Disorders, 238*, 680–688.

Buzzella, B. A., Whitton, S. W., & Tompson, M. C. (2012). A preliminary evaluation of a relation-ship education program for male same-sex couples. *Couple and Family Psychology: Research and Practice, 1*(4), 306.

Cahill, S., Valadéz, R., & Ibarrola, S. (2013). Community-based HIV prevention interventions that combat anti-gay stigma for men who have sex with men and for transgender women. *Journal of Public Health Policy, 34*(1), 69–81.

Dank, M., Lachman, P., Zweig, J. M., & Yahner, J. (2014). Dating violence experiences of lesbian, gay, bisexual, and transgender youth. *Journal of Youth and Adolescence, 43*(5), 846–857.

DeGue, S., Valle, L. A., Holt, M. K., Massetti, G. M., Matjasko, J. L., & Tharp, A. T. (2014). A sys-tematic review of primary prevention strategies for sexual violence perpetration. *Aggression and Violent Behavior, 19*(4), 346–362.

De Silva, P. (2001). Impact of trauma on sexual functioning and sexual relationships. *Sexual and Relationship Therapy, 16*, 269–278. doi:10.1080/14681990123900

Dinno, A. (2017). Homicide rates of transgender individuals in the United States: 2010–2014. *American Journal of Public Health, 107*(9), 1441–1447.

Eisenberg, M. E., Lust, K., Mathiason, M. A., & Porta, C. M. (2017). Sexual assault, sexual orientation, and reporting among college students. *Journal of Interpersonal Violence, 36*(1–2), 088626051772641.

Eubanks-Carter, C., & Goldfried, M. R. (2006). The impact of client sexual orientation and gender on clinical judgments and diagnosis of borderline personality disorder. *Journal of Clinical Psychology, 62*(6), 751–770.

Ford, M. P., & Hendrick, S. S. (2003). Therapists' sexual values for self and clients: Implications for practice and training. *Professional Psychology: Research and Practice, 34*(1), 80.

Fortenberry, J. (2019). Condoms on and off: A review of prophylactic barrier use and youth sexual well-being. *Adolescent Medicine: State of the Art Reviews, 30*(1), 45–59.

Fortenberry, J. D. (2016). Adolescent sexual well-being in the 21st century. *Journal of Adolescent Health, 58*(1), 1–2.

Foubert, J., & Newberry, J. T. (2006). Effects of two versions of an empathy-based rape prevention program on fraternity men's survivor empathy, attitudes, and behavioral intent to commit rape or sexual assault. *Journal of College Student Development, 47*(2), 133–148.

Galinsky, A. M., & Sonenstein, F. L. (2013). Relationship commitment, perceived equity, and sexual enjoyment among young adults in the United States. *Archives of Sexual Behavior, 42*(1), 93–104.

Gidycz, C. A., Orchowski, L. M., & Berkowitz, A. D. (2011). Preventing sexual aggression among college men: An evaluation of a social norms and bystander intervention program. *Violence Against Women, 17*(6), 720–742.

Gower, A. L., Rider, G. N., McMorris, B. J., & Eisenberg, M. E. (2018). Bullying victimization among LGBTQ youth: Critical issues and future directions. *Current Sexual Health Reports, 10*(4), 246–254.

Graham, L. F. (2014). Navigating community institutions: Black transgender women's experiences in schools, the criminal justice system, and churches. *Sexuality Research and Social Policy, 11*(4), 274–287.

Harris, A. J., Terry, K. J., & Ackerman, A. R. (2019). Campus sexual assault: Forging an action-focused research agenda. *Sexual Abuse, 31*(3), 263–269.

Harris, S. M., & Hays, K. W. (2008). Family therapist comfort with and willingness to discuss client sexuality. *Journal of Marital and Family Therapy, 34*(2), 239–250.

Isely, P. J., & Gehrenbeck-Shim, D. (1997). Sexual assault of men in the community. *Journal of Community Psychology, 25*(2), 159–166.

Jozkowski, K. N. (2015). Beyond the dyad: An assessment of sexual assault prevention education focused on social determinants of sexual assault among college students. *Violence Against Women, 21*(7), 848–874.

Jozkowski, K. N., & Ekbia, H. R. (2015). "Campus craft": A game for sexual assault prevention in universities. *Games for Health Journal, 4*(2), 95–106.

Jozkowski, K. N., Peterson, Z. D., Sanders, S. A., Dennis, B., & Reece, M. (2014). Gender differences in heterosexual college students' conceptualizations and indicators of sexual consent: Implications for contemporary sexual assault prevention education. *Journal of Sex Research, 51*(8), 904–916.

King, M., & Woollett, E. (1997). Sexually assaulted males: 115 men consulting a counseling service. *Archives of Sexual Behavior, 26*(6), 579–588.

Lutfey, K. E., Link, C. L., Litman, H. J., Rosen, R. C., & McKinlay, J. B. (2008). An examination of the association of abuse (physical, sexual, or emotional) and female sexual dysfunction: Results from the Boston area community health survey. *Fertility and Sterility, 90*(4), 957–964.

Malamuth, N. M., Sockloskie, R. J., Koss, M. P., & Tanaka, J. S. (1991). Characteristics of aggressors against women: Testing a model using a national sample of college students. *Journal of Consulting and Clinical Psychology, 59*(5), 670.

Maltz, W. (2002). Treating the sexual intimacy concerns of sexual abuse survivors. *Sexual and Relationship Therapy, 17*, 321–327.

Mann, R. E., & Hollin, C. R. (2007). Sexual offenders' explanations for their offending. *Journal of Sexual Aggression, 13*(1), 3–9.

Mellins, C. A., Walsh, K., Sarvet, A. L., Wall, M., Gilbert, L., Santelli, J. S., … Benson, S. (2017). Sexual assault incidents among college undergraduates: Prevalence and factors associated with risk. *PLoS One, 12*(11), e0192129.

Miller, E., Tancredi, D. J., McCauley, H. L., Decker, M. R., Virata, M. C. D., Anderson, H. A., …, & Silverman, J. G. (2012). "Coaching boys into men": A cluster-randomized controlled trial of a dating violence prevention program. *Journal of Adolescent Health, 51*(5), 431–438. https://doi.org/10.1016/j.jadohealth.2012.01.018

Miller, S. A., & Byers, E. S. (2008). An exploratory examination of the sexual intervention self-efficacy of clinical psychology graduate students. *Training and Education in Professional Psychology, 2*(3), 137.

Miller, S. A., & Byers, E. S. (2009). Psychologists' continuing education and training in sexuality. *Journal of Sex & Marital Therapy, 35*(3), 206–219.

Miller, S. A., & Byers, E. S. (2010). Psychologists' sexual education and training in graduate school. *Canadian Journal of Behavioural Science/Revue Canadienne Des Sciences Du Comportement, 42*(2), 93.

Miner, M. H. (2007). Is this any way to develop policy? *Sexual Offender Treatment, 2*(1).

Mizock, L., & Lundquist, C. (2016). Missteps in psychotherapy with transgender clients: Promoting gender sensitivity in counseling and psychological practice. *Psychology of Sexual Orientation and Gender Diversity, 3*(2), 148.

Muehlenhard, C. L., & Peterson, Z. D. (2005). III. Wanting and not wanting sex: The missing discourse of ambivalence. *Feminism & Psychology, 15*(1), 15–20.

Mustanski, B., Birkett, M., Greene, G. J., Hatzenbuehler, M. L., & Newcomb, M. E. (2014). Envisioning an America without sexual orientation inequities in adolescent health. *American Journal of Public Health, 104*(2), 218–225.

Najman, J. M., Dunne, M. P., Purdie, D. M., Boyle, F. M., & Coxeter, P. D. (2005). Sexual abuse in childhood and sexual dysfunction in adulthood: An Australian population-based study. *Archives of Sexual Behavior, 34,* 517–526. doi:10.1007/s10508-005-6277-6

O'byrne, R., Rapley, M., & Hansen, S. (2006). "You couldn't say 'no', could you?": Young men's understandings of sexual refusal. *Feminism & Psychology, 16*(2), 133–154.

O'Driscoll, C., & Flanagan, E. (2016). Sexual problems and post-traumatic stress disorder following sexual trauma: A meta-analytic review. *Psychology and Psychotherapy: Theory, Research and Practice, 89*(3), 351–367.

Potter, S. J., Fountain, K., & Stapleton, J. G. (2012). Addressing sexual and relationship violence in the LGBT community using a bystander framework. *Harvard Review of Psychiatry, 20*(4), 201–208.

Pulverman, C. S., Boyd, R. L., Stanton, A. M., & Meston, C. M. (2017). Changes in the sexual self-schema of women with a history of childhood sexual abuse following expressive writing treatment. *Psychological Trauma, 9,* 181–188.

Reissing, E. D., & Giulio, G. D. (2010). Practicing clinical psychologists' provision of sexual health care services. *Professional Psychology: Research and Practice, 41*(1), 57.

Robinson, B., Bockting, W. O., Simon Rosser, B. R., Miner, M., & Coleman, E. (2002). The sexual health model: Application of a sexological approach to HIV prevention. *Health Education Research, 17*(1), 43–57.

Rosser, B. S., Bockting, W. O., Rugg, D. L., Robinson, B. E., Ross, M. W., Bauer, G. R., & Coleman, E. (2002). A randomized controlled intervention trial of a sexual health approach to long-term HIV risk reduction for men who have sex with men: Effects of the intervention on unsafe sexual behavior. *AIDS Education and Prevention, 14*(3Suppl.), 59–71.

Schick, V. R., Zucker, A. N., & Bay-Cheng, L. (2008). Safer, better sex through feminism: The role of feminist ideology in women's sexual well-being. *Psychology of Women Quarterly, 32*(3), 225–232. doi:10.1111/j.1471-6402.2008.00431.x

Seto, M. C. (2019). The motivation-facilitation model of sexual offending. *Sex Abuse, 31*(1), 3–24. doi:10.1177/1079063217720919

Spengler, E. S., Miller, D. J., & Spengler, P. M. (2016). Microaggressions: Clinical errors with sexual minority clients. *Psychotherapy, 53*(3), 360.

Sun, C. J., Anderson, K. M., Mayer, L., Kuhn, T., & Klein, C. H. (2019). Findings from formative research to develop a strength-based HIV prevention and sexual health promotion mHealth intervention for transgender women. *Transgender Health, 4*(1), 350–358.

Thompson, M. P., Kingree, J. B., Zinzow, H., & Swartout, K. (2015). Time-varying risk factors and sexual aggression perpetration among male college students. *Journal of Adolescent Health, 57*(6), 637–642.

Thompson, M. P., Swartout, K. M., & Koss, M. P. (2013). Trajectories and predictors of sexually aggressive behaviors during emerging adulthood. *Psychology of Violence, 3*(3), 247.

Todahl, J. L., Linville, D., Bustin, A., Wheeler, J., & Gau, J. (2009). Sexual assault support services and community systems: Understanding critical issues and needs in the LGBTQ community. *Violence Against Women, 15*(8), 952–976.

Turchik, J. A. (2012). Sexual victimization among male college students: Assault severity, sexual functioning, and health risk behaviors. *Psychology of Men & Masculinity, 13*(3), 243.

Turchik, J. A., & Edwards, K. M. (2012). Myths about male rape: A literature review. *Psychology of Men & Masculinity, 13*(2), 211.

Turchik, J. A., Hebenstreit, C. L., & Judson, S. S. (2016). An examination of the gender inclusiveness of current theories of sexual violence in adulthood: Recognizing male victims, female perpetrators, and same-sex violence. *Trauma, Violence, & Abuse, 17*(2), 133–148.

van Clief, L., & Anemaat, E. (2020). Good sex matters: Pleasure as a driver of online sex education for young people. *Gates Open Research, 3*(1480), 1480.

Wells, S. Y., Glassman, L. H., Talkovsky, A. M., Chatfield, M. A., Sohn, M. J., Morland, L. A., & Mackintosh, M. A. (2019). Examining changing in sexual functioning after Cognitive Processing Therapy in a sample of women trauma survivors. *Womens' Health Issues, 29,* 72–79.

Woerner, J., Abbey, A., Pegram, S. E., & Helmers, B. R. (2018). The effects of alcohol intoxication and sexual interest on men's sexual persistence and hostility in a dating simulation. *Aggressive Behavior, 44*(5), 537–547.

World Health Organization. (2020a). *Gender and human rights.* Retrieved from https://www.who.int/reproductivehealth/topics/gender_rights/sexual_health/en/

World Health Organization. (2020b). *Sexual violence.* Retrieved from https://www.who.int/reproductivehealth/topics/violence/sexual_violence/en/

Zinzow, H. M., & Thompson, M. (2015). Factors associated with use of verbally coercive, incapacitated, and forcible sexual assault tactics in a longitudinal study of college men. *Aggressive Behavior, 41*(1), 34–43.

Chapter 20

THE GLOBAL GAG RULE EXPANDED

Caitlin E. Gerdts

On his fourth day in office, US President Donald Trump signed an executive order reinstating a policy known commonly as "The Global Gag Rule" (The White House, 2017). This is an antiabortion policy first implemented in 1984 by the Reagan administration that prohibited any nongovernmental organization receiving funding earmarked for reproductive health activities from the US government from promoting, providing access to, referrals for, counseling or information about abortion—even if the funds used for such activities came from other sources (Crane & Dusenberry, 2004). In a chilling expansion of the rule, the executive order issued by the Trump administration seeks not only to prevent reproductive health organizations from engaging in any abortion-related activities but to also prevent organizations receiving any global health assistance from "all departments or agencies" in the US government from doing the same.

Past iterations of the global gag rule have impeded the work of a range of organizations around the world to provide comprehensive sexual and reproductive health services, and decreased access to and use of family planning services (Brooks, Bendavid, & Miller, 2019), erected barriers for people in need of abortions from accessing safe abortion services—even where abortion is legal (Singh & Karim, 2017). In addition, contrary to the policy's stated aim of reducing the number of abortions that occur globally, research has demonstrated consistently that during periods when the global gag rule was in place, the rate of abortions increased significantly in countries highly impacted upon by the policy when compared to periods of time when the gag rule was not in place (Brooks et al., 2019). In its construction and application, the global gag rule violates numerous international human rights doctrines and undermines established human rights principles. This latest global gag rule of the Trump administration goes far beyond past interpretations of the policy, however, because it has the potential to result in devastating effects on a range of health services including access to family planning and HIV services, comprehensive sexual and reproductive education and counseling, maternal and newborn health services, vaccination programs, interventions to reduce zika virus transmission and other infectious disease prevention efforts (Mavodza, Constancia, Cooper, & Goldman, 2019), alongside the intended impact on reducing information about and access to safe abortion (Pugh, Desai, Ferguson, Stöckl, & Heidari, 2017). In such ways the new gag rule is extending sexual illiteracy globally.

Excerpt from "Memorandum of March 28, 2001—Restoration of the Mexico City Policy"

Ineligibility of Foreign Nongovernmental Organizations that Perform or Actively Promote Abortion as a Method of Family Planning. (1) The recipient agrees that is will not furnish assistance for family planning under this award to any foreign nongovernmental organization that performs or actively promotes abortion as a method of family planning in USAID-recipient countries or that provides financial support to any other foreign nongovernmental organization that conducts such activities.

[…].

To actively promote abortion means for an organization to commit resources, financial or other, in a substantial or continuing effort to increase the availability or use of abortion as a method of family planning. (A) This includes, but is not limited to, the following: (I) Operating a family planning counseling service that includes, as part of the regular program, providing advice and information regarding the benefits and availability of abortion as a method of family planning; (II) Providing advice that abortion is an available option in the event other methods of family planning are not used or are not successful or encouraging women to consider abortion (passively responding to a question regarding where a safe, legal abortion may be obtained is not considered active promotion if the question is specifically asked by a woman who is already pregnant, the woman clearly states that she has already decided to have a legal abortion, and the family planning counselor reasonably believes that the ethics of the medical profession in the country requires a response regarding where it may be obtained safely); (III) Lobbying a foreign government to legalize or make available abortion as a method of family planning or lobbying such a government to continue the legality of abortion as a method of family planning; and (IV) Conducting a public information campaign in USAID-recipient countries regarding the benefits and/or availability of abortion as a method of family planning.

Excerpt from "Presidential Memorandum of January 23, 2017—Regarding the Mexico City Policy"

"I direct the Secretary of State, in coordination with the Secretary of Health and Human Services, to the extent allowable by law, to implement a plan to extend the requirements of the reinstated Memorandum to global health assistance furnished by all departments or agencies."

As we take stock of the insidious and intentional efforts of the Trump administration to undermine the sexual and reproductive health and human rights of all people, perhaps most especially of women and girls, it is, nevertheless, critical to acknowledge and celebrate the dedication, creativity and perseverance of existing efforts to combat the negative impacts of the Global Gag Rule. While so many in the global sexual and reproductive health, rights and justice communities are engaged in this fight, I want to specifically focus here on the role of grassroots, feminist organizations—working primarily in countries where abortion is legally restricted—to ensure equitable access to safe abortion for all people regardless of geography or legal context through *abortion accompaniment* (Zurbriggen, Keefe-Oates, & Gerdts, 2018).

Abortion accompaniment is the emerging model through which evidence-based information, counseling and support through the medication abortion process is provided virtually or in person to people who self-manage abortions.[1] Abortion accompaniment groups exist in more than 20 countries around the globe, and each group employs a slightly different model, but all of them provide people in need of abortions with information about and support through (either virtually—by phone or secure online platform, or sometime in person) the medication abortion process. A majority of these organizations provide accompaniment through 12 weeks' gestation—following WHO protocols. Anyone contacting an accompaniment group receives standardized and compassionate pre-abortion counseling about the process and what to expect including how the medications function, how to manage pain, what the products of conception will look like, management of products of conception, how to manage retained products of conception, how to recognize complication signs, potential interactions with medical personnel in case of emergency treatment seeking, how to confirm abortion completion, what to expect after the abortion, management of emotions and prevention of future unwanted pregnancies. Gestational age is most often ascertained by asking the caller to recall the first day of their last menstrual period (LMP). Once a caller can confirm that they have reliable medications in hand, the accompanier will describe the medication abortion protocol (how and when to take the medications) and will ensure that the caller knows how to be in touch throughout the process if they need additional support. While each group employs their own unique approach, the work that they do is not only grounded in evidence and clinical best-practice but also employs a feminist and human-rights lens to deliver person-centered care before, during and after the abortion process for those who cannot or choose not to, access abortion care within the formal health sector. The feminist and human rights perspective embodied by abortion accompaniment groups is the view that in a just world we all would have the resources we need—including information, access to services, supportive policies and power—to make the best choices for ourselves, our families and our communities without discrimination or coercion, and to choose whether and when to have children, and to raise them with dignity. But because of long histories of economic inequality, racism, gender inequality, homophobia many other linked systemic oppressions, many people across the world lack access to quality sexual and reproductive health information, services and care, and are prohibited from exercising their human right to sexual and reproductive health.

---

1 For the purposes of this essay, self-managed abortion (also called self-induced, self-sourced, self-administered or "DIY" abortion) can be defined as "any action a person takes to end a pregnancy without clinical supervision" (Moseson et al., 2019).

Given the political context of the United States in 2019, it is unsurprising that media coverage (Contributor, 2018; Liss-Schultz, n.d.; Shugerman, 2019) and new research (Aiken, 2018; Aiken et al., 2017; "Demand for Self-Managed Medication Abortion through an Online Telemedicine Service in the United States," n.d.; Moseson et al., 2019) demonstrate a growing awareness of the option to self-manage abortion outside of the formal health care system. But of course, self-managed abortion is not new, and has, in fact, been documented throughout history and across cultures to include a range of actions such as ingesting herbs recommended by a traditional healer, purchasing misoprostol from a local pharmacist, inserting objects into the vagina, using medication under the guidance of a safe abortion hotline or accompaniment group, a combination of these methods or other methods (Moseson et al., 2019). Nonetheless, now more than ever, we are learning about people's experiences with self-managed abortion in the United States (Conti & Cahill, 2019). Recent evidence indicates between 1 and 7 percent of abortion patients in the United States have taken or done something to try to end their current pregnancy (Jones & Jerman, 2017). The reasons people attempt to self-manage an abortion are varied, but they are often related to the very real barriers to accessing clinic-based care now extant in America, as well as a preference for self-care. It is, of course, critical to remind ourselves that as barriers to access and legal restrictions increase in the United States, those who self-manage abortions and those assisting them may be targeted, reported, prosecuted or even jailed (Tasset & Harris, 2018)—low-income people, people of color and immigrant people disproportionately face this risk (Paltrow & Flavin, 2013)—those for whom comprehensive sexual literacy is most critical now.

Those of us in the Global North can learn a great deal from the researchers, activists and practitioners who bring years of experience to this issue in legally restricted settings in the Global South. For example, from the Soccoristas en Red in Argentina who, for decades, have advocated for a more expansive interpretation of the concept of "health" within the existing abortion law that allows for abortion when a woman's health is at risk. Under the expanded framework—one championed by the World Health Organization— the physical, emotional and social dimensions of health would all be taken into consideration when evaluating eligibility for legal abortion based on how a person's health might be jeopardized by pregnancy and birth. And, in 2015, the Soccoristas along with activists and grassroots feminists from many sectors in Argentina came together under the banner "Ni Una Menos" (meaning "Not One Less"), to spur a movement that championed calls for abortion-law reform. While the legislature ultimately rejected legal reform for abortion in 2018, the Soccoristas have continued to be at the forefront of the movement for expanded access to safe abortion and legal reform—which will result in another attempt at legalizing abortion in Argentina in 2020.

We have much to learn about improving access to and quality of abortion care for all people, however they choose to, need to or want to access it. A growing consensus is emerging in the global community that abortion medications are safe regardless of where they are taken (Erdman, Jelinska, & Yanow, 2018; Organization & Health, 2015), but evidence is still needed to help us understand peoples' preferences for abortion care, how to best deliver the information and the resources people need in order for them to have the abortion experiences that will be best for them. Additionally, we need to help clinics and formal sector services adapt to this changing landscape (Ibis Reproductive Health, 2018).

Nevertheless, we know from talking to women, and from research documenting what women care about, that safety and effectiveness is only one part of a good abortion experience (Aiken, Broussard, Johnson, & Padron, 2018; Aiken, Gomperts, & Trussell, 2017; Moseson et al., 2019; Zurbriggen et al., 2018). To more fully understand the interpersonal qualities that make for good abortion experiences, we must interrogate how different models of abortion care that take place within and outside of formal health care settings, contribute to feelings of autonomy, well-being and dignity. Exploring alternative models of care such as abortion accompaniment from a more holistic lens of abortion quality may provide additional insights.

Abortion accompaniment models profiled here often exemplify the characteristics of high-quality abortion service delivery in their provision of widely accessible, safe, effective and person-centered services. Documenting and exploring the abortion experiences of those who have been supported to self-manage by abortion accompaniment groups helps us to better understand and conceptualize different ways in which positive abortion experiences can occur. In addition, accompaniment models often center their approach within feminist principles and rely on a human rights framework that espouses that all people deserve access to reliable information and comprehensive reproductive health services. It follows, then, that many of these organizations see their role also as a source of reproductive activism and advocacy through the provision of person-centered, feminist abortion care and as a tool through which to normalize and destigmatize abortion. By providing this care and publicly advocating for abortion access in a range of legal and social settings, they have situated themselves as leaders in the efforts to normalize abortion among those seeking care, and within society as a whole.

In the end, the new analysis of abortion accompaniment in the face of the global gag rule comes down to the reality that people are the experts in their own lives, and it is the courageous efforts of advocates and activists like those who are expanding access to abortion accompaniment, that will, despite broad and sustained global attacks on reproductive health and freedom, allow for improved access to and quality of abortion care in and out of clinic settings; lay the foundation for the de-medicalization of medication abortion service delivery models regardless of legal context; and ultimately shift global norms about abortion in a more positive direction.

References

Aiken, A. R. (2018). Self-sourced online and self-directed at home: A new frontier for abortion in the United States. *Contraception, 97*(4), 285–286.

Aiken, A. R., Broussard, K., Johnson, D. M., & Padron, E. (2018). Motivations and experiences of people seeking medication abortion online in the United States. *Perspectives on Sexual and Reproductive Health, 50*(4), 157–163.

Aiken, A. R., Digol, I., Trussell, J., & Gomperts, R. (2017). Self reported outcomes and adverse events after medical abortion through online telemedicine: Population based study in the Republic of Ireland and Northern Ireland. *BMJ, 357*, j2011.

Aiken, A. R., Gomperts, R., & Trussell, J. (2017). Experiences and characteristics of women seeking and completing at-home medical termination of pregnancy through online telemedicine in Ireland and Northern Ireland: A population-based analysis. *BJOG: An International Journal of Obstetrics & Gynaecology, 124*(8), 1208–1215.

Brooks, N., Bendavid, E., & Miller, G. (2019). USA aid policy and induced abortion in sub-Saharan Africa: An analysis of the Mexico City Policy. *The Lancet Global Health, 7*(8), e1046–e1053. Retrieved from https://doi.org/10.1016/S2214-109X(19)30267-0

Conti, J., & Cahill, E. P. (2019). Self-managed abortion. *Current Opinion in Obstetrics and Gynecology, 31*(6), 435–440.

Contributor, G. (2018, February 5). Safe and supported: Inside the DIY abortion movement. Our bodies ourselves. Retrieved from https://www.ourbodiesourselves.org/2018/02/safe-and-supported-inside-the-diy-abortion-movement/

Crane, B. B., & Dusenberry, J. (2004). Power and politics in international funding for reproductive health: The US Global Gag Rule. *Reproductive Health Matters, 12*(24), 128–137.

Demand for Self-Managed Medication Abortion through an Online Telemedicine Service in the United States. (n.d.). *AJPH*. Retrieved November 15, 2019, from https://ajph.aphapublications.org/doi/abs/10.2105/AJPH.2019.305369

Erdman, J. N., Jelinska, K., & Yanow, S. (2018). Understandings of self-managed abortion as health inequity, harm reduction and social change. *Reproductive Health Matters, 26*(54), 13–19.

Ibis Reproductive Health, Advancing New Standards in Reproductive Health, Gynuity Health Projects. (2018). *A roadmap for research on self-managed abortion in the United States.* Retrieved from https://ibisreproductivehealth.org/publications/roadmap-research-self-managed-abortion-united-states

Jones, R. K., & Jerman, J. (2017). Abortion incidence and service availability in the United States, 2014. *Perspectives on Sexual and Reproductive Health, 49*(1), 17–27.

Liss-Schultz, N. (n.d.). American women can now get abortion pills shipped to their homes. *Mother Jones.* Retrieved November 15, 2019, from https://www.motherjones.com/crime-justice/2018/10/american-woman-self-induced-abortion-diy-pills-mail/

Mavodza, C., Cooper, B., & Goldman, R. (2019). The impacts of the global gag rule on global health: A scoping revie. *Global Health Research and Policy, 4*(1), 26.

Moseson, H., Herold, S., Filippa, S., Barr-Walker, J., Baum, S. E., & Gerdts, C. (2019). Self-managed abortion: A systematic scoping review. *Best* Practice & Research Clinical Obstetrics & Gynaecology, 63, 87–110. doi: 10.1016/j.bpobgyn.2019.08.002

Paltrow, L. M., & Flavin, J. (2013). Arrests of and forced interventions on pregnant women in the United States, 1973–2005: Implications for women's legal status and public health. *Journal of Health Politics, Policy and Law, 38*(2), 299–343.

Pugh, S., Desai, S., Ferguson, L., Stöckl, H., & Heidari, S. (2017). Not without a fight: Standing up against the Global Gag Rule. *Reproductive Health Matters, 25*(49), 14–16. https://doi.org/10.1080/09688080.2017.1303250

Shugerman, E. (2019, January 5). These women say DIY abortion is nothing to fear. *Daily Beast.* Retrieved from https://www.thedailybeast.com/what-back-alley-these-women-say-diy-abortion-can-be-empowering

Singh, J. A., & Karim, S. S. A. (2017). Trump's "global gag rule": Implications for human rights and global health. *Lancet Global Health, 5*(4), e387–e389. https://doi.org/10.1016/S2214-109X(17)30084-0

Tasset, J., & Harris, L. H. (2018). Harm reduction for abortion in the United States. *Obstetrics & Gynecology, 131*(4), 621–624.

The White House. (2017). *Presidential memorandum regarding the Mexico city policy.* Retrieved from https://www.whitehouse.gov/the-press-office/2017/01/23/presidential-memorandum-regarding-mexico-city-policy

World Health Organization. (2015). *Health worker role in providing safe abortion care and post abortion contraception*. Author.

Zurbriggen, R., Keefe-Oates, B., & Gerdts, C. (2018). Accompaniment of second-trimester abortions: The model of the feminist Socorrista network of Argentina. *Contraception, 97*(2), 108–115.

Chapter 21

A RECKONING: MARXISM, QUEER THEORY AND POLITICAL ECONOMY

Holly Lewis

The critique of political economy may seem a world away from debates about critical sexuality. The term *economics* conjures a certain sexlessness: mathematical formulae, the smooth interface of banking apps, the peaks and valleys of charts and graphs. However, once we crack this illusory shell, we see that what we call "the economy" is nothing less than the ever-shifting totality of human social relationships as well as humanity's relationship to the planet itself. A general theory of sexual literacy cannot ignore how the contemporary mode of production and consumption shapes our bodies and our desires, and, in fact, not only shapes them but also relies upon them.

Emerging out of the poststructuralist milieu in the early 1990s, queer theory analyzed sexuality and gender through a discursive lens; subjects are understood to be enmeshed within signifying systems that shape bodies through desiring and discipline where desire is understood as a path to agency[1] and discipline is understood as a hegemon's attempt to tame it. For this reason, the central political theme of queer theory is the reclamation of desire and the subversion of normativity.

Originally, economics appeared as extrinsic to the fundamentals of queerness as mathematics or physics;[2] in fact, the word "economics" itself connotes the kind of

---

1 Though not queer theory proper, Lacan's *Ethics of Psychoanalysis* (year) detached Freudian psychoanalysis from body essentialism.
2 This argument morphed over time, particularly as Marxist-feminists criticized queer theorists regarding their divorce from material social life. Judith Butler's exchange with Nancy Fraser here is key. It is interesting, however, that when Butler *agrees* that economics is crucial to queer oppression, that the capitalist mode of production produces heteronormativity, is precisely when Nancy Fraser (the materialist) insists that heteronormativity is not really important in the capitalist schema, that, in fact, *Marxist economics is not really pertinent* to queer politics and that injustice to queer people is more akin to misrecognition. To make queer experience external to economics implies that a unitary Marxist theory of oppression is untenable. To make queer oppression a matter of misrecognition caricatures the role heterosexism plays within capitalism. See, Judith Butler's (1997) *Merely Cultural*, and Nancy Fraser (1998) in *Heterosexism, Misrecognition, and Capitalism: A Response to Judith Butler*. It should be noted that Rosemary Hennessey's important book, *Pleasure and Profit*, criticizes Butler but rejects Fraser's premise that capitalism has no real connection to sexuality.

instrumental rationality poststructuralism existed to critique. Marx, the primary theoretician of economic liberation, appears in early queer theory as a mere footnote in critical theory's intellectual lineage when he wasn't outright rejected as teleological or patriarchal (Warner, 1993). This dismissal was out of hand and not through immanent critique; the very notion of serious engagement with Marx was foreclosed. This foreclosure suggests that rejection of Marx's work was less a specific rejoinder to his writings on political economy than a reaction to ostensibly socialist states' poor record on queer liberation during the twentieth century, alongside the failure of Marxist movements to incorporate sexual liberation into their projects. But somewhere along the line, this desire to theorize beyond "mere" economic relations became a rejection of serious, sustained critique of such relations. For queer theory, the capitalist mode of production became just another site of domination, another disciplinary apparatus to be criticized, denounced and *problematized*.

This post-Marxist framework shaped the political role queer theory played in both the academy and everyday life at the turn of the millennium. Without a systemic analysis of material relations, queer economic critique was largely limited to bemoaning gay consumerism and the commercialization of gay culture. Two contradictory demands then formed the blurry horizon of queer political liberation: queer space and queer inclusion. These projects were especially fraught in the United States where taking space required reproducing the logic of settler colonial capitalism. How does one occupy space in the gentrifying city? How does one occupy space in the countryside without wedding queer liberation to land ownership?[3] Likewise, demands for queer inclusion meant integration into the market economy and the nation-state; such a politics could only maintain a radical patina by disavowing its own success.

Because these demands were not inherently anticapitalist, some anticapitalists assumed that queer theory and, by extension, queer politics was *inherently neoliberal*. The term *neoliberal* is often deployed as a vague pejorative, but it has a specific meaning. Neoliberalism names the restoration of economic liberalism (free-market economics) that occurred in the late twentieth century after so-called democratic nation-states began to weaken the mid-century regulations they had used to stabilize laboring households—households often politically sentimentalized by the term *working-class families*. Neoliberalism was not a mere ideological shift, not just a new way of *thinking* about the economy; neoliberalism developed from the logic of capitalism itself. The advent of satellites and computer technologies transformed economic production and logistics. Inventories could be tracked from anywhere in the world. Capital could invest where labor was cheapest and divest from labor strongholds. Capital and commodities could move anywhere in the world, while workers were bound by local conditions. This is today's capitalism.

Neoliberalism was (and is) an attack on people who work, people who are more often than not organized into households. Queer theory is a critique of gender and sexual norms and of the family. However, queer politics is not an attack on people who are

---

3   See Mark Rifkin (2014), *Settler Common Sense: Queerness and Everyday Colonialism in the American Renaissance*.

organized into households. There is nothing inherently neoliberal in queer analysis itself. And there is certainly nothing inherently anticapitalist about the family. But as early queer theory abandoned economic questions for discursive ones, it was incapable of mounting a challenge against the dominant order it intuitively opposed. While our bodies are indeed enmeshed in discursive relations and subject to discipline, the question is for what or whom are we being disciplined. Reifying that which disciplines us as "power" or "apparatuses" or "dominant discourses" begs the question and in doing so denies the possibility of an answer. Through its reluctance to name the ongoing and historical processes of material domination, queer theory became neoliberal by default.

This is in part because modern capitalist economics, as a discipline, is designed to confound and intimidate, and uses mathematized charts and graphs about vertical aggregate supply curves and real GDP to obscure exploitative practices (Keen, 2011). This separating of economics from context in the name of providing technical support for a planet triumphantly settled into capitalist development is, in fact, the consummate *grand narrative* of our time.[4] As the story goes, though the market is almost impossible to understand, its whirling packages will always land in the manner most beneficial to human life; the only remaining debate is whether or not this very-best-system-ever needs tweaking. Intervention, especially by ignorant outsiders, necessarily results in scarcity and totalitarian calamity. Queer thinkers cannot ignore the economic sphere without unwittingly upholding this characterization of capitalism as *mysterious spirit* (hegemon, force, apparatus, Adam Smith's "invisible hand," etc.), which reinforces the idea that capitalism is an insurmountable fact. One can oppose capitalism and still internalize this narrative; one need only to accept that this best-of-all-possible-worlds is still inherently tragic, perhaps even poetically so.

A second way queer politics unwittingly ideologically abetted neoliberalism was its move away from the political toward the ethical: emphasis on bodily practice, care of the self, resisting discipline and resisting consumption. This reduction of politics to individual habit and ethics mirrored the capitalist canard that "all economics is local because exchange occurs between two entities." Narrowing material–social relations to consumer habits and market exchange (as opposed to, say, labor power and land occupation) shifts the focus from the mode of production to the circulation of commodities; or, in Marxist terms, mystifies via commodity fetishism.

Although queer theory did not mount a critique of contemporary political economy, a number of heterodox economists' criticisms of the neoclassical (i.e., normative capitalist economics) model provide fuel for a fuller queer anticapitalist analysis. These economists have criticized neoclassical orthodoxy as an intentionally obscurantist, logically incoherent, enterprise that is not reflective of empirical reality (Keen, 2011), and perhaps more akin to religious doctrine than science (Wolff & Resnick, 2012). Queer thought need not shy away from economic inquiry on the grounds that it is inherently logocentric or divorced from lived experience. It is useful to remember that the term *economics* itself comes from the Greek *oikonomia*, meaning household development. If economics

---

4 Jean-Francois Lyotard's *The Postmodern Condition* calls for a departure from grand narratives.

simply means analysis of the organization of our material–social existence—connections between money flows, household reproduction, raw materials, land, waged and unwaged labor, imperialist violence, unemployment, even the organization of time itself[5]—then questions of gender and sexuality are certainly not alien to it. What we refer to as economic life informs the development of all human identities and desires. Neoclassical economics may be a poor paradigm for understanding any aspect of material reality, including queer existence, but capitalist economics in the Marxian sense simply means *material–social relations* between impermanent groups. It takes as its terrain questions about who produces commodities and why, how technology inherently genders labor power, the role of land seizure and colonialization in producing modern power relations, and how labor time disciplines bodies and produces culture.[6]

Recently, Marxist feminists and queer Marxists have produced new work on how material–social relations affect the development of gender and sexuality. These are not functionalist analyses in the sociological sense—that is to say, queer Marxist-feminists do not argue that humans develop genders and sexualities to serve particular functions that stabilize societies. Nor are these arguments determinist: subjects' horizons are not fundamentally bound by heteronormativity or assigned gender. Marx's thought (particularly in *Capital*, 1867?) is nonessentialist in ways that are compatible with queer analysis. For example, Marx is not interested in unchanging, Platonic natural kinds. Unlike neoclassical theory, for Marx, pre-formed humans are not dropped into environments a la Robinson Crusoe. Although the material–social relations of the production and reproduction of life do not narrowly determine what we can be, such relations comprise the conditions of what we become. This becoming is intentionally shaped by those who stand to benefit most from capitalist commodity production (i.e., the capitalist class); but more usually, our becoming is shaped by the common sense that emerges from navigating particular social experiences within the capitalist mode of production: factory organization, distribution chains, militarization, transportation, property development, shopping and leisure, social media, travel, education and so forth. Here follows an analysis of the relevant components linked with sexuality and gender effects.

Origins of Gender

Friedrich Engels' *Origins of the Family, Private Property and the State* is, indeed, a paean to monogamous heterosexual love (though monogamy did not seem to interest Engels very much personally). Marx and Engels' heteronormativity has been explored at length since

---

5   See Jonathan Martineau's *Time, Capitalism, and Alienation: A Socio-Historical Inquiry into the Making of Modern Time*, Stavros Tombazos's *Time in Marx: The Categories of Time in Marx's Capital* and Massimiliano Tomba's *Marx's Temporalities*.

6   The cigarette is exemplary in this sense. Machines accelerating the mass production of cigarettes correlated with rise in use, which itself was an expression of factory time; while the leisurely cigar became emblematic of boss culture, the 10-minute cigarette break became a working-class demand and then an eroticized sign of mid-twentieth-century working-class masculinity.

the height of the gay liberation movement.[7] However, Marx and Engels' Victorian mental limitations are of less interest than their work's potential. The use of the word *origins* is exemplary. To have an origin is to have a beginning. Something that has a beginning is not eternal or essential. By outlining the shifting forms of gendered human cooperation over millennia from sedentarization to industrialization, Engels denaturalizes gender oppression; by showing how these gendered relations influenced the rise of private property, which Engels seeks to abolish, he opens the possibility of the abolition of the family itself (despite explicit denial of this aim).

The family form, as Engels notes, serves to keep inherited wealth inside politically dominant families and communities. But within our current mode of production, the family form also creates an unpaid workforce capable of caring for laboring individuals when they are too old or too young to produce value in a capitalist economy. Family norms thus exist to uphold the existing order; however, blanket calls for the abolition of empirical families are not inherently anticapitalist. Capital has a double relationship with the family. It is a method of generating reproductive labor, but there are also situations where the heteronormative family obstructs the profitability. In those instances, profit takes precedence. Such examples are gender-segregated dormitory labor in China, male mining communities in mid-twentieth-century South Africa, and prison labor in the United States. The colonial violence from which the original industrial capitalists accumulated the raw materials to set mass commodity production in motion destroyed both hierarchical gender regimes *and* complex indigenous genders and sexualities. Such colonial violence imposed heterosexual norms onto indigenous people while creating conditions where the imperialist forces themselves established homosexual partnerships to reproduce their capacity to act as agents of occupation (Aldrich, 2003, pp. 83–105).

Production

While Engels' work sheds light on how gender relations shifted with the development of class society, Marx's *Capital* sheds light on the role gender plays in the production of profit within the capitalist mode. Some additional basics of Marx's economic analysis might be helpful here.

Marx begins his economic analysis with the commodity in order to unpack it, to demystify it. Against utilitarians such as John Stuart Mill, Marx separates the use of a commodity from its exchange value. The commodity is a *queer* thing: its purposiveness is fluid and contextual. Its use value is distinct from its value, which is how much socially necessary labor time went into producing it. Profit is extracted from surplus value or, simply put, profit happens when the total value of the commodities working people make is not returned to the working people. Profit is a cut taken by those who own a given society's industry. There are two ways to take this cut. Surplus value is absolute when more people in a family or community enter the work force, when machines and

---

7   Beginning with Jeffrey Weeks, "Where Engels Feared to Tread." *Gay Left: A Socialist Journal Produced by Gay Men 1*(3) (Autumn 1975).

time-saving technologies speed up production. Surplus value is relative when a capitalist can make more profit relative to other capitalists through cheapening the value
of labor power (cheapening the creation and maintenance of human life) itself. This
occurs when the cost of education is low, when laborers consume lower cost commodities; when the cost of elder care and childcare is low, then wages can go lower. If this
sounds contradictory—if wages are lower then people can purchase less, if childcare is
a free service provided by women then women can't enter the labor market, if care is
nonexistent the workforce will die of disease, child care and elder care are also profitable
businesses—that's because it is contradictory. Different capitalists put different demands
on the system. The contradictions are the very reason why the system is unstable. It is also
the reason why Marx's analysis of capital is neither teleological nor functionalist.

The organization of care has specific effects on working people's bodies. Capitalists
also choose certain aspects of bodies to complete certain tasks within capitalist production. Industrial manufacturing meant a shift from upper-body strength—associated with
masculinity—to small, quick hands, associated with women and children.[8] Women bore
more children during industrialization, not because the "bosses needed labor" or even
because of lack of birth control (proletarian birth rates were often higher than peasant birth
rates) but because of incentives for workers to marry young. Working children had good
reason to emancipate themselves as quickly as possible as to not to have to hand over their
wages to their parents; earlier sexual activity led to more pregnancies over a lifetime.[9] The
urbanization attendant to industrialization (and, in many places, the privatization of family
land) sent young people flocking to the cities, where they were able to cut ties with their families of origin, a precondition for modern gay identities (D'Emilio, 1983), while Kevin Floyd
(2009) has argued that gay male desire was reified as a specific social identity in mid-century
American production regimes.

Reproduction

Queer theory was dismissive toward Marxist feminism, in part because the latter had
not yet broken away from the more gender essentialist strands of second wave feminism
(c1970 in the United States), but also because the terrain of much early Marxist feminism, the inequality of the housewife, was outside the scope of queer activism. Thus,
the traditional family was precisely the construct queers were either fleeing or, given the
status of queer people in the 1970s and early 1980s, the situation they were forced to
flee. After all, families of origin, mothers included, were among those who abandoned
their queer children during the early years of the HIV crisis; what's more, the US labor
movement was slow to take up HIV/AIDS as a political demand.[10]

---

8 See Heather Brown, *Marx on Gender and the Family*; and Donna Haraway, *A Manifesto for Cyborgs*.
9 See Wally Seccombe, *A Millennium of Family Change*.
10 The labor movement did eventually make rights-based demands for workers with HIV/AIDS
     in the 1990s, but only after ACT-UP pushed the traditional left toward such concern. In other
     words, neither Marxist-feminists nor the labor movement were the engine of social change in

However, there is no way to flee the family without a concerted social policy that takes the burden of care off those assigned to live as women. One can refuse to serve the family, but one cannot refuse its services when there are no other social relations to rely upon. One can leave one's family of origin, but without public laundry service, free child-care, home health aides, public eating houses, counseling and public education, one will have to create family anew to take up these burdens. "Chosen families" and "families of choice" are still organized around the logic of family.

Social reproduction theory is a Marxist-feminist project that seeks to unravel the complexities of how labor power is replenished and developed, and in particular how it is developed *noncapitalistically* through the family for the benefit of the capitalist system; the value of socially necessary labor power, the source of the production of values system-wide, is calculated relatively through the expenditures socially necessary to maintain and develop the laborers themselves. When life is cheap, profits are high. Some of this life-sustaining work does not produce immediate profit for a capitalist (home birth, taking care of one's elderly parents, educating children, cleaning toilets in one's own household) but sometimes the survival and development of workers is subsumed into the formal capitalist economy and does, in fact, produce profit for capitalists (home-health care services, for-profit tutoring centers, maid services, coffee shops). However, if workers need to pay tutoring services, pay for home-health care and eat fast food in the car on the way to work—their wages must be enough to compensate the workers who work for such privatized "providers" and must also be enough for the bosses who take their cut. And workers who do reproductive labor must also receive care. This, and not "supply and demand," is why reproductive labor is poorly compensated when not ideologically coerced through gender norms.

In other words, capitalism organizes the biopotentials of working people to produce cheap labor power. Gender differentiation streamlines the tasks and familial love spiritualizes the uncompensated care that lowers labor costs.

Consumption

In the capitalist mode, pleasure is coded as both consumption and nonproduction. The concept of pleasure has been weaponized to socially delegitimize queer people: heterosexuals are industrious and procreative; queers are shallow, idle pleasure-mongers. The heteronormative left echoes these stereotypes (and also echoes the logic of capitalist production and reproduction) when it insists that heterosexual household demands are serious and "economic," while queer demands are merely about identity recognition. When radical queer politics emphasizes the unethical consumption habits of gay men, it becomes heteronormative in this sense.

We can now return to a critique of consumption, but with our perspective rooted in politics rather than ethics. In Marxian economics there are two kinds of

---

this case. See the International Labor Organization's *Toolkit for Trade Unions on HIV and AIDS* (2010), which dates union concern for HIV/AIDS "as early as 1994" (p. 7).

consumption: end-consumer consumption and productive consumption, the latter being consumption in the course of capitalist production, consumption that is ultimately productive of capital (e.g., the water, steel and machinery consumed in mass production). While we are not commodities (we are not traded and consumed; our *labor power* is), we must make ourselves desirable to sell our labor on the market, especially in service-oriented economies. Commodities are not just hedonistic use-values, but also factors that figure into how we are waged. In the past decades, commodities not only shaped the value of our labor power, but they have also come to mediate our sociality. And with the advent of social media, our sociality has itself become a commodity, what Richard Seymour (2019) calls the *social industry*. Our data and user habits are recorded, surveilled and traded, blurring the lines between leisure and labor (Dean, 2010). Sexualities harden into empirical categories. But in the data-mapped universe, the actual content is less important than the fact that it is content. Our global communication—whether gendered, political, familial, health-related or relating sexual desire—is mediated by a privatized data collection schema. The form/coding itself shapes the content to better extract data from us. We perhaps could call this *consumptive production*. Moreover, the gig economy is blurring the line between what is ours to consume and what is consumed in the course of laboring: a sex worker's cam and computer, an Uber driver's car repairs, an online transcriptionist's home office. Production and consumption are dialectically entangled.

The capitalist mode of production is a global set of social relations with no exterior. Our material relationships to one another are both global and local, gendered and anonymous, sexual and de-eroticized. In fact, in an age of pandemic, global commodity exchange has never been more haunted with the specter of workers' bodies and the traces we leave upon one another. We are not simply sovereign, atomized, localized individuals, but deeply interconnected through the objects we make, distribute and consume, and through the services we render. Queer analysis is not meaningless in this paradigm; however, to understand the apparatuses that discipline us, we must not just talk about the disciplining, but name and describe capitalism, the mechanism that shapes us. If we want to go beyond the family and the norms that bind us, we have to acknowledge the material system that produces us.

References

Aldrich, R. (2003). *Colonialism and homosexuality*. New York: Routledge.

Brown, H. (2013). *Marx on gender and the family*. Chicago: Haymarket Books.

Butler, J. (1997). Merely cultural. *Social Text: Queer Transexions of Race, Nation, and Gender, 15*(52/53), 265–277. Durham, NC: Duke University Press.

Dean, J. (2010). Communicative capitalism: Circulation and the foreclosure of politics. In M. Boler (Ed.), *Digital media and democracy: Tactics in hard times* (pp. 1–24). Cambridge, MA: MIT Press.

D'Emilio, J. (1983). *Sexual politics, sexual communities: The making of a homosexual minority* (1st ed.). Chicago: University of Chicago Press.

Floyd, K. (2009). *Reification of desire: Towards a queer Marxism*. Minneapolis: University of Minnesota Press.

Fraser, N. (1997). Heterosexism, misrecognition, and capitalism: A response to Judith Butler. *Social Text: Queer Transexions of Race, Nation, and Gender*, 52/53, 279–289. Durham, NC: Duke University Press.

Haraway, D. (1987). A manifesto for cyborgs: Science, technology, and socialist feminism in the 1980s. *Australian Feminist Studies*, 2(4), 1–42.

Hennessy, R. (2000). *Profit and pleasure*. New York: Routledge.

ILO Bureau for Workers' Activities (ACTRAV). (2010). *Toolkit for trade unions on HIV and AIDS*. Geneva: International Labour Organization.

Keen, S. (2011). *Debunking economics* (rev. ed.). London: Zed Books.

Lyotard, J. (1984). *The postmodern condition: A report on knowledge*. Minneapolis: University of Minnesota Press.

Martineau, J. (2016). *Time, capitalism, and alienation: A socio-historical inquiry into the making of modern time*. Chicago: Haymarket Books.

Rifkin, M. (2014). *Settler common sense: Queerness and everyday colonialism in the American renaissance*. Minneapolis: University of Minnesota Press.

Seccombe, W. (1995). *A millennium of family change*. London: Verso.

Seymour, R. (2019). *The Twittering machine*. London: The Indigo Press.

Tomba, M. (2013). *Marx's temporalities*. Chicago: Haymarket Books.

Tombazos, S. (2015). *Time in Marx: The categories of time in Marx's capital*. Chicago: Haymarket Books.

Warner, M. (Ed.). (1993). *Fear of a queer planet: Queer politics and social theory*. Minneapolis: University of Minnesota Press.

Weeks, J. (1975). "Where Engels Feared to Tread". *Gay left: A socialist journal produced by gay men*, 1, 3–5.

Wolff, R. D., & Resnick, S. (2012). *Contending economic theories: Neoclassical, Keynesian, and Marxian*. Cambridge, MA: MIT Press.

PART THREE

SEXUAL LITERACY IN DIVERSE COMMUNITIES

Chapter 22

BECOMING CRITICALLY GLOCAL: BEYOND NORTH AND SOUTH, INDIVIDUALS AND CULTURES IN UNDERSTANDING SEXUAL LITERACIES

Margaret Jolly

Our editors Gilbert Herdt, Michelle Marzullo and Nicole Polen-Petit espouse a critical situated analysis of sexualities, sexual literacies and sexual inequalities to move us beyond "stale discussions of relativistic devolutions and risky universalisms" (p. 2). This is a great aspiration that I share. Yet we also need to be constantly aware of the continuing legacies of imperial genealogies in discussions of both differences and similarities in human sexual experience and knowledge. This lingers in a tendency to focus on sexual literacies for individuals in certain places and collectivities and cultures in others.

Sexual literacies are not just sexual knowledges inscribed in texts, like the famous *ars erotica*[1] of the East: the *kamasutra* of India or the *shunga*, the spring pictures, erotic paintings and woodblock prints of Japan's "floating world." Or the vast suite of sexology texts, marriage manuals and self-help books promoting both pleasure and discipline in western sexual and reproductive life. Sexual literacy embraces diverse sexual knowledges circulating in oral and embodied form—from adults to children, between peers, witnessing or emulating the sexualities of others and, increasingly, viewing images circulating in connected virtual and digital worlds. As the editors aver: "Our stance in this collection is that sexual literacy is a process rather than a destination. The construct conceptually links human social and developmental processes whereby individuals learn a set of life-long abilities and skills—intellectual or cognitive as well as emotional—needed to access, comprehend, critically evaluate and effectively utilize the dominant sexual systems of their culture for personal, interpersonal and communal development" (p. 1). They stress that sexual literacies are increasingly glocal—creolizing global with local elements in

---

1 I am here alluding to Foucault's (1974) distinction between the *ars erotica* of the East directed toward pleasure and the *scientia sexualis*, the sexual science emergent in Europe from the eighteenth century with the emergence of capitalism, which he sees extracted from individual confessions about sexual feelings and practices. He expressly critiqued Freud's repressive hypothesis, witnessing rather an excess of solicitation and talk about the secret of sex. See Jolly and Manderson (1997

ways that are differentially configured in diverse situations. Hence the situated knowledge and situated analysis this collection espouses.

Yet this new spirit of analysis has to contend with *imperial genealogies*—knowledges that were created and disseminated as an integral part of European imperialism. This is especially palpable in "sexual science," preoccupied with questions of sameness and difference in sexual experiences across humanity. Differences were typically plotted in time and space. Chiang (2009) discerns a "double alterity" in much sexology, that is, the "other" is seen at a distance in both space (remote, exotic) and time (archaic, traditional). For example, eighteenth-century European explorations charted sexual regimes in Oceania on a continuum from west to east *and* from savagery to civilization. Thus, the gender and sexual regimes of places we now know as New Caledonia and Vanuatu were adjudged "savage," whereas those in islands such as Tahiti and Hawai'i were viewed as approaching the "ancients" of Europe's past and the supposedly elevated state of contemporaneous Europe (Jolly, 2012).

In the early twentieth century, Freud and his followers posited both a universal pattern in the formation of psychosexual development and desire and also cultural differences whereby the bourgeois forces of the late nineteenth-century Western civilization and Viennese patrilineal conformity repressed individual libidinal desires more forcefully than in allegedly "savage," non-Western societies (Freud, [1930] 2002). He drew an analogy between the phases of the libidinal development of the individual and the alleged stages in the development of civilization.

In his ethnography of the Trobriand Islands in Papua New Guinea (PNG), Bronislaw Malinowski (1927, 1929) challenged Freud's generalizations and in particular his claims for the universality of the Oedipus complex.[2] Rather, Malinowski depicted a matrilineal society that traced descent through women, and wherein sexuality was celebrated, adolescents were free to find pleasure with several desired partners before marriage, heterosexual couples were expected to experience mutual pleasure and where divorce was easy and rather frequent (1929).

In the same period, Margaret Mead's studies of "coming of age" in Samoa (1927) suggested a less traumatic transition to adulthood than American teenagers and greater sexual freedom for both adolescent women and men. On the basis of her ethnographic research, she suggested that adolescent girls engaged in secretive sexual adventures, and that hard work was more important than virginity in a prospective bride. Young men were encouraged to be hard working and aggressive, including in sexual competition for young women. Marriage was seen to diminish a woman's status but potentially elevate that of

---

2   The Oedipus complex is named after the Greek myth in which Oedipus unwittingly kills his father Laius and marries his mother Jocasta. It was, according to Freud, the unconscious sexual desire of the child for the opposite-sex parent and hatred of the same-sex parent. He suggested it manifest as castration anxiety in boys and penis envy in girls. He claimed that the successful resolution of the complex was when the child ultimately identified with the same-sex parent. As well as anthropological critiques such as that by Malinowski this concept, like much Freudian psychoanalytic theory, has been extensively critiqued for its masculinist and heteronormative presumptions.

a man. After Mead's death her analysis of Samoan gender and sexuality was caustically critiqued by Derek Freeman, who stressed the crucial importance of premarital virginity, for Samoan women at least (Freeman, 1983).[3] Successive studies of sexual cultures across Oceania and Africa have suggested that sexual abstinence, restraint or in Freud's terms *repression*, was hardly unique to the European bourgeoisie, nor solely the result of conversion to Christianity in the context of colonialism. Moreover, sexual abstinence is not always easily equated with repression. For instance, taboos after birth and linked to ritual cycles may be thought to intensify rather than dampen desire (e.g., Jolly, 2001).

More recently, social analysts have plotted differences in human sexual cultures in diverse spatiotemporal terms—such as the West and the non-West, the developed and the underdeveloped world and the current moniker, the Global North versus the Global South. This volume challenges these "historically bifurcating" frames (p. 2). Using the language of the cardinal points risks naturalizing geopolitical inequalities, reifying borders and condensing images of the globe with the anatomy of the human body, in notions of "above" and "below" (Jolly, 2008). We live in a palpably divided and very unequal world but typifying differences in this way freezes what we might rather hope could be fluid and changing geopolitical contours. Bifurcating the world, that is, dividing it into two parts, also hides the flows of sexual knowledge and sexual experiences across space and time.

For example, Fuechtner, Hayes, and Jones (2017) in their studies of the emergence of "sexual science" are alert to the presence of "false cultural universals," promulgated by European scholars, who have presumed a unilinear stadial evolution to their own civilizational superiority. This is apparent in the sexual science of early anthropology, such as that of Edward Westermarck in Morocco (see Leck, 2017) as much as in the psychoanalysis of Freud. In this process "others" have been banished from the realms of sexual civilization or the sexual modernity of the West.

Historically, models of Western sexual modernity often hinged on the celebrated value of the "self" as an individual abstracted from social context, transcending collective norms in a way allegedly unavailable to nonmodern "others." But, Fuechtner, Hayes, and Jones (2017) argue, non-European interlocutors and actors were also crucial in the emergence of global sexual science as ideas circulated multidirectionally in travel, exchanges and encounters. For example, Magnus Hirschfeld, the German doctor and sexual scientist, acknowledged the foundational influence of the *kamasutra* on his lecture tour of India in 1931, while Swami Shivananda drew on both Havelock Ellis and Marie Stopes in developing Ayurvedic principles of sexual restraint (Fuechtner, Hayes, & Jones, 2017, pp. 1–2).

In this twenty-first century we can witness "glocal" sexual literacies. First, I draw on two ethnographic studies in the Pacific, and second, upon *Unorthodox* (Karolinska & Schrader, 2020), a fictionalized TV series based on a memoir by Deborah Feldman. These examples all reveal how local and global elements creolize in specific situations. Creolization, a word first used to describe how introduced languages become indigenous,

---

3 The Mead–Freeman controversy has been exhaustively even exhaustingly analyzed. For a forensic appraisal, see Shankman (2009) and for a recent distillation, see Shankman (2018).

has been extended to depict a process whereby indigenous and imported cultural elements combine to form a new configuration, which is then seen as "of the place." Further, I suggest that problematic, bifurcated understandings of sexual literacies can still persist when there is a fixated focus on communities in "traditional" locales versus individuals in "modern" locales.

Sexual Literacies in the Contemporary Pacific: Individual and Culture in Papua New Guinea

Ever since Malinowski's early ethnography of the Trobriand Islands there has been an accumulating corpus of literature on sexualities in PNG. In earlier ethnographies, this was often rather chastely sequestered in studies of male–female relations, initiation rituals, pollution or later "gender." But, especially from 1987 when HIV emerged and later spread in epidemic waves across PNG, anthropologists, biomedical specialists, epidemiologists and public health professionals engaged in direct and detailed studies of sexual practices and knowledges across the country, which still boasts 800 distinct living languages among its 7.7 million inhabitants. From this vast literature I discuss two exemplary anthropological studies—that of Gilbert Herdt (1981, 1987) with the Sambia (a pseudonym), a large ethnic group in the Eastern Highlands, and that of Katherine Lepani with the Trobriand Islanders (2012, 2015). I choose these two examples since they offer illuminating contrasts in indigenous sexual values (ritual regulation versus pleasurable freedom), because both authors deal critically with the relation of individual and culture in sexual experiences, and because both demonstrate how local and global influences have creolized in the configuration of "glocal" sexual literacies.

Gilbert Herdt initiated research with Sambia people in 1974, a year before PNG became independent, and continued ethnographic work over several decades. He entered a region where earlier anthropologists had reported a pervasive "sexual antagonism" between men and women, endemic warfare and the celebration of male warriorhood, staunch patrilineal and patrilocal norms, pronounced male domination and profound gender segregation. The Sambia fitted this rather formal, functionalist portrait in many ways, but Herdt (1981) revealed some of the deeper philosophies underlying both quotidian and ritual sexual practices. Fundamental to both was the notion that female and male bodies were ontologically different, in both their corporeal essences and their maturation, that girls matured naturally, and more quickly, generating the potent, polluting blood of menstruation and childbirth, while boys were required to ingest semen by fellating unmarried older men over many years in rituals of initiation. This was believed to expel emasculating maternal blood and thus allow the achievement of mature masculinity and warrior capacity. This was effected through their participation in a complex series of ritual initiations starting from seven years old through to early adulthood as a married man and a father.

Herdt initially called this "ritualized homosexuality" (e.g., Herdt, 1984a, 1984b, see also Knauft, 2003) but, from his first publications he stressed that for Sambia men homoerotic practice did not entail a homosexual identity but was rather a necessary precursor to heterosexual relations and fatherhood. He later changed his depiction to "boy insemination" (Herdt, 1987, 1991). The secret, sacral character of the rites was crucial, with practices at successive stages hidden both from women and noninitiates. Pleasure and terror combined in these rites. Herdt analyzed the intimate relation between the domination of older males over younger with the forceful domination of men over women. Premarital heterosexuality was forbidden and marital sex was an anxious affair, given persisting fears of the loss of bodily fluids and of mutual pollution. This was exacerbated if men achieved the ideal of polygyny, having two or more wives. Marital sex was also ritualized, rule-bound and saturated by taboos, which prescribed the timing and duration of oral sex and later vaginal sex and its meaning and purpose (Herdt, 2019). Still, rare for anthropologists of the period, Herdt engaged both women and men in conversations about their sexual pleasure. He suggests that whereas men saw oral sex as mandatory and especially pleasurable, women preferred vaginal sex, and sometimes linked their sexual desires with the sensuality of breastfeeding (Herdt & Stoller, 1990). Herdt's ethnographic corpus is distinctive—in discussing Sambia sexual lives he writes not just of *the* Sambia, but of named individuals—men, women and an intersex person. He portrays initiation rituals not just as collective cultural performances but practices that engaged the subjectivities of individuals and indeed his own subjectivity.

In his latest publication on the Sambia, Herdt (2019) discerns the profound rupture in Sambia sexual lives over the decades since his first research. Pacification, colonization, out-migration, primary schooling and especially conversion to Seventh Day Adventist Christianity combined to catalyze the demise of the male cult, and a transformation from highly ritualized and regulated sexual practice to nonritualized, more individualistic sexual relations. The ritual homoerotic practices of the past were abandoned as sinful while heterosexual courtship, romance and new monogamous Christian marriages celebrated a modern, mutual intimacy between couples rather than anxious, tightly regulated sexual practices. Oral sex, once universal and mandatory, has largely disappeared from intimate relations. Women now have far more agency and autonomy in choosing partners and husbands and in their sexual and reproductive lives. Still, some of the fears of the past, and especially fears of mutual pollution, continue to haunt the present and were reanimated by the appearance of HIV and "sikAIDS" in the Sambia Valley, as across many regions of PNG, from the late 1980s (see also Wardlow, 2006, 2014).

Islands of Love, Islands of Risk (2012) by Katherine Lepani is expressly a study of Trobriand Islanders in the context of that HIV epidemic. The indigenous configuration of gender, sexuality and reproduction is in stark contrast to that of the Sambia. Although Lepani challenges many aspects of Malinowski's depiction of the Trobriands, she also suggests similarities and continuities—women's expansive agency exercised through the value and practice of matriliny, the celebration of sexuality for both female and male adolescents, the pursuit of mutual pleasure in marriage and the mutability of marriage.

Lepani extended her own relationship to the Trobriand community, initially as an in-law, to that of a researcher concerned with questions of public health and sexuality. She is, like Herdt, intensely reflexive about her own positionality. Trobrianders, like most people in the Milne Bay Province of PNG, were exposed to diverse colonial agencies—traders and labor recruiters, planters, officials from the colonizing powers of Britain and Australia and Fijian Christian missionaries from the late nineteenth century.

This history of colonial influences occurred decades prior to indigenous peoples in the Highlands of PNG who first witnessed European incursions from the late 1920s and 1930s. Trobrianders earlier converted to mainstream denominations—Methodism and Catholicism; and although there have been recent reconversions to more evangelical Christian churches, there is not the same pervasive sense of a sharp rupture between the indigenous and the exogenous, the non-Christian and the Christian, as witnessed for the Sambia. Christianity has been profoundly indigenized in the Trobriands and there has not been the stark revolution in gender relations and sexuality which Herdt (2019) discerns for the Sambia. Emblematic of this continuity, is how introduced cloth that is used to make modern Christian clothes has been incorporated alongside indigenous banana leaf fiber bundles and skirts created by women for distribution in complex mortuary ceremonies in which women play a central role (Lepani, 2017).

The "islands of love" label, generated by Malinowski's research and many other foreign observers is, though locally criticized for its exoticism, still central to Trobrianders' own and other Papua New Guineans' perceptions of the region. The celebration of consensual and pleasurable sexuality, fundamental to forming and sustaining social relations in the Trobriands, embraces sexual freedom in adolescence, mutual erotic pleasure and fertility for heterosexual couples (but not homosexual couples) and comparative ease in ending marriages. All of this continues to be core to Trobrianders' sense of their cultural distinction.

But, with the advent of HIV in PNG from 1987, the sexual cultural distinction of the Trobriands became a cause for concern since it was perceived as a problematic "hot spot" in the public health response to the epidemic. Lepani's nuanced ethnography (2012) reveals how Trobrianders themselves interpreted HIV—how they tried to grapple with the dissonances between an approach to sexuality, which stressed danger and death rather than pleasure and fertility, between an approach to sexuality focused on individuals at risk rather than relational persons. She clearly demonstrates how Trobrianders' understanding of HIV was profoundly influenced by preexisting ideas of the body, of health and illness, of gender and sexuality. But, rather than a bifurcated world in which Trobriand sexual literacy focuses on shared collective norms, relationality and reciprocity, and the introduced regime of biomedical public health in the context of HIV focuses on individuals, Lepani argues that notions of relationality and of individual autonomy are equally indigenous (see also Jolly, 2018; Wardlow, 2006). Her article, aptly titled "I am Still a Young Girl if I Want," offers an analysis of the life stories of two young women (2015). It shows how their sense of individual agency, of an autonomous mind (*nanola*), is central to both their narratives and to their embodied social relations, evincing "how the power of love magic transfers agency from one individual to another, and how individual assertions and acts are ultimately expressions of situated relationality" (2015, p. 51).

Unorthodox

Finally, I turn to the fictionalized life story of another young woman that has been globally circulating via Netflix. Here I explore further the question of how the relationship between collective and individual sexual literacies is often orchestrated as a bifurcation between the "traditional" community and the "modern" individual, breaking free.

The Netflix series *Unorthodox* (Karolinska & Schrader, 2020), released to critical and popular acclaim in March 2020, is a fictional recreation of a memoir by Deborah Feldman (2012) who grew up in the Satmar community of ultraorthodox Hasidic Jews in Brooklyn, New York. After an arranged marriage at 17 and the birth of her first child, a son, at 19, Feldman sensed her future trajectory was oppressive and, in 2010, "escaped" the community. The Satmar community was founded by refugees from the Jewish population of the town of Satmar in Hungary, many of whom were survivors of Nazi genocide and the Holocaust. Although their community is but a few decades old, they articulate a sense of embattled survival, connecting the Holocaust to the ancient persecution of Jews by the Pharaohs of Egypt. They speak Yiddish, strictly adhere to many orthodox rituals and daily practices of Judaism, the strict segregation of men and women, strong gender-based sartorial codes and patterns of early, arranged marriage and heterosexual relations dominated by ideas of fulfilling male desires (the husband is the "king" of the bedroom) and ultimately ensuring high fertility (given the history of pogroms and genocidal attacks on Jewish people). Women are celebrated first as chaste and pious girls and then as faithful and fertile mothers and are denied access to public education and public libraries and to communication with the cosmopolitan culture of New York which surrounds them.

Esty (Shira Haas), the central female character in a story based on Feldman's own experience, is "different." Wedded at 17 to an equally naïve young man Yanky (Amit Rahav) she is struggling to deal with the requirements of becoming a wife and a mother. In their elaborate, joyous wedding ceremony she is dressed in a shimmering white dress and celebrated, but as a married woman she must have her head shaved and wear a *sheitel*, a wig or a cloth covering. Her daily wardrobe is modest dresses and suits, her nocturnal wardrobe a coverall nightgown. She must succumb to the sexual desires of her husband. It seems neither she, growing up with her grandparents, nor he, growing up with his parents, has learnt how to cultivate mutual sensual pleasure or sexual intimacy. Scenes of their first and subsequent attempts at sex are as excruciating to watch as they are for Esty and Yanky to suffer. No kissing, no cuddling, no foreplay—just a nervous young husband mounting his young wife who is grimacing in pain. Her pain and hurt is exacerbated by the intrusions of Yanky's mother urging her to please her son, and suggestions that Esty can cure her "vaginismus" by inserting ever larger phallic sex aids. Ultimately, she bears the pain and Yanky climaxes with an orgasm that leaves him momentarily fulfilled and her pregnant. But before she can confide her news to him, Yanky declares he wants a divorce, since their marriage has failed to be fulfilling or fertile. She decides to leave.

After pawning her jewelry, including her marriage ring, Esty flees to Berlin, where it is revealed, her estranged mother Leah (Alex Reid), like herself, was married young but to an alcoholic, abusive and mentally deficient husband (a backstory based on Feldman's own experience). After Esty was born, she resisted continuing the union, was banished by the community and Esty was then taken from her and brought up by her grandparents. In Berlin, Esty, suffering poverty and homelessness, is adopted by a group of young musicians studying at a conservatorium, a cosmopolitan group from all around the world. They are engaged in consensual pleasurable relationships—heterosexual and homosexual. On a fine summer day, Esty goes with her young musician friends to a lake nearby; here she immerses herself and floats in untrammeled freedom in the water. Her wig comes off to reveal her shaved head underneath—a fashionable hairstyle of the period but also echoing images of Jewish people in Nazi concentration camps. Her relocation to Berlin is a cruel paradox—escaping her own personal trauma she is reentering the space where the greatest collective trauma for the Jewish people was devised and orchestrated.

The rabbi in New York instructs her husband to travel to Berlin with a sleazy companion Moishe (Jeff Wilbusch) to bring her and her baby back. They hole up in the Westin Hotel and try to hide the long, curly sidelocks of their orthodox hair styles with American-style baseball caps. Their long black coats are harder to divest. Ultimately, through a stealthy break-in at Esty's mother's apartment, Moishe tracks her down to the conservatorium where she is scheduled to perform an entrance audition as a pianist. She switches to voice in the midst of her performance, breaking the rules both of the conservatorium and more profoundly the injunction against Orthodox women singing in public, with a poignant performance of the wedding song in Yiddish. This is witnessed not just by staff and students at the conservatorium but also by her mother, Leah, and her estranged husband, Yanky. She agrees to visit him at his hotel. He pleads for her to come back to him, even cuts his curly sidelocks and offers her novel freedoms. But in a moving, tearful scene, she declares that it is "Too late, too late." *Unorthodox* ends without a sense of closure but the hopeful prospect of support from new friends as well as her mother when Esty herself becomes a mother.

Powerful as this drama is—it effectively replays not just the drama of Feldman's own life but a hegemonic opposition between a hyper-regulated and oppressive insular tradition and an open and free individualist modernity. The sexual freedom that Esty experiences in Berlin is, in my view, not just an individual expression but a collective sexual culture, shared by her newfound community of friends. This contrast between two forms of sexual literacy, a traditional culture versus a modern individual has often been situated in the Global South versus the Global North. As the research by Herdt and Lepani suggests, this bifurcation is deeply problematic. As we have seen, the values of collective relationality and individual autonomy are co-present in the contemporary sexual lives of Trobrianders, and the heteronormative modernity of Sambia people in the twenty-first century, though portrayed as a "choice" for a more individualist, modern form of sexuality, is similarly saturated with collective cultural, Christian expectations.

As anthropologist Bruce Knauft (2003, p. 3) suggested in reflecting on his ethnography with the Gebusi people of PNG, there is a great danger in constructing past "traditional" sexual practices as fixed and inflexible and "modern" sexual practices as fluid and flexible. There can be a tyranny in the celebration of individuated choice not just in the commodity cultures of late capitalism but in the inculcation of modern sexual literacies.

So, looking critically at sexualities across the world today entails hard empirical and theoretical work to transcend the problematic opposition between a fixed and inflexible traditional culture and a fluid and flexible individualist modernity, an opposition that has suffused much European sexual science for more than a century. New models that bifurcate our world—between the Global North and the Global South—can perpetuate earlier imperial oppositions between the civilized and the savage, the modern and the traditional. The complex relation between individual and collective experience in sexual and reproductive life needs to be witnessed in all places and all times in human history. There have been dynamic flows between sexual knowledge and practice in different locales throughout human history, but these have intensified with the hyper-connectivity of contemporary digital and virtual worlds. Thus, understanding and analyzing sexualities anywhere today has to acknowledge the interpenetration of local and global elements in diverse "glocal" situations. This volume amply reveals the diversity of glocal sexual literacies and attests to the critical importance of situated analysis.

References

Chiang, H. H. (2009). Double alterity and the emergence of sexuality as a global possibility. *e-pisteme*, *2*(1), 33–52.

Feldman, D. (2012). *Unorthodox: The scandalous rejection of my Hasidic roots. A memoir.* New York: Simon and Schuster.

Foucault, M. (1974). *Histoire de la sexualité 1.: La volonté de savoir.* Paris: Editions Gallimard.

Freeman, D. (1983). *Margaret mead and Samoa: The making and unmaking of an anthropological myth.* Boston, MA: Harvard University Press.

Freud, S. (2002). *Civilization and its discontents.* London: Penguin. (Originally published in 1930.)

Fuechtner, V., Douglas, E. H., & Ryan, M. J. (Eds.). (2017). *A global history of sexual science, 1880–1960.* Berkeley: University of California Press.

Herdt, G. H. (1981). *Guardians of the flutes: Idioms of masculinity.* New York: McGraw Hill.

Herdt, G. H. (Ed.). (1984a). *Ritualized homosexuality in Melanesia.* Berkeley: University of California Press.

Herdt, G. H. (1984b). Introduction. In G. Herdt (Ed.), *Ritualized homosexuality in Melanesia* (pp. 1–81). Berkeley: University of California Press.

Herdt, G. H. (1987). *The Sambia: Ritual and gender in New Guinea.* Fort Worth, TX: Holt Rinehart and Winston.

Herdt, G. H. (1991) Representations of homosexuality in traditional societies: An essay on cultural ontology and historical comparison. *Journal of the History of Sexuality*, *2*(2), 603–632.

Herdt, G. H. (2019). Intimate consumption and new sexual subjects among the Sambia of Papua New Guinea. *Oceania*, *89*(1), 36–67.

Herdt, G. H., & Stoller, R. J. (1990). *Intimate communications: Erotics and the study of culture.* New York: Columbia University Press.

Jolly, M. (2001). Damming the rivers of milk? Fertility, sexuality, and modernity in Melanesia and Amazonia. In T. Gregor and D. Tuzin (Eds.), *Gender in Amazonia and Melanesia: An exploration of the comparative method* (pp. 175–206). Berkeley: University of California Press.

Jolly, M. (2008). The South in *Southern Theory*: Antipodean reflections on the Pacific. *Australian Humanities Review*, *44*(March), 75–100. Retrieved from http://epress.anu.edu.au/ahr/044/pdf/essay05.pdf

Jolly, M. (2012). Women of the East, women of the West: Region and race, gender and sexuality on Cook's Voyages. In K. Fullagar (Ed.), *The Atlantic world in the antipodes* (pp. 2–32). Newcastle: Cambridge Scholars Press.

Jolly, M. (2018). Gender and personhood (individual, dividual). In H. Callan (Ed.), *International encyclopedia of anthropology* (pp. 2540–2549). Hoboken, NJ: Wiley Blackwell.

Jolly, M., & Lenore, M. (1997). Introduction: Sites of desire/economies of pleasure in Asia and the Pacific. In L. Manderson & M. Jolly (Eds.), *Sites of desire, economies of pleasure: Sexualities in Asia and the Pacific* (pp. 1–26, notes 293–296). Chicago: University of Chicago Press.

Karolinska A. (Producer), & Schrader, M. (Director). (March 2020). *Unorthodox* [Television Series]. Studio Airlift, Real Film Berlin Gmbh.

Knauft, B. (2003). What ever happened to ritualized homosexuality? *Annual Review of Sex Research, 14,* 137–159.

Leck, R. (2017). Westermarck's Morocco: The epistemic politics of cultural anthropology and sexual science. In V. Fuechtner, D. E. Haynes, & R. M. Jones (Eds.), *A global history of sexual science, 1880–1960* (pp. 70–96). Berkeley: University of California Press.

Lepani, K. (2012). *Islands of love, Islands of risk.* Nashville, TN: Vanderbilt University Press.

Lepani, K. (2015). "I am still a young girl if I want": Relational personhood and individual autonomy in the Trobriand Islands. *Oceania, 85*(1), 51–62.

Lepani, K. (2017). *Doba* and ephemeral durability: The enduring material value of women's work in the Trobriand regenerative economy. In A. Hermkens & K. Lepani (Eds.), *Sinuous objects: Revaluing women's wealth in the contemporary Pacific* (pp. 37–59). Canberra, Australia: ANU Press.

Malinowski, B. (1927). *Sex and repression in savage society.* Cleveland: Meridian.

Malinowski, B. (1929). *The sexual lives of savages in North-western Melanesia.* New York: Harcourt, Brace and World.

Mead, M. (1927). *Coming of age in Samoa.* New York: William Morrow.

Shankman, P. (2009). *The trashing of Margaret Mead: Anatomy of an anthropological controversy.* Madison: University of Wisconsin Press.

Shankman, P. (2018). The Mead-Freeman controversy. In H. Callan (Ed.), *International encyclopedia of anthropology.* Hoboken, NJ: Wiley Blackwell.

Wardlow, H. (2006). *Wayward women: Sexuality and agency in a New Guinea society.* Berkeley: University of California Press.

Wardlow, H. (2014). Paradoxical intimacies: The Christian creation of the Huli domestic sphere. In H. Choi & M. Jolly (Eds.), *Divine domesticities: Christian paradoxes in Asia and the Pacific* (pp. 325–344). Canberra: ANU Press.

Chapter 23

SEXUAL RISKS IN MIGRATIONS TO REACH WESTERN EUROPE

Lynellyn D. Long

People flee persecution, conflict, chronic unemployment and famine. During their migrations, they are exposed to sexual violence and exploitation. Young adults, LGBTI (Lesbian, gay, bisexual, transgender and intersex) persons and unaccompanied children are particularly at risk of sexual abuse and exploitation.

The 70.8 million people forcibly displaced (UNHCR, 2018a) remain trapped in some of the world's most volatile conflicts;[1] inhabit the poorest regions;[2] and are directly impacted by climate change.[3] Many will not obtain asylum but those who do characteristically contribute to their host communities even when discriminated against and rejected. Many perform essential labor and services in their host societies and economies.

While on the move, refugees and migrants form glocal communities that reflect origin and local, host communities and interactions with state and international actors. State and international responses to these new glocal communities vary from neglect or containment to safe haven and asylum. How glocal communities evolve is shaped by local relationships and by larger state and international forces that determine access to status, security and resources. This essay focuses on the forms of sexual- and gender-based violence and exploitation that refugees and migrants face in uprooting and flight, transit and resettlement, and the sexual literacies required to protect these glocal communities. Specific examples cross ethnic and national groups migrating from Africa, the Middle East and Eastern Europe to Western Europe.

Uprooting and Flight

In uprooting and flight, families may become separated. Children, constituting some 52 percent of refugees (UNHCR, 2018a), young women traveling on their own, and

---

1 Over half are from regions of conflict: Syria (6.3 million), Afghanistan (2.6 million) and South Sudan (2.4 million) (MacGregor, 2019).
2 "Developing countries" host 85 percent of the refugees and the least developed countries provide asylum to one-third of the world's total asylum seekers (UNHCR, 2017).
3 The impact of climate change on uprooting and conflict is evidenced in the Sahel and one of the stressors in Syria's conflict was extreme drought between 2006 and 2009.

those escaping political, personal or ethnic persecution, are targeted by smugglers and traffickers with promises of reaching a safe haven.

Traditional gender hierarchies and primogeniture in face of resource scarcity have intensified pressures on a second son, "lesser" wives' children or daughters, who have less status, to migrate. With declines in cash crops or grazing lands in rural areas, only the eldest son may inherit the farm or livestock herds. Daughters may be expected to bring a bride price or requiring a dowry that the family cannot afford, to leave home. Traditional marriage and inheritance practices in face of resource scarcity are a source of local conflict, causing youth, especially young women, to migrate.

LGBTI persons in parts of Africa and the Middle East, face risks of violence and exploitation from families, communities and governments. As MacGregor (2019, para. 15) reports, "In at least ten countries worldwide, homosexuality and transsexuality are punishable with the death penalty. In many other countries the sentence is long-term imprisonment." The European Parliament (2018, p. 2) reports that same-sex acts are illegal in 72 countries and punishable by death in 8. Sexual orientation or gender also increases the risks of sexual abuse and violence during migration. LGBTI refugees seek asylum in Western Europe to live safely again. However, they also suffer the trauma and loss from knowing that they may never be able to return home.

Married women migrate to escape domestic abuse and violence. They may take children with them or be forced to leave the children behind as a condition of leaving. Girls report being forced into an early marriage for a bride price or without the financial means for a dowry, trafficked to support families back home. They may flee a forced marriage to escape abuse and enslavement, to continue their education and/or because they do not want to be a lesser wife to an older man.

Young women, who suffer sexual abuse and rape in their communities, workplaces and conflict, may be stigmatized and blamed rather than their perpetrators. They are forced to leave to avoid shame or at worst, escape honor killings. Women fleeing such situations report that when they reach their destinations, they are still expected to send remittances for children's and parents' care.

Children may be uprooted for enslavement. Destitute parents, who sold their 4-year-old daughter, believed that they were giving her an opportunity to attend school. On the pretext of furthering the girl's education, an aunt trafficked the child to the UK to work for her son's household. Regularly beaten, the child was, at times, denied food so as to do what her employers required. She was also raped by the husband and his friends. Later on, she might have been sold to a brothel, but the son's wife put her out on the streets.

Young men and women, orphaned or abandoned by families, are at increased risk of slavery and trafficking. Growing up in orphanages in Eastern Europe, young women report being turned out on the streets at 18 years of age to fend for themselves. They are easy prey for traffickers, gang members and armed militia. A young Roma woman reported being beaten and forced to beg and provide sexual favors for powerful male clan leaders. Some were sold to local brothels or to traffickers from Western Europe.

In conflict, sexuality is weaponized by acts of rape, sexual slavery and forced prostitution, pregnancy and sterilizations. The Rome Statute of the International Criminal Court (1998) defined and established jurisdiction over acts of genocide, crimes against humanity, war crimes and acts of aggression. Sexual violence in conflict is committed to deny the humanity and human rights of one's enemy and of the other person. Rape, forced sterilization and sexual slavery, as evidenced in Bosnia-Herzegovina, South Sudan, Democratic Republic of the Congo, are also used to humiliate and disempower men and to destroy another ethnic, whole communities, or national group.

Sexual violence and abuse are endemic during uprooting and flight. Young adults who survive rape and torture, may face dishonor and shame and the risk of honor killings from male relatives. Those who have endured these experiences acknowledge that they may never return home. The stigma can be so terrible for young men that they rarely discuss what happened. Women may not wish to raise children who are the outcome of rape; and many of these children are abandoned by their home communities as well.

The Journeys

Refugees and migrants form glocal communities in well-organized, villages, towns and enclosed camps; loosely organized, urban shanty towns; and prisons, brothels and labor camps. These new communities often put strains on surrounding, local populations to provide basic services, water and sanitation and infrastructure. In transit communities, refugees and migrants may also wait years, even generations, in limbo for a "durable solution": to return safely home again, to be integrated into the local population and/or to be accepted for permanent resettlement.

The majority of the worlds' refugees (60%) and internally displaced persons (80%) live in urban areas (UNHCR, 2018a). Yet, international humanitarian assistance is largely provided to maintain people in camps and settlements. In urban settlements, interethnic conflicts are common in glocal communities. Urban refugees and migrants report increased trafficking, sexual abuse, the lack of security and lawlessness, where urban, unemployed youth gangs prey upon children, young adults and LGBTI persons. Funding and services to address sexual violence against refugees and migrants in urban settlements are limited to nonexistent. Many are also reluctant to seek such services as they then face hostility, stigma and danger from within their own communities.

In internationally and state-organized refugee and migrant settlements, young adults also report incidents of sexual abuse and violence from armed groups. In a North African settlement, a group of young women explained how best to handle threats and attacks at night. The women initially call the local community police hotline. If attackers are armed, the local police, who did not bear arms, can do little. Next, they call the UN Border Relief Operation emergency hotline. Although UNBRO may patrol settlement perimeters 24/7, they lack the force capacity to confront armed militia, particularly in camps with tens and hundreds of thousands. Not speaking the local language compounds UNBRO's difficulties in responding to situations. They are satisfied if they can arrest and temporarily detain perpetrators. The young women's final course of action is to obtain a medical exam and rape kit at the local health clinic. Given community stigma, men who are sexually violated rarely reported such incidents. Both men and women survivors are also afraid to report the perpetrators, given the revenge that could follow.

Where early marriage is still practiced, girls and young women report being forced by fathers and camp leaders to leave school to marry an older man. After the marriage, the girl or young woman may be expected to remain in the camp to establish a source of food and services to support the husband, fighting back home and an extended family. Young women, married off to refugee or migrant men in urban areas, found that they were immediately expected to bring in income and forced to sell sexual services. As the girls in several camps and settlements observed, education is critical to their future survival. However, once married off, they could only hope to escape an unwanted relationship or be released by the husband from further obligation.

Humanitarian aid workers and peacekeepers may also be perpetrators of sexual exploitation and abuse (SEA). In 2002, UNHCR and Save the Children (SCF), UK, found 67 allegations of sexual exploitation of refugee children, committed by workers from 40 aid agencies and 9 peacekeeping forces in Liberia, Guinea and Sierra Leone (House of Commons, 2018, p. 9). In the ensuing years, SEA offenses were committed by: (1) UN peacekeepers and aid workers in the Democratic Republic of Congo aid workers in Kenya, Namibia and Thailand (2007–8); (3) peacekeepers and aid workers in the Haiti, Cote d'Ivoire, and South Sudan camps (2008); (4) French peacekeepers in Central African Republic (2015); and (5) aid workers against girls and women in Syria (2018).[4] In February 2018, *the Times* reported that the Oxfam UK country director and staff in Haiti had paid local young women for sex (House of Commons, 2018, p. 8). The UK Government, esta blishing a "zero tolerance" policy, recommended better coordination of international "protection against sexual exploitation and abuse" (PSEA; House of Commons, 2018, p. 6). In November 2018, the international community adopted its "Inter-Agency Standing Committee (IASC) Champions Strategy" to hold perpetrators to account and prevent them from moving to other humanitarian and aid organizations (UN OCHA, 2020).

Despite the documented abuses in organized camps and settlements, the EU's current policy is to address asylum claims offshore. Following agreements in 2016, Western European governments transferred funds to Turkey, and other countries, to hold migrants and refugees; and to force people to file refugee and asylum applications from outside the EU (Henley, 2018). A refugee or migrant today is most likely to settle semipermanently in Lebanon, Jordan, Turkey and Uganda. These four countries host the highest proportion of refugees to their local populations (Wood, 2019). With international development assistance cutbacks, local communities in some of the poorest cities are also bearing a major financial burden for hosting migrants and refugees.

---

4   The House of Commons (2018) cites: UNHCR and Save the Children UK (2002); the Independent (2004); Shotton, A. (2006). UN Department of Peacekeeping Operations; Humanitarian Partnership (2007); Czaky, C. (2008); Save the Children. (2015). Syria GBV Focal Point, UNFPA (2018).

Reception

The 1951 Treaty of Paris was intended not only to restructure the European economies into common markets but also to prevent another war in Europe. However, current nativist movements signal a new era of hostility toward peoples of different ethnic, religious, racial, and national background and sexual orientation. Hungary, Italy and Austria with nationalist parties or coalitions are refusing new asylum seekers; and anti-immigrant rhetoric is increasing in the UK, Denmark and Germany (Human Rights Watch, 2019). Mainstream European parties are also promising migration controls and quotas as part of election platforms (Human Rights Watch, 2019). The current level of intolerance is fragmenting the EU itself and could end in conflict.

Following the post-World War II returns and until the Syrian conflict, Europe did not take large numbers of refugees, displaced or asylum seekers. During the height of the Syrian crisis in 2015, Chancellor Merkel opened the countries' borders. In the ensuing years, Germany accepted some 1.3 million refugees and asylum seekers from several war-torn countries. Although Merkel's acceptance could have brought down her Government, the Christian Democratic Union (CDU) party maintained its lead even after: (1) the Berlin Christmas market terrorist attack; (2) the mass sexual harassment of women at New Year's by men of North African/Arab descent at Cologne railway station; and (3) intense, internal debates on German national identity (Mohdin, 2017).

For those fleeing repression, persecution and gender-based violence, Western Europe still remained a safe haven. In 2011, the Council of Europe had adopted and signed the Istanbul Convention, ratified by most Member States except Bulgaria (European Parliament, 2018). The Convention provides a legal framework for preventing and combating domestic violence and violence against women. The European Convention on Human Rights includes LGBTI rights. The EU has also initiated a UN Declaration for worldwide decriminalization of homosexuality (European Parliament, 2018). EU law recognizes sexual orientation as grounds for discrimination (e.g., in the workplace) but still does not cover discrimination related to social protection, healthcare, education and access to goods and services. Three EU Directives—Free Movement, Family Reunification and Qualification (the granting of asylum on the basis of belonging to a particular social group with reference to sexual orientation and gender identity)—protect LGBTI refugees, migrants and asylum seekers (European Parliament, 2018, p. 5). In June 2018, the EU Court of Justice ruled that same-sex spouses of EU citizens are entitled to free movement in any member state, even if a member state's laws (e.g., Romania) prohibit same-sex marriages (European Parliament, 2018).

A 2015 EU Survey of 93,000 LGBT persons found that 58 percent versus 46 percent in 2012 reported discrimination based on sexual orientation/gender identity; and almost half reported personal discrimination or harassment in the previous year (European Parliament, 2018). Young people (57%), Lesbian women (55%) and poorer LGBT persons (52%) predominated in reporting discrimination (European Parliament, 2018). As the EU Parliamentary Report (2018) acknowledged, verbal and physical attacks have occurred in all member states. LGBTI asylum seekers who may fear arrest and deportation are unlikely to report these incidents to local authorities or even participate in surveys.

In Western Europe, increased levels of intolerance are leading to the closing of asylum. Survivors of sexual abuse, trafficking and persecution may currently wait years for cases to be considered. During that time, they cannot legally work or access public services, education and housing. Depending on extended families, immigrant communities and charities, many work online or in informal economies, which if discovered can lead to the denial of asylum. New glocal communities are formed in homeless shelters, on the streets and in transport stations. In limbo, they face increased risks of being sexually abused and exploited.

Those whose asylum claims are denied, face risks of being required to pay bribes to avoid being re-trafficked, imprisoned and even killed.[5] If they came to Europe as young children, they may no longer have family or communities to which they can return. LGBTI returnees risk violence in returning and if they go underground, increasing intolerance from religious groups, ethnic communities and states such as Austria and Hungary.

Despite the cold climate, refugees and immigrants bring resources to destination communities (Maxmen, 2018). They continue to benefit from and contribute skills and critical labor to Western Europe; and often, remittances, new ways of thinking and development to their origin communities.

Conclusions

Refugees and migrants encounter sexual risks at each stage of their migration. Initially, they may flee sexual- and gender-based violence. Children and young adults are sold to traffickers and enslaved. Because of a sexual identity or orientation, some face state-sanctioned violence from families, communities and governments. Women suffering spousal abuse flee to save their lives and their children's.

During flight, refugees and migrants often have to depend on smugglers and traffickers. If they reach a temporary camp or settlement, they face new sexual risks from warring militia groups. Refugees and migrant sexualities are weaponized by armed groups and militia; they may become commodities of smugglers and traffickers; and as LGBTI persons, they risk being harmed and killed. They cannot count on local police, international community protection or traditional support systems. In adapting to local norms and communities, they may adopt new beliefs and practices about gender and sexuality, which put them in conflict with origin communities.

Those fortunate enough to reach intended destinations, continue to be exploited and abused. If trafficked, they are forced to provide sexual services for employers and clients. Receiving asylum, they may be treated as outsiders even when providing essential

---

5   In air deportations, migrants are hand and foot cuffed and accompanied by police. They are met by government officials, who may be in the pay of traffickers and taken to a nearby brothel. They may also have to bribe local officials to avoid imprisonment.

goods and services to communities. Interventions at each stage of migration are needed to safeguard people's sexual rights. For refugees and migrants, sexual literacy requires finding ways to protect their rights in different glocal communities and situations; and for humanitarian workers and peacekeepers, when and how to respond effectively to prevent sexual abuse and violence.

References

British Broadcasting Corporation (BBC). (2016, March 4). Migrant crisis: Migration to Europe explained in seven charts. *BBC News*. https://www.bbc.com/news/world-europe-34131911

British Broadcasting Corporation (BBC). (2019, November 13). Europe and right-wing nationalism: A country-by-country guide. *BBC News*. https://www.bbc.co.uk/news/world-europe-36130006

Development Initiatives (2019). *Global humanitarian assistance report 2019* [PDF file]. Retrieved from https://reliefweb.int/sites/reliefweb.int/files/resources/GHA%20report%202019_0.pdf

European Asylum Support Office. (EASO; 2019, October). *Latest Asylum trends*. https://www.easo.europa.eu/latest-asylum-trends

European Parliament. (2018). *The rights of LGBTI people in the European Union* [PDF file]. Retrieved from http://www.europarl.europa.eu/RegData/etudes/BRIE/2018/621877/EPRS_BRI(2018)621877_EN.pdf

Fisher, M., & Bennhold, K. (2018, July 3). Germany's Europe-shaking political crisis over migrants, explained. *New York Times*. https://www.nytimes.com/2018/07/03/world/europe/germany-political-crisis.html

Henly, J. (2018, June 27). EU migration crisis: What are the key issues? *World News, The Guardian*. https://www.theguardian.com/world/2018/jun/27/eu-migration-crisis-what-are-the-issues

Henriksen, R. (2019). Libya: Lawlessness and armed groups. In S. Jesperson, R. Henriksen, A.-M. Barry, & M. Jones (Eds.), *Human trafficking: An organized crime* (pp. 51–54). London: C. Hurst.

House of Commons, International Development Committee. (2018, July 23). *Sexual exploitation and abuse in the aid sector* (Eighth Report of Session 2017–19). Retrieved from https://publications.parliament.uk/pa/cm201719/cmselect/cmintdev/840/840.pdf

Human Rights Watch. (2019). *European Union: Events of 2018*. World Report 2019. Retrieved from https://www.hrw.org/world-report/2019/country-chapters/european-union#b742e7

International Criminal Court. (1998, July 17). *Rome Statute of the International Criminal Court* [PDF File]. Retrieved from https://www.icc-cpi.int/resource-library/documents/rs-eng.pdf

MacGregor, M. (2019, February 13). *Changing journeys: Migrant routes to Europe.* InfoMigrants. https://www.infomigrants.net/en/post/15005/changing-journeys-migrant-routes-to-europe

Maxmen, A. (2018, June 20). *Migrants and refugees are good for economies*. Nature. https://www.nature.com/articles/d41586-018-05507-0

The Migration Observatory. (2019, November 8). *Migration to the UK: Asylum and resettled refugees*. The Migration Observatory, University of Oxford. https://migrationobservatory.ox.ac.uk/resources/briefings/migration-to-the-uk-asylum/

Mohdin, A. (2017, September 22). *How Germany took in one million refugees but dodged a populist uprising*. Quartz. https://qz.com/1076820/german-election-how-angela-merkel-took-in-one-million-refugees-and-avoided-a-populist-upset/

United Nations High Commissioner for Refugees. (2014). *Text of the 1954 convention relating to the status of stateless persons* [PDF file]. Retrieved from https://www.unhcr.org/ibelong/wp-content/uploads/1954-Convention-relating-to-the-Status-of-Stateless-Persons_ENG.pdf

United Nations High Commissioner for Refugees. (2018a). *Global trends: Forced displacement in 2018*. https://www.unhcr.org/globaltrends2018/

United Nations High Commissioner for Refugees. (2018b). *Population statistics—Data*. http://popstats.unhcr.org/en/overview

United Nations High Commissioner for Refugees. (2019, June 17). *UNHCR welcomes meaningful new UK commitment to refugee resettlement*. https://www.unhcr.org/uk/news/press/2019/6/5d07830e4/unhcr-welcomes-meaningful-new-uk-commitment-refugee-resettlement.html

United Nations Office for the Coordinator of Humanitarian Affairs (OCHA). (2020). *Protection against sexual exploitation and abuse (PSEA)*. https://www.unocha.org/protection-against-sexual-exploitation-and-abuse-psea.

Wood, J. (2019, March 19). *These countries are home to the highest proportion of refugees in the world*. World Economic Forum. https://www.weforum.org/agenda/2019/03/mena-countries-in-the-middle-east-have-the-highest-proportion-of-refugees-in-the-world/

Chapter 24

IMPACT AND EXPANSION OF SOCIAL NETWORKING ON SEXUAL AND GENDER-DIVERSE YOUNG PEOPLE'S SEXUAL LITERACY

Alexander L. Farquhar-Leicester

During the nineteenth and twentieth centuries, individuals who self-identified as lesbian, gay, bisexual, queer (LGBQ), transgender and gender-diverse (TGD) did not have the opportunity, nor the capability, to engage with or utilize social networking sites (SNSs) and applications. Instead, the exploration of their identity and association with other sexual and gender-diverse individuals was often limited to brick-and-mortar locations that were classified as *queer* (Chauncey, 1994; D'Augelli & Patterson, 1995). Myriad different brick-and-mortar sites—such as restaurants, bars, coffee shops, clubs, theaters, parks, streets, bath houses, neighborhoods and others—functioned as the social spheres where sexual and gender-diverse people could develop robust social relations including communication, companionship and romance (Savin-Williams, 1996). In some places, such as New York City, Los Angeles and San Francisco, California, entire urban ghettos served as queer meccas—dense city spaces that supported people with diverse sexual orientations and gender identities (Meeker, 2005).

However, as the availability of the Internet grew in the mid-to-late 1990s, individuals with diverse sexual orientations and gender identities suddenly gained access to an immense amount of information, media and connectivity, which provided new ways of communicating with, learning from and meeting others that transcended boundaries of time and space (Boyd, 2008). Now, Internet use is nearly ubiquitous among adults in the United States, with 90 percent of people aged 18 to 29 using it in 2019. Among adults, YouTube and Facebook are the most commonly used SNS, with 72 percent using the former and 69 percent using the latter. Nearly 95 percent of adolescents in the United States use a smartphone. SNSs and applications are also relevant to the lives of adolescents in the United States, with YouTube (85%), Instagram (72%) and Snapchat (69%) being the most commonly used sites and applications among this population (Pew Research Center, 2019).

Notably, the availability and use of SNSs and applications have proliferated during the last two decades (Manago, 2014). Boyd and Ellison (2007) define SNSs as an Internet-based service that allow users to "(1) construct a public or semi-public profile within a bounded system, (2) articulate a list of other users with whom they share a connection, and (3) view and traverse their list of connections and those by others within the system" (p. 211). Applications (e.g., apps) refer to software programs that run specific SNSs on a mobile device, tablet or wristwatch. Since the emergence of the Internet, people have become interested in how virtual landscape—especially mass media, social media and SNSs and applications—impact people's lives. This essay will focus on the various uses and affordances of SNSs and applications among LGBQ and TGD youth and young adults, while outlining and proposing the various ways that such virtual landscapes are catalysts for developing and furthering sexual literacy. Since digital media use is only increasing by the year (Pew Research Center, 2019), the future impact of SNSs and applications will also be discussed.

LGBQ Youth and Young Adults

Research has shown that SNSs and applications have become pivotal for the identity development processes of LGBQ youth and young adults (Craig & McInroy, 2014; Fox & Ralston, 2016; Hiller, Mitchell, & Ybarrra, 2012). SNSs and applications have served as a vehicle for LGBQ youth and adults to virtually explore, develop and narrate their identities and lives virtually among like-minded and/or similar others. SNSs and applications can be used by LGBQ youth as a way to search, find and share sexual health information (Bargh & McKenna, 2004; Flanders, Pragg, Dobinson, & Logie, 2017; Magee, Bigelow, DeHaan, & Mustanski, 2012). This exploration and exchange of information engenders broader sexual health consumption and knowledge (Bargh & McKenna, 2004).

SNSs and applications have enabled and spurred LGBQ youth and young adult's social learning, traditional learning, experiential learning, teaching and obtaining sexual health information (Craig & McInroy, 2014; Fox & Ralston, 2016; Hiller et al., 2012; McInroy, Craig, & Leung, 2019). For example, LGBQ youth and young adults use SNSs and applications to acquire information about sex and sexual orientations as well as to identify, communicate with and thus learn from role models (i.e., friends, peers, celebrities) (Fox & Ralston, 2016). What's more, young LGBTQ college students may use more specific SNSs and applications geared toward sexual encounters and dating, such as Grindr and Tinder, to explore and understand, to hook up and to express specific sexual thoughts, feelings and desires (Gudelunas, 2012; Farquhar-Leicester & Polen-Petit, 2020).

Safety and anonymity are especially important considerations for these populations, as not all LGBQ youth and young adults are comfortable—or even able, for various safety reasons—to be visible in or self-disclosing within more public spheres. SNSs and applications provide digitally mediated spaces where LGBQ youth can participate, explore, connect and communicate with similar others in a safe and sometimes anonymous manner (Lucero, 2017). For instance, SNSs and applications have become integral to the facilitation of the coming out process, whereby LGBQ youth and young adults use Facebook and YouTube—among other platforms—to scaffold and/or engage in the disclosure of a sexual orientation (Albert & Bettez, 2012; Alexander & Losh, 2010).

In fact, some LGBQ youth may use SNSs and applications as a means to test out the disclosure of their identity online in order to avoid possible discrimination or aversive responses and become more comfortable (Craig & McInroy, 2014).

TGD Youth and Young Adults

The lives of TGD youth and young adults have also been significantly impacted by SNSs and applications, though there is still little research available. Similar to LGBQ youth and young adults, SNSs and applications have also afforded TGD youth and young adults with a place to access resources and information online, explore and construct identity, find likeness and come out digitally (Craig & McInroy, 2014). However, the visibility and representation may be less favorable for TGD (McInroy & Craig, 2015)—although improving—than for LBGQ people. In this case, SNSs and applications may be particularly salient and important for TGD people as they seek out information and navigate various identity processes.

Instagram, Twitter, SnapChat, YouTube and Facebook are commonly used by TGD adults. They report Facebook as being a platform that is particularly useful for receiving social support by joining online groups and communities, gathering relevant information about various transgender topics and issues, and learning about personal and medical resources that can be accessed in the offline community (Doss, 2018). Facebook offers public and private groups for TGD people who focus on transitioning updates and processes. These online groups and communities can be either public or private, offering TGD people the option of anonymity and safety. Young, transgender adults may use SNSs to explore, experiment, traverse with and foster a transgender identity (Cavalcante, 2018; Doss, 2018).

Consider how Tumblr has become a social and cultural hub for young, TGD adults. It has provided a virtual, queer landscape for seeking information, identity affirmation, empowerment and social justice (Cavalvante, 2018). As elegantly summarized by Cavalcante (2019), "Tumblr can provide a kind of queer utopia that sustains [transgender and gender-diverse] users' sense of self, encourages them to talk back and alters what they expect from the people and institutions they encounter in everyday life" (p. 1726) In other words, SNSs afford TGD users a type of agency, possibility, community and hope regarding identity and the environment in which they are embedded.

YouTube, a video-sharing-based SNSs and application, also provides an avenue through which TGD adults may advance their understanding of TGD-related issues and phenomena. As an autobiographical medium, video blogging acts as a narrative medium through which transgender or gender-diverse people may create, explain and/ or understand their identity and the multifaceted and perhaps nonlinear trajectory of that identity development. TGD people may either create or view videos about the transition process. In this way, video blogging may also be utilized as an affective archive of personal and/or identity-based growth and change through the transition process, which can provide a sense of support, reassurance and empowerment for both—those making and watching the videos (Raun, 2015).

Sexual Literacy: SNSs and Applications

Increasingly, the virtual world impacts how people have contributed to our understanding of how LGBQ and TGD youth and young adults utilize SNSs and applications as part of their identity and sexual lives to further identity, connection, knowledge acquisition and relationship building. The myriad ways in which online narratives of sexuality, gender, pleasure, intimacy, the body and identity are constructed and disseminated personally, socially, and politically is, in itself, a multiplexed and interactive event of sexual literacy. From our current understanding, SNSs and applications fuel the expression—and even online community creation—of information, identities, practices and discourses of LGBQ and TGD youth and young adults that are interdicted in the everyday, brick-and-mortar, routinely heteronormative world. For LGBQ and TGD youth and young adults, learning how to converse, fluently and critically, about sexuality, sex and gender is very important both in developing and furthering individual sexual literacy, especially for subpopulations of abjected social groups.

More generally, SNSs and applications are a means for exploring and acquiring information that is pertinent to the LGBQ and TGD identities and expressions—information that is often obscured or not available offline. Information about and representation of LGBQ and TGD identities may not be accessible to youth and young adults in the United States, especially for those who live in more conservative or rural areas, where social and political barriers may prevent identity construction and exploration as well as the acquisition of knowledge pertaining to sexual health. In this sense, SNSs and applications are home to social microcosms that contain bubbles of information that afford LGBQ and TGD youth and young adult in gaining important knowledge and experience of self-discovery needed to further their literacy apposite to sex, sexuality and gender. These SNS and application microcosms may help promote LGBQ and TGD youth and young adults to think differently, diversely and more expansively about their current knowledge and understanding of their and others' identities, sexualities and sexual lives.

More specifically, though, SNSs and applications have become an avenue for LGBQ and TGD youth and young adults to engage in personal storytelling, digitally narrating their own and others' knowledge, identity and lives. This storytelling is crucial for youth and young people who incessantly face deleterious social marginalization in everyday off-line life, as it acts as a facilitating mechanism for the individual as well as community-based construction of identity, pride and a sense of social belonging. In this sense, storytelling and the act of self-narration on SNSs and applications can be a means through which LGBQ and TGD youth and young adults are able to advance the self-determination of their identities and lives—and thus sexual literacy.

Moving Forward: The Future

The Internet and its associated technologies, such as SNSs and applications, will remain crucial spaces wherein people with sexual and gender-diverse identities can find community, foster empowerment, further development and knowledge of themselves, and create collective resistance and support in a heteronormative gender-essentialist world. Indeed,

SNSs and applications are devices whose anonymity and accessibility can host progressive as well as hateful information and spaces, but this essay provides evidence of the positive effects of SNS and application use among LGBQ and TGD communities. There is growing concern, however, for SNSs and applications as capitalism and globalization advances in the United States and abroad. For instance, privacy may become more of a concern as Internet technologies advance, which may limit LGBQ and TGD youth and young adult's ability to self-narrate their own identities, comfort and safety. Furthermore, Internet-based oppression such as cyberbullying may also become a potentially harmful effect of using SNSs and applications for LGBQ and TGD youth and young adults.

Owing to the rapidly changing landscape of the technological world, it is quite hard to consider, prospectively, how SNSs and applications or other communicative technologies will impact the lives of LGBQ and TGD youth and young adults. Nevertheless, with future technological advances, it is likely that SNSs and applications will become even more omnipresent and ubiquitous in the lives of LGBQ and TGD youth and young adults. Current technological developments such as augmented and virtual reality may provide LGBQ and TGD youth and young adults with the opportunity to have more experientially impactful connections and interactions with similar others, which may result in important changes in sexual literacy and identity development.

References

Albert, C., & Bettez, S. (2012). Opening the closet door: Exploring the role of social media in the coming out process for individuals who self-identify as lesbian, gay, bisexual, and/or LGBQ. *AMCIS 2012 Proceedings*, 1–7. Retrieved from http://aisel.aisnet.org/amcis2012/proceedings/SocialIssues/17

Alexander, J., & Losh, E. (2010). A YouTube of one's own? "Coming out" videos as rhetorical action. In C. Pullen & M. Cooper (Eds.), *LGBT identity and online new media* (pp. 37–50). New York: Routledge.

Bargh, J. A., & McKenna, K. Y. A. (2004). The Internet and social life. *Annual Review of Psychology*, *55*, 573–590.

Boyd, D. M. (2008). Why youth (heart) social network sites: The role of networked publics in teenage social life. In D. Buckingham (Ed.), *Youth, identity, and digital media* (pp. 119–142). The John D. and Catherine T. MacArthur Foundation Series on Digital Media and Learning. Cambridge, MA: MIT Press.

Boyd, D. M., & Ellison, N. B. (2007). Social network sites: Definition, history, and scholarship. *Journal of Computer-Mediated Communication*, *13*(1), 210–230. https://doi.org/10.1111/j.1083-6101.2007.00393.x

Cavalcante, A. (2018). Tumbling into queer utopias and vortexes: Experiences of LGBTQ social media users on Tumblr. *Journal of Homosexuality*, *66*(12), 1715–1735. https://doi.org/10.1080/00918369.2018.1511131

Chauncey, G. (1994). *Gay New York: Gender, urban culture, and the making of the gay male world, 1890–1940*. New York: Basic Books.

Craig, S. L., & McInroy, L. (2014). You can form a part of yourself online: The influence of new media on identity development and coming out for LGBTQ youth. *Journal of Gay & Lesbian Mental Health*, *18*(1), 95–109. https://doi.org/10.1080/19359705.2013.777007

D'Augelli, A. R., & Patterson, C. (1995). *Lesbian, gay, and bisexual identities over the lifespan: Psychological perspectives*. New York: Oxford University Press.

Doss, B., (2018). *Exploring the role of social media in the identity development of trans individuals (MSU graduate theses)*. Retrieved from https://bearworks.missouristate.edu/theses/3317

Farquhar-Leicester, A., & Polen-Petit, N. (in press). Subjective sexual well-being among LGBTQIA and pansexual college students: An exploration of the role of social networking sites and applications. *Undergraduate Research Journal of Psychology at UCLA, 7*, 23–39. Retrieved from https://urjp.psych.ucla.edu/wp-content/uploads/sites/76/2020/09/URJPFinal.pdf

Flanders, C. E., Pragg, L., Dobinson, C., & Logie, C. (2017). Young sexual minority women's use of the internet and other digital technologies for sexual health information seeking. *Canadian Journal of Human Sexuality, 26*(1), 17–25. https://doi.org/10.3138/cjhs.261-A2

Fox, J., & Ralston, R. (2016). Queer identity online: Informal learning and teaching experiences of LGBTQ individuals on social media. *Computers in Human Behavior, 65*, 635–642. https://doi.org/10.1016/j.chb.2016.06.009

Gudelunas, D. (2012). There's an app for that: The uses and gratifications of online social networks for gay men. *Sexuality & Culture, 16*, 347–365. doi: 10.1007/s12119-012-9127

Hiller, L., Mitchell, K. J., & Ybarra, M. L. (2012). The internet as a safety net: Findings from a series of online focus groups with LGB and non-LGB young people in the United States. *Journal of LGBT Youth, 9*(3), 225–246. doi:10.1080/19361653.2012.684642

Lucero, L. (2017). Safe spaces in online places: Social media and LGBTQ youth. *Multicultural Education Review, 9*(2), 117–128. https://doi.org/10.1080/2005615X.2017.1313482

Magee, J. C., Bigelow, L., DeHaan, S., & Mustanski, B. S. (2012). Sexual health information seeking online: A mixed-methods study among lesbian, gay, bisexual, and transgender young people. *Health Education & Behavior, 39*(3), 276–289. https://doi.org/10.1177/1090198111401384

Manago, A. M. (2014). Identity development in the digital age: The case of social networking sites. In K. C. McLean & M. Syed (Eds.), *The Oxford handbook of identity development*. doi:10.1093/oxfordgb/9780199936564.013.031

McInroy, L. B., & Craig, S. L. (2015). Transgender representation in offline and online media: LGBTQ youth perspectives. *Journal of Human Behavior in the Social Environment, 25*(6), 606–617. https://doi.org/10.1080/10911359.2014.995392

McInroy, L. B., Craig, S. L., & Leung, V. W. Y. (2019). Platforms and patterns for practice: LGBTQ+ youths' use of information and communication technologies. *Child and Adolescent Social Work Journal, 36*(5), 507–520. https://doi.org/10.1007/s10560-018-0577-x

Meeker, M. (2005). *Contacts desired: Gay and lesbian communications and community, 1940s–1970s*. Chicago: University of Chicago Press.

Pew Research Center. (2019. *Fact sheets*. Retrieved from http://www.pewinternet.org/factsheets

Raun, T. (2015). Video blogging as a vehicle of transformation: Exploring the intersection between trans identity and information technology. *International Journal of Cultural Studies, 18*(3), 365–378. https://doi.org/10.1177/1367877913513696

Savin-Williams, R. C. (1996). Dating and romantic relationships among gay, lesbian, and bisexual youths. In R. C. Savin-Williams and K. M. Cohen (Eds.), *The lives of lesbians, gays, and bisexuals: Children to adults* (pp. 166–178). Fort Worth, TX: Harcourt Brace College.

Chapter 25

SOCIAL MEDIA AND SEXUAL/GENDER DIVERSITY AMONG YOUNG PEOPLE IN THAILAND

Jan-Willem de Lind van Wijngaarden

In the 1990s, there was vigorous discussion among social scientists about the impact of globalization on societies and cultures. On one side of the debate there were those who feared that globalization would lead to less cultural diversity—to a "global" monoculture of Pepsi, McDonald's, Toyota and Coca-Cola. Multinational corporations would dominate the globe, and capitalism would gradually make every human being part of the same system—with the same wants and needs, and, eventually, the same language and culture. On the other hand, were those who saw opportunities in the rise of globalization, especially in the spectacular rise of the Internet. Instead of creating a global monoculture, these scholars argued, the Internet could, by allowing people from minority cultures, genders and sexuality to connect across the globe, allow for cultural diversity to flourish like never before.

For some commercial production, the first group of scholars was probably right. Electronics firms such as Apple, Samsung and Huawei dominate the computer- and mobile phone market, with smaller companies gradually taken over or pushed into bankruptcy.

But how does this debate apply to the topic of sexual and gender diversity?

The LGBT liberation movement can be described as a multinational movement that has created hope and purpose for millions of individuals scattered across the globe. They long and struggle for freedom of expression and freedom to live and love free from the pressures of heteronormativity and patriarchy, under the banner of the common rainbow flag. At the same time, LGBT's most powerful constructs (the identity labels of gay, lesbian, bisexual and transgender) have entered into local sexual cultures and gender landscapes and created an alternative universe. Locally evolved labels for people who do not fit the heterosexual mainstream may gradually be pushed into oblivion. For a while, scholars believed that soon, across the globe, all people attracted to the same sex/ gender would call themselves gay, or lesbian, or if attracted to both, bisexual. Goodbye to the Thai *Kathoey*, the Indonesian *Waria* and the Bangladeshi *Hijra*, all of which can be described as "indigenous" third- or alternative gender identities.

The example from Thailand shows that this is not at all the case. Before the introduction of "LGBT ideology" in urban, well-educated and well-connected circles, sexual attraction between men was completely "gendered," meaning that it was learned and expressed using masculine and feminine gender stereotypes. Men either identified as feminine, in which case their sexual behavior was presumably receptive ("bottom") and they would show their femininity (and sexual availability) by adopting feminine linguistic expressions and dress. These men took on the label of the Kathoey. Their sexual partners considered themselves "men," in the sense that they were "penetrators" when it came to sex. These men saw sex with other men as pleasurable, but not as a ground for a new or different identity. They were just men—whether they penetrated women or other men did not really matter. The Kathoey often saw themselves as inferior to "real" women—for the simple reason that they could never become mothers, which is the highest attainable goal for Thai women in traditional Thai societies, and the main reason why men would get married to them.

Enter the gay revolution! Gay provided a new concept that allowed men to love, pursue and have sex with other men without choosing a "masculine" or "feminine" gender identity. Who cares if a man is top or bottom? Under this new paradigm, all men who were attracted to other men were gay—just gay. This was convenient for many reasons, not the least that gay men did not need to show themselves as different in terms of their use of language or dress, so they "fitted in" easier in modernizing Thai urban areas. It was also considered to be less embarrassing to parents and other family or community members to be able to pass as a man, rather than be a feminine-looking or sounding man.

So, did gay liberation lead to the demise of the importance of gender in order to make sense of homosexual desire in Thai society? If only things were that easy. As soon as the concept of gay was introduced, Thai men started to add a classifier to the term. Immediately after you were identified as gay, the question came: Are you top or bottom? Read, between the lines: are you a feminine or a masculine man? Are you a girl or a boy?

A decade or so later, the "real" gay finally emerged. In Thailand he is called *Gay Both*—"both" refers to their ability to be both top and bottom. Not long after this, more detailed labels still emerged: the *Both Ruk* (means: both-insertive) and *Both Rab* (both-receptive), referring to their preference—but not an exclusive preference.

At the same time, the introduction of the term "bi" for bisexual led to a "heterofication" of the Thai word for "man" (phu chaai). In the past, every Thai man was intrinsically bisexual, in the sense that there was no boundary for Thai men to cross if they had insertive sex with another man. Their masculinity was implicit in their penetrative sexual behavior. With the term "bisexual" making inroads, a phu chaai who has sex with men is no longer a phu chaai, but either gay or bisexual. Phu chaai is now increasingly used as a term to describe a man who exclusively has sex with women. The term bisexual has, similar to the term "gay," also been upgraded with numerous specifying adjectives: *Bi Ruk, Bi Rab, Bi Both*—with "bi" being a classification that the person has, at least once, had sex with a woman. This makes him sound/look more masculine and, for many people, more desirable. If anything, the proliferation of gender/sexuality identity labels under the influence of the gay revolution has led to higher value being placed on masculine demeanors. Gay/bi is "in," is "hot," is "modern," and the feminine men, the kathoey, are often associated with backwardness.

The Internet played a pivotal role in the development of this diverse Thai sexuality/gender-scape and the appreciation of masculine same-sex imagery and self-presentation. I like to describe what is happening as two rivers merging—the gendered homosexuality river with its kathoey and phu chaai is merging with the gay river. Young people in rural areas are exposed to ideas about gender and sexuality from their conservative rural heterosexual environment from the moment they are born, and many translate their desire for other boys/men to the conclusion that they must, in fact, be females (Kathoey); they are firmly part of the old river. The idea that one can love a man without being/feeling like/acting like a woman, which is implicit in the LGBT revolutionary river, has not yet reached to all nooks and corners of the Thai periphery.

It is often via the Internet that young rural same-sex attracted persons become exposed to these new identity labels, and to what they mean. For some of them, the Internet provides an opportunity to escape from the kathoey label that often has attached to them since they were little children. They pick new pictures on their Facebook or Instagram profiles (or create entirely new profiles, for that matter) that show them look masculine—with short hair and masculine dress, without powder and lipstick, often abruptly changing their gender online from feminine to masculine. Often this leads to immediate success in terms of finding a boyfriend or sex partner who is interested in them. It also often leads to improved relationships with parents and teachers, who usually prefer heteronormative masculine looks in young men to the presentation as a Kathoey.

The Internet also allows for a safe distance from which rural young people can experiment with new language, new concepts and a new way to represent oneself. If it does not work out, try again with a new person to chat with tomorrow. And if it does not work out at all, delete the profile and create a new one—one that better suits/fits one's emerging sense of self. Thai culture is highly hierarchical and is characterized by carefully scripted communication between older and younger, richer and poorer people and between men and women. The Internet throws all these rules, in principle, to the wind. One can present oneself as older or younger, richer or poorer, more or less masculine than one really is. And, while one cannot make oneself younger or richer in real life with a few strokes on one's keyboard, when it comes to creating a more desirable presentation of one's gender/sexuality, practice makes perfect.

The Internet can therefore have an empowering effect on sexual and gender minority populations, especially for those who are young and/or relatively isolated. With hundreds of thousands of young people familiarizing themselves with new ways of living and experience their gender and sexuality, innovative new labels and concepts are continuously emerging, which are in turn passed on to others and changed and given new meaning as they grow older. "Older" labels such as that of the kathoey never disappear: new people take them on, and sometimes the older labels are taken on again when people get older. With the Thai education system failing young people so dramatically when it comes to comprehensive sexuality education, the Internet remains our best hope to provide young same-sex attracted and gender-diverse Thai people with a safe space to learn from each other and to express themselves.

Chapter 26

QUEER VISIBILITY AND RECOGNITION ONLINE

Daniel Cockayne and Jen Jack Gieseking

A common way of understanding lesbian, gay, bisexual, transgender and queer (LGBTQ) bodies, spaces and experiences is that they are "invisible" or "unseen" to populations of heterosexuals and, at times, to one another. The narrative of invisibility emerged most especially within the framework of LGBTQ politics of visibility in the 1970s in response to the painful and pervasive "silence, invisibility, and isolation" they experienced (D'Emilio, 1983, p. 1). Thus, LGBTQ people have framed their agenda and strategies of resistance through a politics of visibility that idealized being out as *the* path toward recognition, justice and liberation (Darsey, 1991). For example, LGBTQ organizations have consistently used spatialized rallying cries such as: "Whose streets? Our streets!" in the first Christopher Street March (renamed the Pride Day march) in June 1970; "Out of the bars and into the streets!" by Harvey Milk, circa 1977; "Out of the closet, and into the streets!" by ACT-UP, circa 1987; "We're everywhere!" by the Lesbian Avengers, circa 1992; "We're here, we're queer!" by *Queer Nation*, circa 1990. At the same time, the politics of visibility, in and beyond LGBTQ communities, also came to appeal to the "secular, commodity-driven" aspects of neoliberal, American society, which is "dominated by the realm of the visible" (Alcoff, 2005, p. 6).

Since the 1990s, however, LGBTQ spaces and their visibility have changed dramatically with the rise of a widely and publicly available, commercial Internet and associated technologies that include web browsers, smart phones, social media and digital applications. Given that LGBTQ people have historically had few visible spaces in which to gather—many of which were and are still located within urban areas—the digital sphere has become a space that shapes the everyday lives of LGBTQ people (Cockayne & Richardson, 2017). Digital spaces have afforded some LGBTQ people a greater sense of community, and increased access to history and resources (Lingel, 2017). In her work on rural queers' use of social media in the 2000s, Mary Gray called these digital spaces "boundary publics" that she defines as "iterative, ephemeral experiences of belonging that happen both on the outskirts and at the center(s) of the more traditionally recognized and validated public sphere of civic deliberation" (2007, p. 53).

Still others have faced the same homophobic, transphobic, heteronormative and/ or cisnormative discrimination online that they experience in real life (IRL). Many drag queens as well as Indigenous peoples had their accounts removed from Facebook in

2014 because they did not allow the use of "preferred names" or names that were not considered "real" names (i.e., legal/birth names). The public outcry in response to this deletion led to many of these accounts to be reinstated, but all the while revealed how much power corporations have in defining who is "real" is done so through White, colonial, heteronormative politics (Lingel & Golub, 2015). This came after many people had heralded Facebook as a LGBTQ leader earlier that year when it launched over 70 gender options, only to then realize that the algorithms within Facebook still labeled you in the binary of male or female (Bivens & Haimson, 2016). These examples, both from the same social media site, reveal the contradictory experiences that LGBTQ people have online. These experiences are characterized by an ambivalent mix of both opportunity for progressive politics and reproduction of prior forms of discrimination "offline."

Other writers have highlighted how digital spaces are necessary to the survival of both a heterosexual culture offline, and an Internet that, as noted above, is often also hostile toward LGBTQ users. The politics of visibility is then still a radical act for many LGBTQ people. Olu Jenzen (2017) examines how Tumblr and YouTube provide necessary resources for transgender youth who may not be able to discuss their gender identity or transition with friends or family in offline spaces. In Jenzen's research, many trans people note that trans video diaries and montages on YouTube have been essential means of support, solidarity and information. Some videos serve an educational purpose both for trans youth and cis audiences. Other trans people document hormone use and bodily changes alongside personal reflections on transitioning, providing insight into challenges and successes, while some offer more general advice on a wide range of topics including relationships, school, family, clothes and emotional experiences. Still others provide more practical advice including guides to binding and make-up, and give advice on navigating health care systems, especially for young people who may not be able to purchase necessary materials or have difficulty accessing essential services. In a different way, these patterns around visibility politics replicate George Chauncey's (1994) argument that for gay men in the 1890s to 1930s in New York City and other North American, European and Euro-colonized cities, "privacy could only be had in public." While gay men of the past were unable to meet or take rooms together in private lest they be arrested, trans youth today are geographically disconnected and must carve out their own conversations in the digital "public" sphere.

Tumblr also provides a kind of counter-cultural space for trans youth online, against the "cis-normative Internet" that can include Google, Facebook, Twitter, Reddit and 4chan for their often overt homophobic and transphobic content (Jenzen, 2017, p. 1629). Tumblr is a microblogging platform that allows the curation of mostly image- and video-based, but also text-based, content. Although users can publish their own material, the focus on Tumblr is on curating existing content online through reblogging to create highly personalized pages that reflect particular interests. Against more rigidly structured social media sites such as Facebook, Instagram and Twitter, Tumblr's functionality is more open-ended and dynamic. Tagging content allows users to make images or videos relevant in different contexts defined by the user. Overall, Tumblr allows more opportunity for the construction of and play with multiple and different gender and sexual identities through both this built-in dynamism and the ease of creating multiple pages for different purposes. These platforms may be a necessary source of everyday survival for trans youth, especially in the absence of support from family and friends. Blake Hawkins and Jack Gieseking (2017) write that trans communities on Tumblr use the site to share and find medical information, including feedback on surgeons and information about the outcomes of hormone usage. Yet, all the authors mentioned above caution that these sites are not unilateral spaces of support for queer, trans and gender nonconforming youth, and that they can also be sites that conform to the cis-heteronormativity of the broader Internet.

While the politics of visibility has changed over time for some LGBTQ people, inclusion and acceptance in mainstream society is often experienced mostly strongly by White, middle-class, cisgender, able-bodied gay men. The ethos of "privacy could only be had in public" continues for most LGBTQ people, especially transgender and gender nonconforming youth, LGBTQ youth of color, and Indigenous youth who still often rely on similar models of sharing information and forming community online. Poor and homeless LGBTQ youth remain disenfranchised, and are also a group least likely to be able to benefit from support structures that exist online, since they are unlikely to have regular or consistent access to online spaces. For decades, patterns of gentrification across cities, once linked to LGBTQ people as a sign of acceptance, has displaced most LGBTQ neighborhoods and places like bars, so that those physical spaces too must be reproduced elsewhere. These more marginalized individuals and groups also must repeatedly reshape and redefine these spaces in the forces of conservative, religious cis-heteropatriarchal policies. In 2019, the *Not Suitable for Work (NSFW)* ban that eliminated images from social media deemed "inappropriate" in the United States drastically redefined these spaces as large amounts of sex positive, body positive and pornographic content was erased from various sites such as Tumblr and Instagram. In response, LGBTQ people have been forced—and may be forced again and again in the future—to locate one another by producing new hashtags, using different sites or apps, and inventing veiled forms of image and video sharing that would mask bodies.

Beyond a focus on queer youth, other writers have looked to online dating sites as having opportunities for and challenges to the issue of queer visibility online for adult LGBTQ people. In a nominal sense, digital dating platforms have a lot of promise, given that they may be able to easily filter out homophobia by connecting LGBTQ people with one another. They also appear to provide safety through relative anonymity and privacy in the sense that you can talk with other LGBTQ people online without "offline" friends and family knowing. Yet many have shown how dating sites such as Grindr, Tinder and OkCupid also amplify and reify other forms of discrimination. Shaka McGlotten, for example, examines racism on Grindr, an (originally) gay men's smartphone application with a focus on hook-ups rather than relationships, through the prevalence of discriminatory language designed to exclude people of color from contact (McGlotten & Sender, 2018). This discrimination is communicated through offensive and racist language such as, "no spice, no rice," to Asian users, implying that persons of a given race or skin color should not contact the owners of these profiles. Jack Gieseking (2017) notes how dating sites such as OkCupid attempt through their algorithms to estimate what the site has deemed "attractiveness," which included a range of factors such as how many users click through to your profile within a given space of time after you create it and/or how many users with whom you match or do not match (cf. Coyne, 2012; Rey, 2010). Given the racial, sexist and transphobic biases of humans/software users, as well as coders (cf. McPherson, 2011), the algorithms behind the app and site—which build upon earlier code—begin to affect if not define who is desirable and/or available to whom.

Scholars have used a variety of approaches and methods to explore queer visibility and recognition online (Rogers, 2019). In particular, qualitative methods such as interviews, surveys, ethnography and participant observation have been used to examine many of the online communities and platforms discussed above. Digital platforms can also be used as tools to recruit participants in research on those very platforms. Some scholars have used ethnography to investigate more immersive spaces such as online video games (McGlotten, 2013). Visual and content analysis is also common as a way to interrogate online spaces, a method that does not necessitate direct contact with human participants (Rose, 2016). Others have used digital spaces to create online archives and databases as ways to share and showcase their work with both academic and popular publics, for example, Adrienne Shaw's database of LGBTQ characters and themes in videogames (Shaw, 2015). These techniques can also be used in combination with offline methods, for example, using digital platforms to recruit participants for in-person interviews, focus groups or workshops (Eaves, 2013). Many also use qualitative analysis software such as Atlas.ti or NVivo to process large amounts of text-based and visual data.

In this chapter, we have highlighted some of the ways in which digital spaces are significant for LGBTQ people in challenging the politics of visibility that has characterized LGBTQ history. We have identified discrimination in online spaces and research that calls large parts of the Internet cis- and heteronormative. The Internet can be a space of opportunity and is a necessary space of survival for many LGBTQ people, especially for transgender youth. We have also explored several ways in which the Internet and digital spaces can be used in research as a specific research method, for example through content analysis, or digital ethnography. Overall, the examples above demonstrate that it is essential to take online spaces into account in understanding the LGBTQ politics of visibility in a world that is increasingly defined by the intermingling of online and offline spaces. Yet it is also important to note that not only the benefits for users and experiences of online (just as in physical) spaces remains highly uneven but also that access to these online spaces is also uneven. Many people in the Global South, as well as in rural and remote areas of the Global North including Indigenous, Native American and First Nations reservations, do not have consistent or sometimes any access to the Internet. This digital divide and effect of the net's nonneutrality reveal that many people are unable to access digital spaces that may provide community and solidarity (Greene, 2016).

Once online, as the examples in this chapter highlight, these spaces may reproduce many of the inequalities that exist in "traditional" spaces and create new avenues for discrimination, but at the same time provide opportunities for the development of progressive politics, communities and content. Digital spaces are a key arena for understanding the evolving relationship between LGBTQ people and the politics of visibility. As the limitations of liberal identity politics and representation are further reified and exposed, digital spaces may provide key sites for working out radical and progressive alternatives for LGBTQ lives in the vein of a neither conformist nor separatist queer politics.

References

Alcoff, L. M. (2005). *Visible identities: Race, gender, and the self.* Oxford: Oxford University Press.

Bivens, R., & Haimson, O. L. (2016). Baking gender into social media design: How platforms shape categories for users and advertisers. *Social Media + Society, 2*(4), 1–12.

Chauncey, G. (1994). *Gay New York: Gender, urban culture, and the making of the gay male world, 1890–1940.* New York: Basic Books.

Cockayne, D. G., & Richardson, L. (2017). Queering code/space: The co-production of socio-sexual codes and digital technologies. *Gender, Place & Culture, 24*(11), 1642–1658.

Coyne, C. (2012). Is being one of the "most attractive people on OKCupid" a permanent status? Retrieved from https://www.quora.com/Is-being-one-of-the-most-attractive-people-on-OKCupid-a-permanent-status-If-I-change-my-photo-or-people-react-to-my-profile-differently-can-I-lose-this-status-What-can-I-do-to-maintain-it?share=1

D'Emilio, J. (1983). *Sexual politics, sexual communities.* Chicago: University of Chicago Press.

Darsey, J. (1991). From "gay is good" to the scourge of AIDS: The evolution of gay liberation rhetoric, 1977–1990. *Communication Studies, 42*(1), 43–66.

Eaves, L. (2013). Space, place, and identity in conversation: Queer Black women living in the rural US South. In A. Gorman-Murray, B. Pini & L. Bryant (Eds.), *Sexuality, Rurality, and Geography* (pp. 111–128). Plymouth: Lexington Books.

Gieseking, J. (2017). Messing with the attractiveness algorithm: A response to queering code/space. *Gender, Place & Culture, 24*(11), 1659–1665.

Gray, M. L. (2007). From websites to Wal-Mart: Youth, identity work, and the queering of boundary publics in small town, USA. *American Studies, 48*(2), 5–15.

Greene, D. (2016). Discovering the divide: Technology and poverty in the new economy. *International Journal of Communication, 10*, 20.

Hawkins, B., & Gieseking, J. (2017). Seeking ways to our transgender bodies, by ourselves: Rationalizing transgender-specific health information behaviors. *Proceedings of the Association for Information Science and Technology, 54*(1), 702–704.

Jenzen, O. (2017). Trans youth and social media: Moving between counter publics and the wider web. *Gender, Place & Culture, 24*(11), 1626–1641.

Lingel, J. (2017). *Digital countercultures and the struggle for community.* Cambridge, MA: MIT Press.

Lingel, J., & Golub, A. (2015). In face on Facebook: Brooklyn's drag community and sociotechnical practices of online communication. *Journal of Computer-Mediated Communication, 20*(5), 536–553.

McGlotten, S. (2013). *Virtual intimacy: Media, affect, and queer sociality.* Albany: State University of New York Press.

McGlotten, S., & Sender, K. (2018). Intimate immanence: A conversation between Shaka McGlotten and Katherine Sender. *First Monday, 23*(7). https://doi.org/10.5210/fm.v23i7

McPherson, T. (2011). US operating systems at mid-century: The intertwining of race and UNIX. In L. Nakamura & P. Chow-White (Eds.), *Race after the Internet* (pp. 21–37). New York: Routledge.

Rey, P. J. (2010). *OkCupid grants special privileges to attractive users.* Sociology Lens https://www.sociologylens.net/topics/communication-and-media/okcupid-grants-special-privileges-to-attractive-users/6629

Rogers, R. (2019). *Doing digital methods.* London: Sage.

Rose, G. (2016). *Visual methodologies.* London: Sage.

Shaw, A. (2015). *Gaming at the edge: Sexuality and gender at the margins of gaming culture.* Minneapolis: University of Minnesota Press.

Chapter 27

ERRANCY AND KARMA IN THAILAND: GLOCAL SEXUAL HEALTH LITERACY IN THE NAME OF THE AESTHETIC OF EXISTENCE

Narupon Duangwises

Glocal sexual health literacy needs to focus on integrating adjustable knowledge and contextual understandings rather than following some scientific formula of uncertain rationality. My major examples in this essay come from studies in South East Asia that demonstrate the dynamics of how the knowledge of sexually transmitted diseases (STDs) and sexually transmitted infections (STIs) intersects with the situated understanding of homosexuality.

In Thailand since 2017, HIV, tuberculosis, and STIs have fallen under the department of disease control in the ministry of public health. This follows the strategy to reduce new HIV infections to less than 1,000 people and reduce deaths from HIV/AIDS to less than 4,000 people by 2030. Importantly, it is expected that within the next 10 years, there will be a reduction in the discrimination and stigmatization of HIV-infected people to 10 percent of THE GENERAL POPULATION. However, this is just a quantitative expectation; but in terms of medical practices, the important policy to focus on is how this brings gay and transgender identifying people into the clinic to test their blood. This strategy is known as RRTTR, which means "reach, recruit, test, treat and retain." This public health strategy focuses on how the epidemiological human body is made into an object for medical examination and remedies only.

Thailand, like most developing countries around the world, adopted the guidelines of the United Nations Program on HIV/AIDS (UNAIDS) long ago (Tosanguan, Kingkhaew, Pirapattanaphokin, & Tirawattananon, 2013). The HIV and AIDS Recommendation, from 2010 (No. 200), provides sound guidance on addressing HIV through the promotion of human rights, job security and enhancing access to HIV prevention, treatment, care and support services from a workplace perspective. The global campaign of attaining the vision of—*Zero new HIV infections. Zero discrimination. Zero AIDS-related deaths*—is a complex effort that leads to accelerating the number of risk groups required not only to have blood tests in hospitals and public health centers but also required increased awareness of the sociocultural context and life experience of each person. Everyone who comes in to draw blood will be in the same situation, coldly investigated by public health officials.

In this respect, Boellstorff (2011) has pointed out that the emergence of men-who-have-sex-with-men (MSM) category that was created from a "universal" concept that makes MSM in every society seem to reduce them to the same identity, and erases the historical context as well as the individual's personal feelings about relationships, sex and life.

When I observed the work of an officer in a private health service unit in Bangkok, I found that each staff member was interested in a medical job rather than focusing on the needs and feelings of those who come to receive services. The procedure for HIV testing is a strict working method and process. In addition, health centers also provide online HIV testing. The first step is calling to talk with and seeking advice from staff. Subsequently, the staff will send the blood test equipment to the client at home. When receiving the blood test equipment, the counselor will recommend a blood test procedure for every step via online video, which the client must follow. This is an example of biomedical and scientific knowledge that neglects the different life experiences and educational backgrounds of individuals via automated processes and distancing from a collaborative medical care group. Gay, transgender and bisexual are treated the same way. This method has been standardized under the supervision of government officials, which wants to succeed with getting to zero policy via bringing risk group into the test, treatment and retain process to achieve quantitative goals—yet people are not widgets on an assembly line of care and history teaches us that humans need a more nuanced approach to care.

During the past 20 years, the HIV/AIDS prevention campaign in Thailand was based on epidemiology and medicine. In the last decade, there were changing meanings of HIV/AIDS discourse that described this epidemic now as a *chronic illness* that requires regular medication. Also, there have been huge advances in medical technology, such as PEP (postexposure prophylaxis) and PrEP (pre-exposure prophylaxis) drugs that help people to have more choices in prevention and treatment. Nevertheless, there remains the entrenched idea that HIV/AIDS is a contagious disease that must be urgently treated, and individuals must know how to prevent infection and thus they are influenced by biomedical knowledge creation and framings (Fee & Krieger, 1993). Recent medical advancements are a phenomenon of the post-AIDS era; yet there are still many factors that affect different sexual experiences, attitudes and lifestyles among gay men, such as age, geographic and generation differences, the ascendancy of the biomedical and the technosexual defined as using gadgets and electronics for sexual pleasure and satisfaction and the supremacy of neoliberal politics that impact glocally. This is the intersectional approach that is driving current AIDS education to focus on various knowledge about health care that is related to human sexual activities in daily life (Bredstrom, 2006; Nyatsanza & Wood, 2017). In this regard, Gary Dowsett (2017) has pointed out that what is bigger than gay health problems is the social, political and economic environment that enables and pressures gays into conforming to the new norms of intimate citizenship.

Thus, new norms of intimate citizenship form the technique of power that exists and deploys in various "knowledge" institutions in which people will use knowledge as a formative of the aesthetics of existence. Following Foucault's idea, intimate and sexual citizenship is formed and shaped by the politics of life (Foucault, 1986, 1988). In the post-AIDS era situated in the neoliberal regime, individual knowledge of sexual health and desire is constituted as an instrument, while sexual literacy is a practice of an autonomous subject—namely the self. Under this logic, sexual literacy is a self-technique that is related to the culture of consumption and investment in a good life and a healthy body. We should reconsider how the global rational science of biomedicine and epidemiology are not the only basis in knowledge to construct and represent a quality of life. Others, local implicit knowledge systems found in private, personal and religious practices and beliefs are also a part of the meanings of better living.

In the Thai younger gay community, since the 2010s, the display and demonstration of sexual desire and pleasure has been based on social media channels, such as Gay Line group (groups and multiperson chats application), live streaming platform, gay application, gay chat and messenger on Facebook. However, recent studies in Thailand often focus on how gay men show their masculine images, body and identity to encourage and lure partners into sexual attraction (Bussabokkaew, 2010; Samakkekarom, Boonmongkon, Ojanen, & Guadamuz, 2012). Some studies explain the relationship between social media influence and openness in sex seeking (Faditthee, 2009). Other study indicates that gay social media is used as a channel that reduces stress in life (Samakkekarom & Boonmomgkon, 2011; Soontravaravit, Boonprakarn & Banthomsin, 2011). Modern social media technology is therefore viewed both positively and negatively in promoting sexual freedom and causing dangerous and risky sexual glocal contact. What is missing in many studies is the emotional and sensational dimensions of which gay and transgender express their own life and social existence.

In Thai society and the ASEAN (Association of Southeast Asian Nations) region, knowledge and literacy about HIV/AIDS epidemic, STIs and sexual health is easy to find in online media via smartphone and computer. At the same time gay men frequently seek sexual pleasure via online media, which produce and disseminate knowledge of sexual relations and intimacy arguably packaged and controlled by a neoliberal consumerism. In these mediascapes, there are more than one type of sexual learning process.

I propose that learning about sexual health, desire and practice is a complex and continuous glocal process. From my talking to many gay men in Bangkok, I have found that Thai people were aware of HIV/AIDS and STIs and their own sexual desire at the same time. They recognize and acknowledge both things at different times and contexts. This sexual awareness depended on different life experiences, social classes and educational backgrounds. In the sociocultural dimension, a most important driver of sexual awareness is that people have their own sexual imagination.

Each person's sexual intercourse history and activity are impacted by no fixed set of behavioral rules. In the case of which gay and transgender people may come to frame their sexual conduct as unprotected and a risk, they usually express the nervousness and anxiety; - in the Thai context, this feeling is defined as *Plaad* which -means errancy, a concept that derives from Buddhism. Their fear of HIV infection makes them think of medical treatment and trying to comfort themselves by bringing into focus the Buddhist belief in Karma to explain their sexual behaviors in term of "bad destiny." During this uneasy time, many experience a turning point and try to integrate in an intersectional way of many kinds of knowledge systems applied as technique of the self. They will decide to go for a blood test after considering their sexual contact. If they know that they are infected they will continue the medical treatment process. In this situation, blood tests are like a transitional ritual or rite of passage. Medical treatment is illustrated as a healing ritual.

This Buddhist context of belief and feeling is very important to Thai healing but has largely been ignored by the epidemiological paradigm in the glocal conjunctions between Thai and UNAIDS approaches.

The transitional period between knowing and unknowing one's HIV infection status is very important, because HIV/AIDS may create vagueness and anxiety. One approach to understanding the errancy and Karmic intersections embedded within sexual literacy techniques of the self are for hospitals and clinics to prepare a specific area of care for those who have just found out that they have HIV positive status. There are other models available that provide simple settings of a friendly atmosphere with counseling staff who listen and guide a person through their *Plaad*. Just suggesting links to groups that support people with HIV or encouraging creative activities push to indeed decrease external and internal discrimination regarding this infection to better support Vision Zero.

Thus, this is a whole tradition of social and practical knowledge that should be applied in the Thai setting in which biomedicine and sexual desire are appropriated within a local aesthetic of existence—an existence that is otherwise known as living a full life, no matter their HIV status.

References

Boellstorff, T. (2011). But do not identify as gay: A proleptic genealogy of the MSM Category. *Cultural Anthropology, 26*(2), 287–312.

Bredstrom, A. (2006). Intersectionality a challenge for feminist HIV/AIDS research? *European Journal of Women's Studies, 13*(3), 229–243.

Bussabokkaew, T. (2010). *Linguistic devices and the presentation of self-identity by the "Online Gays"* (Master's thesis). Bangkok: Chulalongkorn University.

Dowsett, G. (2017). Abjection. Objection. Subjection: Rethinking the history of AIDS in Australian gay men's futures. *Culture Health & Sexuality, 19*(9), 1–13.

Faditthee, C. (2009). Gay website: A public sphere for marginal people. *Damrong Journal of the Faculty of Archaeology, Silpakorn University, 8*(1), 81–101.

Fee, E., & Krieger, N. (1993). Thinking and rethinking aids: Implications for health policy. *International Journal of Health Services, 23*(2), 323–346.

Foucault, M. (1986). *The Use of Pleasure: The History of Sexuality Volume 2* (R. Hurley, trans.). London: Penguin.

Foucault, M. (1988). *The history of sexuality, Volume 3* (R. Hurley, Trans.). London: Penguin.

Nyatsanza, T., & Wood, L. (2017). Problematizing official narratives of HIV and AIDS education in Scotland and Zimbabwe. *SAHARA, 14*(1), 185–192.

Samakkekarom, R., & Boonmomgkon, P. (2011). Cyberspace, power structure, and gay sexual health: The sexuality of Thai men who have sex with men (MSM) in the Camfrog On-line Web-cam Chat Rooms. In P. Jackson (Ed.), *Queer Bangkok. 21st Century markets, media and rights* (pp. 121–140). Hong Kong: Hong Kong University Press.

Samakkekarom, R., Boonmongkon, P., Ojanen, T. T., & Guadamuz, T. E. (2012). Online sexuality, globalization of gay sexual citizenship and sexual representation in smartphone. *Journal of Sexuality Studies, 2*(2), 181–196.

Soontravaravit, N., Boonprakarn, K., & Banthomsin, P. (2011). Image and identities of gay in cyberspace. *Journal of Liberal Arts*, *3*(2), 117–130.

Tosanguan, K., Kingkhaew, P., Pirapattanaphokin, W., & Tirawattananon, Y. (2013). Economic evaluation of comprehensive HIV prevention interventions targeting those most at risk of HIV/AIDS in Thailand (CHAMPION). Retrieved from http://www.hitap.net/wp- content/ uploads/2014/09/full_report_hiv-marps.pdf

Chapter 28

A PALM SPRINGS POSTCARD: UNDERSTANDING SEXUAL LITERACY AMONG OLDER GAY MEN

Brian de Vries

Greetings from Palm Springs!

Probably thousands of postcards have begun with a similar such salutation sent from this beautiful Southern California desert city (a "resort" town of about 48,000 full-time residents, doubling in size during the winter months, Palm Springs, California, Population, 2019), with streets lined with palm trees, oddly lush green lawns and cacti gardens, at the base of the massive San Jacinto mountain and at the northern end of the Coachella Valley. Many postcards would likely then go on to speak of the weather—it is part of the attraction and the wonder of this city. Summer temperatures regularly exceed 110 degrees; winter daytime temperatures in the 70s and above are often the envy of many other parts of the country and beyond—the city especially welcomes large numbers of "snowbird" Canadians, and other northerners, over the winter months.

Palm Springs has an extraordinary presence of midlife and older gay men. Many (older) LGBT people, often proudly report that Palm Springs is "50:50": 50 percent people over 50 years of age and 50 percent LGBT persons (mostly gay men), although perhaps this is overstated. The gay male presence is pervasive and something on which people often remark in restaurants and grocery stores, in the gyms, in movie theaters and on airplanes as you fly into the city. The city council similarly has a profound LGBT presence: two gay men (including the mayor), a bisexual woman, a transgender woman and a Latina woman serve as city council members. Palm Springs is also the host community of many midlife and older gay men (and non-LGBT persons) relocating from across the state and elsewhere in the country. Many describe feeling pulled to Palm Springs by the climatic and social features of the area; some report feeling pushed out of their former communities by exploding housing costs (and the comparative affordability of Palm Springs, though home prices are still beyond the reach of many). The city is also primarily White: estimates are that over 80 percent of the population is White, and diversity is more often characterized in terms of age and gender, rather than ethnicity and race.

However, the city (and area) has successfully attracted younger people for pool party weekends, music festivals (notably the annual Coachella Valley Music and Arts Festival happens in Coachella, a city about 25 miles from Palm Springs), and college spring breaks—their presence is noticeable during these times and mostly welcomed. Several LGBT events are included among these attractions (in addition to Pride and film festivals): the annual White Party brings an estimated 30,000 primarily gay men into the city for a long weekend of pool parties and music; Club Skirts, which hosts the "Dinah Shore weekend," is also an annual music festival and party directed primarily toward lesbians welcoming an estimated 20,000 women ("20,000 Lesbians in the Desert," 2016).

There is also, of course, a strong Los Angeles influence on Palm Springs owing to its nearness to LA (about two hours, depending on Southern California traffic!). Much has been written about the old Hollywood influence on such desert communities because many of Hollywood's Golden Age stars sought to escape the judgmental control and glare of the studio, press and gossipmongers. They found comforting anonymity behind large hedges and the walls of their Palm Springs residences ("About Palm Springs," 2019). This flight to safe anonymity remains especially meaningful for those whose sexualities differ from the norm or are not strictly heterosexual (e.g., Wallace, 2008, "A City Comes Out").

All of these dimensions (the preponderance of midlife and older gay men, the location and history of this "resort" city, the social and physical climate, the relative homogeneity of the area) exert an influence on daily life—and sexual literacy—in Palm Springs. Just the presence of so many older gay men in so many city settings, for example, has a kind of common everydayness effect—with strong hints of the former gay enclaves of the Castro (in San Francisco) and Greenwich Village (in New York City). In informal discussions with older gay men, it is not uncommon to hear expressions of nostalgia for their former lives and times, as they describe bars, restaurants and other public gathering spots in Palm Springs that represent community and connectedness—a sense that this is "our town"—and along with it an implicit sexual citizenship that includes them. Even in many of the condominium complexes of the city, and perhaps especially on the decks of pools, which are ubiquitous in desert communities and around which many of the complexes are built, there is a noteworthy presence of midlife and older gay men. The conversations in these settings often include the exchange of knowledge, views and perspectives ranging from the best dining spots to navigating life, age and sexuality. Such conversations flow from a shared, geographic sense of sexual citizenship: the rights and responsibilities of being a citizen (of this city, state and country) and the provision of both physical and psychological space for the consideration of what this means for identities and interactions (Bell & Binnie, 2006).

The "resort" nature of the city also exerts an influence on people's expectations and experience of Palm Springs. That is, many LGBT visitors come to the Palm Springs area on vacation (frequently from much more sexually and socially restrictive towns and cities); this "vacation mode" may serve to free them of the roles and masks that otherwise obscure their authentic selves back home. The comfort afforded from being in "our town," described above, may offer both the impetus and opportunity to explore more hidden, transgressive and/or guarded aspects (e.g., thoughts, behaviors) of the self. Of course, this experience of Palm Springs extends to people beyond LGBT communities as well; the many heterosexual, cisgender visitors (and residents) are afforded a more inclusive everydayness of the company of midlife and older gay men—with implicit (and sometimes explicit) messages informing their own sexual literacy, such as, for example, questioning traditional sexual (and gender) norms.

To serve the legions of LGBT visitors, there are perhaps dozens of resorts catering to LGBT tourists, mostly gay men, the majority of which offer clothing optional settings—websites boast that no other city in the United States has as great a number of gay (and clothing optional) resorts. A sizable proportion of these resorts also offer day passes—for those "seeking action," as several websites announce. There is a "sexual energy" in many of these resorts, and surrounding area, that is similarly reminiscent of the formative more open years of the 1970s for the gay men who migrated from the gay enclaves in San Francisco and New York and elsewhere. It is also important to counter this image of sexual liberty, however, with the rather mundane ordinariness of life for many in Palm Springs; outside of the resorts and bars and other meeting areas, it is not uncommon to hear of Palm Springs "rolling up the sidewalks" early in the evening.

Perhaps related to the freedom of sexual expression implied above, sexually transmitted infections (STIs) are of concern in Palm Springs and surrounding areas. For example, the Desert Sun (the local daily newspaper) published a story (see "The Quiet Scare," 2015) noting that the city's syphilis infection rate was 20 times the national average, linking these rates to both HIV and the significance of Palm Springs as a travel destination for gay men. These demographics are associated with the challenges of sexual literacy among older gay men: sexual health messaging (e.g., from the Desert AIDS Project [DAP] and others) and reporting (such as the news article noted above) that reaches a much wider audience; such broad casting contributes to what is, arguably (and worthy of empirical pursuit), a glocal sexual literacy process that is deeper and more nuanced than what might be expected for a city this size.

The recent social history of Palm Springs carries with it the history of supporting people living with HIV who have migrated to the desert area, to find community, support and available services, such as the DAP. There is a significant presence of people living with HIV/AIDS: the rate of infection in the Coachella Valley is 400 times greater than the national average, according DAP (see "About DAP," 2019). Coachella Valley is home to the highest proportion of people living with HIV/AIDS in the county, Riverside (see "Estimates of People Living with HIV/AIDS In Riverside …," 2019).

Despite its international gay profile and long status as a secure refuge from a hostile world, Palm Springs is not devoid of homophobia or other pernicious forms of discrimination. For example, in 2009, in what became an embarrassment for the city and its police department, an undercover public sex sting targeted gay men (in a region of the city known for gay male resorts) for lewd conduct; police were caught on tape using vulgar slurs and defense attorneys were able to prove that the police department had never arrested a straight person for the same behavior ("After Warm Sands Gay Sex Sting," 2017). The relationship between the LGBT community and the police department suffered through such interactions with heightened suspicious and mistrust of the police on the part of LGBT persons. Since then, considerable outreach to the LGBT community has taken place and the relationship with the police department is much improved. There have also been anti-LGBT attacks, relatively rare though disturbing.

Similarly rare are overt expressions of ageism, perhaps not surprising, given the pre-ponderance of older people among city residents and a welcome respite from more prevalent experiences of ageism among gay men in general (Wight, Leblanc, Meyer, & Harig, 2015). This is not to say that ageism is not present, there is a subtleness to ageism found in everyday discourse applied to self and others ("you don't look 65") and Palm Springs is not exempt. Racist expressions are also infrequent, though the segregated his-tory of Palm Springs recently was in the news. An area of land, initially outside of city limits in the late 1950s, was developed by Lawrence Crossley, known as the first African American resident of Palm Springs; his goal was to create a place to live for African American families who worked in Palm Springs—but were barred from living there. On land adjacent to this "Crossley Tract" and a few years later, a golf course and luxury condominiums were being developed; a row of tamarisk trees were planted along the 14th fairway blocking views of the African American neighborhood from those living and playing on the golf course—and blocking the mountain views of those living in the "Crossley Tract," serving to maintain depressed property values ("In Palm Springs, Trees Once Planted for "Racist" Reasons Will Be Removed," 2017). The trees have stood as a reminder of this racist past and many of the trees have only recently been removed—unearthing memories and discussion of the segregated past of Palm Springs.

Some have wondered if there is an emerging homonormativity to gay (and lesbian) life in Palm Springs. The answer to this question helps us understand better the nature of sexual literacy barriers in this unique city. Homonormativity has been conceptualized in a couple of distinctive ways (Rosenfeld, 2009): postwar and neoliberal. A postwar con-ceptualization is associated with a type of "passing" or gender conformity to traditional masculine or feminine expectations, which does not challenge the view that acceptable homosexuality should adhere to heteronormativity, which is "a public privilege of hetero-sexuality" (Rosenfeld, 2009, p. 621). Here we see echoes from the former "gay ghettoes" in New York and San Francisco in the 1970s and 1980s that were places where gay men fought to find each other and that also generally linked gay sexual identity to preferred traditional cisgender expressions and identities. The neoliberal conceptualization takes a different point: being a gay man or lesbian is represented through maintaining and seeking inclusion in heterosexist institutions and values (Duggan, 2003), such as same-sex marriage and a kind of depoliticization of sexual and gender rights that intentionally downplays these for improved class mobility (e.g., de Oliveira, Costa, & Nogueira, 2013). Homonormative people in this broader neoliberal framework work within the status quo and do not prioritize seeking radical change, such as rejecting marriage for other queer kinship models, or organizing with economically marginalized people with similar sexual orientations. In both instances, heteronormativity for gay men sets the stage and provides the constructs and language for the creation of "respectable" gay and lesbian culture, or LGBTQ respectability politics (e.g., Clarkson, 2006; Robinson, 2012). The dual conceptualizations of homonormativity have temporal implications of relevance especially to the lives of older lesbian and gay persons—and hence Palm Springs.

Many observers have commented on the somewhat singular focus on marriage equality that has dominated LGBT political efforts in North America—privileging what is seen as a heterosexist construct obscuring some of the many other intersectional domains such as gender (and gender identity) rights, social economic inequalities, institutional racism, among many others. A homonormative interpretation is consistent with this focus and application to the Palm Springs example; this application may be further reinforced by the gender, age and racial homogeneity of the city overshadowing these other domains that demand attention and action as ways of building a more inclusive sexual citizenship (as seen in other larger, more diverse centers, like San Francisco, for example; see Josephson, 2016).

And this critical sexuality interpretation offers a poignant paradox: older (White) gay men both stand out in Palm Springs by virtue of their demography and yet blend in by virtue of LGBTQ respectability politics that constrain the expression of which "gay community" appears. There is so much packed into this Palm Springs social experience of relevance to advocating sexual literacy for older adults, across the spectrum of sexuality and gender, from representations and understanding dominant sex and sex role and gender role ideologies to the efforts at finding a place and a voice for those confronting sexual discrimination.

Wish you were here…

References

20,000 Lesbians in the Desert: Welcome to the Dinah, a World without Men (2016). Retrieved from https://www.theguardian.com/lifeandstyle/2016/apr/07/dinah-lesbian-festival-women-palm-springs

About DAP. (2019). Retrieved from https://www.desertaidsproject.org/about-us/

About Palm Springs. (2019). Retrieved from https://www.visitpalmsprings.com/about-palm-springs

After Warm Sands Gay Sex Sting Case, Judge Accused of Homophobic Comment in Secret Recording. (2017). Retrieved from https://www.desertsun.com/story/news/crime_courts/2017/11/01/after-warm-sands-gay-sex-sting-case-judge-accused-homophobic-comment-secret-recording/801395001/

Bell, D., & Binnie, J. (2006). Editorial: Geographies of sexual citizenship. *Political Geography*, *25*, 869–873.

Clarkson, J. (2006). "Everyday Joe" versus "pissy, bitchy, queens": Gay masculinity on StraightActing.com. *Journal of Men's Studies*, *14*(2), 191–207. doi/10.3149/jms.1402.191.

de Oliveira, J. M., Costa, C. G., & Nogueira, C. (2013). The workings of homonormativity: Lesbian, gay, bisexual, and queer discourse on discrimination and public displays of affection in Portugal. *Journal of Homosexuality*, *60*(10), 1475–1493.

Duggan, L. (2003). *The twilight of equality? Neoliberalism, cultural politics, and the attack on American democracy.* Boston, MA: Beacon Press.

Estimates of People Living with HIV/AIDS in Riverside County Were Significantly Under-Reported. (2017, November 29), *The Desert Sun.* Retrieved from https://www.desertsun.com/story/news/local/2017/11/29/over-2000-more-cases-hiv-aids-coachella-valley-than-previously-reported/902781001/

In Palm Springs, Trees Once Planted for "Racist" Reasons Will Be Removed. (2017, December 19), *The Desert Sun.* Retrieved from https://www.rgj.com/story/news/2017/12/19/palm-springs-trees-once-planted-racist-reasons-removed/964448001/

Josephson, J. J. (2016). *Rethinking sexual citizenship.* Albany: University of New York Press.

Palm Springs, California, Population (2019). Retrieved from http://worldpopulationreview.com/us-cities/palm-springs-population/

The Quiet Scare: Confronting Syphilis in Palm Springs. (2015). *The Desert Sun*. Retrieved from https://www.desertsun.com/story/news/health/2015/08/21/palm-springs-syphilis-stds/32059429/

Robinson, B. A. (2012). "Is this what equality looks like?": How assimilation marginalizes the Dutch LGBT community. *Sexuality Research and Social Policy, 9*, 327–336. doi:10.1007/s13178-012-0084-3 https://link.springer.com/article/10.1007/s13178-012-0084-3

Rosenfeld, D. (2009). Heteronormativity and homonormativity as practical and moral resources: The case of lesbian and gay elders. *Gender & Society, 23*, 617–638.

Wallace, D. (2008). *A city comes out. How celebrities made palm springs a gay and lesbian paradise*. Ft. Lee, NJ: Barricade Books.

Wight, R. G., Leblanc, A. J., Meyer, I. H., & Harig, F. A. (2015). Internalized gay ageism, mattering, and depressive symptoms among mid-life and older gay-identified men. *Social Science and Medicine, 147*, 200–208.

Chapter 29

GLOCALITY IN THE U.S. LGBT RIGHTS STRUGGLE

Sean Cahill

Struggles over LGBT equality and rights in the United States have long been "glocal." We are a country in which most residents are descended from immigrants, refugees or indentured servants, except for indigenous people and the descendants of enslaved people. While with the Internet and social media, the world is increasingly connected, there has long been a strong interplay between what is happening in other countries and what happens in the United States.

Henry Gerber, a German immigrant, formed the first US homosexual rights organization in 1924—the Society for Human Rights in Chicago. Gerber, who fought for the United States during the First World War and then lived in Germany from 1920 to 1923, was inspired by German homosexual and transsexual rights activist and sexologist Dr. Magnus Hirschfeld's Scientific-Humanitarian Committee, which sought to overturn Germany's statute criminalizing same-sex behavior. Gerber published the first publication for a homosexual audience in the United States, Friendship and Freedom. Following a police raid, arrest and imprisonment and seizure of his documents, Gerber and half a dozen other members disbanded the group in 1925 (Janega, 2013). A few years later, in May 1933, Nazis destroyed Hirschfeld's Institute for Sexual Research in Berlin and burned thousands of books (Bauer, 2014).

Brendan Fay along with Thea Spyer, a key figure in a landmark marriage equality case, are two other immigrants and refugees to the United States who have created glocal change, as did Spyer's wife Edie Windsor. Fay is an Irish gay man who came to America in the 1980s for economic as well as cultural reasons. Fay got involved in the fight to allow the Irish Lesbian and Gay Organization (ILGO) to participate in the New York City Saint Patrick's Day Parade in 1991. After appearing on television defending ILGO, Fay was fired from his job teaching at a Catholic school. He eventually formed an alternative, inclusive Saint Patrick's Day celebration in his Sunnyside/Woodside neighborhoods of Queens, New York, that also celebrated the racial and ethnic diversity of Queens. This "Saint Pats for All" project, as well as a growing boycott of the main New York Saint Patrick's Day Parade by elected officials due to its discrimination, eventually caused the organizers to allow LGBT organizations to participate in 2016—a more than 35-year struggle (Allen, 2017).

In 2016, I marched up Fifth Avenue in New York with Fay and other friends. I had marched in Boston's Saint Patrick's Day Parade in 1993 with the Irish Gay, Lesbian and Bisexual Committee under court order and with police escort. As an Irish American, this was important for me because the exclusion and silencing we experienced by Saint Patrick's Parade organizers was symbolic of the broader discrimination and stigma many of us experienced within our families and churches. Also marching with us in 2016 in Manhattan was Edie Windsor, fresh from her 2015 US Supreme Court victory striking down the US government's nonrecognition of same-sex marriages enshrined in the 1996 Defense of Marriage Act. This was a personal and political glocal moment for me.

Fay's connection with Windsor is another glocal story. Edie Windsor and her long-time partner Thea Spyer married in Toronto in 2007. They were part of a group of New York same-sex couples who traveled to Toronto to marry as part of Fay and Jesus LeBron's Marriage Freedom Trail project (LeBron & Fay, 2004). At that point marriage was legal in Canada but not in most of the United States, including New York. Windsor and Spyer met in Greenwich Village in 1963, and they started dating in 1965. Spyer came to the United States from Amsterdam as a child Jewish refugee from Nazism (Fairyington, 2014). Upon Spyer's death, Windsor, who was the executor of Spyer's will, received a federal tax bill of $363,053. Had they been a heterosexual couple, Windsor would not have received this tax bill. Windsor paid the bill and then challenged it, all the way up to the US Supreme Court.

In its landmark ruling in United States vs. Windsor, the US Supreme Court struck down Section 3 of the discriminatory Defense of Marriage Act (1996), which banned federal recognition of same-sex marriages. The court ruled that DOMA was a violation of the equal liberty of persons that is protected by the Fifth Amendment to the US Constitution as well as basic due process and equal protection principles enshrined in the Constitution (*United States v. Windsor*, 2013).

Fay is skilled at media advocacy. On his frequent trips home to Drogheda, Ireland, he engaged Irish media and government officials, who also frequently visited New York. The exclusion of gay groups from the Boston and New York Saint Patrick's Day parades caused many in Ireland to revisit the socially conservative views that had caused many people like Fay to emigrate in the first place. In 1993, Dublin allowed its first gay float in its Saint Patrick's Day Parade (Allen, 2017). Twenty-two years later, in 2015, Ireland became the first country in the world to legalize marriage equality in a ballot referendum, by a 62–38 margin. Two years later, Ireland elected as Taoiseach (Prime Minister) Leo Varadkar, a gay man and the son of an Indian immigrant (Cahill, 2018).

Another international kerfuffle emerged in 2008 when the antigay President of Poland, Lech Kaczynski, attacked Fay and his husband, Tom Moulton. In a national address urging Poles to reject the Lisbon Treaty, which Kaczynski said would force Poland to adopt sexual orientation nondiscrimination legislation, he did the following, as reported in the New York Times.

As part of his five-minute speech, Mr. Kaczynski displayed a wedding photograph of Mr. Fay and his partner, Dr. Thomas A. Moulton; showed a video clip of their 2003 wedding in Canada; and even pointed to a photo of their wedding certificate (Chan, 2008).

I attended Brendan and Tom's wedding. They took their vows in kilts, a traditional Gaelic garment. I wonder if the Polish President chose them because they appeared in what to Kaczynski was gender nonconforming dress. Fay was soon contacted by Polish and other media, which asked if he had consented to the Polish President use of his wedding photos. Fay wrote a letter to the Polish consul general in New York, stating, "We are frustrated to hear that images from such a joyous day are used to spread intolerance [...] We would never have agreed to permit our photographs as part of a homophobic campaign" (Chan, 2008). Fay and Moulton then traveled to Poland, seeking a meeting with Kaczynski, to no avail (Chan, 2008). They have since returned repeatedly to support LGBT activists in Poland. Many Poles are especially receptive to Fay, because thousands of Poles have immigrated to Ireland.

Two years after the Windsor court ruling, the US Supreme Court in Obergefell v. Hodges, 576 U.S.644 (2015) struck down state laws prohibiting same-sex marriages and more limited forms of partner recognition, like civil unions (*Obergefell v. Hodges*, 2015). The Court ruled that the right to marry is guaranteed by the equal protection and due process clauses of the 14th Amendment to the US Constitution.

In reaction to marriage equality in the United States, the religious right reacted strongly, promoting religious refusal policies at the state and federal level (Cahill, 2017), antitransgender ballot campaigns at the local and state level (Wang & Cahill, 2018), and mobilizing to elect a Republican to replace the very pro-LGBT President Obama. They succeeded in elected President Trump.

President Trump has appointed religious right activists throughout his administration. Vice President Pence is the first member of the religious right or Christian right to hold such a high office. Previous Republicans, from Ronald Reagan to George W. Bush, used opposition to gay rights issues to get elected, but were not of that community themselves (Cahill, 2004). Between his judicial appointments and his promotion of religious refusal policies, Trump has probably gone further than Reagan or the two Bushes to implement the religious right's agenda.

Among the actions the Trump Administration has taken that harm LGBT people and women are:

- Issuing federal regulations that would allow health care and social service providers to refuse to care for patients who conflict with their "religious belief or moral conviction" or force them "to act contrary to one's belief";
- Placing transgender inmates of the Federal Bureau of Prisons, especially transgender women, at much higher risk of sexual assault by incarcerating them according to their sex assigned at birth instead of their affirmed gender identity;
- Dismissing Peace Corps volunteers and Air Force service members who tested positive for HIV and refusing to provide pre-exposure prophylaxis for HIV prevention (PrEP) to at-risk Peace Corps volunteers;
- Ending the practice of issuing G-4 visas to same-sex domestic partners of foreign diplomats or employees of international organizations—such as the World Bank or the United Nations—who are working and living in the United States;

- Sending Secretary of State Mike Pompeo to attend the inauguration of Brazil's new president Jair Bolsonaro, who campaigned on a racist, misogynistic and homophobic platform and signed an executive order just hours after being sworn into office prohibiting the country's human rights ministry from hearing any concerns from Brazil's LGBT community;
- Preventing transgender people from serving in the military;
- Filing a brief with the US Supreme Court arguing that gender identity is outside of the scope of Title VII of the Civil Rights Act of 1964, which prohibits discrimination based on "race, color, religion, sex and national origin";
- Ending the US Department of Education's practice of hearing complaints from transgender students regarding their access to school facilities such as bathrooms and locker rooms that correspond to their gender identity;
- Appointing numerous anti-LGBT judges, including Supreme Court Justices Gorsuch and Brett Kavanaugh;
- Removing sexual orientation and gender identity questions from several surveys, including the National Crime Victimization Survey (which measures intimate partner violence, as well as other violent acts), a national disability survey and a national aging survey (Cahill, Wang, & Jenkins, 2019).

In 2019, the Trump Administration finalized a health care regulation that works as a federal-level religious refusal rule to "protect" the "statutory conscience rights" of health care providers (U.S. Department of Health and Human Services, 2019a). Under this rule, providers and staff who have religious objections to certain procedures can refuse to participate. While the rule focuses on abortion, assisted suicide and sterilization, the language of the rule mirrors the language of religious refusal laws in 12 states that authorize the denial of services, including health care, on the basis of religious or moral beliefs. Potential conduct protected by the final rule could include a refusal to provide care to LGBT people (*Ward v. Wilbanks*, 2010), same-sex couples or spouses/partners (White House Presidential Memorandum, 2010) and their children (Phillip, 2015). The Trump Administration also proposed to roll back a 2016 rule prohibiting discrimination on the basis of gender identity in federally funded health care facilities and programs. The original rule also prohibits some forms of sexual orientation discrimination that constitutes sex stereotyping. The administration also said that faith-based homeless shelters can refuse to admit transgender people. This same proposed rule would also have a cascading discriminatory effect by removing explicit sexual orientation and gender identity nondiscrimination language from several other programs, including federal and state health insurance exchanges and Qualified Health Plans, Medicaid and the Program of All-Inclusive Care for the Elderly (PACE), which serves nursing-home-eligible elders. These proposed changes could allow health care providers to broadly discriminate against LGBT people. Anti-LGBT discrimination in health care is widespread (Lambda Legal, 2010), and can act as a barrier to accessing both preventive and emergency health care.

President Trump has announced a push to get more than 70 countries that criminalize homosexuality to repeal their laws (Signorile, 2019). While this move is welcome, ultimately, the State Department confirmed that there was no new initiative. Rather, in a rare exception, the Trump administration was actually continuing a pro-LGBTQ effort from the Obama era [which prioritized LGBT rights in US foreign policy]. Then, a few months later in yet another rollback, the State Department banned the display of rainbow flags outside embassies, clearly undercutting [the initiative] (Signorile, 2019; brackets added for clarity).

Furthermore, the federal-level religious refusal rule finalized in May 2019 (U.S. Department of Health and Human Services, 2019a) also threatens expanded HIV prevention efforts with gay and bisexual men and transgender women in Africa and elsewhere that have been supported by the US. President's Emergency Plan for AIDS Relief over the past decade. It states that funding recipients cannot be required to "endorse, utilize, make a referral to, become integrated with, or otherwise participate in any program or activity to which the organization has a religious or moral objection" (U.S. Department of Health and Human Services, 2019a, pp. 15–16). This could mean that organizations working in the Global South could refuse to work with LGBT people, sex workers, people who use drugs, prisoners, migrant workers and others who are at elevated risk of HIV infection and already extremely marginalized and vulnerable.

As a result of this rule, LGBT advocates in Uganda and elsewhere are now experiencing a twofold setback of (1) neocolonial anti-LGBT policies being pushed in their national legislatures by US-based evangelical groups like Focus on the Family and (2) religious refusal policies promoted by the Trump Administration that will allow religious organizations to receive US HIV prevention and care money and refuse to serve gay and bisexual men and transgender women, who are disproportionately at risk for HIV infection (Kaoma, 2014; Semugoma, Nemande, & Baral, 2012).

Sometimes, in the case of Fay, Windsor and Spyer, glocalism can work to the benefit of LGBT people. Other times, as in the case of the Trump Administration's policies, it can undermine the ability of LGBT communities to organize and access basic services like health care. Spyer and Fay are examples of refugees and immigrants who help their adopted country advance toward greater equality. Fay has also supported Polish LGBT activists, who are currently facing a situation in which more than 80 Polish towns have declared themselves "LGBT-free zones" amid a rise in anti-LGBT rhetoric from the governing Law and Justice Party (Hume, 2019).

It is important that glocal sexual literacy projects take a political stance in favor of equality and liberation, and understand that sexual rights are human rights. This perspective was articulated in the 2006 Yogyakarta Principles, in which international human rights experts articulated a set of international principles related to sexual orientation and gender identity (Yogyakarta Principles, n.d.). It was then articulated by Secretary of State Hillary Clinton in 2011, when she said that "gay rights are human rights, and human rights are gay rights."

We should support local LGBT activists in Poland, Uganda and elsewhere who are organizing to live free of violence, whether it emanates from the mob or from the state. LGBT activists in sub-Saharan Africa, the Caribbean, the former Soviet bloc and the majority Muslim and Arab countries are the most vulnerable to persecution and violence (United Nations Office for the High Commissioner for Human Rights, 2015).

Many countries funded by the US PEPFAR program are also in these regions. In the 2000s, PEPFAR funded anti-LGBT organizations such as Samaritan's Purse to promote "Abstinence, Be faithful, and [as a last resort] Condoms" in Africa and elsewhere (Cahill, 2008). Most countries engaged in exclusively heterosexual HIV prevention messaging, leading many African gay and bisexual men to believe that they were not at risk of HIV. Today under President Trump, the United States allows PEPFAR recipients to refuse to work with LGBT people, sex workers, people who inject drugs, prisoners and other populations to which they have a religious or moral objection—all populations bearing a disproportionate burden in the HIV epidemic. A glocalist analysis underlines the responsibility that US activists have to resist and reverse these policies here and support grassroots LGBT activists around the world who are seeking to transform their societies to be more accepting of LGBT people.

References

Allen, S. (2017, March 9). LGBT veterans fight Boston St. Patrick's Day Parade ban. *The Daily Beast.* Retrieved from https://www.thedailybeast.com/lgbt-veterans-fight-boston-st-patricks-day-parade-ban

Bauer, H. (2014). Burning sexual subjects: Books, homophobia and the Nazi destruction of the institute of sexual science in Berlin. In G. Partington & A. Smyth (Eds.), *Book destruction from the medieval to the contemporary* (New Directions in Book History), pp. 17–33. London: Palgrave Macmillan.

Cahill, S. (2004). *Same-sex marriage in the United States: Focus on the facts.* New York: Lexington Books.

Cahill, S. (2008, July). How the U.S.-based Christian right shapes HIV/AIDS policies abroad and in international fora (poster). International AIDS Society conference, Mexico City.

Cahill, S. (2017, June 12). Refusal laws threaten LGBT health care access. *Public Health Post.* Retrieved April 2, 2021, from https://www.publichealthpost.org/?s=Cahill%2C+S.+%282017%2C+June+12%29.+Refusal+laws+threaten+LGBT+health+care+access.+Public+Health+Post.

Cahill, S. (2018, September 26). "Same-sex marriage referendum in Ireland 2015," at forum on "Public health wins in Ireland: Reflections on same-sex marriage and abortion rights." Harvard Chan School of Public Health, Boston.

Cahill, S., Wang, T., & Jenkins, B. (2019, January). *Trump Administration continued to advance discriminatory policies and practices against LGBT people and people living with HIV in 2018.* Boston, MA: Fenway Institute.

Chan, S. (2008, March 19). A New York activist, a wedding photo, and the future of Poland. *New York Times.* Retrieved from https://cityroom.blogs.nytimes.com/2008/03/19/a-queens-activist-a-wedding-photo-and-the-future-of-poland/

Fairyington, S. (2014, February 14). Inside the love story that brought down DOMA: An interview with the filmmakers who put Edith Windsor in the national spotlight. *The Atlantic.* Retrieved from https://www.theatlantic.com/national/archive/2014/02/inside-the-love-story-that-brought-down-doma/283840/

Hume, T. (2019, December 19). More than 80 Polish towns have declared themselves "LGBTQ-Free Zones." *Vice News.* Retrieved from https://www.vice.com/en_us/article/xgq8mq/european-parliament-tells-poland-to-stop-declaring-lgbtq-free-zones

Janega, J. (2013, October 30). "First gay rights group in the U.S. (1924)." *Chicago Tribune.* Retrieved from https://www.chicagotribune.com/business/blue-sky/chi-first-gay-rights-group-us-1924-innovations-bsi-series-story.html#targetText=Henry%20Gerber%2C%20immigrant%20and%20World,of%20gays%20in%20American%20society

Kaoma, Rev. K. (2014, March 23). How anti-gay Christians evangelize hate abroad. *Los Angeles Times*. Retrieved from http://www.latimes.com/opinion/op-ed/la-oe-kaoma-uganda-gays-american-ministers-20140323-story.html

Lambda Legal. (2010). *When health care isn't caring: Lambda Legal's survey of discrimination against LGBT people and people with HIV*. New York: Lambda Legal.

LeBron, J., & Fay, B. (2004, March 31). A bus ride to the freedom trail. *Gay City News*. Retrieved from https://www.gaycitynews.com/a-bus-ride-to-the-freedom-trail/

Phillip, A. (2015, February 19). "Pediatrician refuses to treat baby with lesbian parents and there's nothing illegal about it." *Washington Post*. Retrieved from https://www.washingtonpost.com/news/morning-mix/wp/2015/02/19/pediatrician-refusestotreat-baby-with-lesbian-parents-and-theres-nothing-illegal-about-it/

Semugoma, P., Nemande, S., & Baral, S. (2012). The irony of homophobia in Africa. *The Lancet*, *380*(9839), 4–5.

Signorile, M. (2019, August 20). Trump has a devastating record on LGBTQ rights. Don't deny the truth. *Washington Post*. Retrieved from https://www.washingtonpost.com/opinions/trump-may-want-you-to-think-hes-lgbtq-friendly-dont-be-fooled/2019/08/20/c2b7a7be-c36b-11e9-b72f-b31dfaa77212_story.html

U.S. Department of Health and Human Services, Office of the Secretary. (2019a, May 2). 45 CFR Part 88 RIN 0945-AA10, Protecting statutory conscience rights in health care; delegations of authority. Final Rule [Pdf file]. Retrieved from https://www.hhs.gov/sites/default/files/final-conscience-rule.pdf

U.S. Department of Health and Human Services. (2019b, May 24). *HHS proposes to revise ACA Section 1557 rule to enforce civil rights in healthcare, conform to law, and eliminate billions in unnecessary costs* [Press release]. Retrieved from https://www.hhs.gov/about/news/2019/05/24/hhs-proposes-to-revise-aca-section-1557-rule.html

United States v. Windsor, 570 U.S. 744. (2013). https://www.oyez.org/cases/2012/12-307

United Nations Office for the High Commissioner for Human Rights. (2015, May 4). *Discriminatory laws and policies and acts of violence against individuals based on their sexual orientation and gender identity*. Geneva. Retrieved from https://www.ohchr.org/Documents/Issues/Discrimination/LGBT/A_HRC_29_23_One_pager_en.pdf

Wang, T., & Cahill, S. (2018). Anti-transgender political backlash threatens health, access to care. *American Journal of Public Health*, *108*(5), 609–610. Ward v. Wilbanks, 09-CV-11237, 2010 WL 3026428 (E.D. Mich. 2010, July 26), rev'd and remanded sub nom. Ward v. Polite, 667 F.3d 727 (6th Cir. 2012), dismissed with prej. by Ward v. Wilbanks, 09-CV-11237 (E.D. Mich. Dec. 12, 2012) (case settled).

The White House, U.S. Office of the Press Secretary. (2010, April 15). *Presidential Memorandum – Hospital Visitation* [Press Release]. Retrieved from http://www.whitehouse.gov/the-press-office/presidential-memorandum-hospital-visitation

Yogyakarta Principles. (n.d.). Retrieved from https://yogyakartaprinciples.org/

Chapter 30

LIFELONG SEXUAL LITERACY: A UNIVERSAL HUMAN RIGHT FOR SEXUAL MINORITIES AND MAJORITIES

Gilbert Herdt and Stefan Lucke

This chapter advocates for lifelong sexual literacy as a universal human right for all people. Historically, human rights advocacy began in the aftermath of and as reaction to the atrocities of World War Two and was aimed at the most basic universal protections of human life. As time advanced, other protections were added to international laws and policies, the protection of women, the poor, protections of reproductive health and disempowered minorities, including sexual and gender minority people. Human rights have a deep place in western civilization and democracy (Hunt, 2007), and with the start of the new millennium, the "idea of the universality of international human rights law had gained substantial ground" (Lassen, 2014, p. 43). In this essay, we think of this general framework as protecting the inherent dignity and right to sexual, gender and reproductive freedom of expression, including the most basic of all rights, to live, and to seek out the means to well-being, across the course of life. Pleasure is a part of such a positive and respectful approach (Petchesky, Correa & Parker, 2010). The international bulwark of this set of conventions and principles is particularly critical to the foundation of the World Health Organization, whose vision of rights is well explored in Chapter 10 by D. Bhana, E. Yankah, and P. Aggleton (also see Weeks, 2011, pp. 87–90; WHO, 2015). Yet, the *interpretation* and *balancing* of human rights remain anchored in different world religions and cultures, especially regarding the topics of sexuality and gender equality, fueling an ongoing discourse about the universalism and relativism of such rights (Lassen, 2014). In spite of the inherent slowness, frustration and obstacles to these ultimate goals and principles inherent to our lifelong sexual literacy approach, there is "no better structure available for confronting these issues" (Hunt, 2007, p. 213).

Gradually as well a movement for comprehensive sex education has arisen in western countries, often coming out of local concerns that became more widely used, even in the Global South. These sex education efforts are not typically linked back to human rights (Correa, Petchesky, & Parker, 2008). Within the sex education discourse, there has been a strong tendency to focus on *negative* rights: that is, safeguarding from risk or harm, such as protecting women from being reproductively coerced. Rarely have the universal concerns for human rights been stated in the proactive and positive way that establishes and affirms local or "glocal" regional sexuality education. Notably, curricula for comprehensive sexual education were designed largely for the heterosexual majority, as well as for disease and pregnancy prevention and, later, HIV prevention. We might think of some of these "negative" rights as "glocal" in the sense that they advanced local concerns to help people with regional or global knowledge and practices. Likewise, employing an international understanding of human rights is glocal in that such rights are intended to serve individuals in their local setting. Gradually, a notion of comprehensive sexuality education has seeped into these discussions of universal rights. However, this proactive direction stopped short of addressing people of all ages; for example, there has never been an advocacy of sexual education for seniors, or for young children, at the level of international rights covenants. In both these ends of the spectrum, elders and children, the western assumption continued that they were asexual, sexually innocent or some such ideology, which made policies and interventions into these populations seem unnecessary, intrusive, irrelevant and always controversial. It is time to expand the operating definition of human sexual nature to include all the different age groups of people in protecting their negative *and positive* sexuality rights.

Lifelong sexual literacy is concerned with all humans at all the epochs of the life course. Sexual literacy is here defined as the development of sexual knowledge, skills and proactive plans and behaviors that assure sexual well-being and life satisfaction. Thus, compared to prior comprehensive sexual education visions, lifelong sexual literacy is aimed at sexual majorities and minorities alike. Moreover, we advocate a more encompassing lifelong system of knowledge and life skills necessary to promote and protect sexual health and well-being, gender identity and reproductive health. To make this new vision of lifelong sexual literacy succeed, it cannot remain confined to institutions of primary or secondary education.

Historically, *comprehensive* sex education, which emerged from health education and the praxis of disease prevention early in the twentieth century (Irvine, 2002), was designed to deal with the needs of young people coming of age and transitioning into adulthood, and—as critics may add—to instill cultural sexual norms. Much like the basic literacy movement promoted by the United Nations since 1946, which is focused on children and the amelioration of social and economic inequities, a life-course perspective on issues of literacy and sexuality has seldom resulted in ongoing programmatic efforts (UNESCO, 2019). Comprehensive sexuality education was expanded through the incredible efforts of NGOs such as Planned Parenthood Federation of America and SIECUS (formerly, Sex Information and Education Council of the United States, now Sex Ed for Social Change, located in New York) in the 1960s and 1970s to encompass the earlier teenage years (reviewed in Chapter 14 by L. Valin). Thus, in the popular discourse of the past two generations, sex education came increasingly to mean "teenage preparation for sex." Notice, however, that in the essays in this volume by Moore and Reynolds (Chapter 6) and Lucke (Chapter 7), respectively, it is abundantly clear that sexuality education for children remains tabooed in the United States, whereas sexual literacy for elders is largely unknown (see Diamond, Fagundes, & Butterworth, 2010).

Perhaps these gaps were understandable in the situation of postwar Europe and America, when resources were scarce and the average age in populations younger. Many critics would argue, however, that the taboo on sex education for young children in the

United States is a direct result of seeing in them an "innocence" and lack of sexual curiosity that is no longer defensible (Lucke, 2020). But given the much greater resource base today, and the aging populations of the world in highly developed countries such as Italy, Japan and the United States, this dearth of sexual literacy training across the life course hardly makes sense (Schwartz, Diefendorf, & McGlynn-Wright, 2014). Indeed, the continued absence of attention to elders has created an acute information gap that is urgently in need of fixing.

Our call to action for lifelong sexual literacy also represents a new changing social and behavioral reality for individuals and communities. The rapid changes in sexual, gender and reproductive health and life in the later twentieth century (e.g., the invention of hormonal contraception, the Internet, increased LGBTQ acceptance) have resulted in new populations in search of a new framework for teaching and learning. Late modern theoretical frameworks of sexual motivation have decentered the (purportedly, sole or exclusive) reproductive goal of sex in favor of foregrounding relationships, love, recreation, pleasure, not to mention the forces of the sexual marketplace (Sigusch, 2005). In other words, age groups outside of the younger, normative family-founding young adulthood era are expressing their sexuality in a variety of creative ways, including online communications and dating in the context of the Covid-19 pandemic. It is obvious that significant numbers of these sexual encounters do *not* aim to produce babies. The concept of lifelong sexual literacy needs to reflect and inform these new proactive relationships with the necessary supportive interventions to help people stay healthy and productive.

Viewed historically, and especially from the perspective of the emergence of the HIV pandemic in the 1980s, comprehensive sexuality education that was once focused on heterosexual disease prevention and pregnancy prevention was burdened further with HIV disease reduction; the result was an increase in curricular efforts directed to the sexual minorities of the time, namely, gay men (Herdt & Lindenbaum, 1992). In the more extreme variants of the risk reduction curricula—the failed "Abstinence Only" policies exported by the American government (DiMauro & Joffe, 2009)—reducing sexual risk behavior became the sole focus, as Douglas Kirby (2012) has well critiqued (also see Kocsis, 2019). Notably, this discourse not only instilled fear, anxiety and avoidance of young people's sexual relations—that is, it continued some of the silence surrounding young people's sexuality (Irvine, 2002); it also perpetuated denial of the desires of women, especially their desire for pleasure (Garland-Levett & Allen, 2018; McGeeney & Kehily, 2016; Tolman, 2002), and especially of people of color (Moore, 2012).

Today it is indeed very hard to imagine how programs of sexuality education *of any kind* could ignore sexual freedom, desire, pleasure, fulfillment, relational satisfaction and sexual variation, because these surely are core elements of human sexual nature and culture (Herdt & Polen-Petit, 2021). Nevertheless, it is undeniable that many curricula still disregard these core elements when they do not address the particular needs of sexual and gender minorities such as transgender or gender nonbinary people, or individuals with physical or mental disabilities (Monaco, Gibbon, & Bateman, 2018; Riggs & Bartholomaeus, 2018).

Our call for lifelong sexual literacy aims to encompass all these groups and to be in this way more comprehensive, empowering and proactive than earlier or traditional approaches to sex education. Sexual literacy has to start in early childhood, as implemented through parents, families, teachers, communities and the institutions of a society, including schools and churches, temples or synagogues. Sexual literacy must also encompass *media literacy* for older children, teens and adults, as the Internet in our global data age has become a major source of glocal (sexual) information and exchange (Döring, 2009, 2014; Ragonese, Bowman & Tolman, 2017). Early sexuality learning and subjective understanding, especially when positively oriented toward enhancement, enrichment, support and protection of age-appropriate cognitive and emotional nuances of sexual skills, meanings, ethical reasoning (i.e., trusting one's own feelings as valid and worthwhile) and plans for future action, can lay a solid foundation for all subsequent and continuing education.

What does "sexuality" include when it comes to the cognitive and emotional domains of being, doing, feeling and reasoning out when it comes to lifelong sexual literacy? The answer in general is: everything the person says that pertains to their own unique sexuality, which of course includes their position in their own community and society. The necessary life skills, for example, might include how to talk about sex, to negotiate sexual challenges or to stay silent, when dealing with provocative agents; how to say "no" and "yes" to intimate sexual advances; how to understand and respond to the cues of intimate partners, as well as to formulate plans that enable enhancement and enrichment of existing relationships. And when it comes to the knowledge component, sexual literacy includes the ability to seek and identify sources of accurate information, for example, about sexual frustration and sexual satisfaction, about the end of a relationship and the beginning of new ones, pregnancy complications, loss or decline of sex drive in later life and so on.

Even traumatic events across the course of life, due to the imponderables of death, sickness, violence, poverty, loss of friends or family members, separation and divorce, prolonged isolation in the pandemic and other actual events in life, may have a better outcome, with increased resilience (cf. Lerner et al., 2013), when good early knowledge, skills and plans for life are laid down (Chopra & Tanzi, 2018). Viewed in such an expansive way, of course, sexual literacy must be thought of as a relational and developmental system: both accretive and accumulative, each step of the way influencing the shape and experience of the next phase of life. This view goes hand-in-hand with recent paradigm shifts in developmental science: Cognitive development begins to be understood not only as a mental process in the brain but to include embodied action, somatic processes, and an extension into our material, technological and cultural world. In sociocultural development, the notion of individual development and culture as interacting but distinct entities is being succeeded by an emergent understanding of how both entities are codetermined, coconstructed and codeveloped (Overton & Molenaar, 2015).

Since the life course is a universal in our species, as is sexuality, we imagine that the combination of very particular events across the course of time that have sexual outcomes enable us to better link the local, the glocal and the species-wide perspectives of H. Sapiens sapiens. In other words, our approach is a means of linking the microenvironments with the macroenvironments of human sexual development. In this way, lifelong sexual literacy training is reminiscent of creating the embodied habits of an avocation, for example, that is, to become a truly accomplished musician, mathematician, dancer, swimmer or performing artist, the training starts in early life, perhaps even ages 2 or 3. As experience accumulates, skills and knowledge expand into increasing competence, enhanced performance and self-assurance. Experientially, sexual literacy is learned consciously and unconsciously in life circumstances, a combination of knowing, intuition and leaps of conviction when good sense is required. Then as practice leads to knowledge, and knowledge to the larger awareness required of relationship formation, we can see refinements in intimate communication and the respect and trust needed for critical life decisions, such as entering into long-term relationships. In this way, for some individuals, aging may increase rather than decline their ability to have satisfying intimate relationships later in life.

The concept of sexual literacy implicitly aims to both expand the targeted population range beyond normative heterosexual couples and remove cognitive and emotional constraints around sexual matters that still exist for many people. The knowledge, practice and avocation of being sexually literate should not be limited to society's traditional ideas and assumptions about "ideal" (heterosexual) relationships, sexual practices, gender roles and intimate fulfillment. Metaphorically speaking, there are multiple "dialects" of sexuality in a society; to understand and wield the grammar and vocabulary of sexuality, it is helpful not only to be literate in one dialect but in several of them, despite if individuals prefer a certain "language" or dialect for themselves. Furthermore, the sexually literate person will understand that there are many other vocabularies or dialects that one might not yet understand or be fluent in, but which are equally as valid and interesting as any variation and personal uniqueness in human sexuality.

This expanded vision of sexual literacy takes the pressure off of sexual and gender minorities and other marginalized populations who often feel compelled to explain, advocate, and to educate the majority while they already deal with the adverse consequences of oppression and normativity (see Graham & Padilla, 2014). Yet, also the sexual majority can be empowered as this vision of sexual literacy allows them to shed the straightjackets of their own, socially expected adherence to sexual norms. We feel that, ultimately, sexual literacy needs to go *beyond* the sexual and address awareness of the particularities and needs of *any* human being, regardless of being considered a (sexual) minority or majority. In that, sexual literacy points to the importance of intersectionality as a core principle in the understanding of human sexuality. Lifelong sexual literacy, understood in that way, then enables a general understanding of human, sexual rights that is universal and glocal; it appreciates that the adherence to and support of human rights might have a different shape for different sexual groups or for each individual.

Here are several practical steps and likely obstacles that we would like to pose in summing up. Advocating for lifelong sexual literacy as a human right raises some practical considerations that shall help to achieve these goals. When persuading states and governmental institutions to adhere to human rights, research on human rights practices suggest that NGOs and other nonstate actors often play a bigger role for a positive outcome than the official signing of international human rights conventions (Mitchell & Flett, 2014). NGOs (e.g., the aforementioned SIECUS) and other potential advocates and allies, such as American Association of Retired Persons (AARP), Teacher's Unions or parents' interest groups, should monitor the progress on educational programs, curricula and policy that establish and support sexual literacy. Researchers, scholars and policy makers could assist such monitoring and develop criteria for evaluation (e.g., what counts as a violation of the right to sexual literacy or create a standardized "report card" for states). Economic health and democratic political structures also play a major role for the adherence to human rights in any given society (Mitchell & Flett, 2014), so improvements in these areas will indirectly support the rights to sexual literacy.

In conclusion, we would like to underline the perennial problem of the status of children's sexual rights in the larger arena of lifelong sexual literacy and human rights. Even though *The Convention on the Rights of the Child* (CRC) has been accepted by most countries as a legal standard (unfortunately, not by the United States), various parties do not agree on the theory and reasoning behind such rights. The disagreements point at adultism, developmentalism and other epistemological arguments that question if children have rights per se or have rights granted to them, that make assumptions about children's best interests, or that differ in their understanding of children as a social group (Cordero Arce, 2015). We reiterate our central concern that lifelong sexual literacy training must begin in early childhood or else human beings will lack the necessary foundation for forward-feeding, positive sexual development. Of course, our model inevitably requires us to advocate for children's rights generally, as we accept the paradigm that considers children an oppressed minority in regard to *both age and sexuality* (Cordero Arce, 2015). It also means that we have to be cautious not to err on the side of an adultist notion that we, as adults, simply know what is best for "the child" and for all children, especially when sexual science has repeatedly failed to produce the necessary empirical data allowing us to examine core elements of childhood sexual development and well-being.

We cannot escape the conclusion that sexual literacy must contain the right for each disenfranchised group, including children and the elderly, to choose and demand their own educational content or to even refuse the offer. Similar, though not identical, issues exist for many other groups and categories of people, various forms of physical, emotional and mental impairments at any age, including the general denial of sexual rights. Lifelong sexual literacy imagines that the social and policy solutions to these challenges will not be easy in the course of human development, but it is certainly necessary for upholding human dignity and freedom.

References

Chopra, D., & Tanzi, R. E. (2018). *The healing self: A revolutionary new plan to supercharge your immunity and stay well for life*. New York: Crown.

Cordero Arce, M. (2015). Maturing children's rights theory. *International Journal of Children's Rights, 23*(2), 283–331. doi:10.1163/15718182-02302006

Correa, S., Petchesky, R., & Parker, R. (2008). *Sexuality, health and human rights*. New York: Routledge.

Diamond, L. M., Fagundes, C. P., & Butterworth, M. R. (2010). Intimate relationships across the life span. In M. E. Lamb & A. M. Freund (Eds.), *The handbook of life-span development: Social and emotional development* (vol. 2, pp. 379–433). Hoboken, New Jersey: John Wiley. doi:10.1002/9780470880166.hlsd002011

DiMauro, D., & Joffe, C. (2009). The religious right and the reshaping of sexual policy: Reproductive rights and sexuality education during the Bush years. In G. Herdt (Ed.), *Moral panics, Sex panics* (pp. 47–103). New York: New York University Press.

Döring, N. M. (2009). The internet's impact on sexuality: A critical review of 15 years of research. *Computers in Human Behavior, 25*(5), 1089–1101. doi:10.1016/j.chb.2009.04.003

Döring, N. (2014). Consensual sexting among adolescents: Risk prevention through abstinence education or safer sexting? *Cyberpsychology: Journal of Psychosocial Research on Cyberspace, 8*(1), article 9. doi:10.5817/CP2014-1-9

Garland-Levett, S., & Allen, L. (2018). The fertile, thorny, and enduring role of desire and pleasure in sexuality education. In J. Gilbert & S. Lamb (Eds.), *The Cambridge handbook of sexual development* (pp. 521–536). Cambridge: Cambridge University Press. doi:10.1017/9781108116121.027

Graham, L. F., & Padilla, M. (2014). Sexual rights for marginalized populations. In D. L. Tolman, L. M. Diamond, J. A. Bauermeister, W. H. George, J. G. Pfaus, & L. M. Ward (Eds.), *APA handbook of sexuality and psychology, vol. 2: Contextual approaches* (pp. 251–266). Washington, DC: American Psychological Association. doi:10.1037/14194-008

Herdt, G., & Lindenbaum, S. (1992). *The time of AIDS: Social analysis, theory and method.* Thousand Oaks, CA: Sage.

Herdt, G., & Polen-Petit, N. (2021). *Human sexuality: Self, society, and culture.* McGraw Hill.

Hunt, L. (2007). *Inventing human rights: A history.* New York: W. W. Norton.

Irvine, J. (2002). *Talk about sex.* Berkeley: University of California Press.

Kirby, D. (2012). *Reducing sexual risk behavior among young people: A training toolkit for curriculum developers.* Scotts Valley, CA: ETR Associates. Cited in Kantor, L. M., Rolleri, L., & Kolios, K. (2014).

Kocsis, T. (2019). *A critical analysis of sexuality education in the United States: Toward an inclusive curriculum for social justice.* New York: Routledge. doi:10.4324/9780429454684

Lassen, E. M. (2014). Universalism and relativism. In A. Mihr & M. Gibney (Eds.), *The SAGE handbook of human rights* (pp. 39–55). Los Angeles: Sage.

Lerner, R. M., Agans, J. P., Arbeit, M. R., Chase, P. A., Weiner, M. B., Schmid, K. L., & Warren, A. E. A. (2013). Resilience and positive youth development: A relational developmental systems model. In S. Goldstein & R. B. Brooks (Eds.), *Handbook of resilience in children* (pp. 293–308). Springer. doi:10.1007/978-1-4614-3661-4_17

Lucke, S. (2020). Researching childhood sexuality. In Z. Davy, A. C. Santos, C. Bertone, R. Thoreson, & S. E. Wieringa (Eds.), *The SAGE handbook of global sexualities* (vol. 1, pp. 99–118). Thousand Oaks, CA: Sage. doi:10.4135/9781529714364.n5

McGeeney, E., & Kehily, M. J. (2016). Young people and sexual pleasure—where are we now. *Sex Education, 16*(3), 235–239. doi:10.1080/14681811.2016.1147149

Mitchell, N. J., & Flett, B. N. (2014). Human rights research and theory. In A. Mihr & M. Gibney (Eds.), *The SAGE handbook of human rights* (pp. 3–21). Los Angeles: Sage.

Monaco, E. A. H., Gibbon, T., & Bateman, D. (2018). *Talking about sex: Sexuality education for learners with disabilities.* Lanham, MD: Rowman & Littlefield.

Moore, M. (2012). Intersectionality and the study of black, sexual minority women. *Gender & Society, 26,* 33–39.

Overton, W. F., & Molenaar, P. C. M. (2015). Concepts, theory, and method in developmental science: A view of the issues. In W. F. Overton, P. C. M. Molenaar, & R. M. Lerner (Eds.), *Handbook of child psychology and developmental science. Volume 1: Theory and method* (7th ed., pp. 1–8). Hoboken, NJ: Wiley.

Petchesky, R., Correa S., & Parker, R. (2010). Reaffirming pleasures in a world of dangers. In P. Aggleton and R. Parker (Eds.), *Routledge handbook of sexuality, health and rights* (pp. 401–411). New York: Routledge.

Ragonese, M., Bowman, C. P., & Tolman, D. L. (2017). Sex education, youth, and advocacy: Sexual literacy, critical media, and intergenerational sex education(s). In L. Allen & M. L. Rasmussen

(Eds.), *The Palgrave handbook of sexuality education* (pp. 301–325). London: Palgrave Macmillan. doi:10.1057/978-1-137-40033-8_15

Riggs, D. W., & Bartholomaeus, C. (2018). Transgender young people's narratives of intimacy and sexual health: Implications for sexuality education. *Sex Education, 18*(4), 376–390. doi:10.1080/14681811.2017.1355299

Schwartz, P., Diefendorf, S., & McGlynn-Wright, A. (2014). Sexuality in aging. In D. L. Tolman, L. M. Diamond, J. A. Bauermeister, W. H. George, J. G. Pfaus, & L. M. Ward (Eds.), *APA handbook of sexuality and psychology, vol. 1: Person-based approaches* (pp. 523–551). Washington, DC: American Psychological Association. doi:10.1037/14193-017

Sigusch, V. (2005). *Neosexualitäten* [Neo-Sexualities]. New York: Campus.

Tolman, D. (2002). *Dilemmas of desire: Teenage girls talk about sexuality.* Cambridge, MA: Harvard University Press.

United Nations Educational Scientific and Cultural Organization. (UNESCO). *Literacy.* Retrieved from https://en.unesco.org/themes/literacy

Weeks, J. (2011). *The languages of sexuality.* New York: Routledge.

World Health Organization (WHO). (2015). *Sexual health, human rights and the law.* Retrieved from http://apps.who.int/iris/bitstream/10665/175556/1/9789241564984_eng.pdf

PART FOUR

SEXUAL LITERACY IN HEALTH, WELL-BEING AND PRACTICE

Chapter 31

SEXUAL LITERACY AND HEALTH: A GLOBAL CHALLENGE

Deevia Bhana, Ekua Yankah and Peter Aggleton

Literacy/Sexual Literacy: How Well Are We Doing?

Since 1946, UNESCO (United Nations Educational, Scientific and Cultural Organization) has spearheaded global mass literacy efforts, underpinned by principles of human rights and dignity, to promote lifelong learning. Beyond concern for reading, (w)riting and (a)rithmetic (known collectively as the three Rs), UNESCO identifies literacy throughout the life course as "a means of identification, understanding, interpretation, creation, and communication in an increasingly digital, text-mediated, information-rich and fast-changing world" (UNESCO, 2019). Jones (1990) suggests that UNESCO's development of literacy is as much political process as it is educational, in that it seeks to open up opportunities and promote social inclusion.

UNESCO prioritizes formal schooling to achieve global technological demands while seeking to produce standard learning outcomes across the world. UNESCO also focuses on adult literacy as a remedial process to compensate for the poor provision of formal and primary schooling—especially in contexts of the Global South such as low- and middle-income countries in Africa, Asia, Latin America and the Caribbean. Notwithstanding debates around standardization, improving literacy is vital to address hunger, poverty, gender inequalities, inclusive societies and health (2030 Agenda for Sustainable Development, 2015) as well as economic and social development in this momentous era of digitalization, migration and climate change. Despite the rise in literacy rates, however, UNESCO (2019) reports that 750 million people, especially in the Global South, lack literacy skills with wide gender disparities in literacy that marginalize women and girls:

> When looking at literacy across regions, we know that southern Asia is home to almost one-half of the global illiterate population. In addition, 27 per cent of all illiterate adults live in sub-Saharan Africa, 10 per cent in eastern and south eastern Asia, 9 per cent in northern Africa and western Asia, and about 4 per cent in Latin America and the Caribbean. (UNESCO, 2019)

These statistics illustrate the urgent need for improving global literacy attentive to gender inequalities and structural fractures that marginalize literacy efforts in Africa, Asia, Latin

America and the Caribbean. Consequently, UNESCO (2019) proposes a global plan of action to "put the world back on track." While these efforts to increase global literacy are laudable, they remain "off track" not simply because of their narrow focus on the three Rs and their limited reach but also because of the notable absence of concern for literacy in a broader sense, encompassing sexual literacy.

Sexual Health and Sexual Literacy

Across the globe, significant sexual health and rights challenges include rampant HIV and other sexually transmitted infections (STIs); teenage pregnancy as the result of lack of information; gender and sexual diversity, inequality; choice restrictions in family planning; and infringements on fundamental human rights, such as poor response to sexual assault, violence and rape. The adverse effects of sexually related health challenges are vast and uneven. In sub-Saharan Africa for instance, HIV remains a major cause of morbidity and mortality (Dwyer-Lindgren et al., 2019). HIV hotspots including South Africa, UNAIDS (2019) report that young girls are eight times more likely to be living with HIV than their male peers. Global data also suggest that young people transition into adulthood ill-prepared for their sexual lives. Approximately 16 million girls aged 15–19 years and 2.5 million girls under 16 years give birth every year in developing countries (Neal et al., 2012; UNFPA, 2015). Complications during pregnancy and birth are the leading cause of death in this age group (WHO, 2016). Additionally, every year nearly 3.9 million girls aged 15–19 years undergo unsafe abortion (Darroch, Woog, Bankole, & Ashford, 2016).

This grim reality holds true not only for young people. While many women want to avoid pregnancy, approximately 225 million adult women worldwide are not using an effective contraceptive method (Singh, Darroch, & Ashford, 2014). A recent study by Robles et al. (2016) indicated that transgender adults in Mexico used hormonal contraception without proper access to medical care and treatment, and a similar situation pertains in many other majority world contexts. Moreover, too many women and girls are the victims of violence including child marriage, predatory sexual practices, intimate partner violence, sexual assault, human trafficking and rape (UN Women, 2010).

Writing in a US context, Herdt and Howe (2007, p. 3) define sexual literacy as:

> The ways in which people become knowledgeable and healthier human beings, protecting themselves from HIV and STIs, avoiding unintended pregnancies, and understanding sexual violence [it also] centers on the positive side of sexuality—learning to enjoy and appreciate sexual identities, the body, romance, pleasure and intimate relations. [Importantly,] the process of becoming sexually literate links individuals to larger communities and ultimately to society, supporting individual development and democracy. [brackets added for clarity]

Extending such an analysis slightly, sexual literacy is an important aspect of "identifying, understanding, interpreting, creating and communicating in a fast changing world" (UNESCO, 2019). Recognizing and improving sexual literacy is vital for improving sexual health, but such literacy must adopt a glocal approach as to be situational, taking heed of local culture and driven by people's diverse interests and needs, while also understanding global information circulation digital, text-mediated, information from far-away places. For instance, as part of HIV literacy campaigns, addressing gender norms and developing female sexual agency is critical to the task of sexual literacy. So too is the need to address structural fault lines. Racial inequalities, class, sexuality, faith and xenophobia increase adverse health outcomes (see, e.g., Davis, 2019; Parker, 2002). Addressing sexual literacy requires recognition of these complex processes based on and driven local by contexts.

Moreover, a focus only on the negative sexual health outcomes and morbidity is untenable in both the short- and longer term. In its current working definition, the World Health Organization (WHO) understands sexual health as:

> A state of physical, emotional, mental and social well-being in relation to sexuality; it is not merely the absence of disease, dysfunction or infirmity. Sexual health requires a positive and respectful approach to sexuality and sexual relationships, as well as the possibility of having pleasurable and safe sexual experiences, free of coercion, discrimination, and violence.
>
> For sexual health to be attained and maintained, the sexual rights of all persons must be respected, protected, and fulfilled. (UNESCO, 2019)

Sexuality thus includes pleasure, intimacy, desire and attraction. Sexuality is shaped by myriad social, psychological and biological processes. It is deeply contextual. Sexual expression interacts with (and is to a degree determined by) cultural, political, socio-economic and historical factors making it a complex experience that ties the individual to a broader social system. While personal agency is critical to improving sexual health, communities, gender power relations, poverty and access to sexual and reproductive health services all affect what is possible for people to do, or not to do. To improve sexual health throughout the lifespan, identifying, communicating, interpreting and understanding matters relating to sex and sexuality are all vital (Guzzetti, Bean, & Dunkerly-Bean, 2019). Conjoining literacy with sexual health offers strategic benefits in mobilizing attention to sex and sexuality in all its diversity and complexity.

Sexual literacy, albeit complex, must take heed of all these factors since sexuality as pleasure, desire and danger is situated in the broader sociopolitical, economic and cultural context. Sexual literacy underpinned by these complexities, as we argue, is key to the development of positive sexual health outcomes. A wide range of studies now reveals a positive correlation between sexual literacy and sexual health outcomes (Aggleton, Boyce, Moore, & Parker, 2012; Ford et al., 2017). Research suggests that girls and women who have knowledge of sexual and reproductive health measures such as contraception are more likely to use family planning (Lloyd, 2005). There is also a negative correlation between education (literacy) and low birth rates and education—in other words, the more educated a woman is the more likely she plans her pregnancies and is able to therefore more freely plan her own life. Thus, within sexual literacy advocacy is the ethical imperative for gender and economic enhancement focused on women, their children and families and their communities—inclusive of educating men and others about these issues.

To maximize these benefits and to advance sexual health, sexual literacy must be optimized throughout the life course. Put quite simply, sexual health cannot be achieved if people are not literate about the things that matter to them in their own lives—they themselves must become sexually literate to attain such control. This awareness requires an understanding of sexual literacy in ways that encompass understandings of sexuality and health based on conceptions that include rights, pleasures, intimacy and desires while addressing risk via attending to the knowledge of structural violence and power imbalances (Ford et al., 2019).

But what does sexual literacy mean in a global context? In addressing this huge question, we draw from participants in a recent International Planned Parenthood Federation Africa Region consultation, who suggested the following:

> Sexuality literacy means accessing the right knowledge about rights and responsibilities on sexuality [...] Sexual literacy empowers the people to seek the right information [...]
>
> Sexual literacy is knowledge of sexual health and well-being. It promotes development in that it prevents unintended pregnancy.
>
> Sexual literacy is a form of empowerment with regard to information or awareness of sexual health and wellbeing.
>
> Sexual literacy to me is the information or knowledge required for having/protecting good and sexual health and wellbeing.
>
> (https://ippfar.org/blogs/sexual-literacy-calling-brave-dialogues-about-sex)

What these grassroots messages tell us is that sexual literacy goes well beyond biological issues related to gender and sexuality. Sexual literacy, like all literacy, is political, rights-based and requires talking about sexuality in ways that address pleasure, consent, desire and intimacies as well as structural issues such as men's control over women or lack of investment in health care systems and economic opportunity that increase sexual risks.

Like the UNESCO definition of literacy, sexual literacy involves communication, understanding, creativity, knowledge and sexual competencies to allow people to flourish as sexual beings in society. Sexual literacy is thus not simply about danger, morbidity and personal risk—but also about developing the capacity to have a fulfilling sexual life vis-à-vis knowledge of the self and the particular situation one is experiencing. Being sexually literate allows individuals to understand the "logics" of gender, sexuality, race, age, class and geohistorical context (and their complex intertwinings), to address domination and privilege while alert to sexual expression and action that allows people to critically challenge and resist unequal relations of power. Sexual literacy is hence not a "cul de sac" but an ongoing process through which people's understanding of sexuality is developed. This involves recognition of and the ability to engage with gender and sexual systems in ways that show an understanding of domination while critically evaluating and engaging with the possibility of change.

We have illustrated ample evidence positioning sexual literacy as both an important global endeavor and a major challenge. As scholars have attested, knowledge of sexuality (sexual literacy) can improve girls' and women's ability to communicate about safe sex

(UNESCO, 2018). Sexual literacy can improve conditions to communicate about what pleasure and choice might look like in intimate partner relations (Guzzetti et al., 2019). Contemporary struggles around LGBTQA+ diversity and citizenship point to the capacity of sexuality to change life and circumstances for the better (Aggleton, Cover, Leahy, Marshall & Rasmussen, 2019). Yet for all these positives, challenges remain that inhere at the individual, community and structural levels.

Challenges to Global Sexual Literacy

Sexual literacy is steeped in notions of sex and sexuality that are heavily stigmatized and discriminated against. Efforts to promote inclusive sexuality, sexual literacy and sexual health often face barriers in local communities, health care settings and broader society. Indeed, it can be argued that matters concerning sexual health only receive credence when they focus on health risks, which means that the more positive aspects of sexuality such as pleasure, rights and desire are rarely scripted into everyday talk about sexual health. Moreover, social media and communication technologies are restricted to particular sectors of the globe with many parts of the world such as the Global South, the Middle East and China lacking access (through lack of provision, censorship and in other ways) to eHealth and other forms of formal sexual literacy information provisioning. These challenges are exacerbated in the context of refugees and immigrants who often face xenophobic violence. Mass migration conflicts frequently expose people to abuse, sexual trauma and violence.

Another issue that must be considered in the challenge facing global sexual literacy concerns the intersections between race, class and gender. Since the sociopolitical and cultural context shapes how individuals conceive of their sexuality and become sexually literate, these social conditions produce both possibilities and constraints. In contexts where gender and sexual diversity, for example, is legally prohibited, the expansion of sexual literacy to encompass respect for such diversity will be constrained. There are also challenges to questions about age-appropriate sexual knowledge. Sexual consent remains problematic especially as consensual sex assumes equality in decision-making skills. Sexual literacy is often stymied when young people and children are defined as "not yet ready" to develop the skills, values and knowledge associated with sex and sexuality (Guzzetti et al., 2019). Child marriage challenges these developmental ideals of sexuality but also raises the question of sexual literacy as it pertains to child brides and their husbands-to-be.

Queering sexual literacy requires addressing gender, age and sexual norms, but following Rasmussen and Allen (2014), sexual literacy must be both radical and political. By this we mean that sexual literacy cannot be "cordoned off" to just one set of learning outcomes as an end point. Rather sexual literacy must be seen as "mutating, changing, unfolding," endlessly creating new possibilities based on what matters to people. Sexual literacy is thus a lifelong process, variable and may encompass disparate concerns dependent on geographical and regional location.

Internationally, we have a long way to go in the pursuit of sexual literacy, what it means and what it will take to allow sexual literacy to thrive. However, it is important to normalize the diversity of sexuality in relation to literacy and health beyond disease risk and danger. We must recognize wide variations in expectations and experience, and the structural inequalities and stigma associated with heteronormative imperative that surveils and constrains sex and sexuality. Despite the challenges, we need to harness possibilities to place sexual literacy high on the agenda in pursuit of beneficial sexual health outcomes.

Conclusion

This chapter has argued that unless global literacy efforts are conjoined with sexual literacy, poor health outcomes are more likely to continue especially in local contexts where they matter the most. By linking literacy, sexual literacy and sexual health toward an aim of glocal sexual literacy efforts to normalize a range of sex and sexuality, while also addressing sexual stigma and increasing possibilities for knowledge and action, it is possible to enhance positive sexual health outcomes (Epstein & Mamo, 2017). To advance sexual literacy and sexual health then requires us to address literacy throughout the life course. Since sexuality changes through the lifespan, sexual literacy initiatives must reflect the changing force of developmental sexuality as not only an issue of the young but for all ages. To be clear, this force interacts with other social forces. Sexual literacy is thus inextricably tied to broader situational factors such as race, class, gender, history, culture and geography. The development of sexual literacy skills is thus constrained by, or enabled in relation to, specific contexts.

While we are still developing our understanding of sexual literacy, there is need to address these key barriers related to social inequalities. A prime example is the situation in the Global South where literacy skills remain lacking, hampered by structural and historical inequalities (UNESCO, 2019).

Throughout this chapter, we have advanced an approach that highlights the international effort needed. Sexual literacy is a democratic process grounded in grass-roots initiatives involving traditional structures as well as nonformal educational activities (it is neither something a government or health or education department can impose nor a one-off revolutionary exercise). Glocal literacy efforts should be tailored to those who are disproportionately affected by lack of literacy opportunities and address the types of information, competences, skills and appreciations they need most. New strategies are needed for teaching literacy beyond the school context to bring education to community spaces wherein women and girls, gender and sexual minorities and other structurally disadvantaged groups gather.

The challenge lies in finding methods that view sexual literacy not as a problem of individual countries, communities or cultures but as something that is part of a broad, connected social system. If we are to conceive accurate glocal sexual literacy efforts, then it is imperative to understand that local literacy must be conjoined with global sexual health and literacy. Wagner (2011) suggests that the key to ending poor literacy lies in the work of international agencies such as UNESCO and its development partners. However, considering the current context in which both literacy and sexual literacy have not yet permeated the global world, it is impossible to think of containing literacy efforts to these agencies alone.

To summarize, developing sexual literacy is about the development of a critical consciousness, which shows how sexuality is shaped, how heterosexuality is enforced, as well as about the broader social parameters through which sexuality is regulated through gender and power relations (Fahs & McClelland, 2016). Individuals' ability to choose, and to express rights and freedoms are located within heavily constrained circumstances, and these shape what and how literacy is produced and developed. Like the emergent field of critical sexuality studies (Fahs & McClelland, 2016), sexual literacy efforts involves a critical examination of power and privilege that must take heed of "overlooked bodies," focusing on the operation of gender and oppression by a heteronormative imperative. Sexual literacy involves recognizing how sexuality and power collide in contexts but crucially provide knowledge for people to act against oppressive conditions and subvert power toward living lives of their own making. Being sexually literate is thus about building agency (both personal and collective) despite oppressive conditions in order to understand and act in developing a life of one's own.

Thinking, talking and teaching sexual literacy is a multipronged challenge located in all aspects of the social and "online" life. Ultimately, its pursuit is the responsibility of national authorities including governments, state institutions and health and education services along with community organization, groups and individuals within their communities. All must work together to broaden global reach and improve sexual health outcomes to improve thriving for all.

References

Aggleton, P., Boyce, P., Moore, H. L., & Parker, R. (Eds.). (2012). *Understanding global sexualities: New frontiers (Sexuality, culture & health)*, 1st ed. London: Routledge.

Aggleton, P., Cover, R., Leahy, D., Marshall, D., & Rasmussen, M. L. (Eds.). (2019). *Youth, sexuality and sexual citizenship*. London: Routledge.

Darroch, J., Woog, V., Bankole, A., & Ashford, L. S. (2016). *Adding it up: Costs and benefits of meeting the contraceptive needs of adolescents*. New York: Guttmacher Institute.

Davis, D. A. (2019). *Reproductive injustice: Racism, pregnancy, and premature birth*. New York: New York University Press.

Dwyer-Lindgren, L., Cork, M. A., Sligar, A., Steuben, K. M., Wilson, K. F., Provost, N. R., & Hay, S. I. (2019). Mapping HIV prevalence in sub-Saharan Africa between 2000 and 2017. *Nature, 570*(7760), 189–193.

Epstein, S., & Mamo, L. (2017). The proliferation of sexual health: Diverse social problems and the legitimisation of sexuality. *Social Science and Medicine, 188*, 176–190.

Fahs, B., & McClelland, C. I. (2016). When sex and power collide: An argument for critical sexuality studies. *Journal of Sex Research, 53*(4–5), 392–416.

Ford, J. V., Corona Vargas, E., Finotelli, Jr, I., Fortenberry, J. D., Kismödi, E., Philpott, A., ..., & Coleman, E. (2019). Why pleasure matters: Its global relevance for sexual health, sexual rights and wellbeing. *International Journal of Sexual Health, 31*(3), 217–230.

Ford, J. V., Ivankovich, M. B., Douglas, J. M., Hook, E. W., Barclay, L., Elders, J., ..., & Coleman, E. (2017). The need to promote sexual health in America: A new vision for public health action. *Sexually Transmitted Diseases, 44*(10), 579–585.

Guzzetti, B. J., Bean, T. W., & Dunkerly-Bean, J. (Eds.). (2019). *Literacies, sexualities, and gender: Understanding identities from preschool to adulthood*. New York: Routledge.

Herdt, G., & Howe, C. (2007). Introduction. In G. Herdt & C. Howe (Eds.), *21st Century sexualities: Contemporary issues in health, education and rights*. London: Routledge.

International Planned Parenthood Federation of Africa. (2019). Sexual literacy—calling for brave dialogues about sex. Retrieved from https://ippfar.org/blogs/sexual-literacy-calling-brave-dialogues-about-sex

Jones, P. W. (1990). UNESCO and the politics of global literacy. *Comparative Education Review, 34*(1), 41–60.

Lloyd, C. B. (2005). *Growing up global: The changing transition to adulthood in developing countries*. Washington, DC: National Academy Press.

Neal, S., Matthews, Z., Frost, M., Fogstad, H., Camacho, A. V., & Laski, L. (2012). Childbearing in adolescents aged 12–15 years in low resource countries: A neglected issue. New estimates from demographic and household surveys in 42 countries. *Acta Obstetricia et Gynecologica Scandinavica, 91*(9), 1114–1118.

Parker, R. (2002). The global HIV/AIDS pandemic, structural inequalities and the politics of international health. *American Journal of Public Health, 92*(3), 343–347.

Rasmussen, M. L., & Allen, L. (2014). What can a concept do? Rethinking education's queer assemblages. *Discourse: Studies in the Cultural Politics of Education, 35*(3), 433–443.

Robles, R., Fresán, A., Vega-Ramírez, H., Cruz-Islas, J., Rodríguez-Perez, V., Domínguez-Martínez, T., & Reed, G. M. (2016). Removing transgender identity from the classification of mental disorders: A Mexican field study for ICD-11. *Lancet Psychiatry, 3*(9), 850–859.

Singh, S., Darroch, J. E., & Ashford, L. S. (2014). *Adding it up: The costs and benefits of investing in sexual and reproductive health*. New York: Guttmacher Institute.

United Nations. (2015). Transforming our world: The 2030 Agenda for Sustainable Development. Retrieved from https://sustainabledevelopment.un.org/post2015/transformingourworld

UN Women. (2010). Fast facts on violence against women and girls. Retrieved from http://www.endvawnow.org/en/articles/299-fast-facts-statistics-on-violence-against-women-and-girls-.html

UNAIDS. (2019). *Women and HIV: A spotlight on adolescent girls and young women* [Pdf file]. Retrieved from https://www.unaids.org/sites/default/files/media_asset/2019_women-and-hiv_en.pdf

UNESCO. (2018). *International technical guidance on sexuality education (Volume 2)*. Paris: UNESCO.

UNESCO Institute for Lifelong Learning. The global alliance for literacy. Retrieved from http://uil.unesco.org/literacy/global-alliance

UNESCO Institute for Statistics, & Global Education Monitoring Report Team. (2019). *Meeting Commitments: Are countries on track to achieve SDG 4?* Paris, France: UNESCO.

UNFPA. (2015). *Girlhood, not motherhood: Preventing adolescent pregnancy*. New York: UNFPA.

United Nations Educational Scientific and Cultural Organization. (UNESCO). Literacy. Retrieved from https://en.unesco.org/themes/literacy

Wagner, D. A. (2011). What happened to literacy? Historical and conceptual perspectives on literacy in UNESCO. *International Journal of Educational Development, 31*(3), 319–323.

World Health Organization (WHO). (2016). *Global health estimates 2015: Deaths by cause, age, sex, by country and by region, 2000–2015*. Geneva: Author.

World Health Organization (WHO). (2021). Gender and human rights. Retrieved from http://www.who.int/reproductivehealth/topics/gender_rights/sexual_health/en/index.html

Chapter 32

REPRODUCTIVE RIGHTS AND JUSTICE: THINKING THROUGH THE CONNECTIONS, CONTRADICTIONS AND COMPLEXITIES

Elisabeth Berger Bolaza

Human reproductive life is imbued with values, taboos and regulations, due in part to the relationship between human sexuality and the great social significance of reproduction. The rights and justice issues embedded in the reproductive body are patterned by social context and cultural location. Intersecting social forces such as racism and classism also shape reproduction in concrete ways. A holistic sexual literacy would include awareness of reproductive politics, rights and justice. With this in mind, this chapter explores universalized reproductive rights frameworks as they have evolved over time, contrasted with unfolding movements for reproductive justice and the myriad of glocal expressions of reproductive life.

Reproductive Rights

Reproductive rights impact people of all genders and sexualities, cultures and ethnicities, while encroaching into sensitive cultural and religious terrain. One way to conceptualize a glocal understanding of reproduction is to critically examine reproductive rights language and frameworks. Today numerous international documents advance reproductive rights. Reproductive Rights first articulated at the International Conference on Population and Development in Cairo in 1995 (UN, 1994) reads as follows:

> Reproductive rights rest on the recognition of the basic right of all couples and individuals to decide freely and responsibly the number, spacing and timing of their children and to have the information and means to do so, and the right to attain the highest standard of sexual and reproductive health. They also include the right of all to make decisions concerning reproduction free of discrimination, coercion and violence. (UN, 1994)~~WHO, 2019~~

The Universal Declaration of Human Rights drafted by the United Nations (UN) in 1948, formed the critical foundation for all human rights discourse, but omitted reproductive issues. It would be almost 20 years before a major international statement addressed reproductive life, in the *Declaration on Population by World Leaders*, as follows:

The Universal Declaration of Human Rights describes the family as the natural and fundamental unit of society. It follows that any choice and decision with regard to the size of the family must inevitably rest with the family itself, and cannot be made by anyone else. But this right of parents to free choice will remain illusory unless they are aware of the alternatives open to them. Hence, the right of every family to information and the availability of services in the field is increasingly considered as a basic human right and as an indispensable ingredient of human dignity (Ayala & Caradon, 1968, p. 2).

Their primary concern was population growth, which world leaders believed posed a serious threat to the future of humankind (Ayala & Caradon, 1968). The earliest international human rights accord to deal directly with reproduction is the *Convention on the Elimination of All Forms of Discrimination against Women* or CEDAW (Englehart & Miller, 2014). Adopted by the UN in 1979 and signed by 189 nations to date, CEDAW requires signatory states to eliminate sexist discrimination, challenge traditional norms that arise from and perpetuate sexist notions that women are inferior to men, ensure that men and women are equally able to control their reproduction, and prevent and address violence against women and girls. Notably, the United States and Palau have signed but not ratified CEDAW, and it remains unsigned by Iran, The Holy See, Somalia, Sudan and Tonga.

Universal human rights charters did not explicitly include sexuality until the UN convened the Programme of Action of the International Conference on Population and Development (ICPD) in Cairo in 1994. Thanks to the hard work of advocates and activists, this UN conference marked a turning point away from racist and classist preoccupations with curbing population growth, and pivoted toward protecting reproductive rights, autonomy and individual choice (Cook & Fathalla, 1996; Higer, 1999; McIntosh & Finkle, 1995). The resulting ICPD documents proclaim the centrality of sexual and reproductive rights to health and development:

> Sexual and reproductive health and rights spans the lives of both women and men, offering individuals and couples the right to have control over and decide freely and responsibly on matters related to their sexual and reproductive health, and to do so free from violence and coercion. (UN, 1994)

The ICPD articles tackled issues of birth control, maternal and infant mortality, the education of women and mitigating the impact of unsafe abortion (though a universal right to safe abortion care was not named). It also acknowledged that reproductive rights would not be fulfilled in reality without the necessary conditions, including freedom from discrimination, universal access to education and health care and ample funding. The ICPD principles have been expanded, refined and operationalized over time. In 2007, the *Yogyakarta Principles* expanded global human rights language to address sexual orientation and gender identity. These were then expanded further in 2017 to name issues of gender expression and sex characteristics, a victory resulting from a glocal process that integrated findings from various local contexts around the world.

In another step forward, sexual and reproductive health targets were explicitly included in the UN Millennium Development Goals (MDGs). The MDGs, ratified in

2000 by 189 countries, were hailed as a historic achievement in creating a global consensus to achieve measurable progress toward eight shared priorities by 2015. This was a tide shift away from a more passive role in naming rights toward becoming actively accountable for their fulfillment. Reproductive rights and health goals were featured in MDG 5 (maternal health) and MDG 6 (HIV/AIDS, malaria and other diseases). However, critical connections between gender equity, reproductive health and rights were overlooked. When the MDGs outcomes were evaluated in 2015, it became clear that a more nuanced and intersectional approach was needed (WHO, 2015).

Through a massive participatory process involving advocacy and activism from around the globe, the MDGs were improved and expanded into 17 Sustainable Development Goals (SDGs) to be achieved by 2030. These improvements include a broader and interconnected view of reproductive life that focuses on health care and family planning (SDG 3), gender-inclusive equitable education (SDG 4), and gender equality and empowerment broadly (SDG 5). The SDGs address other tough issues related to governance, infrastructure, peacemaking, the environment and economic viability, which surely impact reproductive rights. To be achieved in full by 2030, the SDGs also buck incrementalism. Overall, the SDGs represent bolder and nuanced political analyses guiding current efforts of UN member states (WHO, 2015). And progress continues as sexual and reproductive rights remained a priority of the UN Nairobi Summit in November 2019. Further, seven other international documents assert and define sexual and reproductive rights for particularly marginalized groups including women, children, the disabled, indigenous and sexual minorities. Altogether, the global accords presented here illustrate how the glocal circuit works positively in terms of organizing institutions and states to come together in global-level conventions making joint decisions but then also revising such guidance after application in local contexts.

Yet in spite of such solid global work, certain individual states and localities actively oppose reproductive rights in terms of language and implementation in policies, programs and services. One example is the recent coalition-building efforts by states generally opposing sexual and reproductive rights in international accords, as well as specifically challenging the right to abortion and contraception by the United States, Saudi Arabia, Russia and others (Cha, 2019). This is nothing new. Human rights have never enjoyed universal adoption or assurance. Reproductive rights are no different.

The concept of human rights has not been applied uniformly across the spectrum of reproductive experience for all people (Brown, 2019; Davis, 2019a, 2019b; Ross & Solinger, 2017). For example, in clear violation of human rights accords, public health programs in the United States forced sterilizations on indigenous, Latina and Black women, with cases reported well into the 1980s (Silliman, Fried, Ross & Gutiérrez, 2004; Smith, 2005). Another example is childbirth. Recent studies documenting abuse during childbirth have gained public attention (Bohren et al., 2019; d'Oliveira, Diniz, & Schraiber, 2002; da Silva, Marcelino, Rodrigues, Toro, & Shimo, 2014; Davis, 2019a; 2019b; Diaz-Tello, 2016; Flavin, 2008; Grilo Diniz, Rattner, Lucas d'Oliveira, de Aguiar, & Niy, 2018; Oparah, & Black Women Birthing Justice (BWBJ), 2016; Paltrow & Flavin, 2013). These studies collectively describe many examples of obstetric violence and abuse such as physical assault (including slapping or striking patients in labor), conducting vaginal examinations, surgical procedures (such as episiotomy, cesarean or sterilization), administering medications without informed consent or against explicit refusal and imprisoning birthing people in health institutions involuntarily. Other examples include verbal threats or insults, shroud-waiving, withholding information, providing false information, threatening to or actively engaging authorities to remove newborns from parental custody and other coercive tactics used to force complicity with clinician orders. The WHO has issued statements regarding the rights of people in childbirth as a first step to address the problem in a top-down fashion (WHO, 2014, 2018). However, national level pushback also occurs. For example, the Brazilian Health Ministry issued statements opposing the use of the term "obstetric violence" altogether as unproductive, without issuing any corresponding statements to address the institutionalized abuse of birthing people (Ignacio, 2019). Glocal thinking and analysis reveals gaps between universally promised human rights and lived reality for communities and individuals.

Usefulness and Limitations of Reproductive Rights

Reproductive Rights discourse established in global conventions has created a baseline language, or ways of talking about, the human rights issues embedded in reproduction. This language has been leveraged to enact policy and roll out programming that have reduced maternal mortality and morbidity, addressed unmet need for contraception and sexual health care and assured access to abortion, STI and HIV/AIDS treatment and more. No doubt this language has contributed to the global health movement and impacted the lives of many, particularly in well-resourced parts of the world given greater access to information and general discussion on these topics. Yet, there remain tremendous gaps between the above-stated rights and lived reality for many people, particularly those marginalized by state policy and/or cultural and religious conventions.

In the legal and policy academies there is a good deal of debate as to the nature of human rights discourse, and how it works and for whom. Corrêa, Petchesky, and Parker (2008) argue that human rights are indispensable yet insufficient for human progress, and offer reassurance that social justice efforts are on the right track with their tireless pursuit of rights (pp. 151–163). But is the only shortcoming of rights their insufficiency? While human rights thinkers ponder whether or not human rights are enforceable, "such debates seem academic in the face of overwhelming evidence of persistent abuse" (Farmer, 2005, p. 221). Some have taken a more critical view of human rights discourse as a device. Using the example of "freedom from cruel and unusual punishment and torture," one of the oldest recognized human rights, Higgins (1994) makes the quandary of the situation quite plain:

> No one doubts that there exists a norm prohibiting torture. No state denies the existence of such a norm; and, indeed, it is widely recognized as a customary rule of international law by national courts. But it is equally clear from, for example, the reports from Amnesty International, that the great majority of states systematically engage in torture. If one takes the view that noncompliance is relevant to the retention of normative quality, are we to

conclude that there is not really any prohibition of torture under customary international law? (Higgins, 1994, cited by Steiner, Alston, & Goodman, 2008, p. 141)

As put by Farmer (2010), "Laws are not science; they are normative ideology and are thus tightly tied to power" (p. 235). Rights, and their translations into law, track the interests of power. Some have criticized rights-granting institutions as functioning as a façade or decoy (Farmer, 2010; Žižek, 2002, 2006). Žižek distinguishes a basic incompatibility at the core of human rights discourse, namely between neoliberalism and social justice, an incompatibility that human rights discourse serves to mask (2002, p. 2). Those with the power to declare universal human rights for individuals are also those who maintain the myriad of economic and legal structures that systematically violate human rights. Enter here movements for Reproductive Justice that have long asserted that rights are meaningless without their actualization in the lives of real people, particularly those hard pressed by systems of oppression.

Reproductive Justice: Feminist, Black Feminist and Queer Approaches

Mainstream reproductive health organizing over several decades has accomplished great progress in expanding access to reproductive health services including contraception, abortion, prenatal and birth care (Corrêa et al., 2008; Silliman et al., 2004; WHO, 2015). However, these efforts, led by largely upper-class White-identifying women in Western nations, have too often ignored issues facing women of color (WOC) and queer people of color (QPOC) (Combahee River Collective, 1983; Silliman et al., 2004). For example, in the United States, the most severe reproductive issues are shouldered by WOC and QPOC in most every measurable health outcome (CDC, September 2019, October 2019). The *reproductive justice* framework as developed by WOC organizing in the southern United States and the global south over the last 50 years articulates and challenges dominant understandings of reproductive politics. Structural racism, sexism, classism and violence operate through the myriad of avenues in the institutions where reproductive health is managed—both in preventing unwanted pregnancy and healthfully bearing and raising children. Answering to complex and unaddressed reproductive health challenges, movements for Reproductive Justice continue to be led by women and queer people of color today (Davis, 2019a, 2019b; Ross & Solinger, 2017; Silliman et al., 2004). These movements have defined *Reproductive Justice* as: "the human right to maintain personal bodily autonomy, have children, not have children, and parent the children we have in safe and sustainable communities" (Asian Communities for Reproductive Justice, 2013; SisterSong, 2019).

The *Birth Justice Movement*, for example, is within the umbrella of reproductive justice organizing (Sistersong, 2019). Beginning roughly in the early and mid-2010s, Birth Justice scholarship began to address the intersecting oppressions facing WOC and QPOC specifically in birth and postpartum (Diaz-Tello, 2016; Diaz-Tello & Paltrow, 2012; Oparah & Bonaparte, 2015; Oparah & BWBJ, 2016; Paltrow & Flavin, 2013; Silliman et al., 2004). Birth justice advocates have argued that birth should be explicitly named in the definition of reproductive justice, highlighting particular forms of institutionalized violence many birthing people experience, especially WOC and QPOC (Diaz-Tello, 2016; Diaz-Tello & Paltrow, 2012; National Advocates for Pregnant Women, 2010; Oparah & BWBJ, 2016, pp. 6–7). Birth Justice activists challenge racist, classist, heteronormative and neoliberal frames persistent in the typically White upper-class spaces focused on birth rights, natural birth, breastfeeding as well as mainstream obstetric and maternal public health thinking (Cheyney, 2008; Craven, 2010; Davis, 2019a; 2019b; McCormack, 2005; Oparah & BWBJ, 2016). The Birth Justice Movement acknowledges pregnancy, birth and early parenting as fundamental to broader social justice transformation and empowerment (Oparah & BWBJ, 2016).

Reproductive justice is often conceptualized as a feminist project. There are many feminisms, most of which address reproductive life in some way (Humm, 2014; Luke & Gore, 2014). Feminism, at large, can be understood as multifaceted cultural, political and intellectual movements for the equality of all genders (hooks, 2000). Mainstream feminists have been accused of universalizing and thereby erasing the experiences of marginalized races and classes of people, especially WOC, QPOC, indigenous and disabled people; and thereby reinforcing their oppression (for review, see Gunew, 2019). *Intersectional feminism* is a form of feminism rooted in *intersectionality*, a knowledge project that acknowledges that race, class, sexual orientation, gender and other socially constructed systems and ideologies of hierarchy and power do not exist or exert influence in isolation, but rather intersect, interact and construct each other (Collins, 2015; Crenshaw, 1989). *Black feminism* centers and celebrates Blackness and Black knowledge in the pursuit of gender equity (Carby, 2007). *Decolonizing feminism* endeavors to extract colonial structures of power and reinstate the authority of indigenous and aboriginal ways of knowing and being to liberate all genders from White supremacist patriarchy (Hernandez & Rehman, 2019; Mohanty, 2003; Smith, 2005). Disability is another important piece of this puzzle, as ability and disability pattern reproductive life in significant ways (Garland-Thomson, 2002). Like gender and race, motherhood is itself socially and historically constructed, and that "the category of *mother* is distinct from the category woman and that many of the problems mothers face—social, economic, political, cultural, psychological, and so forth—are specific to women's role and identity as mothers." (O'Reilly, 2016, p. 2). *Matricentric Feminism* can be understood, then, as a mode of feminism "organized from and for the particular identity and work of mothers" (O'Reilly, 2016, p. 2). All of these feminisms are fruitful for reproductive justice work in that they articulate unique positionalities, elucidate specific modes of oppression and reveal levers for activism and advocacy.

Queer theory, a vast field of scholarly discourse related to and distinct from feminist scholarship, contends with all constructions of gender and interrogates gendered terms such as man, woman, mother and father, as heteronormative. Trans, gender nonconforming and intersex folx experience and seek to manage their reproductive capacities and fulfill their reproductive desires in heteronormative institutions and cultures that are openly hostile, render them invisible or are woefully unprepared to serve them (Cipres et al., 2017; Dreger & Herndon, 2009; Light, Obedin-Maliver, Sevelius, & Kerns, 2014; Obedin-Maliver & Makadon, 2016; Ryan, 2013). Assuring that the reproductive rights of all people are fulfilled will require approaches to reproductive justice work that are inclusive of all people whatever their gender, sexuality, race, ability, sociogeographic position or other salient power differentials via local context.

Conclusion

Universal conceptualizations of reproductive rights have been a great step toward ensuring reproductive justice for populations around the world. Reproductive Rights discourses have established important common legal and political ground in the pursuit of reproductive health and justice. The language of reproductive rights has served to inspire action and direct resources on international, national and regional levels for the improvement of the well-being and reproductive autonomy of people across the globe. However, much work remains to be done at local levels where the most egregious reproductive harms and negative outcomes persist. In spite of international accords, great disparities remain. Individuals with requisite means and power (socially or culturally) can secure access to contraception, abortion, assistive reproductive technologies, prenatal and birth-related care and the freedom to parent in environmental and political safety. Those who lack sufficient economic, social or cultural capital (Bourdieu, [1979] 2013) face myriad institutional pressures and constraints that conspire to compromise their reproductive rights and well-being. Social and political forces shape the reproductive lives of everyday people around the world in ways that are profoundly personal. How reproduction is framed and controlled varies with local context depending on some of the glocal influences reviewed in this chapter, including cultural, legal, medical and social norms. Those facing intersecting oppressions such as racism, colorism, classism, sexism, heteronormativity, ableism, ageism and beyond, face the steepest challenges and typically have the worst reproductive health outcomes given the various power imbalances impacting these positionalities. Reproductive justice movements in their many forms are leading the way toward a future where all people enjoy the fullness of their reproductive rights.

References

Ayala, T., & Caradon, L. (1968). Declaration on population: The world leaders statement. *Studies in Family Planning, 1*(26), 1. doi:10.2307/1965194

Bohren, M. A., Mehrtash, H., Fawole, B., Maung, T. M., Balde, M. D., Maya, E., ... & Adeyanju, A. O. (2019). How women are treated during facility-based childbirth in four countries: A cross-sectional study with labour observations and community-based surveys. *Lancet, 394*(10210), 1750–1763.

Bourdieu, P. (2013). *Distinction: A social critique of the judgement of taste.* Oxon: Routledge.

Brown, J. (2019). *Birth strike: The hidden fight over women's work.* Oakland, CA: PM Press.

Carby, H. (2007). White woman listen! Black feminism and the boundaries of sisterhood. In *CCCS selected working papers* (pp. 753–774). Oxon: Routledge.

Centers for Disease Control. (2019, October 10). *Pregnancy mortality surveillance system.* Division of Reproductive Health, National Center for Chronic Disease Prevention and Health Promotion. Retrieved from https://www.cdc.gov/reproductivehealth/maternal-mortality/pregnancy-mortality-surveillance-system.htm

Centers for Disease Control. (2019, September 24). *Data and Statistics*. Division of Reproductive Health, National Center for Chronic Disease Prevention and Health Promotion. Retrieved from https://www.cdc.gov/reproductivehealth/data_stats/index.htm

Cha, A. E. (2019, September 24). U.S. joins 19 nations, including Saudi Arabia and Russia: "There is no international right to an abortion." *Washington Post, Health*. Retrieved from https://www.washingtonpost.com/health/2019/09/24/us-joins-nations-including-saudi-arabia-russia-there-is-no-international-right-an-abortion/?fbclid=IwAR0n1PAC4Gh6JDSRxgsVB-JAJ3ux55OiELwwaB5PsAc8OUDQ4dOWbyL7dFA

Cipres, D., Seidman, D., Cloniger III, C., Nova, C., O'Shea, A., & Obedin-Maliver, J. (2017). Contraceptive use and pregnancy intentions among transgender men presenting to a clinic for sex workers and their families in San Francisco. *Contraception, 95*(2), 186–189.

Collins, P. H. (2015). Intersectionality's definitional dilemmas. *Annual Review of Sociology, 41*, 1–20.

Combahee River Collective. (1983). Combahee River Collective Statement. In B. Smith (Ed.), *Home girls: A black feminist anthology* (pp. 272–282). New York: Kitchen Table: Women of Color Press.

Cook, R. J., & Fathalla, M. F. (1996). Advancing reproductive rights beyond Cairo and Beijing. *International Family Planning Perspectives, 22*(3), 115–121.

Corrêa, S., Petchesky, R., & Parker, R. (2008). *Sexuality, health and human rights*. Oxon: Routledge.

Craven, C. (2010). *Pushing for midwives: Homebirth mothers and the reproductive rights movement*. Philadelphia, PA: Temple University Press.

Crenshaw, K. (1989). Demarginalizing the intersection of race and sex: A Black feminist critique of antidiscrimination doctrine, feminist theory and antiracist politics. *University of Chicago Legal Forum*, 138–167.

d'Oliveira, A. F. P. L., Diniz, S. G., & Schraiber, L. B. (2002). Violence against women in health-care institutions: An emerging problem. *Lancet, 359*(9318), 1681–1685.

da Silva, M. G., Marcelino, M. C., Rodrigues, L. S. P., Toro, R. C., & Shimo, A. K. K. (2014). Obstetric violence according to obstetric nurses. *Revista da Rede de Enfermagem do Nordeste, 15*(4). doi:10.15253/2175-6783.2014000400020

Davis, D. A. (2019a). Obstetric racism: The racial politics of pregnancy, labor, and birthing. *Medical Anthropology, 38*(7), 560–573. doi:10.1080/01459740.2018.1549389

Davis, D. A. (2019b). *Reproductive injustice: Racism, pregnancy, and premature birth*. Manhattan: New York University Press.

Diaz-Tello, F. (2016). Invisible wounds: Obstetric violence in the United States. *Reproductive Health Matters, 24*(47), 56–64.

Diaz-Tello, F., & Paltrow, L. M. (2012). *NAPW working paper: Birth justice as reproductive justice* [PDF file]. Retrieved from National Advocates for Pregnant Women (NAPW) website: http://advocatesforpregnantwomen.org/Birth%20justice%202012.pdf

Dreger, A. D., & Herndon, A. M. (2009). Progress and politics in the intersex rights movement: Feminist theory in action. *GLQ: A Journal of Lesbian and Gay Studies, 15*(2), 199–224.

Englehart, N. A., & Miller, M. K. (2014). The CEDAW effect: International law's impact on women's rights. *Journal of Human Rights, 13*(1), 22–47.

Farmer, P. (2005). *Pathologies of power: Health, human rights, and the new war on the poor*. Berkeley: University of California Press.

Farmer, P. (2010). *Partner to the poor: A Paul Farmer reader*. H. Saussy (Ed.). Berkeley: University of California Press.

Flavin, J. (2008). *Our bodies, our crimes: The policing of women's reproduction in America*. Manhattan: New York University Press.

Garland-Thomson, R. (2002). Integrating disability, transforming feminist theory. *National Women's Studies Association Journal, 14*(3), 1–32. *JSTOR*. Retrieved from www.jstor.org/stable/4316922.

Grilo Diniz, C. S., Rattner, D., Lucas d'Oliveira, A. F. P., de Aguiar, J. M., & Niy, D. Y. (2018). Disrespect and abuse in childbirth in Brazil: Social activism, public policies and providers' training. *Reproductive Health Matters, 26*(53), 19–35.

Gunew, S. (Ed.). (2019). *Feminism and the politics of difference*. New York: Routledge.

Hernandez, D., & Rehman, B. (Eds.). (2019). *Colonize this!: Young women of color on today's feminism*. New York: Seal Press.

Higer, A. J. (1999). International women's activism and the 1994 Cairo Population Conference. In Meyer, M. K., & Prügl, E. (Eds.). (1999). *Gender politics in global governance* (pp. 122–141). New York: Rowman & Littlefield.

Higgins, R. (1994). *Problems and process: International law and how we use it*. Oxford: Oxford University Press.

hooks, b. (2000). *Feminism is for everybody: Passionate politics*. London: Pluto Press.

Humm, M. (2014). *Feminisms: A reader*. Oxon: Routledge.

Ignacio, A. (2019, August 9). Brazil's debate over "obstetric violence" shines light on abuse during childbirth. *World News, Huffington Post, HuffPost Brazil*. Retrieved from https://www.huffpost.com/entry/obstetric-violence-brazil-childbirth_n_5d4c4c29e4b09e72974304c2

Light, A. D., Obedin-Maliver, J., Sevelius, J. M., & Kerns, J. L. (2014). Transgender men who experienced pregnancy after female-to-male gender transitioning. *Obstetrics & Gynecology, 124*(6), 1120–1127.

Luke, C., & Gore, J. (2014). *Feminisms and critical pedagogy*. New York: Routledge.

McCormack, K. (2005). Stratified reproduction and poor women's resistance. *Gender & Society, 19*(5), 660–679.

McIntosh, C. A., & Finkle, J. L. (1995). The Cairo conference on population and development: A new paradigm? *Population and Development Review, 21*(2), 223–260.

Mohanty, C. T. (2003). *Feminism without borders: Decolonizing theory, practicing solidarity*. Durham, NC: Duke University Press.

Obedin-Maliver, J., & Makadon, H. J. (2016). Transgender men and pregnancy. *Obstetric Medicine, 9*(1), 4–8.

Oparah, J. C., & Black Women Birthing Justice (2016). Introduction beyond coercion and malign neglect: Black women and the struggle for birth justice. In J. C. Oparah & A. D. Bonaparte (Eds.), *Birthing justice: Black women, pregnancy, and childbirth* (pp. 1–18). New York: Routledge/Taylor & Francis.

Oparah, J. C., & Bonaparte, A. D. (Eds.). (2016). *Birthing justice: Black women, pregnancy, and childbirth*. New York: Routledge/Taylor & Francis.

O'Reilly, A. (2016). *Matricentric feminism*. Demeter Press.

Paltrow, L. M., & Flavin, J. (2013). Arrests of and forced interventions on pregnant women in the United States, 1973–2005: Implications for women's legal status and public health. *Journal of Health Politics, Policy and Law, 38*(2), 299–343.

Ross, L., & Solinger, R. (2017). *Reproductive justice: An introduction*. Berkeley: University of California Press.

Ryan, M. (2013). The gender of pregnancy: Masculine lesbians talk about reproduction. *Journal of Lesbian Studies, 17*(2), 119–133.

Silliman, J., Fried, M. G., Ross, L., & Gutiérrez, E. (2004). *Undivided rights: Women of color organizing for reproductive justice*. Chicago: Haymarket Books.

Sistersong. (2019). Reproductive justice [website]. Retrieved from https://www.sistersong.net/reproductive-justice

Smith, A. (2005). *Conquest: Sexual violence and American Indian genocide*. Cambridge: South End Press.

UN. (1994). Programme of action adopted at the International Conference on Population and Development, Cairo, September 5–13. New York: United Nations. Document No. A/CONF. 171/13, 18, October. Retrieved from https://www.unfpa.org/events/international-conference-population-and-development-icpd

UN. (2019). Sustainable Development Goals. Retrieved from https://www.un.org/sustainabledevelopment/

UN Department of Economic and Social Affairs. (2019). Reproductive rights. Retrieved from https://www.un.org/en/development/desa/population/theme/rights/index.asp

UN General Assembly. (1948). Universal declaration of human rights. Retrieved from http://www.un.org/en/documents/udhr/

UN Statistics. (2019). Retrieved from https://unstats.un.org/unsd/mdg/Host.aspx?Content=Indicators/OfficialList.htm

World Health Organization. (2014). *The prevention and elimination of disrespect and abuse during facility-based childbirth* [PDF file]. Retrieved from https://www.who.int/reproductivehealth/topics/maternal_perinatal/statement-childbirth/en/

World Health Organization. (2015). *Health in 2015: From MDGs to SDGs* [PDF file]. Retrieved from https://www.who.int/gho/publications/mdgs-sdgs/en/

World Health Organization. (2018). *WHO recommendations: Intrapartum care for a positive child-birth experience* [PDF file]. ISBN: 978-92-4-155021-5. Retrieved from https://www.who.int/reproductivehealth/publications/intrapartum-care-guidelines/en/

Žižek, S. (2002). *Welcome to the desert of the real!: Five essays on September 11 and related dates.* New York: Verso.

Žižek, S. (2006). Against an ideology of human rights. *Displacement, asylum, migration: The Oxford Amnesty Lectures 2004, 56–85.*

Chapter 33

LGBT MINORITY STRESS THROUGH A GLOCAL LENS

Sean G. Massey

For the past week, Megan would come home after school and sit on her bed for hours with the lights off. She felt terrified that if she told her parents about her feelings for Teresa, they'd make her quit drama club, or worse they might kick her out.

At the church fellowship last week, 17-year-old Kim realized he was really attracted to Liang. He knew these feelings were sinful but worried he might not be able to resist temptation. He felt really ashamed and hoped prayer would help.

Even though Jasper had given their preferred name and pronouns during freshman orientation, one of their professors continued to misgender them in class. To make things worse, the professor and Jasper's classmates laughed whenever they pointed it out.

Peter and John became Jimmy's foster parents almost a year ago. Adoption day was only a few months away and a state legislator just introduced a bill that would ban adoption by LGBTQ people.

Juan and Peter were walking home from a friend's party. They were holding hands and Juan leaned his head on Peter's shoulder. They were both a little drunk and didn't notice the group of men that crossed the street in front of them until they started yelling "fucking faggots!" and throwing punches.

Progress and Prejudice

Over the past half-century, LGBTQ people in the United States have achieved significant advances in social acceptance. These advances include challenging pervasive, ongoing and repressive harassment by law enforcement igniting the Gay Liberation Movement; forcing the removal of homosexuality from the list of mental illnesses; persevering, but also strengthening the LGBT community in the face of a devastating plague; advocating and winning legal cases that decriminalized homosexuality; achieving the right to marry (Hammack, Frost, Meyer, & Pletta, 2018); and moving general social attitudes toward LGBT people in a positive direction (Smith, Davern, Freese, & Morgan, 2018).

However, as the vignettes at the start of this chapter are meant to suggest, not all the challenges have been overcome. Attitudes toward LGBT people still vary significantly by region in the United States, and some of the observed positive shift may reflect subtle prejudice replacing overt prejudice, rather than the elimination of prejudice all together (Massey, 2009). A recent Harris Poll, sponsored by Gay & Lesbian Alliance against Defamation (GLAAD), revealed that the positive trend in attitudes among adults toward LGBTQ people, had reversed (GLAAD, 2019). In addition, a recent report by the Williams Institute pointed out that over half of LGBTQ people in the United States live in states without protections against LGBT discrimination in employment, education, public accommodation and housing (Williams Institute, 2019), and efforts to roll back or limit many of these protections are ongoing. According to the National Coalition of Anti-Violence Programs, 2017 had the highest number of LGBTQ hate-related homicides and an increase in the overall severity of anti-LGBTQ violence (NCAVP, 2018). Finally, despite the recent ruling on marriage equality by the US Supreme Court, the legal and social legitimacy of same-sex relationships and parenting rights continues to be debated. Shifting political power within the United States suggests that many of these accomplishments are fragile.

Stress and Minority Stress

Folkman and Larazus (1986) described *stress* as something experienced by a person that they view as too taxing or that exceeds their resources and endangers their well-being. Consequently, living in a sociopolitical environment that fails to support your basic rights or to affirm your dignity, in which you are more likely than others to experience prejudice, discrimination, hostility or even violence, is stressful (Meyer, 2003). Although our bodies are fairly resilient and can handle some amount of stress, too much stress—chronic stress—can negatively affect mental and physical health. Normally, stress is like driving a car and pressing down on the gas pedal to make the car go faster. Cars are made to go fast, and the ability to speed up is really important when you're late to work or you're trying to get someone to the hospital during an emergency. But if you keep your car at full speed all the time, the car will eventually break down. This is what happens with chronic stress.

Stressors are those "events and conditions (e.g., losing a job, death of an intimate) that cause change and that require that the individual adapt to the new situation or life circumstance" (Dohrenwend, 1998, p. 675). Stressors can range in intensity from mild daily hassles to traumatic life events. Stressors can result when a minority group member tries to navigate institutional structures and social interactions that remind them of their social disadvantage (Meyer, 2003), such as being the target of negative attitudes or prejudice, experiencing overt or subtle forms of discrimination, or being the victim of stigma-driven violence (Brooks, 1981; Meyer, 1995). The stress that results from an encounter with these stressors is called *minority stress* (Meyer, 1995), the psychosocial stress one experiences due to one's minority status, above and beyond the stress that is experienced by nonminorities as a result of everyday life (see also Brooks, 1981).

Distal and Proximal Stressors

Minority stress can be caused by both external stressors (also called *distal* stressors), meaning something outside the individual that causes stress, such as discrimination, harassment or violence; and internal stressors (also called *proximal* stressors), meaning how the individual views or reacts to the distal stressors in their environment, such as the expectation of rejection, fear, disappointment, or the need to hide or conceal one's minority status and the internalization of negative social attitudes (Meyer, 2003). Distal minority stressors can also vary in terms of their directness or magnitude, ranging from daily hassles and microaggressions (e.g., trying to fill out a medical form that only provides "husband" or "wife" as the options under "relationship"), to chronic strain (e.g., having to endure a continually hostile work environment) and major life events (e.g., a serious injury resulting from a hate crime) (Meyer, 2015).

Researchers have explored the negative impact minority stress has on LGBTQ health in a variety of contexts. Experiences such as harassment and discrimination in the work-place (Waldo, 1999), unsupportive campus climates for trans and nonbinary and gender nonconforming college students (Budge, Dominguez, & Goldberg, 2019) and stigma-related traumatic experiences while serving in the military (Livingston, Berke, Ruben, Matza, & Shipherd, 2019) have been found to negatively impact on both mental and physical health. The growing list of negative health outcomes associated with minority stress includes: increases in psychological distress (Meyer, 1995), depression (Bockting et al., 2013; Nolen-Hoeksema, McBride, & Larson, 1997), threats to interpersonal and romantic relationships (Frost & Meyer, 2009), increased risks of substance abuse (Hatzenbuehler, Nolen-Hoeksema, & Erickson, 2008; Mays & Cochran, 2001), HIV risk behaviors (Meyer & Dean, 1998), fewer positive health behaviors (Meyer & Frost, 2013), self-reported health problems (Frost, Lehavot & Meyer, 2015) and even suicide (Meyer, 2003).

Coping and Resilience

LGBT people utilize a range of coping strategies and resources to buffer against minority stress, such as finding or increasing social support from family and having or increasing one's sense of connectedness to one's minority community or other minority community members, and strong identification with one's LGBT identity (Meyer, 2003). Some of the LGBT community resources that have been found to help individuals cope with minority stress include LGBT community centers and support groups, information and crisis hotlines, visible LGBT community leaders, laws and institutional policies that protect against discrimination or affirm LGBTQ family and relationships and ongoing organized groups working to confront existing injustice (Meyer, 2015), as well as the social support, role models and the values, norms and feelings of connectedness that come from them (Fergus & Zimmerman, 2005).

Minority Stress in Non-US Cultural Contexts

Early research on minority stress has taken place in a US/North America cultural context, which has a relatively affirming social and legal environment, widespread visibility of LGBT individuals and communities and a vast and growing LGBT-affirming social, educational, legal and economic landscape (Šević, Ivanković, & Štulhofer, 2016). Only a few studies have explored how minority stress is experienced by those with intersecting sexual minority and ethnic/racial minority identities (Ghabrial & Ross, 2018; Huang et al., 2010; Wei, Ku, Russell, Mallinckrodt, & Liao, 2008).

Recently, researchers have begun to explore minority stress among sexual minority populations outside of the United States, including Brazil (Dunn, Gonzalez, Costa, & Nardi, 2014), China (Shao, Chang, & Chen, 2018), Rwanda (Moreland, White, Riggle, Gishoma, & Hughes, 2019), South Africa (McAdams-Mahmoud et al., 2014), Australia and Malaysia (Brown, Low, Tai, & Tong, 2016), Macedonia (Stojanovski, Zhou, King, Gjorgjiovska, & Mihajlov, 2018), Croatia (Šević et al., 2016) and one study comparing experiences across 38 different European countries (Pachankis et al., 2017). Most of these studies have used constructs and approaches established in the United States, and sampled individuals who understood themselves as being LGBT or were connected to an LGBTQ community.

One important strength of the minority stress model is that it acknowledges the importance and interaction of both internal (proximal) and external (distal) stressors. This helps to avoid Western psychology's obsession with the individual (Adams, Estrada-Villalta, Sullivan, & Markus, 2019) and encourages consideration of cultural, structural and institutional forces. This approach encourages flexibility in how internal and external stressors are understood or defined within a particular context, and how they should be operationalized and measured. As the next section demonstrates, studies exploring minority stress in non-US cultural contexts requires reconsideration of some of the assumptions in the LGBT minority stress model. For example, a significant number of studies have documented the negative consequences of identity concealment, which is thought to be both a cause and symptom of internalized homophobia (turning anti-LGBT social attitudes inward toward oneself). However, in some contexts, concealment may be a pragmatic and strategic response to very real threats of homonegativity (i.e., extreme anti-LGBT attitudes that can result in discrimination and violence) and limited LGBT community resources (Hammack, Frost, Meyer, & Pletta, 2018). This raises some concerns about reliance on LGBT identity prominence and LGBT community connectedness as a buffer for distal stressors across countries or cultures.

Studies conducted in cultural contexts of extreme homonegativity found that stressors such as concealment, do not appear to have the same negative impact on mental health as in more accepting communities. For example, participants in a study of men who have sex with men (MSM) in Cape Town, South Africa (McAdams-Mahmoud et al., 2014) reported high levels of perceived stigma and the need to conceal their sexuality, but the participants also reported low levels of internalized homophobia and trauma. The stress they did experience, due to the stigma they perceived, appeared to be reduced or buffered by their affiliation with supportive social networks and community organizations. Similar findings emerged from a study of sexual minority women in Rwanda (Moreland et al., 2019), who reported high levels of external minority stressors in the form of experiences of stigma and discrimination, expectations of rejection and sometimes violence, and concealment strategies were frequently used to cope with these stressors, along with seeking out social support and working on self-acceptance. Another study of sexual and gender minority men in Brazil (Dunn et al., 2014) found significant minority stress related to social condemnation and "enacted stigma" (i.e., the unfair treatment by others, including discrimination and violence, resulting from stigma). Although both internalized homonegativity and concealment behaviors were expressed among the participants, mental health problems were limited only to internalized homonegativity, not concealment. It is possible, then, that in highly homonegative contexts in these countries that concealment is seen as a necessary and pragmatic strategy that buffers distal stressors such as enacted stigma (Dunn et al., 2014).

Cultural variations in the independence and interdependence of self (Kitayama & Markus, 1995) (i.e., the extent to which a person understands or defines themselves in terms of their relationship to others) and in the importance of family connectedness have also been shown to influence minority stress. For example, Shao, Chang, and Chen (2018) explored minority stress in gay, lesbian and bisexual Chinese young adults living in mainland China, where laws prohibiting homosexuality were limited to restricting public displays and discussions on social media, and where significant emphasis was placed on interdependence and family connectedness. In their study, conventional internal minority stress variables such as internalized homophobia, self-concealment and gay-related rejection sensitivity (Pachankis et al., 2008) were not found to significantly affect mental health. Rather, respect for one's parents, and whether one's parents were perceived to be supportive of one's sexual orientation, predicted variation in mental health, highlighting how culture influences the meaning and significance of internal minority stressors.

Economic globalization, social media, as well as the work of NGOs responding to the AIDS epidemic, have all contributed to some extent to the exportation or "mainstreaming" of Western LGBT identities to nonwestern, local or indigenous societies where they did not previously exist (Kole, 2007). However, this proliferation of Western LGBT identities may represent a kind of double-edged sword.

The introduction of Western LGBT healthcare and human rights organizations have provided much-needed resources, expertise and new ways of conceptualizing sexuality and gender that have been useful to many (McAdams-Mahmoud et al., 2014). Knowledge, access to educational resources, social support, advocacy efforts and community connectedness (Meyrowitz, 2005) have all have been found to buffer against minority stressors. However, as anthropologists and other researchers have demonstrated for decades, not everyone across the globe views their sexuality as a significant defining part of their self-concept or understands labels such as "gay and straight." Some may not identify with the LGBT community at all, or fear identification with it in the public domain, or feel that they are not connected to or perhaps some even may not feel the need for an LGBTQ community at all (Frost & Meyer, 2012).

In addition, Western offers of help and assistance are often accompanied by or compliment Western commodities, such as NGOs and cultural and media resources, that then replace local or indigenous solutions; implying tacitly (and sometimes overtly) that Western understanding and organization of sexuality is superior to (i.e., more developed or civilized) local or indigenous understandings of sexuality and gender.

Another concern is that reliance on this assistance can also increase economic dependence on the West (Kole, 2007; Massad, 2002) and adherence to neoliberal ideals. Neoliberalism describes a set of political, social and economic ideas and policies that gained prominence in the 1980s, characterized by the privatization of government services, deregulation of markets and industry, expansion of global trade and emphasis on individual competition in a free market economy. Success and advancement in the neoliberal context are determined by individual merit demonstrated by economic competition unfettered by government intervention (Harvey, 2005). Increases in personal capital and wealth create the conditions for advances in individual freedom (Brown, 2005) where the success of a few (because competition creates winners and losers) will "trickle down" to the many. From this perspective, the best way to address repressive anti-LGBTQ social and governmental policies and practices (as well as many other forms of marginalization) is to create prosperity through the introduction of the global capitalist ideal, where the market solves all problems (Treanor, 2005). Communities, particularly those perceived as backward when it comes to LGBTQ+ issues, are not simply sites for intervention, but are seen as potential markets to export the products of LGBTQ equality.

Several concerns have been raised about this approach. The first is that democratic processes can become secondary to market outcomes. Despite its popularity, the "trickle down" aspect of neoliberalism has little empirical support and has led to increased inequality (McGuigan, 2014; Spence, 2016). Another concern is that neoliberalism is based on the notion of meritocracy (i.e., success is understood as resulting exclusively from an individual's skill and hard work). Explanations for inequality shift away from the possibility of structural injustice to individual failure (Brodie, 2007). Although higher economic status and educational achievement have been found to buffer minority stress in many of these communities, class and educational achievement definitely limit the access of most actors to LGBT-focused resources and organizations, which are often centered in urban and tourist-focused areas (Kole, 2007; McAdams-Mahmoud et al., 2014; Moreland et al., 2019). These economic barriers in turn can limit access to the social identities and resources that might help to buffer the negative effects of stigma and discrimination to those with resources and who are willing and able to play the neoliberal game successfully.

Finally, these resources are sometimes seen as a kind of devil's bargain that creates dependence on Western and US organizations and social, financial and military resources. It is not surprising, therefore, when proliferation of LGBTQ communities and identities are perceived as belonging to middle and upper class and Western milieus associated with economic globalization and Western and US imperialism (i.e., extending the political, economic and cultural influence of one country beyond its borders through the use of political, economic and military power). In fact, this suspicion and criticism of Western influence may have contributed to an increase in anti-LGBTQ cultural and governmental efforts that previously did not exist (Massad, 2002).

These various concerns raised in this chapter are not unique to research on minority stress. Each highlights the importance of proceeding with caution when applying psychological concepts developed in the United States across cultures or to other countries. Researchers who utilize a cultural psychology framework (Adams et al., 2019) warn against generalizing psychological constructs that are derived from research (or standardized using) Western participants to global communities. Adams and colleagues argue that to understand and utilize psychological theories and findings, we must have a critical awareness and willingness to challenge these culture-bound theories and explore the different ways they work or do not work across cultures. Western psychology's tendency to focus on the neoliberal self-favoring psychological essentialism, personal growth/empowerment, individual responsibility and self-esteem management at the expense of interdependence, solidarity and attention to the social and historical forces that shape experience—makes the imposition of theories and knowledge from the West to non-Western contexts at the very least fraught, and at its worst imperialist.

Summary

The LGBT minority stress model can be a useful tool for exploring and better understanding structural and individual threats and challenges some LGBTQ people face during their daily lives, as well as to discover possible sources for resilience and improved health and well-being. However, in order to understand the lives of sexual minorities (only some of whom refer to themselves as LGBTQ) in a glocal context, it is important to proceed with caution. Concepts such as minority stress, resilience and well-being emerging from Western US psychological traditions, can also obscure or supplant local understanding and pathways to resilience and well-being. It is vital to consider the particular culturally specific ways that these concepts are articulated in those contexts. As Segalo, Manoff, and Fine (2015) suggest, this has the best chance of occurring if psychologists and other social scientists begin to listen to researchers and community members who are from, and who live in those contexts, allowing their assumptions to be challenged and, if necessary, allowing those researchers to abandon faulty notions of objectivity that keep them from working alongside, standing in solidarity and sometimes stepping back and bearing witness to communities engaged in local struggles for social justice.

References

Adams, G., Estrada-Villalta, S., Sullivan, D., & Markus, H. R. (2019). The psychology of neo-liberalism and the neoliberalism of psychology. *Journal of Social Issues, 75*(1), 189–216.

Bockting, W. O., Miner, M. H., Swinburne Romine, R. E., Hamilton, A., & Coleman, E. (2013). Stigma, mental health, and resilience in an online sample of the US transgender population. *American Journal of Public Health, 103*(5), 943–951. doi:10.2105/AJPH.2013.301241

Brodie, J. (2007). Reforming social justice in neoliberal times. *Studies in Social Justice, 1*(2), 93–107.

Brooks, V. (1981). *Minority stress and lesbian women.* Lexington, MA: Lexington Books.

Brown, J., Low, W. Y., Tai, R., & Tong, W. T. (2016). Shame, internalized homonegativity, and religiosity: A comparison of the stigmatization associated with minority stress with gay men in Australia and Malaysia. *International Journal of Sexual Health, 28*(1), 28–36. https://doi.org/10.1080/19317611.2015.1068902

Brown, W. (2005). *Edgework—Critical essays on knowledge and politics* (pp. 37–59), Princeton, NJ: Princeton University Press.

Budge, S. L., Domínguez, S., Jr., & Goldberg, A. E. (2019). Minority stress in nonbinary students in higher education: The role of campus climate and belongingness. *Psychology of Sexual Orientation and Gender Diversity.* https://doi-org.proxy.binghamton.edu/ 10.1037/sgd0000360

Dohrenwend, B. P. (1998). Theoretical integration. In B. P. Dohrenwend (Ed.), *Adversity, stress, and psychopathology* (pp. 539–555). New York: Oxford University Press.

Dunn, T. L., Gonzalez, C. A., Costa, A. B., & Nardi, H. C. (2014). Does the minority stress model generalize to a non-U.S. sample? An examination of minority stress and resilience on depressive symptomatology among sexual minority men in two urban areas of Brazil. *Psychology of Sexual Orientation and Gender Diversity, 1*(2), 117–131.

Fergus, S., & Zimmerman, M. A. (2005). Adolescent resilience: A framework for understanding healthy development in the face of risk. *Annual Review of Public Health, 26,* 399–419. http://dx.doi.org/10.1146/annurev.publhealth.26.021304.144357

Folkman, S., Larazus, R. S., Gruen, R. J., & DeLongis, A. (1986). Appraisal, coping, health status, and psychological symptoms. *Journal of Personality and Social Psychology, 50*(3), 571–579.

Frost, D. M., Lehavot, K., & Meyer, I. H. (2015). Minority stress and physical health among sexual minority individuals. *Journal of Behavioral Medicine, 38*(1), 1–8. https://doi-org.proxy.binghamton.edu/10.1007/s10865-013-9523-8

Frost, D. M., & Meyer, I. H. (2009). Internalized homophobia and relationship quality among lesbians, gay men, and bisexuals. *Journal of Counseling Psychology, 56*(1), 97–109. https://doi-org.proxy.binghamton.edu/10.1037/a0012844

Frost, D. M., & Meyer, I. H. (2012). Internalized homophobia and relationship quality among lesbians, gay men, and bisexuals. *Journal of Counseling Psychology, 56*(1), 97–100.

Ghabrial, M. A., & Ross, L. E. (2018). Representation and erasure of bisexual people of color: A content analysis of quantitative bisexual mental health research. *Psychology of Sexual Orientation and Gender Diversity, 5*(2), 132–142. https://doi-org.proxy.binghamton.edu/10.1037/sgd0000286

GLAAD. (2019). *Accelerating Acceptance 2019* [PDF file]. Retrieved from https://www.glaad.org/sites/default/files/Accelerating%20Acceptance%202019.pdf.

Hammack, P. L., Frost, D. M., Meyer, I. H., & Pletta, D. R. (2018). Gay men's health and identity: Social change and the life course. *Archives of Sexual Behavior, 47,* 59–74.

Harvey, D. (2005). *A brief history of neoliberalism.* Oxford: Oxford University Press.

Hatzenbuehler, M. L., Nolen-Hoeksema, S., & Erickson, S. J. (2008). Minority stress predictors of HIV risk behavior, substance use, and depressive symptoms: Results from a prospective study of bereaved gay men. *Health Psychology, 27*(4), 455–462. https://doi-org.proxy.binghamton.edu/10.1037/0278-6133.27.4.455

Huang, Y.-P., Brewster, M. E., Moradi, B., Goodman, M. B., Wiseman, M. C., & Martin, A. (2010). Content analysis of literature about LGB people of color: 1998–2007. *The Counseling Psychologist, 38*(3), 363–396. https://doi-org.proxy.binghamton.edu/10.1177/0011000009335255

Kitayama, S., & Markus, H. R. (1995). Culture and self: Implications for internationalizing psychology. In N. Goldberger & J. Veroff (Eds.), *The culture and psychology reader* (pp. 366–383). New York: New York University Press.

Kole, S. K. (2007). Globalizing queer? AIDS, homophobia and the politics of sexual identity in India. *Globalization and Health, 3*(8). doi:10.1186/1744-8603-3-8.

Livingston, N. A., Berke, D. S., Ruben, M. A., Matza, A. R., & Shipherd, J. C. (2019). Experiences of trauma, discrimination, microaggressions, and minority stress among trauma-exposed LGBT veterans: Unexpected findings and unresolved service gaps. *Psychological Trauma: Theory, Research, Practice, and Policy, 11*(7), 695–703. https://doi-org.proxy.binghamton.edu/10.1037/tra0000464

Massad, J. (2002). Re-orienting desire: The gay international and the Arab world. *Public Culture, 14*(2), 361–385.

Massey, S. G. (2009). Polymorphous prejudice: Liberating the measurement of heterosexuals' attitudes toward lesbians and gay men. *Journal of Homosexuality, 56*(2), 147–172. doi:10.1080/00918360802623131

Mays, V. M., & Cochran, S. D. (2001). Mental health correlates of perceived discrimination among lesbian, gay, and bisexual adults in the United States. *American Journal of Public Health, 91*(11), 1869–1876. https://doi.org/10.2105/ajph.91.11.1869

McAdams-Mahmoud, A., Stephenson, R., Rentsch, C., Cooper, H., Arriola, K. J., Jobson, G., …, & McIntyre, J. (2014). Minority stress in the lives of men who have sex with men in Cape Town, South Africa. *Journal of Homosexuality, 61*, 847–867.

McGuigan, J. (2014). The neoliberal self. *Culture Unbound, 6*, 223–240. Retrieved from http://www.cultureunbound.ep.liu.se/v6/a13/cu14v6a13.pdf

Meyer, I. H. (1995). Minority stress and mental health in gay men. *Journal of Health and Social Behavior, 36*, 38–56.

Meyer, I. H. (2003). Prejudice, social stress, and mental health in lesbian, gay, and bisexual populations: Conceptual issues and research evidence. *Psychological Bulletin, 129*(5), 674–697. doi: 10.1037/0033-2909.129.5.674.

Meyer, I. H. (2015). Resilience in the study of minority stress and health of sexual and gender minorities. *Psychology of Sexual Orientation and Gender Diversity, 2*(3), 209–213. https://doi-org.proxy.binghamton.edu/10.1037/sgd0000132

Meyer, I. H., & Dean, L. (1998). Internalized homophobia, intimacy, and sexual behavior among gay and bisexual men. In G. M. Herek (Ed.) *Stigma and sexual orientation: Understanding prejudice against lesbians, gay men, and bisexuals* (pp. 160–186). Thousand Oaks, CA: Sage.

Meyer, I. H., & Frost, D. M. (2013). Minority stress and the health of sexual minorities. In C. J. Patterson & A. R. D'Augelli (Eds.), *Handbook of psychology and sexual orientation* (pp. 252–266). New York: Oxford University Press. Retrieved from https://search-ebscohost-com.proxy.binghamton.edu/login.aspx?direct=true&db=psyh&AN=2012-32754-018&site=ehost-live

Meyrowitz, J. (2005). The rise of glocality: New senses of place and identity in the global village. In K. Nyíri (Ed.), *A sense of place: The global and the local in mobile communication* (pp. 21–30). Vienna: Passagen Verlag.

Moreland, P., White, R., Riggle, E. D. B., Gishoma, D., & Hughes, T. L. (2019). Experiences of minority stress among lesbian and bisexual women in Rwanda. *International Perspectives in Psychology: Research, Practice, Consultation, 8*(4), 196–211.

National Coalition of Anti-Violence Programs (NCAVP). (2018). *Lesbian, gay, bisexual, transgender, queer and HIV-affected hate and intimate partner violence in 2017* [PDF file]. Retrieved from http://avp.org/wp-content/uploads/2019/01/NCAVP-HV-IPV-2017-report.pdf

Nolen-Hoeksema, S., McBride, A., & Larson, J. (1997). Rumination and psychological distress among bereaved partners. *Journal of Personality and Social Psychology, 72*(4), 855–862. https://doi-org.proxy.binghamton.edu/10.1037/0022-3514.72.4.855

Pachankis, J. E., Goldfried, M. R., & Ramrattan, M. E. (2008). Extension of the rejection sensitivity construct to the interpersonal functioning of gay men. *Journal of Consulting and Clinical Psychology, 76*(2), 306–317. https://doi-org.proxy.binghamton.edu/10.1037/0022-006X.76.2.306

Pachankis, J. E., Hatzenbuehler, M. L., Mirandola, M., Weatherburn, P., Berg, R. C., Marcus, U., & Schmidt, A. J. (2017). The geography of sexual orientation: Structural stigma and sexual attraction, behavior, and identity among men who have sex with men across 38 European countries. *Archives of Sexual Behavior, 46*(5), 1491–1502. https://doi.org/10.1007/s10508-016-0819-y

Segalo, P., Manoff, E., & Fine, M. (2015). Working with embroideries and counter-maps: Engaging memory and imagination within decolonizing frameworks. *Journal of Social and Political Psychology, 3*(1), 342–364. https://doi.org/10.5964/jspp.v3i1.145

Šević, S., Ivanković, I., & Štulhofer, A. (2016). Emotional intimacy among coupled heterosexual and gay/bisexual Croatian men: Assessing the role of minority stress. *Archives of Sexual Behavior, 45*, 1259–1268.

Shao, J., Chang, E. S., & Chen, C. (2018). The relative importance of parent-child dynamics and minority stress on the psychological adjustment of LGBs in China. *Journal of Counseling Psychology, 65*(5), 598–604.

Smith, T. W., Davern, M., Freese, J., & Morgan, S. (2018). *General social surveys, 1972–2018* [machine-readable data file]. National Opinion Research Center at the University of Chicago, the GSS Data Explorer. Retrieved from gssdataexplorer.norc.org.

Spence, L. K. (2016). *Knocking the hustle: Against the neoliberal turn in black politics.* Brooklyn, NY: Punctum Books.

Stojanovski, K., Zhou S., King, E., Gjorgjiovska, J., & Mihajlov, A. (2018). An application of the minority stress model in a non-western context: Discrimination and mental health among sexual and gender minorities in Macedonia. *Sex Research and Social Policy, 15,* 367–376.

Treanor, P. (2005). Neoliberalism: Origins, theory, definition. Retrieved from http://web.inter.nl.net/users/Paul.Treanor/neoliberalism.html

Waldo, C. R. (1999). Working in a majority context: A structural model of heterosexism as minority stress in the workplace. *Journal of Counseling Psychology, 46*(2), 218–232. https://doi-org.proxy.binghamton.edu/10.1037/0022-0167.46.2.218

Wei, M., Ku, T.-Y., Russell, D. W., Mallinckrodt, B., & Liao, K. Y.-H. (2008). Moderating effects of three coping strategies and self-esteem on perceived discrimination and depressive symptoms: A minority stress model for Asian international students. *Journal of Counseling Psychology, 55*(4), 451–462. https://doi-org.proxy.binghamton.edu/10.1037/a0012511

Williams Institute. (2019). *LGBT people in the U.S. not protected by state nondiscrimination statutes* [PDF file]. Retrieved from https://williamsinstitute.law.ucla.edu/wp-content/uploads/LGBT-Nondiscrim-Statutes-Mar-2019.pdf

Chapter 34

REDEFINING SEXUAL COMPETENCE

Stefan Lucke

At first glance, the concepts of *sexual literacy* and *sexual competence* may mean similar things and indeed they do overlap in several keyways. This chapter delineates the differences between them and provides a rationale for keeping them separate. In a nutshell, if sexual literacy is to be understood as a cultural mission, a human right, a social justice endeavor and a demand to expand sexuality education (Herdt, 2007; Herdt & Lucke, this volume; Moore & Reynolds, 2018a), then sexual competence is how sexual literacy manifests itself in the individual as a desired outcome. One main aspect of sexual competence is its focus on the positive aspects of sexual development as opposed to a commonly employed emphasis on sexual risks. Moreover, sexual competence leans on understanding the formation of competence as a cascading, forward-feeding, *developmental process*[1] that begins in infancy and extends into all life spans and ages. This process has been found to be especially critical during the fast developmental changes that typically happen in childhood and adolescence. Importantly, recent paradigm shifts in childhood studies suggest that children have agency and may exert some control over their own development (Esser, Baader, Betz, & Hungerland, 2016), a point that has largely been ignored so far in studies of sexual development.

Framing competence as a *process* means that becoming increasingly competent is understood *not* as a succession of predetermined, universal stages of maturity, but as *multidimensional continua* that occur differently for each individual. Applied to sexuality, conventional notions such as "age-appropriateness," "consent" or "maturity" are often employed in a binary fashion that minimizes the processual characteristic of human development, while such terms actually and inherently refer to an *underlying ability* that I conceptualize as sexual competence. I further argue that this concept allows a more fluid and nuanced understanding of *individual* sexual development and its implications for the areas of education, policy and clinical intervention. Sexual competence intentionally poses challenges to the idea of childhood innocence, developmentalism, ableism and age-based school curricula or laws. For example, pedagogy cannot simply assume that the content of a sexual literacy curriculum for fifth graders will be suitable and

---

1 Located inside a decidedly postdevelopmentalist stance (compare Diamond, Bonner, & Dickenson, 2015; Halfon, Forrest, Lerner & Faustman, 2018; Lerner et al., 2019; Robinson & Davies, 2015).

supportive for all children in that age group as the level and shape of children's existing sexual competence, their social backgrounds and thus their individual needs, might vary greatly. Likewise, in the arena of policy and law, the conceptual step forward is to ask if a (young) person is *competent enough* to process certain sexual information or to engage in certain sexual activity, instead of simply asking *how old* they are (see Morrow, 2013; cf. Moore & Reynolds, 2018b).

Framing competence as an *ability* or *capability* thus foregrounds the scientific inquiry about positive contexts and factors that support developing sexual competence, or to rephrase: My goal for theorizing sexual competence is the empowerment of sexual human beings. Yet, these frames are just one part of sexual competence, so let us look closer at its definition and attributes and also critically approach this emerging concept in the following.

Properties and Attributes of Sexual Competence

The concepts of literacy and competence can be distinguished by their scientific history. The theory and research of competence are a complex and diverse body of scholarship that originated in cognitive psychology already in the 1950s, partially in answer to the inadequate simplicity of Freud's theory of innate drives (see White, 1959). Definitions and approaches to competence are plentiful, and the inflationary use and semantic broadness of the term has rightfully invited criticism (Höhne, 2007). Recent discussions can predominantly be located in the two domains of business/organizational management or education/pedagogy (Klieme & Hartig, 2008). Educators especially have an interest in the *assessment* or diagnostics of competence to verify or quantify learning in schools, while attempting to optimize the educational system. Psychology and related disciplines have rekindled an intense discussion about the theory behind competence since the beginning of the 2000s (Klieme & Leutner, 2006).

As a *general* definition, Weinert (2001, pp. 27–28) describes competences as cognitive abilities and skills that individuals have available or can learn in order to solve certain problems, as well as the associated readiness and motivational, volitional and social abilities to use these problem solutions in variable situations successfully and responsibly. Klieme and Leutner (2006, p. 879), on the other hand, define competencies as context-specific, cognitive dispositions for performance, which relate functionally to situations and demands in certain domains. As Bayer (2015) points out and as exemplified by the two preceding definitions, one dominant conceptual approach to competence highlights *cognition*, and situational and contextual *solving of problems* in certain specific areas. It is thus an approach that is favored in studies measuring performance in school; its goal is quantification. The other dominant approach stems from a humanistic pedagogical tradition and employs a general, broader concept of competence: an *ability to act* autonomously or together with others, or to utilize certain instruments and tools, in the sense of key or life skills (Bayer, 2015). Both dominant approaches can be historically aligned with more quantitative or, respectively, qualitative research methods (cf. Martens & Asbrand, 2009). While these approaches to competence hold some merit as a starting point, they fall short when applied to the sexual life trajectories of human beings.

Sexual competence is not simply equivalent to the cognitive ability to solve a math problem but is much more complex. Human sexuality deals with bodies, somatic processes, emotions, attractions, desires, relations between people, norms, laws and many other dynamic and very complicated elements. Moreover, the stakes are high with respect to the sexual well-being of oneself, of one's sexual partners and of others. Especially the dimensions of embodiment, somatic experience and emotion are not currently covered in conventional definitions of competence: for example, the somatic experience of touching and being touched, the feelings of pleasure, comfort or discomfort that touch can elicit in oneself or others, the right balance between "too rough" or "too light" stroking. Such nuances are core components of sexual competence; they must be experienced, given and received, practiced and refined throughout the life course. Touch and its erotic function exemplify a type of deep, developmental body-learning that is only secondarily cognitive and which allows to recognize the different sexual and tactile individuality of other people.

Existing competence definitions thus need to be enlarged and redefined for the realm of sexuality, that is, considering the critical experiences of emotion, the somatic self and practical learning in addition to sole cognitive abilities. Moreover, handling the cultural and moral dimensions of sexuality must be part of competence as well, beyond just "giving a nod" to context: Developing a sexual moral compass includes the awareness of which actions, statements or attitudes might be perceived as sexually offensive and transgressive, or beneficial and welcome by others—and the reasons why. In a sexually competent person, such moral awareness should inherently allow to critically interrogate cultural norms, gender roles and common moral positions about their positive or negative effects on each individual. Conventional theories of moral development have typically ignored the child's sexual self, owing to the presumption that children are sexually innocent (Lucke, 2020).

Therefore, I propose a new definition: *Sexual competence is an individual's context-specific ability to **integrate** sexually relevant cognitive, emotional, somatic and behavioral dimensions and capacities of oneself and as perceived in others, while critically considering the cultural and macrosocial aspects of sexuality. Sexual competence, applied, leads to actions, attitudes and modalities that promote sexual health, sexual well-being and sexual rights for oneself, sexual partners and all people.* Juxtaposing literacy and competence, I consider sexual literacy to be one major contributing factor for the development of sexual competence, more centered on the side of cognition and applicable in the field of education. Sexual competence, as a future, fully evolved model, ultimately aims to be the foundation of a *developmental theory of sexuality*, investigating *how* young people become sexually competent and resilient while including new paradigms in social and developmental theory of childhood.

Defining sexual competence as an ability allows to envision two sides of a coin: On the one hand, sexual competence can be understood as the current state of an ability, a momentary snapshot at a point of time inside a developmental process that could potentially be assessed; as such, it is a construct that is both outcome and predictor of a developmental trajectory (Lerner, Lerner, Bowers, & Geldhof, 2015, p. 643). On the other hand, sexual competence entails this lifelong, developmental process itself, which can be theorized and investigated. The necessarily pithy definition of sexual competence above aims to describe the ontological side of the concept, that is, its parts and relations that can be idealistically conceived under a social constructivist lens. Even though the important aspect of an individual's macrosocial setting is part of this expanded definition, it does not yet explain the developmental workings of how competence is acquired, fostered or hindered in regard to an individual's situatedness that includes the whole ecological system (Bornstein, Leventhal, & Lerner, 2015; Bronfenbrenner, 1993)—family, peers, institutions, governmental organizations, local and global cultures. In short, my approach also aims to account for all the structures of power that assign or withhold rights, resources and opportunities, which prescribe norms and prohibitions, to both oppress or privilege. Thus, sexual competence (as a state) can be a positive or negative indicator of how an individual has been able to develop sexually inside a particular sociocultural system with its distinct values, normativities, stereotypes and isms. However, a fully established approach to sexual competence (as a process) will ultimately help us to understand the complicated interactions between individual and society, during the lifelong formation of competence and its challenges.

Let us illustrate these workings by using a foundational part of sexual development, namely body image, as an example. Having a positive body image can be understood in my approach as a mark or result of high sexual competence, which might include successful negotiation or indeed a complete rejection of constraining or competing ideals of beauty, sex appeal and gendered performance in contemporary media. An affirmative body image might also support confidence with being naked in a sexual situation and appreciating the partner's body, creating a forward-feeding positive effect upon further development of sexual competence. Later in life, then, keeping a positive body image while aging could pose an ongoing challenge to personal well-being that might require different competence skills. To what extent a person really has control over such processes will be critically discussed in the next sections.

Sexual competence is not a value-free analytical proposition because it involves evaluation: When regarding a person as competent, certain underlying frames of reference are employed that define and elaborate what is deemed critically significant for competence, what optimal sexual development should resemble and what purpose sexual competence should serve. For example, if appreciating all sexual orientations and gender identities as valid and coequal is regarded as a component of sexual competence, then the belief in equality and individual sexual freedom is at work at a higher level—a belief that might be contested. This is the axiological side of sexual competence. When the above definition of sexual competence mentions "promoting sexual health, sexual well-being, and sexual rights," these values need to be explained and defended, that is, by employing a global human rights framework (see Yogyakarta Principles, ICJ, 2007, 2017) or subscribing to the WHO definition of sexual health (World Health Organization, 2006). Whereas these terms can represent desirable outcomes for a sexually competent person, developmental processes are unique for each individual and not a universal trajectory (Overton, Molenaar, & Lerner, 2015).

This approach to sexual competence aims to create a new emphasis on the positive markers and results of sexual development in previously shunned areas. As is well known, research and theory are still lacking and dismal in regard to understanding and conceptualizing positive and healthy sexual development and outcomes in children and adolescents (Lucke, 2020; cf. Russell, 2005). For example, the conceivable developmental effects of masturbation, especially the potential benefits, are insufficiently theorized and hardly empirically verified (Driemeyer, 2013). Conversely, sexual science has often focused on the mitigation of problematizations and dangers of sexuality, such as LGBT discrimination, sexually transmitted infections or sexual abuse—especially concerning youth (Egan & Hawkes, 2009; Jenkins, 2003; Weeks, 2016). I do not mean to negate sexual dangers; instead, the construct of sexual competence allows to integrate risk as a necessary vulnerability that can be managed by resilient and competent (young) actors (Lucke, 2020).

However, the mere prevention of the *negative* is simply not sufficient for establishing the *positive*: the sexual well-being of the person. *Sex positivity*, for one, is an emerging approach that goes hand in hand with the notions of *sexual health* and *sexual rights* (Burnes, Singh, & Witherspoon, 2017; Diamond, 2006; Glick, 2000; Williams, Thomas, Prior, & Walters, 2015). Together, these concepts are needed to investigate ignored areas and to redefine the positive aspects of sexuality that are so important to establishing sexual competence as a distinct, analytical lens. A new paradigm is needed to empower children and adults alike: to claim their sexual well-being and individuality as a right and demand, and to provide scientific backing for their ability to actively take part in this effort (Moore & Reynolds, this volume). In the following, let us discuss and engage critically with this new paradigm.

Agency and Structure, Choice, Performance

Contemporary childhood studies (cf. Esser et al., 2016; Hanson, 2016; Stoecklin & Fattore, 2018), developmental science (Sokol, Hammond, Kuebli, & Sweetman, 2015) and social theory (Ritzer & Stepnisky, 2017, pp. 334–82) suggest that people of all ages, including children, have *agency*. Agency means that individuals are able to actively influence their own development to some extent, make autonomous decisions and choices, ascribe meanings and take deliberate action or inaction (Sokol et al., 2015). This process can be reflected, conscious and intentional (Egan & Hawkes, 2009). For example, children may question their heterosexuality despite living in a heteronormative society (Carver et al., 2004) or they deliberately decide what to reveal about their own sexual knowledge to adults (Bhana, 2016). Agency can also take the form of resistance to power and resilience to adverse circumstances (compare Lerner et al., 2013; Seery, 2011). When theorizing the formation of sexual competence, *personal agency* thus must be taken into account. Whereas children's actions may also be based on unconscious motivations, such actions shall not fall under the definition of agency for the purpose of disambiguation in this section, despite that unconscious, experiential (sexual) behavior can be part of the formation of sexual competence, as mentioned before. Moreover, Sparrman (2015) warned not to confuse agency with competence: "Saying that children are agentive and actors is not synonymous with saying that children per se are competent, mature and rational" (p. 125). The interesting issue regarding agency and competence is how much control a person can actually exert over their own development vis-à-vis their social surroundings.

One of the core questions that social theory grapples with is how social structures, societies and cultures shape an individual's roles, actions, attitudes and social power—and vice versa, how individuals produce and change social structures and systems. In other words, competing theories deal with the relationship between agency and social structure, or between the socially microscopic and macroscopic (Ritzer & Stepnisky, 2017). Although my approach to sexual competence assumes agency on the side of the individual, it does not simply assume that the onus of successful competence formation is located only on the individual; obviously, many other factors are to be considered besides personal agency, especially in the case of children who are mostly dependent on adults and the availability of education. And while this approach centers on the individual as the *unit of analysis*, the whole *levels of analysis* extend from the individual and *intra*personal into the *inter*personal, societal, cultural and global realms (Della Porta & Keating, 2008), striving for a critical analysis of the interaction between agency and structure. Let us also not forget that—contrary to the typical use of these terms—agency may be ascribed to bigger social groupings or institutions, and structures may exist in individuals and dyads as well (Ryan, 2005).

Bay-Cheng (2018) provided helpful illustrations for the limits of personal agency in connection to societal structure. The author critically engaged with the notion of *choice* as used in sexuality education for youth: *Neoliberal ideology* tends to purport that individuals are powerful agents who determine their lives by making the right sexual choices (and are to blame and responsible for poor choices). Making good choices in one's lived sexual experience can look, on the surface, like a sign of agency and competence. Yet this appearance of agency is illusionary if the available options are pre-ascribed or limited to choices detrimental to a person, due to challenging circumstances (Bay-Cheng, 2018; cf. Herdt, 2006). For example, sexual consent is a murky proposition regarding agency, choice and gendered or age-related power differentials. For a person who is economically or emotionally dependent on a sexual partner, giving affirmative consent might not be a viable choice or option but become a foregone conclusion. Such a choice can further be more problematic if contraception or STI protections are not available (Bay-Cheng, 2018). As these illustrations show, agency and choice as singular approaches are not sufficient to avoid practical and theoretical challenges. A truly holistic concept of sexual competence thus needs an embedding theoretical framework for agency.

The macrosocial situatedness of an individual as well as operative power structures cannot be analyzed separately from agency; the contingent process of sexual competence development must always consider the productive interaction between the individual and the society. Therefore, I consider social theories of *agency–structure integration* the most relevant and useful as theoretical context to sexual competence. Next to Pierre Bourdieu's theory of *Habitus and Field* (Bourdieu, 2019), Anthony Giddens' *Structuration Theory* (Giddens, 1984) provides a helpful approach to understanding the development of sexual competence as a process. Broadly speaking, in Structuration Theory, agency and structure are perceived as a duality that cannot be conceived as separate from one another. Structure can both enable and constrain agency. Giddens conceptualizes power as a prerequisite to agency without ignoring the constraints of structure. Most interestingly, to bridge the structure–agency duality, both Bordieu and Giddens focus on their respective notions of (social) *practice*, roughly understood as routinized and habitual ways of acting that involve bodily performance and mental activity (Ritzer & Stepnisky, 2017, pp. 334–82; Stoecklin & Fattore, 2018). This kind of theorizing is especially applicable for sexual competence since sexuality is located on the body.

In my approach to sexual competence, I include not only the behavioral dimension of action but also (deliberate) inaction. One critical point of debate is how actual performance (behavior) is related to competence, in terms of causality or being equivalent: A lack of performance cannot be equated with a lack of competence; successful performance might not be solely based on competence; or it might be difficult to assess competence *without* assessing some behavior that is performed (Bos, 2010). Judith Butler's (2006, 2011) theory of *performativity* provides a similar contention: When gender or a sexual role is performed via speech or behavior, we can question if competence is inherently in the origin of performance, or is actually *produced by* recursive performativity. Similarly, Sophian (1997) suggested that children might develop competence *from* performance and behavior, by trying different strategies to solve a problem. In human development, (conceptual) competence should not be understood to always cognitively precede successful performance; the process is actually bidirectional "such that cognitive competences not only guide performance but also are shaped by it" (Sophian, 1997, p. 281). Considering this complicated relationship between competence and performance is thus critical for establishing the research design when setting out to investigate sexual competence. Reiterating the example of human sexual touch, competence in providing pleasurable touch may, arguably, be less a preexisting cognitive concept than it is much more the result of repeatedly receiving and giving such touch, and then reflecting upon or embodying the sensations or the feedback of others. But if competence is only partially the origin of (touching) behavior, where does, by contrast, the *motivation* to gaze, touch or kiss come from? Sexual desire can be characterized as a deeply emotional source that spawns sexual behavior, potentially sidelining cognition as a modifier and being an unconscious process, particularly at an early age (compare Herdt & McClintock, 2000). For theorizing sexual development, these important distinctions suggest that the development of sexual competence over time entails increasing emotional awareness and consciousness. Furthermore, the aforementioned notion of *social practice* as proposed by Bourdieu (2019) and Giddens (1984) may derive from a different kind of social motivation, but may also be theorized as a base element for the early development of sexual competence.

In conclusion, sexual competence may serve as a new and fertile conceptual vehicle for both empirical study and the refinement of developmental and sexual theory. In (initially explorative) empirical research, found topics germane to sexual competence may be compared between different groups (e.g., by gender, age, sexual orientation, culture, ethnicity, ability or geography) and probed in regard to their particular individual and social meanings. Subsequent research could then investigate the interactions between individual and macrosocial structure and their implications for the development of sexual competence. These empirical results may successively allow for a deeper conceptualization of sexual competence. Especially the areas of sex and relationship education (SRE), policy and clinical intervention could benefit by using a sexual competence model that fosters the empowerment of human beings with their particular sexual selves. In the realm of policy and law, sexual competence would have the biggest impact once it can be assessed or measured. People with mental or physical disabilities, who are often deemed sexually incompetent or incapable to consent, should find conceptual backup inside a positive sexual competence framework that focuses on what could be achieved and supported (compare Arstein-Kerslake, 2015; Mackenzie & Watts, 2013). Whereas this chapter has focused on young age regarding development, it is important to emphasize that sexual competence is a topic that concerns the complete life span of any individual. And as a construct that may be used in any cultural setting, sexual competence is a proponent of a "glocal" perspective.

References

Arstein-Kerslake, A. (2015). Understanding sex: The right to legal capacity to consent to sex. *Disability & Society*, *30*(10), 1459–1473. doi:10.1080/09687599.2015.1116059

Bay-Cheng, L. Y. (2018). Bad choices: How neoliberal ideology disguises social injustice in the sexual lives of youth. In J. Gilbert & S. Lamb (Eds.), *The Cambridge handbook of sexual development* (pp. 180–197). Cambridge: Cambridge University Press. doi:10.1017/9781108116121.010

Bayer, M. (2015). Bildung, Leistung und Kompetenz [Education, performance and competence]. In A. Lange, C. Steiner, S. Schutter, & H. Reiter (Eds.), *Handbuch Kindheits- und Jugendsoziologie* (pp. 135–147). Wiesbaden: Springer Fachmedien. doi:10.1007/978-3-658-05676-6_7-1

Bhana, D. (2016). *Childhood sexuality and AIDS education: The price of innocence*. New York: Routledge.

Bornstein, M. H., Leventhal, T., & Lerner, R. M. (Eds.). (2015). *Handbook of child psychology and developmental science. Volume 4: Ecological settings and processes* (7th ed.). Hoboken, NJ: Wiley.

Bos, W. (2010). *Kompetenzforschung: Erfahrungen aus Schulleistungsstudien* [Competence research: Experiences from studies of school performance]. Institut für Schulentwicklungsforschung, Technische Universität Dortmund. Retrieved from http://www.forschungsnetzwerk.at/downloadpub/Bos_Kompetenzforschung_Vechta_2005.pdf

Bourdieu, P. (2019). *Habitus and field: General sociology, volume 2 (1982–1983)*. Cambridge: Polity Press.

Bronfenbrenner, U. (1993). Ecological models of human development. In M. Gauvain & M. Cole (Eds.), *Readings on the development of children* (2nd ed., pp. 37–43). New York: Freeman.

Burnes, T. R., Singh, A. A., & Witherspoon, R. G. (2017). Sex positivity and counseling psychology: An introduction to the major contribution. *The Counseling Psychologist*, *45*(4), 470–486. doi:10.1177/0011000017710216

Butler, J. (2006). *Gender trouble: Feminism and the subversion of identity*. New York: Routledge.

Butler, J. (2011). *Bodies that matter: On the discursive limits of "sex"*. New York: Routledge.

Carver, P. R., Egan, S. K., & Perry, D. G. (2004). Children who question their heterosexuality. *Developmental Psychology*, *40*(1), 43–53. doi:10.1037/0012-1649.40.1.43

Della Porta, D., & Keating, M. (2008). Introduction. In D. Della Porta & M. Keating (Eds.), *Approaches and methodologies in the social sciences: A pluralist perspective* (pp. 1–15). Cambridge: Cambridge University Press.

Diamond, L. M. (2006). Introduction: In search of good sexual-developmental pathways for adolescent girls. *New Directions for Child and Adolescent Development*, *2006*(112), 1–7. doi:10.1002/cd.158

Diamond, L. M., Bonner, S. B., & Dickenson, J. (2015). The development of sexuality. In R. M. Lerner & M. E. Lamb (Eds.), *Handbook of child psychology and developmental science: Volume 3: Socioemotional processes* (pp. 888–931). Wiley. doi:10.1002/9781118963418.childpsy321

Driemeyer, W. (2013). Masturbation und sexuelle Gesundheit—ein Forschungsüberblick. [Masturbation and sexual health—a research overview]. *Zeitschrift für Sexualforschung*, *26*(04), 372–383. doi:10.1055/s-0033-1356159

Egan, R. D., & Hawkes, G. L. (2009). The problem with protection: Or, why we need to move towards recognition and the sexual agency of children. *Continuum: Journal of Media & Cultural Studies, 23*(3), 389–400.

Esser, F., Baader, M. S., Betz, T., & Hungerland, B. (Eds.). (2016). *Reconceptualising agency and childhood: New perspectives in childhood studies.* New York: Routledge.

Giddens, A. (1984). *The constitution of society: Outline of the theory of structuration.* Berkeley: University of California Press.

Glick, E. (2000). Sex positive: Feminism, queer theory, and the politics of transgression. *Feminist Review, 64*(1), 19–45. doi:10.1080/014177800338936

Halfon, N., Forrest, C. B., Lerner, R. M., & Faustman, E. M. (Eds.). (2018). *Handbook of life course health development.* New York: Springer Science+Business Media. doi:10.1007/978-3-319-47143-3

Hanson, K. (2016). Children's participation and agency when they don't "do the right thing". *Childhood, 23*(4), 471–475. doi:10.1177/0907568216669222

Herdt, G. (2006). Sexual development, social oppression, and local culture. In M. Kimmel (Ed.), *The sexual self: The construction of sexual scripts* (pp. 211–238). Nashville, TN: Vanderbilt University Press.

Herdt, G. (2007). What is sexual literacy, and why is it needed now? In G. Herdt & C. Howe (Eds.), *21st century sexualities: Contemporary issues in health, education, and rights* (pp. 17–19). London: Routledge.

Herdt, G., & McClintock, M. (2000). The magical age of 10. *Archives of Sexual Behavior, 29*(6), 587–606. doi:10.1023/a:1002006521067

Höhne, T. (2007). Der Leitbegriff "Kompetenz" als Mantra neoliberaler Bildungsreformer. Zur Kritik seiner semantischen Weitläufigkeit und inhaltlichen Kurzatmigkeit. [The guiding term 'competence' as mantra of neoliberal educations reformers. Critiquing its semantic broadness and contained shortness of breath]. In L. A. Pongratz, R. Reichenbach, & M. Wimmer (Eds.), *Bildung – Wissen – Kompetenz* (pp. 30–43). Bielefeld: Janus Software Projekte.

International Commission of Jurists (ICJ). (2007). *Yogyakarta principles—principles on the application of international human rights law in relation to sexual orientation and gender identity.* Retrieved from http://yogyakartaprinciples.org/wp-content/uploads/2016/08/principles_en.pdf

International Commission of Jurists (ICJ). (2017). *The Yogyakarta principles plus 10—additional principles and state obligation on the application of international human rights law in relation to sexual orientation, gender expression and sex characteristics to complement the Yogyakarta principles.* Retrieved from http://yogyakartaprinciples.org/wp-content/uploads/2017/11/A5_yogyakartaWEB-2.pdf

Jenkins, P. (2003). Watching the research pendulum. In J. Bancroft (Ed.), *Sexual development in childhood* (pp. 3–20). Bloomington: Indiana University Press.

Klieme, E., & Hartig, J. (2008). Kompetenzkonzepte in den Sozialwissenschaften und im erziehungswissenschaftlichen Diskurs. [Competence concepts in social sciences and in pedagogical discourse]. In M. Prenzel, I. Gogolin, & H.-H. Krüger (Eds.), *Kompetenzdiagnostik* (pp. 11–29). Wiesbaden: VS Verlag für Sozialwissenschaften. doi:10.1007/978-3-531-90865-6_2

Klieme, E., & Leutner, D. (2006). Kompetenzmodelle zur Erfassung individueller Lernergebnisse und zur Bilanzierung von Bildungsprozessen. [Competence models for measuring individual learning results and for accounting of educational processes]. *Zeitschrift für Pädagogik, 52*(6), 876–903.

Lerner, R. M., Agans, J. P., Arbeit, M. R., Chase, P. A., Weiner, M. B., Schmid, K. L., & Warren, A. E. A. (2013). Resilience and positive youth development: A relational developmental systems model. In *Handbook of resilience in children* (pp. 293–308). Springer. doi:10.1007/978-1-4614-3661-4_17

Lerner, R. M., Lerner, J. V., Bowers, E. P., & Geldhof, G. J. (2015). Positive youth development and relational-developmental-systems. In W. F. Overton, P. C. M. Molenaar, & R. M. Lerner (Eds.), *Handbook of child psychology and developmental science.* Volume 1: Theory and method (7th ed., pp. 607–651). Hoboken, NJ: Wiley.

Lerner, R. M., Tirrell, J. M., Dowling, E. M., Geldhof, G. J., Gestsdóttir, S., Lerner, J. V., ... Sim, A. T. R. (2019). The end of the beginning: Evidence and absences studying positive youth development in a global context. *Adolescent Research Review, 4*(1), 1–14. doi:10.1007/s40894-018-0093-4

Lucke, S. (2020). Researching childhood sexuality. In Z. Davy, A. C. Santos, C. Bertone, R. Thoreson, & S. E. Wieringa (Eds.), *The SAGE handbook of global sexualities* (vol. 1, pp. 99–118). Thousand Oaks: Sage.

Mackenzie, R., & Watts, J. (2013). Sexual health, neurodiversity and capacity to consent to sex. *Tizard Learning Disability Review, 18*(2), 88–98. doi:10.1108/13595471311315119

Martens, M., & Asbrand, B. (2009). Rekonstruktion von Handlungswissen und Handlungskompetenz—auf dem Weg zu einer qualitativen Kompetenzforschung. [Reconstruction of knowledge to act and competency to act—on the way towards qualitative competence research]. *Zeitschrift für Qualitative Forschung, 10*(2), 201–217.

Moore, A., & Reynolds, P. (2018a). Sexual literacy. In *Childhood and sexuality: Contemporary issues and debates* (pp. 197–224). London: Palgrave Macmillan.

Moore, A., & Reynolds, P. (2018b). The age of consent. In *Childhood and sexuality: Contemporary issues and debates* (pp. 79–98). London: Palgrave Macmillan.

Morrow, V. (2013). What's in a number? Unsettling the boundaries of age. *Childhood, 20*(2), 151–155. doi:10.1177/0907568213484199

Overton, W. F., Molenaar, P. C. M., & Lerner, R. M. (Eds.) (2015). *Handbook of child psychology and developmental science: Volume 1: Theory and method* (7th ed.). Hoboken, NJ: Wiley.

Ritzer, G., & Stepnisky, J. (2017). *Modern sociological theory* (8th ed.). Sage.

Robinson, K. H., & Davies, C. (2015). Children's gendered and sexual cultures: Desiring and regulating recognition through life markers of marriage, love and relationships. In E. Renold, J. Ringrose, & R. D. Egan (Eds.), *Children, sexuality and sexualization* (pp. 174–190). New York: Palgrave Macmillan.

Russell, S. T. (2005). Conceptualizing positive adolescent sexuality development. *Sexuality Research & Social Policy, 2*(3), 4–12. doi:10.1525/srsp.2005.2.3.4

Ryan, M. (2005). Micro-macro integration. In G. Ritzer (Ed.), *Encyclopedia of social theory* (pp. 502–503). Thousand Oaks, CA: Sage. doi:10.4135/9781412952552.n194

Seery, M. D. (2011). Resilience. *Current Directions in Psychological Science, 20*(6), 390–394. doi:10.1177/0963721411424740

Sokol, B. W., Hammond, S. I., Kuebli, J., & Sweetman, L. (2015). The development of agency. In W.F. Overton, P. C. M. Molenaar, & R. M. Lerner (Eds.), *Handbook of child psychology and developmental science: Volume 1: Theory and method* (7th ed., pp. 284–322). Hoboken, NJ: Wiley.

Sophian, C. (1997). Beyond competence: The significance of performance for conceptual development. *Cognitive Development, 12*(3), 281–303.

Sparrman, A. (2015). Seeing (with) the "sexy" body—young children's visual enactment of sexuality. In E. Renold, J. Ringrose, & R. D. Egan (Eds.), *Children, sexuality and sexualization* (pp. 123–140). New York: Palgrave Macmillan.

Stoecklin, D., & Fattore, T. (2018). Children's multidimensional agency: Insights into the structuration of choice. *Childhood, 25*(1), 47–62. doi:10.1177/0907568217743557

Weeks, J. (2016). *What is sexual history?* Malden, MA: Polity.

Weinert, F. E. (2001). Leistungsmessungen in Schulen—eine umstrittene Selbstverständlichkeit. [Measurement of performance in schools—a controversial obligation]. In F. E. Weinert (Ed.), *Leistungsmessungen in Schulen* (pp. 17–32). Weinheim: Beltz.

White, R. W. (1959). Motivation reconsidered: The concept of competence. *Psychological Review, 66*(5), 297–333. doi:10.1037/h0040934

Williams, D. J., Thomas, J. N., Prior, E. E., & Walters, W. (2015). Introducing a multidisciplinary framework of positive sexuality. *Journal of Positive Sexuality, 1*(6), 11.

World Health Organization. (2006). *Defining sexual health.* Retrieved from http://www.who.int/reproductivehealth/topics/sexual_health/sh_definitions/en/

Chapter 35

THE MEDICALIZATION OF THE DSM: RECONCEPTUALIZING HUMAN SEXUALITY AND GENDER

Megan Neitling

In this essay, I dismantle the current medicalization of human sexuality and gender as framed by the Diagnostic and Statistical Manual of Mental Disorders (DSM). I advocate that clinicians and human sexuality educators must focus on alternative methods of conceptualizing, naming and treating human sexuality and gender. The terminology needed to reconceptualize folx's[1] realities and clinical concerns are in some ways pre-discursive. As sexuality scholars and clinicians, we must move as far away as possible from these hierarchical models, or in the perfect world completely dismantle them, devising new models of taxonomy, nosology and diagnosis of human sexuality and gender in order to promote positive change in Western society and glocally.

Clinicians trained in social work, clinical mental health, and psychology in Western society are taught to embrace and employ the DSM in their clinical work. Professionally referred to as "the DSM," this text is the main diagnostic classification system utilized by mental health clinicians or therapists (Wincze & Carey, 2001). Afterall, according to the American Psychological Association (APA) the DSM is the "authoritative guide" (2020a) on mental diagnoses and the classification of disorders. Budding professionals are taught in their clinical training programs, and as part of their curriculum or accrediting standards, how to use the DSM (CACREP, 2020). Clinicians are taught the DSM's diagnostic criteria and how to pathologize behaviors using a medical model. The DSM provides everything clinicians need to diagnose and classify, or does it?

Eriksen and Kress (2005) however suggest that "the DSM represents only one model, one story, for understanding human problems—the medical model" (p. x). The DSM, like any model, they argue, has real limitations (Eriksen & Kress, 2005; Kotov et al.,

---

1 Folx is used to refer to a person or a group of people. Folx is inherently gender neutral. Folx is inclusive and affirming of all genders as this term rejects the social construct of the gender binary. Folx is intentionally utilized because it affirms individuals with expansive gender identities or gender expressions while also respecting folx's chosen pronouns.

2017). The process of medicalization within the DSM, for example, provides clues for the limitations. Medicalization refers to the process of framing and describing human sexuality and gender in a tautological way whereby defining sexual behavior or gender using medical language, using a medical framework to understand it and then conveniently using medical interventions to "treat" or "cure" it, causing human sexuality and gender to be seen as a medical problem.

Historically, we can see evidence that the "medicalization of sex proliferated new sexual categories, vocabularies and hierarchies effecting an evaluative shift from 'badness' to 'sickness,' a judgment often just as socially negative" (Irvine, 2005, p. 6). Cacchioni (2015) describes the medicalization of sexual deviance, which "includes scientific, medical, psychoanalytic, and psychiatric attempts at defining and classifying 'normal' sexual desire and expression across social locations of gender, race, class, and so forth" (p. 436). When diagnosing human sexuality and gender within clinical work became more pervasive, the reactions of sexologists or sex researchers was to invent "devises to observe, measure, and time bodily contractions and secretions toward the goal of quantifying maleness and femaleness" (Irvine, 2005, p. 7). Thus, as the medicalization of human sexuality and gender continued to prevail in Western society, the present-day reaction of licensed psychotherapists and counselors as well as many sex researchers is frequently medicalizing their research, diagnoses and psychological treatment methods.

As of 2020, the Council for Accreditation of Counseling and Related Educational Programs (CACREP) has no universal standard regarding the requirement to provide human sexuality training or education on the DSM's criteria for sexual diagnoses, gender identity or paraphilias to all clinicians. For example, according to the 2016 CACREP standards, the standards utilized for my master's degree in licensed mental health counseling (LMHC) in Indiana, there is no required human sexuality coursework or clinical training in treating or diagnosing sexual issues or gender (CACREP, 2020). Wieck (2010) agreed that "CACREP does not require programs to offer a human sexuality course as a required or elective course. Therefore, human sexuality learning is at the discretion of counseling programs' interpretation of CACREP standards" (p. 40). Bidell (2013) found the limitations of multicultural counseling education "likely contribute to counsellors' and psychotherapists' frequent reports of being unprepared, poorly trained, and marginally competent to provide LGBT-affirmative counselling and mental health treatment" for issues related to human sexuality or gender (p. 301). Notably, only two states in the United States, Florida and California, require human sexuality training for counseling professionals to become licensed (see 2 B.P.C. § 16 in California Behavioral Board of Sciences, 2020; Florida Board of Clinical Social Work, Marriage & Family Therapy and Mental Health Counseling, 2020), whereas CACREP, as an accrediting body for various disciplines within mental health counseling, do not require such education or training.

Unfortunately, some clinicians who have graduated from reputable clinical programs often do not have adequate or accurate information about human sexuality or gender. According to the APA (2020b), the DSM is "intended to facilitate an objective assessment of symptom presentations in a variety of clinical settings" (para. 2). However, my main argument in this chapter is that the DSM is a moral and ethical book that predetermines what is appropriate, normal and healthy behavior for all folx regardless of the setting or circumstances. Indeed, Eriksen and Kress (2005) go further and suggest that the DSM has "historically oppressed certain groups" of people including people that are gay or lesbian, people of color and women (p. 56). Today, the DSM-5 is arguably oppressing people who are transgender or gender-nonconforming along with those who practice alternative sexual lifestyles.

Understanding the structural limitations of any model means understanding its history. The system of diagnostic classification in the DSM was formed exclusively using White European American men, which meant there was not any inclusion of diverse participants (Eriksen & Kress, 2005). The DSM is positioned to define how people should *not behave* by diagnosing what is a problematic behavior or identity. Thus, the DSM's medicalized stance on sexual behavior and gender presents diagnoses as moral and ethical issues that are harmful to the world, Western society and clinicians because we treat clients in a clinical setting that is globally intertwined (Eriksen & Kress, 2005; Greenberg, 2013). The APA (2020b) states that the DSM is used globally in "much of the world" but scholars dispute this. For example, Frances (2013) from the *Psychiatric Times* states that the DSM is not utilized or widely accepted outside of the United States in places such as China or Germany. So why frame it as a global tool when it was not nor was actually meant to be such?

Again, medicalization is defined by Conrad in 1992 as "a process whereby nonmedical problems become defined and treated as medical problems, usually in terms of illnesses or disorders" (p. 210). It is apparent that medicalization of human sexuality and gender has to be contextualized inside broader glocal sociopolitical context. The DSM-5's diagnoses of sexual disorders and gender dysphoria are overly pathologized and diagnosed as illness for folx to receive treatment suggesting medicalization. In other words, there are various "macro factors" within society including "colonialism, capitalism, patriarchy," White supremacy, heteronormativity, mononormativity and cisnormativity that all influence the growth of "scientific and medical epistemologies" with the intention of diminishing new ways of understanding and treating sexual health (Cacchioni, 2015, p. 449). The way that the medicalization of human sexuality and gender vis-à-vis the DSM reads, it works to maintain a society of reproductive cisgender heterosexuality and by framing this as "globally" adopted, the manual promotes this limited view of human sexuality worldwide—glocal in the worst sense (Cacchioni, 2015). "The medicalization of sexual deviance includes scientific, medical, psychoanalytic, and psychiatric attempts at defining and classifying 'normal' sexual desire and expression across social locations of gender, race, class, and so forth" (Cacchioni, 2015, p. 436).

Conrad (1992) explained that medicalization occurs anytime a medical framework, or medical definition, is used to understand or treat an issue such as gender dysphoria. Cacchioni (2015) agrees that the medicalization of "sexuality has been most evident in its classification, treatment, and monopolization over (1) sexualities deemed as deviant (2) sexual reproduction and (3) sexual functioning" (p. 24). As the medicalization of human sexuality and gender has developed and intertwined with the field of psychotherapy, there have been "new forms of sexual measurement, diagnosis, and classification, along with therapeutic techniques to both define and effect personal sexual fulfillment" (Irvine, 2005, p. 6).

Conrad's example of gender dysphoria being medicalized was written many decades ago yet, despite the time lapse, the act of diagnosing gender a pathological ailment is still an ongoing issue and debate within the DSM-5 and within modern Western society. The implications of medicalizing gender have reified broad social practices of oppressing folx, which today include but are not limited to those who identify as: agender, bigender, gender diverse, gender fluid, gender queer, gender questioning, gender variant, intersex, nonbinary, pangender or transgender. The central argument of this chapter is that the DSM-5 is a prime example of a form of glocal social control, especially on issues of sexuality and gender (Braun-Harvey & Vigorito, 2016; Conrad, 1992; Drescher, 2015; Greenberg, 2013).

Thus, the DSM is a device that continues to pathologize diversity and exploits its monetary power vis-à-vis clinicians (Eriksen & Kress, 2005; Greenberg, 2013). As we have seen, there has long been a line of critical thinking by sex therapists, sex researchers, sexologists and sexuality educators have retheorized and disputed various ways that the DSM pathologizes sexual behavior as "abnormal" through discourse on such categories as Bondage and Discipline, Dominance and Submission, Sadism & Masochism (BDSM), kinks, fetishes, sexual orientation and gender identity (Braun-Harvey & Vigorito, 2016; Drescher, 2015; Greenberg, 2013). It also disciplines therapists, who hold licenses and are engaged in billing via insurance companies, to conceive human sexuality and gender in ways defined by the manual. This has two effects: it normalizes this pathologizing of various sexuality and gender issues that arguably hold no moral or ethical threat or harm to an individual, and it translates the labor of the therapist into a use value for insurance companies to commodify[2] on the market—this dialectic I argue is the process through which the DSM pathologizes sexualities and genders that do not conform to monogamous cisgender heterosexual expectations and behavior repertoires. For these reasons, a growing number of scholars and clinicians hold that the DSM should not be the primary standard utilized for clinical diagnosis and treatment.

The Fallacies of Diagnosis

The Book of Woe (2003) was written about the cultural use of the DSM, and in it, Greenberg points out that "the prejudices and fallacies behind psychiatric diagnosis, and even the interest [the diagnosis] serve, are invisible to us" (p. 7) as providers or clinicians. Thus, our "desire to relieve suffering can pull a veil over our eyes and sometimes it takes an incendiary example or two to rip that veil away" (Greenberg, 2013, p. 7). Essentially, a DSM diagnosis means nothing more than "doctors get paid to treat it, scientists could search for its causes and cures, employers could shun its victims, families could urge [clients] to seek help" and clients can justify behaviors or feelings with diagnoseable disorders (Greenberg, 2013, p. 5). Kotov and colleagues (2017) succinctly state that

---

2 Commodification is, from a Marxist's perspective, turning a product, such as services from a therapist, into a commodity that holds a monetary value. The service would be exchanged with a client in order to receive the insurance-driven value associated with the service.

clinically a diagnosis is "expected to help in selection of treatment, but the DSM and ICD are imperfect guides to care" (p. 457).

The DSM does not just provide a manual for clinical diagnosis, the DSM categorizes: it is a taxonomy. The term *nosology* is defined by Merriam Webster (2020) as "a classification, or list, of diseases" and "a branch of medical science that deals with classification of diseases." Essentially, nosology is the best-fit adjective that describes the ways we have classified, pathologized and medicalized sexuality and gender using the DSM. Strand (2011) revealed the first DSM edition was created just after the beginning of the Second World War after the previous edition of *The Statistical Manual for Use of Institutions of the Insane* proved inadequate to detail the mental health nosology of war veterans. The APA created the first draft of the DSM-I, it was described as "a nosological manual" that "objectified psychiatry" and contained "minimal diagnostic material" meaning it had little clinical implications (Strand, 2011, p. 288). Yet, as each edition passed, the DSM morphed into a diagnostic manual of mental illness that was intended to be compatible with the taxonomy produced by the International Classification of Diseases 9th edition (ICD-9) (Strand, 2011).

Thus, Western medicalization has in essence linked almost every clinical issue or ailment back into the idea that there must be a diagnosis to justify our attention to it. Further, that without a diagnosis, there can be no remedy. In line with this ideology, Kotov and colleagues (2017) simply and shockingly state that "no patients are excluded or incompletely described by the system, because everyone can be characterized on a set of dimensions, even those with low levels of pathology" (p. 458). This fallacy and endless cycle of classifying disorders is the foundation of Western mental health treatment and is especially noticeable when addressing clinical issues related to human sexuality and gender.

As the fifth edition of the DSM states, these disorders are created and maintained by over "160 of the top researchers and clinicians from around the world" on the "DSM–5 Task Force." These people are "experts in neuroscience, biology, genetics, statistics, epidemiology, social and behavioral sciences, nosology, and public health" but these folx participated "on a strictly voluntary basis and encompass several medical and mental health disciplines including psychiatry, psychology, pediatrics, nursing and social work" (APA, 2020). Interestingly, the APA does not bode and brag that they have sex therapists, sex researchers, or academics specializing in human sexuality and gender on their task force. Thus, I question how experts can maintain and classify perceived disorders of sexuality and gender that they have little experience work with and little academic knowledge about these specialized topics. Instead, I agree with Braun-Harvey and Vigorito (2016, p. iv) that "pathologizing, stigmatizing, labeling, and criminalizing deviations from what are considered 'acceptable' sexual behavior have not helped individuals." In fact, the DSM and diagnoses has done quite the opposite for many people.

The chief issue I identify within the DSM is its taxonomy, specifically the hierarchical taxonomy. The DSM works to identify a very specific behavioral repertoire in folx that Western society does not like, agree with or endorse as "healthy," "normal" or "safe." By applying this taxonomy to people who are not cisgender, heterosexual and engaging in "vanilla," or nonkink-related sexual fantasies or activity, more and more folx are being diagnosed and pathologized.

A central provocation here is: does Western society still need a taxonomy via the DSM? Many of the disorders listed for human sexuality and gender are binary. The binarizing work of the DSM pathologizes people in such ways as: healthy or unhealthy, well or ill, suffering or thriving, significant clinical distress or other/unspecified. These taxonomies are deeply rooted in both a philosophical Cartesian dualism that is now thousands of years old and backed by a Western Christian lens that uses such moral ideals of heterosex as the primary social norm. Further, clinical taxonomies continue to occur and replicate within society despite the efforts of the DSM to change, remove, edit or alter a taxonomy. Slowly human sexuality and gender diagnoses have been refuted or removed from their medical treatment paradigm; however, many in the medical and counseling communities never stopped pathologizing human sexuality and gender.

Sexual Literacy Exercise

By way of concluding this essay, I would like to offer a space for reflection on the issues raised above. Take a few moments to review the DSM-5's sections on Sexual Dysfunctions, Gender Dysphoria and Paraphilic Disorders.

I invite you to consider the following: who, or what groups of folx, are being pathologized by these diagnoses? Who, or what groups of folx, are not being pathologized by these diagnoses? Why do you think the DSM includes these specific sexual behaviors, symptoms or identities as disorders? What group, or groups, of people do you think are creating and maintaining these diagnostic classifications of sexual behavior and gender in the DSM? What purposes do these diagnoses serve? How do you think a diagnosis impacts the person, or client, labeled with sexual dysfunction, paraphilia or gender dysphoria?

My own reflection leads me to feel that nonnormative behaviors or identities are being pathologized but normative monogamous cis-gender heterosexual penis-in-vagina sex is being idealized as the DSM's clinical norm. These disorders are listed and classified as a way to control society *through our therapeutic interventions* and maintain the cis-heterosex patriarchy. I conclude by urging professors of clinical programs, novice clinicians in their training program, and experienced clinicians to further their own sexual literacy by attending a sex-positive, culturally competent, body positive, kink/fetish affirming, LGBTQIAP+ affirming, and nonmonogamy affirming course or training focusing on the diversities of human sexuality and gender. These courses or trainings should provide educational information and discuss the limitations to the DSM diagnosis. These courses must teach new ways for counselors to conceptualize and think about diverse or nonnormative behaviors and identities. For students or professors interested in creating an inclusive and affirming human sexuality curriculum for their CACREP, or counseling education program, explore the following from the American Association of Sexuality Educators, Counselors and Therapists (AAASECT): the sexual attitude reassessment (SAR), which creates a safe and brave space to explore feelings, attitudes, values and beliefs about sex or gender in one's self and in others, and the human sexuality education core knowledge areas. More information may be found at www.AASECT.org. Additional resources are: *What Every Mental Health Professional Needs to Know About Sex* by

Stephanie Buehler (2016), *Becoming a Kink Aware Therapist* by Caroline Shahbaz and Peter Chirinos (2017), *A Clinician's Guide to Gender-Affirming Care: Working with Transgender and Gender Nonconforming Clients* by Sand Chang, Anneliese Singh, and Lore Dickey (2018), *A Therapist's Guide to Consensual Nonmonogamy: Polyamory, Swinging, and Open Marriage* by Rhea Orion (2018), and *Designing and Leading a Successful SAR* by Patti Britton and Robert Dunlap.

Attaining sexual literacy is a process and a journey for professional clinicians and researchers. Our knowledge about human sexuality education is changing both in Western society and glocally. Western clinicians and clinical educators can be part of the glocal movement to attain sexual literacy by being open to learn new ways to understand human sexuality and gender using a broader, more inclusive and affirming, lens.

References

APA. (2020a). DSM-5: Frequently asked questions. Retrieved from https://www.psychiatry.org/psychiatrists/practice/dsm/feedback-and-questions/frequently-asked-questions

APA. (2020b). About the DSM. Retrieved from https://www.psychiatry.org/psychiatrists/practice/dsm/about-dsm

Bidell, M. P. (2013). Addressing disparities: The impact of a lesbian, gay, bisexual, and transgender graduate counselling course. *Counselling & Psychotherapy Research 13*(4), 300–307. https://doi-org.ciis.idm.oclc.org/10.1080/14733145.2012.741139

Braun-Harvey, D., & Vigorito, M. A. (2016). *Treating out of control sexual behavior: Rethinking sex addiction*. New York: Springer.

Buehler, S. (2016). *What every mental health professional needs to know about sex*. New York: Springer.

Cacchioni, T. (2015). The medicalization of sexual deviance, reproduction, and functioning. In J. DeLamater & R. Plante (Eds.), *Handbook of the sociology of sexualities* (pp. 435–52). Cham, Switzerland: Springer International.

CACREP. (2020). 2016 CACREP Standards. Retrieved from https://www.cacrep.org/for-programs/2016-cacrep-standards/

Chang, S. C., Singh, A. A., & Dickey, L. M. (2018). *A clinician's guide to gender-affirming care: Working with transgender and gender nonconforming clients*. Oakland, CA: New Harbinger.

Conrad, P. (1992). Medicalization and social control. *Annual Review of Sociology, 18*, 209–232. https://doi-org.ciis.idm.oclc.org/10.1146/annurev.so.18.080192.001233

Drescher, J. (2015). Queer diagnoses revisited: The past and future of homosexuality and gender diagnoses in DSM and ICD. *International Review of Psychiatry, 27*(5), 386–395. https://doi-org.ciis.idm.oclc.org/10.3109/09540261.2015.1053847

Eriksen, K., & Kress, V. E. (2005). *Beyond the DSM story: Ethical quandaries, challenges, and best practices*. Thousand Oaks, CA: Sage.

Florida Board of Clinical Social Work, Marriage & Family Therapy and Mental Health Counseling. (2020). Retrieved from https://floridasmentalhealthprofessions.gov/licensing/licensed-mental-health-counselor/

Frances, A. (2013). *The International Reaction to DSM-5*. Retrieved from https://www.psychiatrictimes.com/international-reaction-dsm-5

Greenberg, G. (2013). *The Book of Woe: The DSM and the unmaking of psychiatry*. New York: Blue Rider Press.

Irvine, J. (2005). *Disorders of desire: Sexuality and gender in modern American sexology*. Philadelphia, PA: Temple University Press. Revised and Expanded Edition.

Kotov, R., Krueger, R. F., Watson, D., Achenbach, T. M., Althoff, R. R., Bagby, R. M., … & Zimmerman, M. (2017). The hierarchical taxonomy of psychopathology: A dimensional alternative to traditional nosologies. *Journal of Abnormal Psychology, 126*(4), 454–477. https://doi-org.ciis.idm.oclc.org/10.1037/abn0000258

Merriam Webster. (2020). Nosology. Retrieved from https://www.merriam-webster.com/dictionary/nosology

Shahbaz, C., & Chirinos, P. (2017). *Becoming a kink aware therapist.* New York: Routledge.

Strand, M. (2011). Where do classifications come from? The DSM-III, the transformation of American psychiatry, and the problem of origins in the sociology of knowledge. *Theory and Society, 40*(3), 273–313. Springer Stable.

Wieck, C. R. (2010). *Counselor's comfort levels and willingness to discuss sexual issues with couples they counsel* (Doctoral dissertation). Retrieved from ProQuest Dissertations and Theses (UMI No. 3414807).

Wincze, J. P., & Carey, M. P. (2001). *Sexual dysfunction: A guide for assessment and treatment,* 2nd ed. London: Guildford Press.

Chapter 36

"*OUR BODY IS OUR OWN BODY*": THE COLLECTIVE BODIES OF PUBLIC HEALTH

Katherine Lepani

Public health has a central role in fostering sexual literacy, given its mandate for health promotion and disease prevention at the population level, and the dominance of medical science in defining sexual and reproductive health and structuring clinical services to meet the needs of different groups of people. The epidemiological contours of health and disease associated with sexual practice—fertility, reproduction, contraception, unwanted and unplanned pregnancy, HIV and other sexually transmitted infections and intimate partner violence—are a key focus of standardized public health policies and programs.

Often missing in the application of public health principles in meeting the sexual health needs of different populations is the importance of contextual diversity, structural differentials, such as the basic availability and accessibility of healthcare services and the multiple meanings of sexuality and well-being. Sexual literacy for critical public health requires understanding the differential effects of power and inequalities in people's lives, at both individual and collective levels, and addressing the systemic and entrenched barriers to accessing services. Being mindful of diversity entails providing services not only to individual bodies but in ways attuned to the collective identities and values of groups of people, and recognizing service delivery as a social interaction that involves knowledge translation and exchange, not simply the dissemination of standardized information coupled with instructions. Being attuned to different contexts and knowledge systems also involves bridging the scientific and discursive practices of specialized disciplines and facilitating dialogue with diverse audiences.

This chapter draws on contextual insights from the Trobriand Islands, a group of small coral atolls in the Solomon Sea off the east coast of mainland Papua New Guinea, a country of eight million people north of Australia in the southwest Pacific (Lepani, 2012). My ethnographic research in the Trobriands explored the cultural epidemiology of HIV, that is, the conceptual, discursive and social dimensions of disease, and how these highly social patterns and processes are contextually specific (Trostle, 2005). The declaration of collective subjectivity in the title of this chapter—"Our body is our own body"—was expressed frequently and in various ways by women and men, young and old, during discussions and interviews I held on gender, sexuality and HIV prevention. In these sessions, and in casual conversations, people would often critique what they regarded as prescriptive interventions for sexual health and HIV, which they felt either diminished or disrespected their unique cultural identity.

The Trobriand context offers insights for locating critical sexuality in relation to the importance of collective values and meanings in the promotion of individual sexual health and well-being. The sex-positive culture of the Trobriands challenges conventional public health models of individualized sexual practice based on reductive categories and uniform assumptions about what constitutes identity and behavior, and redirects focus toward public health's collective register in contributing to "glocal" sexual literacy.

Public Health and Its Bodies

Health promotion and disease prevention are the twin promises of public health. This moral and strategic pact for collective well-being is structured by regulatory bodies and health systems, both government and nongovernment, and conveyed to constituent populations by laws, policies, research and services. In turn, individuals and communities are directed, motivated and enabled to access information and services, and make decisions about their health behavior and well-being. To achieve its effects, public health and its various registers—population health, international health, global health—employ interdisciplinary approaches to identify the social determinants of health and their patterns, to examine how these variables interact and are distributed within and between specific populations and geographical areas, and to manage the health concerns of these defined groups. Critical to public health's role are approaches attentive to health inequalities and gaps, and to the relations of power and privilege that structure inequalities on both local and global scales.

The containment and control of disease matters in public health. This objective registers at a universal level to prevent pathogens moving within and between populations and individual bodies, taking into account specific disease ecologies and behavioral environments. Surveillance technologies inform the control and management of the spread of pathogens based on epidemiological assumptions about interactions between disease and human behavior, which are largely framed by degrees of "risk." Protocols involve the collection of health-related statistical data on individual variables, which are then aggregated to chart patterns and trends at the population level. Data might be routinely collected at the facility level, or collected through randomized sampling among different populations, or at sentinel sites to gain information on specific cohorts.

These measurement tools are used to construct the "evidence base," a much-touted notion about the veracity and strength of foundational knowledge. The term conveys firm confidence about the reliability and authority of claims about knowledge built on a seemingly solid body of baseline data from which to mount and manage public health policies and interventions. The term *evidence-based*, used to describe the application of research findings, originated from randomized control trials in laboratory settings, conducted to test the efficacy of medical treatments and improve clinical practice (Barbour, 2000). The term is now part of the everyday language of public health research, policy and decision-making, and it has migrated into other disciplines and fields of study as well (Trostle, 2005).

The public health evidence base largely comprises what can be enumerated, classified and controlled for bias, with units of data defined by assumptions about the risk of exposure, transmission or other social and environmental factors, and analyzed and presented in linear order or in causal association. Standardized baseline data serves the purpose of monitoring and evaluation, the framework and tools of which are used to survey and statistically measure the imagined outcome of public health interventions—behavior change—through a trinity construct of what is deemed to constitute the individual's ability to make rational decisions: knowledge, attitudes and practice (USAID, 2011).

In the practice of public health, this "seduction of quantification," to quote Sally Engle Merry (2016), sets the standards for validity, accountability and rationale for policies and programs. The evidence-based mandate for public health then moves to an accelerated pace of "scaling up," or replicating and adapting interventions on the basis of "best practice"—where methodology can be shown to produce desired outcomes—to extend reach and coverage into multiple locations. For example, scaling the provision of HIV counseling and testing services in resource-poor settings might be guided by surveillance data used to identify "high risk" populations and locations based on assumptions and reductive classifications about sexual identity and practice (Boyce et al., 2007; Dworkin, 2005). In turn, the pace of scaling is determined and constrained by policies and funding, and is accompanied by the often-expressed proviso about the importance of context: "One size does not fit all" (Centers for Disease Control, 2019).

Paradoxically, the reliance on aggregated statistical data to build the public health evidence base often reproduces decontextualized assumptions about individual behavior rather than revealing a richer understanding about the complexities of social life among diverse groups of people in particular locations. The evidence base tends to diminish the value of knowledge that comes not from the power of numbers but from the interpretive, intersubjective accounts and descriptions of everyday lived experience, which involves patterns of *collective* practice, not isolated individual acts, where meaning is found in shared understanding (Dworkin, 2005; Kippax & Stephenson, 2012).

Public health evidence is enriched by the contextual insights that come from qualitative research, not merely as a mixed-method supplement to quantitative research but as the theoretical framework for interpreting evidence through critical descriptive analysis. Qualitative research offers an ethical framework for direct interaction with people in their own settings and on their own terms. This in turn opens the way for exploring contextual diversity, questioning concepts and assumptions, engaging in dialogue that brings ideas to life and learning about sexuality beyond its associations with contagion and disease.

Locating Critical Sexuality in Public Health

While the regulatory scope of public health is directed at populations as a whole, the moral register is decidedly individualistic, prescriptive and often corrective, framed by risk avoidance and measures of deviance from presumed health norms. The binary focus of interventions, and indeed the unilateral authority of "intervening," calls into question the ethical imperative of public health—to advocate the right to health for individuals, communities and populations, and to provide nonjudgmental and equitable access to services.

The effect of public health's regulatory mandate on its populations, or the so-called "target groups" that interventions are aimed at, and its stress on individual responsibility, is particularly noticeable in the sphere of sexuality. The universal and essentialist framing of sex as a biological fact independent of social and cultural factors, and with emphasis on morbidity and dysfunction, tends to shape public health's subjects in static, one-dimensional forms, while overshadowing local agency and knowledge and the ways sexuality is "intimately embedded in social life" (Boyce et al., 2007, p. 18).

For example, public health programs typically conjoin and package sexual and reproductive health services to primarily target antenatal women—women categorized as mothers and wives, or as victims of patriarchal oppression. This not only frames sexuality foremost in terms of risk management and clinical treatment, but it also positions women as passive recipients of services who are nonetheless personally responsible for making the right choices about their health. Moreover, it gives little attention to how women's sexual and reproductive agency is situated within social relations and social practices (Fahs & McClelland, 2016). Less often does the reach of sexual and reproductive health programs extend inclusively to the needs and desires of other members of a community, most immediately to women's sexual and reproductive partners, but equally to men, transgender and intersex people and adolescents and children. Reductive categories not only isolate individuals from social context but they diminish understandings of the spectrum of gender and sexuality, and how it intersects with other factors that shape identity and agency, such as age, ethnicity, kinship, education, income, religion, disability and place of residence.

The critical framing of sexual literacy in the public health domain might instead start with how sexuality is imagined, talked about and practiced, and how this is a highly social process that unfolds differently in different cultural contexts that may be glocally informed. Qualitative research offers an orientation for comparative understandings of sexuality and for rethinking sexual health promotion and prevention strategies by demonstrating how specific cultural contexts and collectivities provide an analytical lens for linking and scaling between individual and collective bodies.

"Our body is our own body": Local Articulations of Sexuality and Public Health

The collective ethos of Trobriand sexual culture, as articulated in the above quote, illustrates the importance of context for public health's role in glocal sexual literacy. The contextual imperative of "one size does not fit all" is made more pronounced when one considers that the Trobriands represents one of over 800 distinct language groups in Papua New Guinea, a country of tremendous cultural and geographical diversity. The assertion of a unified body, which Trobrianders often express when talking about sexuality, is a sharp contrast to the public health imaginary of the universalized body that is sexed and gendered categorically, and measured and counted individually (Connell, 2012). Rather, it represents a cohesive social body that exercises relational agency through collective identity of place and belonging.

More specifically, the assertion of ownership and autonomy can be heard as a form of resistance to the regulatory control of sexual practice by the government and religious bodies that deliver public health messages and services. These colonialist-tinged interventions often promote sexual health by denouncing indigenous culture as the primary source of risk and disease, over that of pathogens and the genetic, environmental and psychosocial stressors that contribute to poor health outcomes. These discursive practices laud individual behavior change as an emancipatory measure in relation to cultural norms and practices that are perceived as stubbornly persistent and, more often than not, oppressive. The blaming of indigenous culture for disease has historical roots in colonialism and the movement of western medicine throughout the world, and continues to echo in the moral register of contemporary public health practice in Papua New Guinea and elsewhere (Andersen, 2004, 2018).

The Trobriand context provides grounding for thinking about how cultural values inherent in collective sociality—such as clan identity, matrilineal regeneration, female sexual agency, consensual desire and pleasure and reciprocity—challenge the predominantly negative public health narratives on sexuality, not only in Papua New Guinea but globally, as communicated by interventionist policies and programs with implicit moral evaluations about what is considered normal and transgressive sexual identity and practice. Trobriand culture validates sexuality as a productive resource for building and reinforcing social relations. Trobriand women exercise sexual autonomy and choose their sexual and marital partners. Consensual, pleasurable sexual activity is regarded as part of a young person's physical and social development into adulthood. The life stage of youth sexuality, *kubukwabuya*, which also means "freedom" in Trobriand language, resonates strongly with the distinct forms of autonomy and interconnected agency within the Trobriand cultural world, wherein the identity of the individual person registers meaning through social relationships, and autonomous decisions and acts are also expressions of collective identity (Lepani, 2015).

The Trobriand lens also provides insights on how people engage with public health services not as individuals but as collective bodies, whether by household, extended family, clan or village groups or peer cohorts of students, workmates and sports teams. This collectivist cultural preference is common in Papua New Guinea, and validated anecdotally, particularly by community development workers who work in various places throughout the country—places that can differ greatly in language and custom even if in close proximity. The collective form of personhood and agency has a deep cultural history in Papua New Guinea, and it has been layered, and exploited, by colonial public health practices that corralled entire populations during periodic health patrols in the early twentieth century (Connelly, 2007; Denoon, 1989; Reed, 1997; Street, 2014). The collective social identity retains a strong presence in health extension work today, including in the application of global development models for mobilizing communities in health promotion activities (Adams & Pigg, 2005).

An example of collective action in accessing health services was conveyed by an older Trobriand woman during a group discussion about gender, sexuality and HIV, which I facilitated with a women's church fellowship group in a village school classroom. The woman fondly recalled a memory of when she was in her early 20s and the birth control pill was first made available in the islands in 1972. Several younger women had been voicing frustration about the unreliable supply of modern contraceptives at the local government-run health center, and this issue prompted the older woman to suddenly stand up in the middle of the group and enact her memory about how she and her agemates—sisters and friends, married and single—donned freshly made bright red banana fiber skirts and proudly walked the three hours from their village to the health center to get the pill. Their collective action was all the more notable given that they were from a Catholic village, and the national policy on family planning services at the time restricted contraceptives to married women and required a husband's written consent.

The women's act of adornment in the festive finery of traditional skirts was a deliberate expression of female sexual and reproductive agency, at once personal and collective. As material objects of exchange made by women for distribution during funeral feasts, these skirts represent women's value and status in Trobriand matrilineal society, and are emblematic of the vitality of sexuality as valued social practice (Lepani, 2012). Inspired by their shared desire to obtain modern contraceptives, the women's trek across the island in traditional dress, in full view of curious onlookers, can be viewed as a form of *cultural activism*, or the strategic mobilization of positive cultural values and aesthetics, grounded in local knowledge and communities of belonging, to promote awareness, dialogue and social change (Parker & Aggleton, 2012).

Whether through dance, music or other forms of creative expression, cultural activism can translate and mediate the resources and tools of sexual literacy within and between collective bodies, and help to shift perceptions and structures that inhibit sexual rights. Cultural activism accounts for identity and relationality in the advocacy and exercise of rights, and it upholds an epistemic and aesthetic preference for models of reciprocity in the provision of health services—responding to people's own articulations of what they want and need.

In the Trobriand context, this illustration of cultural activism emanates from the core cultural value of relational agency in achieving collective well-being—"Our body is our own body." The senior woman's story above also illustrates the intergenerational dimension of collective agency—the transfer of knowledge and lived experience from one generation to the next—and how this too is a potential force for fostering sexual literacy in the public health domain. Her memory was shared in response to the concerns expressed by the younger women, and this opened up unanswered questions about fertility cycles and conception, and further dialogue about health rights and HIV prevention.

My argument here is that there are many positive opportunities for public health to foster sexual literacy in the promise of promotion and prevention by strategically engaging with a diversity of cultural models and people's lived experience of sexual identity and practice. The register for doing this should not be solely focused on the individual body but rather the ways in which the social is collectively experienced. The pedagogical authority of scientific knowledge and technologies should not supplant cultural knowledge but be viewed as complementary in the process of making glocal connections of meaning and value as people exercise their sexual and reproductive rights (Pigg, 2005).

Collective Bodies and Common Ground

Community participation and "ownership" are key modalities for public health practice, and provide an important framework for engaging collective identities to foster sexual literacy. Initiatives that work within communities, and emerge from and reinforce social connectedness, mutual trust, respect and collective action, have greater potential for effecting change (Kippax & Stephenson, 2012). The argument here for critical sexual literacy is not to suggest that the collective body is homogenous and acts in a uniform way. Rather, the common denominator of shared identity and practice offers a mode of action inclusive of diversity *within* groups and populations. The collective body in the Trobriands, and beyond, is about meeting on common ground, exchanging knowledge and making meaningful connections between different ways of knowing.

Public health's longstanding familiarity with community-based approaches, including participatory action research to inform program design and implementation, provides a strong premise for contributing to critical sexual literacy in ways that resonate with collective identities and values. This is not about making sexual literacy a pluralistic exercise, that is, where multiple and distinct knowledge systems coexist and compete within the same space. Rather, critical sexual literacy in a collectivist key is more about integration—maintaining the integrity of different strands of knowledge and action through mutual recognition so that each strand works to bring coherence into view. Importantly, qualitative research can support public health's role in fostering critical sexual literacy by representing collective bodies not as target groups for interventions but as communities of belonging with common values, practices and sexual geographies, and by recognizing how gender power relations and inequalities are structured locally.

The importance of well-functioning local health systems for promoting sexual health cannot be overstated. Communities cannot carry the responsibility for sexual health on their own but require a supportive environment provided by good laws, ethical policies and reliable services. In most places throughout the world, Papua New Guinea included, public health faces the basic challenges of service delivery—ensuring equitable and inclusive access to information, reliable treatments, care and support, in response to the lived experience of disease, marginalization, dispossession, exploitation and trauma (Street, 2014). Whether or not public health systems have the resources and capacity to fulfill the obligation to teach and support learning on sexual identity, expression and intimacy as the promise of promotion and prevention, beyond a focus on the avoidance of disease, is an open question.

In the Trobriand Islands, and in other glocal sites of belonging, sexual literacy cannot be separated from the major issues that define the contemporary context of social change—rapid population growth and mobility, environmental pressures and climate change, increasing economic inequalities and battles for human rights and gender justice. The embodiment of knowledge on sexuality is integral to all aspects of social life, and the role of public health is critical in supporting bodies of collective identity to access and apply sexual knowledge as they navigate this turbulent terrain.

References

Adams, V., & Pigg, S. L. (Eds.). (2005). *Sex in development: Science, sexuality, and morality in global perspective*. Durham, NC: Duke University Press.

Andersen, B. (2018). Cultural competency and rural disorder in PNG health promotion. *Anthropological Forum, 28*(4), 359–376.

Anderson, W. (2004). *Colonial pathologies: American tropical medicine, race, and hygiene in the Philippines*. Durham, NC: Duke University Press.

Barbour, R. S. (2000). The role of qualitative research in broadening the evidence base for clinical practice. *Journal of Evaluation in Clinical Practice, 6*(2), 155–163.

Boyce, P., Huang Soo Lee, M., Jenkins, C., Mohamed, S., Overs, C., Paiva, V., ... & Aggleton, P. (2007). Putting sexuality (back) into HIV/AIDS: Issues, theory and practice. *Global Public Health, 2*(1), 1–34.

Centers for Disease Control. (2019). Global health protection and security. Where we work. Retrieved from https://www.cdc.gov/globalhealth/healthprotection/nphi/wherewework.htm

Connell, R. (2012). Gender, health and theory: Conceptualizing the issue, in local and world perspective. *Social Science & Medicine, 74*, 1675–1683.

Connelly, A. J. (2007). *Counting coconuts: Patrol reports from the Trobriand Islands, Part I: 1907–1934* (Master of Arts in Anthropology thesis). California State University, Sacramento.

Denoon, D. (1989). *Public health in Papua New Guinea: Medical possibility and social constraint, 1884–1984*. Cambridge: Cambridge University Press.

Dworkin, S. L. (2005). Who is epidemiologically fathomable in the HIV/AIDS epidemic? Gender, sexuality, and intersectionality in public health. *Culture, Health & Sexuality, 7*(6), 615–623.

Fahs, B., & McClelland, S. I. (2016). When sex and power collide: An argument for critical sexuality studies. *Journal of Sex Research, 53*(4–5), 392–416.

Kippax, S., & Stephenson, N. (2012). Beyond the distinction between biomedical and social dimensions of HIV: Prevention through the lens of a social public health. *American Journal of Public Health, 102*(5), 789–799.

Lepani, K. (2012). *Islands of love, islands of risk: Culture and HIV in the Trobriands*. Nashville, TN: Vanderbilt University Press.

Lepani, K. (2015). "I am still a young girl if I want": Relational personhood and individual autonomy in the Trobriand Islands. *Oceania, 85*(1), 51–62.

Merry, S. E. (2016). *The seductions of quantification: Measuring human rights, gender violence, and sex trafficking*. Chicago: University of Chicago Press.

Parker, R., & Aggleton, P. (2012). From research to policy and practice. In P. Aggleton, P. Boyce, H. Moore, & R. Parker (Eds.), *Understanding global sexualities: New frontiers* (pp. 232–246). New York: Routledge.

Pigg, S. L. (2005). Globalizing the facts of life. In V. Adams & S. L. Pigg (Eds.), *Sex in development: Science, sexuality, and morality in global perspective* (pp. 39–65). Durham, NC: Duke University Press.

Reed, A. (1997). Contested images and common strategies: Early colonial sexual politics in the Massim. In L. Manderson & M. Jolly (Eds.), *Sites of desire, economies of pleasure: Sexualities in Asia and the Pacific* (pp. 48–71). Chicago: University of Chicago Press.

Street, A. (2014). *Biomedicine in an unstable place: Infrastructure and personhood in a Papua New Guinea hospital*. Durham, NC: Duke University Press.

Trostle, J. A. (2005). *Epidemiology and culture*. Cambridge: Cambridge University Press.

USAID. (2011). The KAP survey model. Retrieved from https://www.spring-nutrition.org/publications/tool-summaries/kap-survey-model-knowledge-attitudes-and-practices

Chapter 37

COVID-19: SEXUAL AND REPRODUCTIVE HEALTH

Terry McGovern, Kathryn Gibb and Batul Hassan

As there is a "before and after 9/11" historical narrative, there will be a "before and after" COVID-19 narrative. Dominant narratives may fill the history books and museums; the effects on those outside positions of power and privilege may be told only through family lore or may simply disappear from the grand historical narrative. Here we hope to disrupt this prophecy by documenting the gendered impacts of COVID-19 and exploring how infectious disease interacts with and exacerbates structural inequalities that shape the contexts of people's sexual and reproductive health, including discussions of the intersections of race and global location. The Coronavirus pandemic (COVID-19) contributes to and illuminates gender and racial injustice. Women and nonbinary people are devalued in the pandemic: policymakers have deemed sexual and reproductive health services "nonessential," gender-based violence (GBV) has spiked during social distancing, and the health and economic consequences of this pandemic on women and sexual and reproductive health provisioning overall are staggering.

Globally, women and girls do three times the amount of unpaid care and domestic work than men and boys do (UN Women, 2020). The COVID-19 pandemic has exacerbated existing burdens of unpaid care work through an increase of dependent relatives, care of sick relatives and increased child care due to school closures; these burdens also fall on mothers who work in formal or informal sectors outside the home (Garijo, 2020). COVID-19's impact on paid work will also disproportionately affect women: Research has shown that the recession following the COVID-19 pandemic will likely most heavily affect sectors with high female employment shares (Alon, Doepke, Olmstead-Rumsey, & Tertilt, 2020).

Globally, women comprise upward of 80 percent of nurses (Turquet & Koissy-Kpein, 2020) and constitute the majority of caregivers to the elderly, in formal facilities as well as home-based care during quarantine. Longer-term outcomes of recessions have shown that women suffer economic impacts more intensely and for longer periods of time as compared to men, and face more significant pay cuts upon returning to work after periods of absence (Alon et al., 2020). The Ebola outbreak showed that health crises pose serious threats to women's workforce participation rates, especially in informal sectors, and can exacerbate existing gender gaps (European Parliament, 2015). This essay explores the gendered impacts of COVID-19 and suggests that a *sexual and reproductive justice approach* that centers human rights, acknowledges intersecting injustices, recognizes power structures and unites across identities is essential for monitoring and addressing the inequitable gender, health and social effects of COVID-19. We also aim to demonstrate here that infectious disease prevention and response is only as strong as the health system's ability to provide integrated primary health care services.

Sex Differences in COVID-19 Cases: Much Is Unknown

Scientists' predictions early on in the HIV epidemic that the novel disease was mostly affecting gay White men ignored the impact of HIV on other populations. This failed prediction provides a cautionary tale. I was lead counsel on a class action in 1990, ultimately successful, which argued that the Centers for Disease Control and Prevention's (CDC) definition of AIDS did not adequately reflect the significance of HIV for women and communities of color. The beginnings of the COVID-19 pandemic feel eerily similar to me: Prediction about risk patterns have not held true thus far. We see the convergence of underlying disease vulnerability with this new virus, causing disparate societal impacts.

Existing evidence demonstrates that men are more likely to die from COVID-19. Scientists have raised sex-specific biological susceptibility, varying behavioral risk factors, and different distributions of underlying comorbidities to explain sex differences in infection risk, infection severity and mortality from COVID-19. Some experts have suggested that the physiologic effects of androgens may explain sex differences in COVID-19 infection (Montopoli et al., 2020). While this hypothesis has not been confirmed, androgens, such as testosterone, are the hormones that play a role in male-specific traits, and these tend to suppress the immune system. Additionally, some have postulated that sex differences in infection severity may be related to higher smoking rates in men than women (Walter & McGregor, 2020), but there is limited evidence of an association between smoking and prevalence or severity of COVID-19 (Cai, 2020). Gendered behavioral response factors may also play a role: Women are 50 percent more likely than men to adopt nonpharmaceutical behaviors such as handwashing, sanitation, avoiding crowds or public transit and mask wearing (Moran & Del Valle, 2016).

The fact is, much is unknown about this virus, and the potential for COVID-19 case undercount is eerily similar to HIV in its early days of the 1980s. Few countries have formally reported complete sex-disaggregated data so far. The World Health Organization (WHO) sex-disaggregated data collected thus far only reflect 41 percent of all cases (UN Women, 2020). Given challenges with data collection and reporting, it is difficult to determine accurate morbidity and mortality. CDC death counts are significantly higher than normal death count averages for this time of year, suggesting that deaths attributable directly or indirectly to COVID-19 are higher than the official count (Katz, Lu, & Sanger-Katz, 2020).

Sexual and Reproductive Health and Rights

Globally, women represent 70 percent of health care workers and an even greater share of informal and formal caregiving roles in society. These care-taking responsibilities and attendant personal risks are magnified with COVID-19. With medical services and resources focused on the COVID-19 response, vital sexual and reproductive health services are the first to be deprioritized, placing the health of millions of women and men, girls and boys at even further risk (UNFPA, 2020). Measures to contain the virus that disrupt one's ability to fulfill the right to sexual and reproductive health will cause long-term damage and disrupt the right to sexual literacy, bodily autonomy and gender identity.

Historical evidence from the 2013–16 Ebola crisis in Sierra Leone provides a critical forecast for the COVID-19 pandemic. Those data showed that the indirect effects of an epidemic on reproductive, maternal and neonatal health outcomes may be at least as significant as the direct effects in fragile health systems. Decreased utilization of maternal and newborn care due to disrupted services, and fear of contagion that hinders seeking treatment during the outbreak contributed to an additional 3,600 stillborn, maternal deaths and neonatal deaths from 2014 to 2015, equivalent to the number of deaths directly related to Ebola during the entire period of the epidemic in Sierra Leone (Sochas, Channon, & Nam, 2017).

In some places, unfortunately, policymakers have deemed sexual and reproductive health services "nonessential." Supply chain shutdowns have halted production, delayed air and sea shipments, complicated customs approvals and restricted in-country transport to hospitals and health care clinics (Ahmed, Sonfield, & Guttmacher Institute, 2020). All of these disruptions may cause contraceptive supply shortages in at least 46 countries within the next six months (UNFPA, 2020a). Service provision has also been disrupted by lockdowns and curfews, which prevent women from accessing family planning and reproductive health care and block service providers from reaching patients in more rural areas.

A major reproductive health organization, *Marie Stopes Kenya*, has estimated that if service provision remains reduced due to social distancing measures, travel restrictions and health care closures through December 2020, the organization could be prevented from averting nearly 100,000 unintended pregnancies, 65,000 unsafe abortions and 500 maternal deaths (Marie Stopes International, 2020). More than one in five of International Planned Parenthood Federation (IPPF) global clinics, which provide essential reproductive and sexual health services including family planning counseling and sexually transmitted infection screenings and treatment have closed because of pandemic-related restrictions; this includes more than 5,000 mobile clinics across 64 countries, the majority of which are in South Asia and Africa (IPPF, 2020). Thus, an estimated 47 million women in 114 low- and middle-income countries may lose access to modern contraceptives if the situation continues for six months, leading to nearly 7 million unintended pregnancies (UNFPA, 2020). Little is yet known about the impacts of COVID-19 on pregnancy and the potential for vertical transmission of the virus.

Global health policies and funding practices that existed prior to the pandemic may compound this situation. In 2019, the United States defunded the United Nations Population Fund (UNFPA) for the third year. The US Mexico City Policy, or "global gag rule," has already prevented millions of dollars from reaching sexual and reproductive health organizations around the world (Government Accountability Office, 2020). Without targeted action to ensure access to reproductive and sexual health care, access to essential services and the quality of any care provided will likely decline.

Within the United States, policymakers who have long opposed abortion and a range of sexual and reproductive health rights have seized upon guidance from the CDC to limit elective and nonurgent services to increase capacity for critical COVID-19 care, using it as a rationale to curtail essential abortion care. Lawmakers have labeled abortion care as "nonessential" and have tried to block access to abortion in Tennessee, Texas, Oklahoma, Arkansas, Alabama and Ohio (Barnes, 2020). While US federal courts blocked orders restricting access in these states, many abortion procedures were canceled as a result of initial state action. Many of the same elected official and policymakers who have attempted to restrict abortion access brought us the domestic "gag rule," which imposed sweeping financial and programmatic limitations on programs funded through the Title X family planning program. These politicians have already reduced the program's capacity to provide contraceptive services by at least 46 percent, adversely affecting about 1.6 million people (Dawson, 2020).

Gender-affirming procedures, including surgical interventions that enable secondary sex characteristics to be more aligned with an individual's gender identity, have been affected by the prohibition of medical procedures deemed nonessential. Evidence suggests that gender-affirming procedures are life-saving and critical to the long-term well-being of individuals in the trans community (Bränström & Pachankis 2019; Glynn et al., 2016). Prior to COVID-19, the trans community struggled to get insurance companies to provide coverage or recognize their care as medically necessary. Health care institutions' use of the term "elective" to describe gender-affirming procedures has consequently prevented trans individuals from receiving this care and may be used as an excuse by insurance companies to deny coverage in the future.

Gendered Impacts of Quarantine/Lockdown

Research demonstrates that pandemics can exacerbate GBV through quarantine, economic insecurity and reduced access to first responders (O'Donnell, Peterman, & Potts, 2020). During the Ebola outbreak in West Africa, for example, women and girls experienced more exploitation, coercion and sexual violence after school closures and quarantines (John, Casey, Carino, & McGovern, 2020). Of course, sexual violence coupled with a reduction or closure of sexual and reproductive health services leads to ongoing blatant violations of human rights.

The COVID-19 pandemic is no different, and the emerging evidence suggests that violence against women and girls, particularly domestic violence, has sharply increased following the implementation of lockdowns. Consider the following global examples. In France, reported cases of domestic violence have risen 30 percent since lockdowns were implemented in mid-April 2020 (Euronews, 2020). In Argentina, calls to the national emergency abuse line were 67 percent higher in April 2020, following the imposition of lockdown, compared to one year earlier (Sigal, 2020). In parts of South America that already see high rates of femicide (the intentional killing of women or girls), rates of GBV have surged amid the COVID-19 pandemic. The mayor of Bogota, Colombia noted that in the first weeks of the lockdown, crime statistics dropped in all categories except violence against women; the police's 24/7 hotline experienced a 225 percent increase in calls (Janetsky, 2020). Demand for shelter has also risen in countries across the globe, including in the United States (UNFPA, 2020).

The scale of this GBV crisis is expected to grow in 193 UN member states, as lockdowns continue. The UNFPA estimated a 20 percent increase in GBV over an average three-month long lockdown. Accounting for high levels of underreporting, the report warned of 15 million additional cases of GBV for every three-month extension of the lockdown. Diversion of resources under COVID-19 will cause disruption in violence prevention and support programs, potentially reducing the impact of preventative GBV services by one-third (UNFPA, 2020).

Intersections of Risk

The intersection of race, gender identity and sexual orientation intensifies social, health and economic vulnerabilities to COVID-19. Racial and ethnic minorities are overrepresented among hospitalized COVID-19 patients in the United States and the UK. In the UK, Black people are more than four times more likely to die from COVID-19 than their White counterparts (Office of National Statistics, 2020). Further social determinants of health that may contribute to higher rates of COVID-19 morbidity and mortality in low-income communities and communities of color include living conditions, working conditions, underlying health conditions and reduced access to care.

The places where people live put them at risk. In the United States, racial residential segregation contributes to adverse health outcomes and the presence of underlying health conditions, which increase the likelihood of COVID-19-related morbidity and mortality (Anthopolos, James, Gelfand, & Miranda, 2011; Bravo, Anthopolos, Kimbro, & Miranda, 2018). Air pollution, which tends to be concentrated in low-income communities and communities of color, is a driver of respiratory illness and cardiovascular disease—known risk factors for COVID-19 (Cosselman, Navas-Acien, & Kaufman, 2015; Ohio State University, 2019). In the UK from 2014 to 2017, studies found overcrowding (which increases the risk of COVID-19 transmission) in 30 percent of Bangladeshi households, 16 percent of Pakistani households, and 12 percent of Black households, compared to only 2 percent of White households (Ministry of Housing, Communities, and Local Government, 2018).

The places where people work put them at further risk of infection too. In the UK, racial and ethnic minorities are more likely to work in frontline roles in the National Health Service [NHS]: nearly 21 percent of staff are from ethnic minorities, compared with about 14 percent of the population of England and Wales. Similar patterns occur in the United States: almost one-fourth of employed Hispanic and Black American workers work in service industry jobs, compared to only 16 percent of non-Hispanic Whites. Hispanic workers account for 17 percent of total employment but constitute 53 percent of agricultural workers; Black Americans make up 12 percent of all employed workers, but account for 30 percent of licensed practical and licensed vocational nurses (Erchick, Barnett, & Upton, 2019). Hispanic workers have lower rates of access to paid leave than White non-Hispanic workers. In 2019, Hispanics were nearly three times as likely to be uninsured as non-Hispanic Whites, and African Americans were almost twice as likely to be uninsured (US Bureau of Labor Statistics, 2019).

LGBT people are particularly vulnerable to COVID-19 due to higher rates of HIV, cancer, smoking, unemployment, poverty and discrimination in the health care system (Addy, 2020; OHCHR, 2020). Owing to experiences of stigma and prejudice, LGBT people may be less likely to reach out to health care providers due to fear of discrimination or harassment (CDC, 2016; OHCHR, 2020). Again, LGBT people who are women-identifying, of color or disabled face intersecting discrimination.

Globally, LGBT communities also face discrimination outside of the context of the health care system and have been blamed for the COVID-19 pandemic in some settings. In Iraq, a political leader blamed the pandemic on the legalization of same-sex marriage (OHCHR, 2020). Stay-at-home restrictions and quarantine orders require LGBT individuals to stay home, restricting access to support networks and traditional means of coping with adversity. This also may increase their exposure to violence, especially among LGBT youth with unsupportive families (OHCHR, 2020). During a time when information to the public is crucial, LGBT groups can be left out of the governmental and public health guidance. In Panama, for example, the government has imposed lockdown measures that restrict movement based on sex, with women and men permitted to leave the house on alternate days of the week (Ott, 2020). This has left transgender and nonbinary people at a heightened risk of discrimination and interaction with law enforcement.

In response, 170 organizations have called for increased protection against discrimination as well as the incorporation of sexual orientation and gender identity into COVID-19 data collection (Addy, 2020). Disaggregated data is key to understanding the impact of the pandemic on these communities (Addy, 2020). It is essential that government agencies and public health authorities work to ensure LGBT individuals are not subjected to discrimination that could prevent them from seeking and accessing health care.

Conclusion: Including Women's Voices in the Response

Generally, national and global COVID-19 leadership and decision-making spaces are unrepresentative of the global population. The White House Coronavirus Task Force is majority White male. A comparison of COVID-19 task forces in 24 countries showed that most were majority male and some had no women members at all (Rajan et al., 2020). This imbalance reflects broader gender inequity: while 70 percent of the global health care workforce is made up of women, only 25 percent of global leaders are female (WHO, 2019). When women do hold higher-level positions in health care decision making, such as in governmental bodies, research shows they tend to bring attention to issues such as gender-based violence and sexual and reproductive health more than their male colleagues (Inter-Parliamentary Union, 2015). Sexual and reproductive justice is not just a women's health issue, of course, and men must be actively engaged in the response to ensure women's voices and the voices of other genders are amplified and that the response addresses how power and privilege affects health justice for all.

The global response must use a rights-based sexual and reproductive health and justice framework that acknowledges existing structures that compound factors of individual and community disadvantage in order to address the unique challenges of COVID-19. An intersectional lens that highlights these gendered imbalances but attends to other identities is required on every level, from the individual to the structural, to ensure the differential needs of women and girls and people who are socially, economically and politically marginalized are addressed in times of crisis. Otherwise, we risk the further entrenchment of gender inequity in the pandemic's aftermath. As many of the essays in this volume show, sexual literacy should be an important aspect of the justice framework in the global response to COVID when considering as it includes a lifelong system of knowledge and life skills necessary to promote and protect sexual health and well-being, gender identity and reproductive health.

References

Addy, J. (2020). *LGBTQ+ and allied organizations issue second open letter urging decisive action to prevent COVID-19 discrimination* [Press release]. Retrieved from https://www.whitman-walker.org/press-and-media/second-covid-19-lgbtq-letter

Ahmed, Z., Sonfield, A., & Guttmacher Institute (2020, April 20). The COVID-19 outbreak: Potential fallout for sexual and reproductive health and rights. *The Guttmacher Institute*. The Guttmacher Institute. Retrieved from https://www.guttmacher.org/article/2020/03/covid-19-outbreak-potential-fallout-sexual-and-reproductive-health-and-rights

Alon, T., Doepke, M., Olmstead-Rumsey, J., & Tertilt, M. (2020). *The impact of COVID-19 on gender equality* (NBER Working Paper 26947, pp. 1–39). Cambridge, MA: National Bureau of Economic Research. https://doi.org/10.3386/w26947

Anthopolos, R., James, S. A., Gelfand, A. E., & Miranda, M. L. (2011). A spatial measure of neighborhood level racial isolation applied to low birthweight, preterm birth, and birthweight in North Carolina. *Spat Spatio-Temporal Epidemiol, 2*(4), 235–246.

Barnes, R. (2020, April 14). Supreme Court avoids one abortion battle, but new lawsuits are being filed. *Washington Post*. Retrieved from https://www.washingtonpost.com/politics/courts_law/abortion-texas-louisiana-tennessee-supreme-court/2020/04/14/c04022e4-7e7e-11ea-a3ee-13e1ae0a3571_story.html

Bränström, R., & Pachankis, J. E. (2019). Reduction in mental health treatment utilization among transgender individuals after gender-affirming surgeries: A total population study. *American Journal of Psychiatry*. doi:10.1176/appi.ajp.2019.19010080

Bravo, M. A., Anthopolos, R., Kimbro, R. T., & Miranda, M. L. (2018). Residential racial isolation and spatial patterning of type 2 diabetes mellitus in Durham, North Carolina. *American Journal of Epidemiology, 187*(7), 1467–1476.

Cai, H. (2020). Sex difference and smoking predisposition in patients with COVID-19. *Lancet Respiratory Medicine, 8*(4), e20. doi:10.1016/S2213-2600(20)30117-X

Centers for Disease Control and Prevention. (2016). Stigma and discrimination. Retrieved from https://www.cdc.gov/msmhealth/stigma-and-discrimination.htm

Centers for Disease Control and Prevention. (2020, February 11). Coronavirus disease 2019 (COVID-19). Retrieved from https://www.cdc.gov/coronavirus/2019-ncov/need-extra-precautions/racial-ethnic-minorities.html

Centers for Disease Control and Prevention. (2020, April 17). *Hospitalization rates and characteristics of patients hospitalized with laboratory-confirmed coronavirus disease 2019—COVID-NET, 14 States, March 1–30, 2020*. Retrieved from https://www.cdc.gov/mmwr/volumes/69/wr/mm6915e3.htm?s_cid=mm6915e3_w

Cosselman, K. E., Navas-Acien, A., & Kaufman, J. D. (2015). Environmental factors in cardiovascular disease. *Nature Reviews Cardiology, 12*(11), 627–642. doi:10.1038/nrcardio.2015.152

Dawson, R. (2020, February 26). Trump administration's domestic gag rule has slashed the Title X network's capacity by half. *The Guttmacher Institute.* Retrieved from https://www.guttmacher.org/article/2020/02/trump-administrations-domestic-gag-rule-has-slashed-title-x-networks-capacity-half

Erchick, E. R., Barnett, J. C., & Upton R. D. (2019). *Health insurance coverage in the United States: 2018* (Current Population Reports, P60-267[RV]). Washington, DC: U.S. Government Printing Office.

Euronews. (2020, March 28). Domestic violence cases jump 30% during lockdown in France. *Euronews.* Retrieved from https://www.euronews.com/2020/03/28/domestic-violence-cases-jump-30-during-lockdown-in-france

European Parliament. (2015). *Report on the Ebola Crisis: The long-term lessons and how to strengthen health systems in development countries to prevent future crises.* Retrieved from https://www.europarl.europa.eu/doceo/document/A-8-2015-0281_EN.html

Garijo, B. (2020, April 24). COVID-19 highlights how caregiving fuels gender inequality. *World Economic Forum.* Retrieved May 13, 2020, from https://www.weforum.org/agenda/2020/04/covid-19-highlights-how-caregiving-fuels-gender-inequality/

Glynn, T. R., Gamarel, K. E., Kahler, C. W., Iwamoto, M., Operario, D., & Nemoto, T. (2016). The role of gender affirmation in psychological well-being among transgender women. *Psychology of Sexual Orientation and Gender Diversity, 3*(3), 336–344. doi:10.1037/sgd0000171

Government Accountability Office. (2020, March 18). *Global health assistance: Awardees' declinations of U.S. planned funding due to abortion-related restrictions.* Retrieved from https://www.gao.gov/products/GAO-20-347#summary

International Planned Parenthood Foundation. (2020, April 9). COVID-19 pandemic cuts access to sexual and reproductive healthcare for women around the world. Retrieved from https://www.ippf.org/news/covid-19-pandemic-cuts-access-sexual-and-reproductive-healthcare-women-around-world

Inter-Parliamentary Union. (2015). *Women in Parliament: 20 years in review* (pp. 1–20). Retrieved from https://www.ipu.org/resources/publications/reports/2016-07/women-in-parliament-20-years-in-review

Janetsky, M. (2020, April 20). Violence against women up amid Latin America COVID-19 lockdowns. *Al Jazeera.* Retrieved from https://www.aljazeera.com/indepth/features/violence-women-surges-latam-coronavirus-quarantines-200420020748668.html

John, N., Casey, S. E., Carino, G., & McGovern, T. (2020). Lessons never learned: Crisis and gender-based violence. *Developing World Bioethics, n/a* (n/a). doi:10.1111/dewb.12261

Katz, J., Lu, D., & Sanger-Katz, M. (2020, April 28). U.S. coronavirus death toll is far higher than reported, C.D.C. data suggests. *New York Times.* Retrieved from https://www.nytimes.com/interactive/2020/04/28/us/coronavirus-death-toll-total.html

Marie Stopes International. (2020). Estimated impact on our services. Retrieved May 8, 2020, from https://www.mariestopes.org/newsletter/

Ministry of Housing, Communities and Local Government. (2018, October 10). *Overcrowded households.* Retrieved May 8, 2020, from https://www.ethnicity-facts-figures.service.gov.uk/housing/housing-conditions/overcrowded-households/latest

Montopoli, M., Zumerle, S., Vettor, R., Rugge, M., Zorzi, M., Catapano, C. V., … & Alimonti, A. (2020). Androgen-deprivation therapies for prostate cancer and risk of infection by SARS-CoV-2: A population-based study (n=4532). *Annals of Oncology.* doi:10.1016/j.annonc.2020.04.479

Moran, K. R., & Del Valle, S. Y. (2016). A meta-analysis of the association between gender and protective behaviors in response to respiratory epidemics and pandemics. *PloS One, 11*(10), e0164541–e0164541. doi:10.1371/journal.pone.0164541

O'Donnell, M., Peterman, A., & Potts, A. (2020). *A gender lens on COVID-19: Pandemics and violence against women and children*. Retrieved from https://www.cgdev.org/blog/gender-lens-covid-19-pandemics-and-violence-against-women-and-children

Office of National Statistics. (2020, May 7). *Coronavirus (COVID-19) related deaths by ethnic group, England and Wales: 2 March 2020 to 10 April 2020*. Retrieved from https://www.ons.gov.uk/peoplepopulationandcommunity/birthsdeathsandmarriages/deaths/articles/coronavirusrelateddeathsbyethnicgroupenglandandwales/2march2020to10april2020

OHCHR. (2020). *COVID-19 and the human rights of LGBTI people*. Retrieved from https://www.ohchr.org/Documents/Issues/LGBT/LGBTIpeople.pdf

Ohio State University. (2019, August 10). Low-income, black neighborhoods still hit hard by air pollution. *Science Daily*. Retrieved from https://www.sciencedaily.com/releases/2019/08/190810094052.htm

Ott, H. (2020, April 10). Trans woman fined for violating Panama's gender-based coronavirus lockdown, rights group says. *CBS News*. Retrieved from https://www.cbsnews.com/news/trans-woman-fined-for-violating-panamas-gender-based-coronavirus-lockdown-rights-group-says-2020-04-10/

Rajan, D., Koch, K., Rohrer, K., Bajnoczki, C., Socha, A., Voss, M., ... & Koonin, J. (2020). Governance of the Covid-19 response: A call for more inclusive and transparent decision-making. *BMJ Global Health*, *5*(5). doi: 10.1136/bmjgh-2020-002655

Sigal, L. (2020, April 27). "Another pandemic": In Latin America, domestic abuse rises amid lockdown. *Reuters*. Retrieved from https://www.reuters.com/article/us-health-coronavirus-latam-domesticviol/another-pandemic-in-latin-america-domestic-abuse-rises-amid-lockdown-idUSKCN2291JS

Sochas, L., Channon, A. A., & Nam, S. (2017). Counting indirect crisis-related deaths in the context of a low-resilience health system: The case of maternal and neonatal health during the Ebola epidemic in Sierra Leone. *Health Policy and Planning*, *32*(Suppl. 3), iii32–iii39. http://dx.doi.org/10.1093/heapol/czx108

Turquet, L., & Koissy-Kepin, S. (2020). *COVID-19 and gender: What do we know; what do we need to know?* Retrieved from https://data.unwomen.org/features/covid-19-and-gender-what-do-we-know-what-do-we-need-know

UN Women (2020). COVID-19: Emerging gender data and why it matters. Retrieved from https://data.unwomen.org/resources/covid-19-emerging-gender-data-and-why-it-matters

UNFPA. (2020a). *Impact of the COVID-19 Pandemic on family planning and ending gender-based violence, female genital mutilation and child marriage*. Retrieved from https://www.unfpa.org/resources/impact-covid-19-pandemic-family-planning-and-ending-gender-based-violence-female-genital

UNFPA. (2020b). *COVID-19: A gender lens. Protecting Sexual and reproductive health and rights, and promoting gender equality*. Retrieved from https://www.unfpa.org/sites/default/files/resource-pdf/COVID-19_A_Gender_Lens_Guidance_Note.pdf

UNFPA. (2020c, May 8). *UNFPA supplies COVID-19 Update No-4*. UNFPA Supplies.

US Bureau of Labor Statistics. (2019). *Labor force characteristics by race and ethnicity, 2018* (Report 1082). Retrieved from https://www.bls.gov/opub/reports/race-and-ethnicity/2018/home.htm

Walter, L. A., & McGregor, A. J. (2020). Sex- and gender-specific observations and implications for COVID-19. *Western Journal of Emergency Medicine: Integrating Emergency Care with Population Health*, *21*(3). http://dx.doi.org/10.5811/westjem.2020.4.47536 Retrieved from https://escholarship.org/uc/item/76f9p924

World Health Organization. (2019, March 20). *Delivered by women, led by men: A gender and equity analysis of the global health and social workforce*. Retrieved from https://www.who.int/hrh/resources/health-observer24/en/

Chapter 38

ADVOCATING FOR SEXUAL LITERACY

Allison Moore and Paul Reynolds

The starting point for a discussion of advocating sexual literacy is to understand that it represents more than simply childhood-focused formal sexual education or the formal/informal transmission of sexual knowledge between peers, parents (or partners) or within individual discursive formations, such as the institutional purviews and pedagogies employed by health professionals, educators, social workers or psychologists (Foucault, 1978).[1] Sexual literacy represents a more cohesive and comprehensive life-long learning project that marries both sexual knowledge with the means of developing practice-focused sexuality skills, including communication strategies, empowering judicious deliberative decision-making and enabling sexual agency. Sexual agency is best understood as the capacities for individuals to make informed and free sexual choices. Thus people—however diverse their identities, genders, ethnicities, national origin, faith, forms of desired relationships and practices and orientations—are provided with and actively build up the knowledge and skills to express their sexual needs and wants (including what they do *not* want) protecting their well-being, safety, agency and self-respect.

These individual needs and wants are mediated by sociocultural and sociolegal values, norms and regulatory regimes, which draw lines between the permissible and impermissible. These lines between permissible and impermissible is often porous, inconsistent, culturally bound, politically controversial and based on historical knowledge and beliefs that range from reasoned attempts to regulate for public safety or against violence or exploitation of individuals, to prejudiced and pathological beliefs. Hence, even where sex work is legal and regulated, there is often prejudice and stigma visited upon sex workers (see Ditmore, Levy, & Willman, 2010; Sanders, O'Neill, & Pitcher, 2009). Likewise, Bondage and Discipline, Domination and Submission, Sadism and Masochism (BDSM) practitioners simultaneously find representations of their sexual pleasures commodified and represented in mainstream culture while still criminalized under laws against assault (Langdridge & Barker, 2013; Thompson, 1994).

---

1 The authors would like to thank the editors for their comments on a previous draft. Some of this essay is informed by, and therefore elaborated in, Moore and Reynolds (2018). We acknowledge the publisher, Palgrave, in permitting us to cite, quote and draw from that text.

Some regimes of sexual regulation are ethically informed, with sound rationales for prohibitions, such as laws prohibiting rape and sexual violence in the late twentieth and twenty-first centuries. Other regimes arise from deep-seated historical and cultural prejudices or pathologies, forming a terrain of sexual constraints and/or internalized inhibitions in contemporary sexual cultures. For example, these punitive regimes may surrender discretionary powers of authoritative interpretation to the state and propagators of orthodoxy and suppression, such as countries that manifest and enforce laws on indecency and obscenity. For example, regimes that practice prejudicial approaches to nonheterosexual identities and relationships, polyamorous relationships and whose ideologies express presumptions of the "unnaturalness" of nongenitocentric (not focused on genital sexual contact and physical orgasm) practices.

Equally, there are people in society who are regulated and disadvantaged or punished because they do not conform to glocally normative constructions of sexual agents. These include: people with significant physical disabilities; people with emotional or learning difficulties; asexual people; younger people below the locally enforced age of consent; older adults and the elderly; people who enjoy playing with pain; people who are deemed unsexual through their bodies being regarded as lacking attraction, such as obese people or people who are very small and tall; and people with genitocentric sexual dysfunctions or restrictive conditions (such as erectile dysfunction and genitopelvic pain/penetration disorder [GPPPD]). Sexual literacy provides a sense of enabling sexual agents to find pleasure within *their* diverse practices, embodiment and relations, while contributing to an open, responsive sexual culture that respects other sexual practices. Enabling a culture of sexual literacy sets up the conditions by which democratic societies reasonably decide what to prohibit, regulate or permit. This underlines the tension between personal pleasures and cultural and social norms, even within an enlightened sexual culture. For sexual literacy, the necessity of regulation and prohibitions is always balanced with the importance of enabling space and knowledge for physical, emotional, sensory and affective sexual pleasure and performance. It recognizes that sexual knowledge and understanding manifest meaning to how a sexual agent self-identifies, how they experience belonging and identity/community and how they pursue their pleasures through the "messy physicality" of sensory experience.

One useful way of expressing this performance and practice struggle strategically is to employ the notion of hegemony/counter-hegemony. A hegemonic project involves a constant remaking in which political and cultural power are exercised, but at the same time, the process and necessity of remaking leaves "gaps", ruptures and opportunities for substantive change. Raymond Williams (1977, pp. 112–13) observes:

> A lived-in hegemony is always a process. It is not, except analytically, a system or a structure. It is a realised complex of experiences, relationships, and activities, with specific and changing pressures and limits. In practice, that is, hegemony can never be singular. Its internal structures are highly complex, as can readily be seen in any concrete analysis. Moreover (and this is crucial, reminding us of the necessary thrust of the concept), it does not just passively exist as a form of dominance. It has continually to be renewed, recreated, defended

and modified. It is also continually resisted, limited, altered, challenged by pressures not at all its own.

Thus, while sexual literacy can be regarded as a coherent approach to making and supporting sexual agency, it is equally a project with diverse and plural strands and interwoven and intersecting complex experiences, connecting people in their intimate subjectivities to larger social structures within an enabling cultural context—linking the personal and the political.

James Sears (1997) summarized sexual literacy—albeit in the context of a sex education model—as comprising teaching *tolerance* to facilitate an imperative to teach sexual diversity by recognizing *difference* as a significant, positive characteristic both in the content and pedagogy of sex education. This is a reflective approach that embeds sex education as part of the learning curriculum, as a cultural subject and not just a specific subject or classroom event in itself. Sears' focus on sexual agency, diversity and the constraints of dominant ideological, cultural forms and power relationships echoes Gayle Rubin's (2011, p. 152) "Charmed Circle" metaphor that distinguished legitimated—dominant—from delegitimated—dissenting—sexualities. It allowed Rubin to graphically distinguish what was seen as good, normal, natural and blessed in sex (heterosexual, married, monogamous, procreative, noncommercial, in pairs, in a relationship, same generation, in private, no pornography, bodies only and "vanilla") from what was seen as bad, abnormal, unnatural and damned (homosexual, unmarried, promiscuous, nonprocreative, commercial, alone or in groups, casual, cross-generational, in public, with pornography, with manufactured objects and sadomasochism). While Rubin made this distinction in 1982, and particular features may have shifted across the dividing line since that time, the principle of inclusion/acceptance and exclusion/disapproval.

Gilbert Herdt and colleagues framed sexual literacy "as the knowledge necessary to promote and protect sexual wellness and the rights of oneself and intimate others" (Stein & Herdt, 2005, p. 1).

Earlier they stated:

> We focus on a positive, integrated and holistic view of sexuality from a social justice perspective. We believe that every person should have the knowledge, skills and resources to support healthy and pleasurable sexuality—and that these resources should be based on accurate research and facts. We examine how race, gender, culture, ability, faith and age intersect with and shape our sexual beliefs. We know that sexuality education and learning should be lifelong. We call this *sexual literacy* (NSRC [National Sexuality Resource Center, 2003, cited in Moore and Reynolds, 2018, p. 199).

Although the NSRC—a nonprofit, mission-driven organization—is no longer in existence, they developed a way of thinking about sexual literacy as informed by its sexpositive mission as:

> to build capacity to advance lifelong sexual literacy and foster healthy sexuality for all Americans.

We do this by:

– creating and disseminating trainings, research and information that are accurate, research-based and promote best practices;
– convening diverse communities of advocates, researchers and academics to actively engage, shape and deepen the concept of sexual literacy;
– mobilizing stakeholders to become activists, educators and advocates for sexual literacy (National Sexuality Resource Center, 2003, cited in Moore and Reynolds, 2018, p. 199).

Even a cursory review of this sex-positive agenda emphasizes the limits and deficiencies of mainstream concepts of sex education and learning, which are problem-focused, time-limited, and emphasize (perhaps necessarily but not exclusively) risks and dangers. Standard approaches to sex education also emphasize the problematic fetishism of the different forms of public sexual bodies of knowledge, such as pornography or media representations of "good" sex or health representations of healthy sex, which often reflect rather than question existing orthodoxies and hierarchies of sexual normality.

The foundations of sexual literacy lie embedded in the rich content of diverse and sometimes contradictory sexual knowledge that can be made available for meaning making, learning and the expression of desires and pleasures. For Meg-John Barker (2013), a psychologist and sex therapist, opening up this knowledge involves *reconceiving* key concepts and ideas—such as "fidelity" or "pleasure"—away from the dominant orthodox meanings and emphasizing their diverse and contingent possibilities. This involves experimenting with and allowing creativity in rewriting and practicing the rules. This reconceptualization is articulated in the language of rules, which allows Barker to show the limitations of rule-based behavior deriving from orthodox meanings—current laws and conventions. Nevertheless, there is a necessity to rules that enable both self and others regarding intimate subject formations, and to provide a framework grounded on ethical judgments and not prejudice. The answer to this is to rewrite the rules as enabling and encouraging creativity rather than adopting a default position of prohibition or discouraging sex outside extant norms. Barker approaches this reconceptualization in the form of a manual for practical applications and exercises to enrich intimate relationships. In this respect, literature like this encourages lifelong sexual literacy practices as well as reflection or analysis. It is possible to find a range of these resources joining informed knowledge and practice-oriented initiatives in the current research/instructional literature (selectively, Barker & Hancock 2017, 2018; Comfort & Quilliam, 2011; Stryker, 2017).

Counter-hegemonic sexual practices such as those in the BDSM community have tended to adopt this "manual" approach to disseminating knowledge in a skills context where both specific explanatory bodies of knowledge and ethical codes are aligned (selectively, Miller & Devon, 1995; Wiseman, 1996). Such knowledges often become co-opted into a porous sexual mainstream as "novel" practices or "acceptable differences," such as with polyamory and open relationships, but through a hegemonic heteronormative lens (Barker & Iantaffi, 2018; Hardy & Easton, 2018; Williams & Williams, 2019). This illustrates the limits to mainstream culture, where some forms of sexual diversity are included only as minority or "peculiar" subcultures. This acts as a form of heteronormative gatekeeping and regulating alternative sexual practices and knowledges, producing partial and provisional accommodations and normalizations. Innovative encouragement of sexual learning is often done at the most agentic and perhaps marginal levels of society, whose aims include supporting changing and enabling glocally informed populations. In respect of youth, for example, some creative sex education is done in social, recreational and support groups, especially for LGBTQA youth (Elley, 2013; Plummer, 1995).

Sexual literacy also requires a more critical approach to language and pedagogy, problematizing the mediums of communication as well as the "sex-positive" message. Alexander (2008, p. 18) characterizes the discursive terms of rewriting sexual scripts through "understanding of the ways in which sexuality is constructed in language and the ways in which our language and meaning-making systems are always already sexualized." This understanding requires a disruption of the conventional "language game" of sex and sexuality, recognizing the way in which language carries value-laden properties sometimes embedded with pathology, prejudice and a bias toward orthodox framings. For example, monogamy, sex between lovers and privacy in sex are often framed with the assumption that they are always positive, while polyamory, casual sex play and public sex are often framed negatively or of less value. Sexual literacy thus involves the development of value-neutral or sex-positive language alternatives that blends erotically open possibilities while also retaining extant ethical values, for example respecting consent as opposed to coercion in relationships (Cameron & Kulick, 2003).

A focus on sex-positive or value-neutral language encourages critical rethinking of the pedagogies by which sex-positivity (as it is often referred to in studies on sex education) is communicated. It is not just the value-laden nature of language but who participates or is excluded in these dialogues—such as younger and less experienced voices or marginalized voices such as those who engage in BDSM practices, or those severely disabled who may have particular sexual requirements to gain satisfaction. Here, a circulatory model of knowledge sharing and acquisition (as opposed to a more traditional hierarchical model) and the plasticity of roles between learners and pedagogues, both implicit in the critical pedagogy of Freire (1996), hooks (1994) and Illich (1995), provide fruitful models for the sharing of sexual knowledge and understanding beyond top-down standard sex education programs with hegemonic, norm-deviant framings.

These theoretical critiques locate sexual literacy within a wider political project of sexual justice and sexual citizenship (selectively, Bamforth, 1997; Bell & Binnie, 2000; Evans, 1994; Kaplan, 1997; Phelan, 2001; Plummer, 2003, 2015; Richardson & Munro, 2012; Weeks, 2000, 2007). At the core of this wider project is the relationship between intentionally enabling sexual agents in their struggles with sexually oppressive, alienating and exploitative, pathological, fetishized and commodified dominant discourses of both sex and its wider cultural, political and social contexts. This raises the question of whether sexual literacy is possible through the incremental erosion of prejudice and pathology without adopting a wider political critique and project. Such thinking connects with the current politically inflected interests in theories that in different ways reject the current dominant orthodoxies, such as queer theory, crip theory, feminist critiques and Marxism (see Lewis, this volume, and selectively Drucker, 2014; Kirsch, 2000; Lewis,

2016; McRuer & Mollow, 2012; Munro, 2005). While they are very different theoretical articulations, they share (to different degrees) the common project of enabling sexual literacy, with a focus on performance and practices, and the making of space, time and resources to practice sexual pleasure and experimentation.

Indeed, "performance and practice" are critical because they *instantiate* diversity and agency via expressing identities, relationships, orientations, behaviors and acts, making these entities real to the performer in the same way as prohibitions, prejudices and pathologies are concretely real and experienced in societal policing, material institutional pathologies and shaming prejudiced speech.

To summarize: Sexual literacy involves performances, practices and discourses that deconstruct and criticize existing orthodoxy, and enable sexual agents to engage in open and fluid relationships of learning, experiencing, understanding and feeling in relation to knowledge. Our framework also invites the following questions (Moore & Reynolds, 2018, pp. 211–220):

- *How do agents inculcate skills and what skills do we inculcate to allow for sexual information to be received critically in a way that enables the sexual agent?* This involves a focus on literacy skills to both produce and receive glocal sexual knowledge and understandings that do not rely on received wisdom and extant forms of knowledge, whether pornography or formal sex education. The point here is not the rejection of orthodoxy and extant forms of knowledge; but rather how to create a capacity to critically appraise all forms of sexual knowledge. These capacities include reading (text and visual), vocabulary and knowledge acquisition, experience and self-reflection, so that information is transformed into knowledge and understanding.
- *How can sexual literacy be promoted as a cultural and communicative subject as well as focused upon the enabling of sexual agency?* This is where the focus on enhancing sexual subjective understanding, experience and agency is translated into a political and counter-hegemonic project. It involves a sensitivity to both agentic and cultural contexts—the cultural milieu within which a literacy strategy is formed and who the relevant agents are within that milieu. Strategies will be different in more or less sexually "free" cultures and with agents who are more sexually recognized (such as those engaged in heterosexual sex play) one whose identities or preferences are desexualized in their cultures. Those whose sexuality is often diminished or negatively stereotyped include older people, people differently abled—physically or intellectually—African/afro-Caribbean's as sexually stereotyped or women whose sexuality is represented as open and visible. At the same time, as cultural sensitivity plays a part, sexual literacy does have universal values, such as opposing sexual violence.
- *What strategies can be used to promote an understanding of extant power/knowledge relations within sexual cultures?* This involves making explicit the power relations that govern existing sexual pedagogies and their drawing lines of legitimacy, illegitimacy and normative preference. Focusing on power promotes a political analysis that uncovers the issues of hegemonies behind "natural", "normal" and current heteronormative (and homonormative), patriarchal (and racial) and monogamous constructs of sexuality. The critical practice that underpins sexual literacy reinforces the skills to rupture

discourses of deceit, taboo, shame, social pressure and contextual challenges such as dominant cultural representations that permeate thinking about diverse sexualities. It also enables agents to recognize extant characteristics that impact on their own sexualities, such as bodily distinctions, inequalities in relations, commitment and feeling, idiosyncrasies in touch and desire and their respect for different appetites or desires in others. Such a concern also extends to reappraising political equity questions, such as the public distribution of resources to support sexual agency both in relation to extant public concerns about sex and other public concerns. For example, are adequate sexual services provided for severely disabled people, who may have problems acquiring sexual partners or have specific sexual desires? Is the balance of support for sexual agency for everyone proportional in importance with sexual health/risk prevention budgets and activities? Should more resources be put into sensual public spaces as opposed to commercial spaces? Sexual literacy is not simply about individual liberation, but also about collective emancipation and support, so sexual lives can be enjoyed within the community and socially recognized as central to well-being.

- *How can sexual agency be enabled as skills and techniques of the body and sexual practice?* This takes sexual literacy beyond understanding what is healthy, what is possible and what rights and justice might be apportioned in society. It is about the "messy physicality" of sexual practice and understanding of that sex play neither necessarily conforms with a genitocentric focus on sexual organs, nor has to or does conform to idealized romantic versions often represented in popular culture in practice. Being a sexual agent involves a recognizable and self-reflective capacity to give and take sexual pleasure. If sexual agents are fearful or ignorant of their bodies and touching others, the anxiety and expectation that is raised by sexual scenarios and relationships diminishes that pleasure and their understanding. In that context, any legal, political and pedagogic support that is provided in preparing the adult for sexual life is of limited comfort. For sexual subjects to be liberated, they need to be liberated in understanding sex as something frequently conditioned by moments of pleasure, physical "fits" and mismatches and a potent mixture of desire/reserve, function/dysfunction and affirmation/self-consciousness. This is affective and phenomenological practice-based experience at the point of pleasure rather than skirting around it: where learning meets doing.

- *Can sexual literacy be promoted without addressing the material means for sexual engagement?* Sexual literacy is enabled partly by knowledge and self-reflexive growth, but also by material circumstances. This involves the means to change the sexual environment, such as providing access to sex toys and fetish paraphernalia, knowledge and spaces. The case for this provision is often persuasively made to benefit meeting the sexual needs for older and/or differently abled people. However, in a sexual literate society, these facilities should be available to all, where availability is supported by principle, such as: "from each according to his ability, to each according to his needs" (Marx, [1875] 1943, p. 14).[2] This extends to changes that might have a significant impact on the way social life is organized, such as having the time and space to explore the sexual self and enjoy

---

2   The quotation in the original is gendered—the principle not so.

sexual other(s), which might require changes to the structuring of the working day. Sexual literacy operates in the context of agentic receptivity that is influenced by economic as well as cultural framings, such as access to sources of knowledge and the time to study and practice. These are critical to the exercise of sexual agency and should not be only the purview of the monied. This suggests a wider linkage between sexual literacy as personal and political projects, rejecting the inequalities and purported pathologies that deprive those who often do not have access to resources or do not conform to normative stereotypes of the means to explore and be themselves. Throughout the life span, these considerations point to a reconceiving of what schooling should involve, how work and leisure should intersect, and what is fundamental and ephemeral in maintaining or enabling in the resources for social life and sexual literacy for all. In short, sexual literacy is a limited concept if it can only be exercised by the wealthy, the time-rich or those who have the resources for protracted study.

These questions constitute an agenda for advocacy that connects sexual literacy with broader political, social and ethical literacies, and as part of a radical—even revolutionary—politics. At the same time, these questions signpost the central issues that can be used to guide individuals toward being enabled sexual agents. Sex is not bounded by its particularities, apart from other aspects of social life, but interweaves pleasure and desires with ways of human organization, reproduction, resource distribution, making relationships and expressing conformity and transgression. As such, following the Freudo-Marxists from Reich to Marcuse and contemporary critics, sexual agency and literacy is bound to social equivalents and cannot be achieved without engagement with wider social and economic problems (Drucker, 2014; Floyd, 2009; Marcuse, 1998; Reich, 1968; Reynolds, 2018).

Sexual literacy involves the immediate responsiveness and agentic capacities to develop our sexual knowledge, judgment and practice *now*, alongside a commitment to change that enables enriched agency within sexual cultures—both being and becoming. In this respect, as we have observed elsewhere (Moore & Reynolds, 2018, p. 219):

> Sexual literacy is not simply a means by which a sexual subject takes charge of resources such as bodies of knowledge or means of understanding and engages in their own pleasures and desires. Nor is it simply an awareness and sensitivity of the rights of other sexual subjects. It involves an understanding of the agent as praxeological. Once practice is informed by thinking, and thinking with practice, the responsibilities, relationships and interactions between sexual subjects cannot return to ignorance. Sexual literacy may be hard work, as the sexual subject seeks to be informed, thinking through relations, make judgements, be aware of the consequences and impacts of pleasures and desires. This is not necessarily an ethical or a regulatory obligation, but it is a condition by which sexual subjects enter into a sexually literate world of others. They cannot retreat to passive thinking on injustice, nor to ill-considered action in relation to the pursuit of desires.[3]

---

3   Praxeological from the Greek *Praxis* or practice. Within the Marxist tradition, it refers to the unity of theory and practice—thinking and doing—as inextricably linked if agents are to exercise free choice with regards to both themselves and others, and the wider social milieu.

This agenda is achieved by the practice of sexual literacy, the ethical regard for self and others in exploring pleasures, and the larger commitment to doing toward sharing a culture and space free from violence and prejudiced repression that is characterized by enabling and enrichment. Individually, it involves the everyday and reciprocating characteristics of care, sexual longing, practiced intimacies, common understandings and balances of responsibilities and entitlements that sexual agents exercise in our relationships. It also involves holding that those individual ethical and intimate values be reflected in our politics, culture and socioeconomic contexts. While there is much critical work to be done on advocating the particularities of sexual literacy, there should also be a recognition of its broader connection with other literacies and change.

References

Alexander, J. (2008). *Literacy, sexuality, pedagogy: Theory and practice for composition studies*. Logan: Utah State University Press.

Bamforth, N. (1997). *Sexuality, morals and justice*. London: Cassell.

Barker, M. (2013). *Rewriting the rules: An integrative guide to love, sex and relationships*. London: Routledge.

Barker, M., & Hancock, J. (2017). *Enjoy sex: How, when and if you want to*. London: Icon Books.

Barker, M. & Hancock, J. (2018). *A practical guide to sex: Finally, helpful sex advice*. London: Icon Books.

Barker, M., & Iantaffi, A. (2018). *Life isn't binary: On being both, beyond and in-between*. London: Icon Books.

Bell, D., & Binnie, J. (2000). *The sexual citizen: Queer politics and beyond*. Cambridge: Polity.

Cameron, D., & Kulick, D. (2003). *Language and sexuality*. Cambridge: Cambridge University Press.

Comfort, A., & Quilliam, S. (2011). *The joy of sex* (revised ed.). London: Mitchell Beazley.

Ditmore, M. H., Levy, A., & Willman, A. (2010). *Sex work matters: Exploring money, power and intimacy in the sex industry*. New York: Zed Books.

Drucker, P. (2014). *Warped: Gay normality and queer anti-capitalism*. New York: Haymarket Books.

Elley, S. (2013). *Understanding sex and relationship education, youth and class: A youth work based approach*. Houndsmill: Palgrave Macmillan.

Evans, D. (1994). *Sexual citizenship: The material constructions of sexualities*. London: Routledge.

Floyd, K. (2009). *The reification of desire: Towards a queer Marxism*. Minneapolis: University of Minnesota Press.

Foucault, M. (1978). *The history of sexuality volume 1: An introduction*. London: Penguin.

Freire, P. (1996). *Pedagogy of the oppressed*. Harmondsworth: Penguin.

Hardy, J., & Easton, D. (2018). *The ethical slut: A practical guide to polyamory, open relationships and freedoms in love and sex*. New York: Ten Speed Press.

hooks, b. (1994). *Teaching to transgress—Education as the practice of freedom*. London: Routledge.

Illich, I. (1995). *Deschooling society* (new ed.). London: Marion Boyars.

Kaplan, M. (1997). *Sexual justice: Democratic citizenship and the politics of desire*. London: Routledge.

Kirsch, M. (2000). *Queer theory and social change*. London: Routledge.

Langdridge, D., & Barker, M. (2013). *Safe, sane and consensual: Contemporary perspectives on sadomasochism*. London: Palgrave Macmillan.

Lewis, H. (2016). *The politics of everybody: Feminism, queer theory and Marxism at the intersection*. London: Zed Books.

Marcuse, H. (1998). *Eros and civilisation*. London: Routledge.

Marx, K. (1943). *Critique of the Gotha Programme*. London: Lawrence and Wishart. (Originally published in 1875.)

McRuer, R., & Mollow, A. (2012). *Sex and disability*. Durham, NC: Duke University Press.

Miller, P., & Devon, M. (1995). *Screw the roses, send me the thorns: The romance and sexual sorcery of sadomasochism*. Fairfield: Mystic Rose Books.

Moore, A., & Reynolds, P. (2018). *Childhood and sexuality: Contemporary issues and debates.* London: Palgrave Macmillan.

Munro, S. (2005). *Genderpolitics: Citizenship, activism and sexual democracy.* London: Pluto.

Phelan, S. (2001). *Sexual strangers: Gays, lesbians and dilemmas of citizenship.* Philadelphia, PA: Temple University Press.

Plummer, K. (1995). *Telling sexual stories: Power, change and social worlds.* London: Routledge.

Plummer, K. (2003). *Intimate citizenship: Private decisions and public dialogues.* Seattle: University of Washington Press.

Plummer, K. (2015). *Cosmopolitan sexualities.* Cambridge, MA: Polity.

Reich, W. (1968). *The function of the orgasm.* London: Panther Books.

Reynolds, P. (2018). Sexual capitalism: Marxist reflections on sexual politics, culture and economy in the 21st century. *tripleC, 16*(2), 696–706. Retrieved from http://www.triple-c.at

Richardson, D., & Monro, S. (2012). *Sexuality, equality and diversity.* Houndmills: Palgrave Macmillan.

Rubin, G. (2011). *Deviations: A Gayle Rubin reader.* Durham, NC: Duke University Press.

Sanders, T., O'Neill, M., & Pitcher, J. (2009). *Prostitution: Sex work, policy and politics.* London: Sage.

Sears, J. T. (1997). Centering culture: Teaching for critical sexual literacy using the sexual diversity wheel. *Journal of Moral Education, 26*(3), 275–283.

Stein, T. S., & Herdt, G. (2005). Editorial: Welcome to SRSP 2005 sexuality research and social policy. *Journal of the National Sexuality Resource Center, 2*(1), 1.

Stryker, K. (2017). *Ask: Building consent culture.* Portland: Thorntree Press.

Thompson, B. (1994). *Sadomasochism.* London: Cassell.

Weeks, J. (2000). *Making sexual history.* Cambridge, MA: Polity Press.

Weeks, J. (2007). *The world we have won: The remaking of erotic and intimate life.* London: Routledge.

Williams, D., & Williams, D. (2019). *The polyamory toolkit: A guidebook for polyamorous relationships.* Independently Published: eroticawakening.com.

Williams, R. (1977). *Marxism and literature.* Oxford: Oxford University Press.

Wiseman, J. (1996). *SM101: A realistic introduction* (2nd ed.). San Francisco, CA: Greenery Press.

CONTRIBUTORS

Peter Aggleton, PhD
School of Sociology, The Australian National University, Canberra, Australia

Deevia Bhana, PhD
Professor, University of KwaZulu-Natal
bhanad1@ukzn.ac.za

Rebecca Blais, PhD
Associate Professor, Utah State University
rebecca.blais@usu.edu

Elisabeth Berger Bolaza, MPH
Doctoral Candidate, Human Sexuality PhD Program, California Institute of Integral Studies
elisabethbolaza.com
ebolaza@ciis.edu

Erika Burns, PhD
Founder & Executive Director, Sacramento Peers on Prevention
sacpop.org
EBurns@sacpop.org

Sean Cahill, PhD
Director, Health Policy Research, The Fenway Institute
Boston University School of Public Health
Northeastern University Bouve College of Health Sciences
scahill@fenwayhealth.org

Hon. Helen Clark
Former Prime Minister of New Zealand
Former Administrator of the United Nations Development Programme

Adele E. Clarke, PhD
Professor Emerita, Sociology and History of Health Sciences, University of California, San Francisco
adele.clarke@ucsf.edu

Carole Clements, MFA, MA
Associate Professor, Contemplative Psychology, Naropa University
carole@naropa.edu

Daniel Cockayne, PhD
Department of Geography and Environmental Management, University of Waterloo
daniel.cockayne@uwaterloo.ca

Jan-Willem de Lind van Wijngaarden, PhD, MPH, MA
Independent Consultant on HIV, sexual health and related human rights
jwdlvw@gmail.com

Brian DeVries, PhD
Professor Emeritus, San Francisco State University
bdevries@sfsu.edu

Janna Dickenson, PhD, LP
Assistant Teaching Professor, University of California, San Diego & Clinical Psychologist
jdickenson@ucsd.edu

Narupon Duangwises, PhD
Sirindhorn Anthropology Centre, Bangkok, Thailand
narupon.d@sac.or.th

Alex Farquhar-Leicester, MA
University of Nebraska, Lincoln
afarquharleicester@gmail.com

Jermisha J. Frazier, MEd
Human Sexuality Doctoral Student, California Institute of Integral Studies
Institutional Review Board Member, Institute of Women and Ethnic Studies New Orleans
Poet / Public speaker
Jermishafrazier.com
contact@jermishafrazier.com

Caitlin Gerdts, PhD, MHS
Vice President for Research, Ibis Reproductive Health
www.ibisreproductivehealth.org
cgerdts@ibisreproductivehealth.org

Kathryn Gibb, MPH
Heilbrunn Department of Population and Family Health, Columbia University Mailman School of Public Health
kg2781@columbia.edu

Jen Jack Gieseking, PhD
Department of Geography, University of Kentucky
jgieseking.org
jgieseking@uky.edu

Christoph Hanssmann, PhD
Assistant Professor, San Francisco State University
chanssmann@sfsu.edu

Batul Hassan, MPH
batulmh@gmail.com

Jerika Loren Heinze
Founder, Fieldwork Initiative
www.fieldworkinitiative.org
fieldworkinitiative@gmail.com

Gilbert Herdt, PhD
Professor Emeritus, Departments of Sexuality Studies and Sociology, San Francisco State University
Director Emeritus, National Sexuality Resource Center
Founder and Director, Amsterdam Institute Sexuality and Society,
Founder, Human Sexuality PhD Program, California Institute of Integral Studies
gilherdt@gmail.com

Margaret Jolly, PhD
Professor/Australian Research Council Laureate Fellow 2010-2016, School of Culture, History and Language, College of Asia and the Pacific, Australian National University

Elliott Kronenfeld, PhD, LICSW, CSTS
Clinical Director, Insight Institute for Sexual and Relationship Health
Supervisor, American Association of Sex Educators, Counselors, and Therapists
www.couplesbyintention.com
elliott@insightbrookline.com

Roger Kuhn
Lecturer, American Indian Studies, San Francisco State University
PhD Candidate, Human Sexuality PhD Program, California Institute of Integral Studies

Katherine Lepani, PhD, MPH
Honorary Senior Lecturer, Australian National University
katherine.lepani@anu.edu.au

Holly Lewis, PhD
Associate Professor of Philosophy, Texas State University

Lynellyn D. Long, PhD
President, HERA (Her Economic Rights and Autonomy) France Association
lynellyn@gmail.com

Stefan Lucke, MA
Doctoral Candidate, Human Sexuality PhD Program, California Institute of Integral Studies
http://erosandmind.net
CriticalSexuality@protonmail.com

Satori Madrone, MA
Doctoral Candidate, Human Sexuality PhD Program, California Institute of Integral Studies
Certified Sexologist
satorimadrone.com
satori@satorimadrone.com

Michelle Marzullo, PhD, MA
Professor and Chair, Human Sexuality Department, California Institute of Integral Studies
ciis.edu/hsx
mmarzullo@ciis.edu

Sean G. Massey, PhD
Associate Professor of Women, Gender, & Sexuality Studies, Binghamton University, State University of New York
smassey@binghamton.edu

Terry McGovern, JD
Professor and Chair, Heilbrunn Department of Population and Family Health, Mailman School of Public Health, Columbia University
tm457@cumc.columbia.edu

Rita Melendez, PhD
Professor, Sociology and Sexuality Studies, San Francisco State University
rmelende@sfsu.edu

Alison Moore, PhD
Reader, Social Sciences, Edge Hill University

Megan Neitling, LMHC, CST
Doctoral Student, Human Sexuality PhD Program, California Institute of Integral Studies
Licensed Mental Health Therapist
American Association of Sex Educators, Counselors, and Therapists (AASECT) Certified Sex Therapist, and Sexualities Educator
www.BloomBehavioralHealth.com
BloomBehavioralHealth@outlook.com

Caroline Paltin, PhD
Assistant Professor and Lead Psychology Faculty, Psychology Department, National University
Licensed Clinical Psychologist

Nicole Polen-Petit, PhD
Interim Associate Dean, College of Letters and Sciences, National University
npolen-petit@nu.edu

Lisa Rapalyea, PhD, AT Ret
University of California, Davis
llrapalyea@ucdavis.edu

Paul Reynolds, PhD
Associate Lecturer, Open University
Chair, Research Ethics Group, University of Limerick

Angela Towne, PhD, MEd
Weidner University
AngieJTowne@yahoo.com

Lisa M. Vallin, PhD, MA
University of Hawai'i, Mānoa
vallin@hawaii.edu

Ekua Yankah, PhD, MPH
Centre for Social Research in Health, University of New South Wales
ekua.yankah@gmail.com

INDEX

4chan 224

AASECT. *See* American Association of Sex
    Educators, Counselors and Therapists
abortion accompaniment model 177–79
abortion (legal) 16, 316
abstinence-only programs 15–16
abstinence-only-until-marriage (AOUM)
    programs 15
Academia 52
Affordable Care Act 16
A–H Guidelines of Abstinence Education 15
AIS. *See* androgen insensitivity syndrome
Alexander, Jonathon 3
American Association of Sex Educators,
    Counselors and Therapists (AASECT)
    154, 302
American Psychological Association
    (APA) 297
American Society of Reproductive Medicine
    (ASRM) 146
androgen insensitivity syndrome (AIS) 135
Angelou, Maya 124–25
anthropology 51–52
antiabortion policy. *See* The Global Gag
    Rule
anti-Black racism 59
APA. *See* American Psychological Association
Apple 219
applications (apps) 214
    definition 214
    future 216–17
    for LGBQ youth 214–15
    sexual literacy and 216
    for TGD youth 215
    for young adults 214–15
ars erotica 195, 195n1
ART. *See* assisted reproductive technology
ASRM. *See* American Society of Reproductive
    Medicine
assisted reproductive technology (ART) 145
Association of Black Sexologists and Clinicians 40

Atlas.ti software 226
axiology 87

BAAITS. *See* Bay Area American Indian
    Two-Spirit Society
Bay Area American Indian Two-Spirit Society
    (BAAITS) 67–71
Bi Both 220
binary sex 105
Bi Rab 220
Birth Justice Movement 271–72
Bi Ruk 220
bisexuality 58
Black, Indigenous and people of color
    (BIPOC) 127
Black feminism 272
Black fluid sexualities 60
Black Lives Matter (BLM) movement
    59, 62–63
Black queer 57, 59–61
Black sexual freedom 57–63
    media analysis 60–63
    sexuality research studies 59–60
Black sexuality education within United
    States 35–40
The Black Teacher Project 40
#BLM (Black Lives Matter movement
    hashtag) 124
The Book of Woe 300
boundary publics 223
The Boys in the Band 143

CACREP. *See* Council for Accreditation of
    Counseling and Related Educational
    Programs
CAH. *See* congenital adrenal hyperplasia
"calling out" 124–28
Calvert v Johnson 144
cancel culture 124–28
capitalism 185–90, 219
capitalist economics 185–90
Catch and Kill (Farrow) 44

CECHR. *See* Council of Europe Commissioner of Human Rights
CEDAW. *See* Convention on the Elimination of All Forms of Discrimination against Women
charmed circle 81–82, 87
Chauncey, George 224
childhood
    "age-appropriate" model 114–20
    maturation 113–14
    naturalized and "normal" developmental model 114–20
    sexuality 114–20
    sexual literacy and 113–20
    sexual precociousness 116
    sexual risks 115–16
Christianity 197, 199–200
cigarette 186n10
Clarke's (revised) situational matrix 24
colonialism 197
commodification 300n2
comprehensive sex education 250
"Comprehensive sexuality education: A foundation for life and love," campaign 13
Compulsory Sex Education (CSE) 116
Comstock, Anthony 96
Comstock Laws of the United States 96
congenital adrenal hyperplasia (CAH) 135
constructionism 81–82
consumption 189–90
Convention on the Elimination of All Forms of Discrimination against Women (CEDAW) 268
conversion therapy 154
Coronavirus pandemic (COVID-19) 1–2, 313–19
    LGBT people and 318
    pregnancy, impacts on 315
    quarantine/lockdown, gendered impacts of 316–17
    risk, intersections of 317–18
    sex differences in cases 314
    sexual and reproductive health and rights 314–16
    women's voices in 318–19
Council for Accreditation of Counseling and Related Educational Programs (CACREP) 298
Council of Europe Commissioner of Human Rights (CECHR) 108

critical sexuality studies (CSS) 5–6, 79–88
    conceptual analysis in 86–87
    doing 85–88
    epistemologies for 86
    situational analysis and 23–29
    thinking criticality in 80–85
Crossley, Lawrence 238
Cruising 143
CSE. *See* Compulsory Sex Education
CSS. *See* critical sexuality studies
cultural activism 310

DAP. *See* Desert AIDS Project
decolonization/decolonizing sexuality 67, 69–70
decolonizing feminism 272
Defense of Marriage Act (1996) 242
Deliverance 143
Desert AIDS Project (DAP) 237
Diagnostic and Statistical Manual of Mental Disorders (DSM)
    CACREP standards and 298
    criteria for sexual diagnoses 298
    diagnosis, fallacies of 300–302
    medicalization within 297–303
    sexual literacy exercise 302–3
Diamond, Lisa 154
differences of sex developments (DSDs) 105–6, 133–35
Dilemmas of Desire (Tolman) 44
distal stressors 278
DSDs. *See* differences of sex developments
DSM. *See* Diagnostic and Statistical Manual of Mental Disorders

Ebola 313
economics 183, 185–86
emotions 94
Engels, Friedrich 186–87
epistemic violence 3, 5, 83
epistemology 80–81
erotic survivance 67–71
errancy 229–32
Evans, Gabrielle 38

Facebook 213, 221, 223–24
Farmer, P. 271
Farrow, Ronan 44
Fay, Brendan 241–43
fear 18
female-to-male (FtM) transgender athletes 135, 137–38

Fieldwork Initiative 49–53
Fieldwork Initiative to Stop Sexualized
    Trauma (FISST) training 49, 52–53
fieldwork preparation, sexual literacy in 49–53
Fight Online Sex Trafficking Act of 2017
    (FOSTA) 84
FISST. *See* Fieldwork Initiative to Stop
    Sexualized Trauma
fluid sexualities 58, 60
Folx 297, 297n1
FOSTA. *See* Fight Online Sex Trafficking Act
    of 2017
Foucauldian genealogical approach 86
Foucault, Michel 101

Gay & Lesbian Alliance against Defamation
    (GLAAD) 277–78
Gay Line group 231
gay men 220, 224
    older, sexual literacy in 235–39
    Palm Springs, California and 235–39
    sexual literacy and 143–50, 235–39
    surrogacy and 145–50
Gay Parenting Assistance Program 145
GCS. *See* gender confirmation surgery
Gebusi people 202–3
gender 183–86
    GI 58, 69, 125, 131–32, 134, 136–38, 153–
        60, 209, 215, 220, 224, 239, 243–45
    origins of 186–87
    violence 49–53
gender confirmation surgery (GCS) 134–35
gender identity (GI) 58, 69, 125, 131–32, 134,
    136–38, 153–60, 209, 215, 220, 224,
    239, 243–45
Gerber, Henry 241
GI. *See* gender identity
GLAAD. *See* Gay & Lesbian Alliance against
    Defamation
The Global Gag Rule 175–79
globalization 219
glocal
    analysis 94–95
    construct 93
    power relations in 4–5
    in practice 8
    sexual health literacy 229–32
    for sexuality 4–5
    sexual literacies 197–200
    in U.S. LGBT rights struggle 241–46
Goldman, Emma 96

gonads 109
Google 224
great fears 100
grounded theory (GT) 23
GSVT policy, in sports 135–37
GT. *See* grounded theory

Habitus and Field (Bourdieu) 292
Hall, Wendasha Jenkins 38–39
health 8
health clinics 7
Heraean games 132
Herdt, Gilbert 2–3, 195, 198–99
heterosexual sex 44
Hijra, Bangladeshi 219
Hirschfeld, Magnus 241
HIV/AIDS pandemic 1–2, 15, 33, 36, 57, 60,
    68, 100–101, 175, 188, 198–200, 215,
    229–32, 237, 243, 245–46, 250–51,
    260–61, 270, 305–10, 314, 318
holocaust 98
homophobia in Ghana 98–99
homosexuality 97–99
Howard, Shamyra 38–39
Huawei 219
human rights 2, 6, 13, 93, 102, 108, 128, 160,
    163, 167, 175–77, 179, 209, 244–45,
    249–54, 260, 267–71, 290, 311
hyperandrogenism 135–36

IAAF. *See* International Association of
    Athletics Federation
ICPD. *See* International Conference on
    Population and Development
ILGO. *See* Irish Lesbian and Gay Organization
imperial genealogies 196
Indigenous scholarship 67
Indonesia 99
Inquisition 96–98
Instagram 213, 221, 224
International Association of Athletics
    Federation (IAAF) 106, 136
International Conference on Population and
    Development (ICPD) 268
International Olympic Committee
    (IOC) 137–38
International Planned Parenthood Federation
    (IPPF) 315
Internet 59, 62, 213–17, 219, 221–26,
    241, 251–52
intersectional feminism 272

intersex
activism 109
as condition/disorder 106–7
global movements 110
information 109
meaning 105–6
people, barriers to sexual literacy 7, 105–10
positionality 106
sexual literacy, considerations in 106–10
stigma 109
variations 105–7
intersex/DSD athletes 135
Intersexion documentary 108–9
in vitro (IVF) fertilization 144
IPPF. *See* International Planned Parenthood
Federation
Irish Lesbian and Gay Organization (ILGO) 241
Islands of Love, Islands of Risk (Lepani)
199–200

Kaczynski, Lech 242–43
kamasutra, India 195, 197
karma 229–32
Kathoey, Thai 219–20
Killing the Black Body (Roberts) 38
Knauft, Bruce 202
kubukwabuya 309

LeBron, Jesus 242
Lee, Frances 126
Leonardi, B. 127
Lepani, Katherine 199–200
lesbian, gay, bisexual, queer (LGBQ) 213–17
LGBQ. *See* lesbian, gay, bisexual, queer
LGBQ youth, SNS for 214–15
LGBT
community resources 279
COVID-19 and 318
identities 281
issues, teaching about 118
liberation movement 219
minority stress 8, 277–83
coping and resilience strategies 279
distal/proximal stressors 278–79
in non-US cultural contexts 279–83
Palm Springs and 235–39
prejudice 277–78
progress 277–78
stress 278
U.S. LGBT rights struggle, glocality
in 241–46

LGBTQ people 93, 127, 223–27
communities 223, 279–82
Facebook and 223–24
Internet and 223
minority stress impact on 279
online recognition 225–26
spaces/visibility 223–27
in the United States 278
lifelong sexual literacy 249–54
love 18

MacKinnon, Catharine 43–47
male sports 131–38
male-to-female (MtF) transgender
athletes 134–35
Marriage Freedom Trail project 242
Marx, K. 184–90
Marxism 184–90
Marxist feminism 188–89
Marzullo, Michelle 195
mass cultural anger 100
masturbation 100
material–social relations 186
matricentric feminism 272
medicalization
within DSM 297–303
of human sexuality and gender 298–303
Men Having Babies (MHB) 145
mental health therapy offices 7
men-who-have-sex-with-men (MSM)
category 230
#MeToo Movement 44, 46, 99, 124
migrations to Western Europe, sexual risks
in 205–11
in journeys 207–8
reception 209–10
in uprooting and flight 205–7
Mill, John Stuart 187
The Minority Sex Report 39
minority stress, LGBT 8, 277–83
coping and resilience strategies 279
distal/proximal stressors 278–79
in non-US cultural contexts 279–83
moral campaigns 100
moral panics 93–102
challenge 102
emotional reaction and 94
examples 95–96
glocal sexual discourse and 94–95
HIV pandemic and 100–101
incidence/frequency of 101

#MeToo Movement and 99
Nazi ideology and 97–98
sexual abuse of children and 98
social life and 98–99
Socrates and 94
of sodomy 97
in twentieth century 98–99
in United States 95–96
in Western countries 99–100
moral shocks 100
mostly straight 58
Moulton, Thomas A. 242
multinational corporations 219

natal biological female (NBF) 131–37
natal biological male (NBM) 131, 133–34
natal (birth) biological sex (NBS) 131, 135, 138
National Collegiate Athletic Association
    (NCAA) 137–38
Nazi Germany regime 97–98
NBF. See natal biological female
NBM. See natal biological male
NBS. See natal (birth) biological sex
NCAA. See National Collegiate Athletic
    Association
NCSI. See non-consensual sexual interactions
necropolitics 98
neoliberalism 184–86
Netherlands 13–14
nonbinary athletes 133
non-consensual sexual interactions (NCSI)
    7, 163–70
    in American culture 165–66
    current prevention approaches,
        problems with
        binary gender bias 165–66
        LGBTQ issues 166–67
    LGBTQ individuals and 166–67
    mental health impact of 164–65
    power and control in 164
    risk for 164
    sex in 163–64
    sexual literacy implications 168–69
    sexual well-being to 167–68
        efficacy 167–68
        as human right 168–69
        messaging in sexual literacy
            campaigns 169
        in treatment 168
nosology 301
NVivo software 226

OAH. See Office of Adolescent Health
Obamacare. See Affordable Care Act
Obergefell v. Hodges, 2015 243
Oedipus complex 196n2
Office of Adolescent Health (OAH) 16
Offor 40
OkCupid 225
older gay men, sexual literacy in 235–39
oppression for women 43–44
oral sex 199
Origins of the Family, Private Property and the State
    (Engels) 186–87

Palm Springs, California 235–39
pansexuality 58, 62
Papua New Guinea (PNG) 98
    culture in 198–200
    Gebusi people of 202–3
    HIV in 200
    individual in 198–200
    sexual literacy in 198–200
    Trobriand Islands 196, 198–200, 305–11
parthenoi 132
PCOS. See polycystic ovary syndrome
pedophilia 100
Perel, Esther 153
penis, 81, 107, 109, 133, 136
penis-in-vagina sex 107–109, 164, 302
penis-vagina penetration 81
phu chaai 220
Planned Parenthood Federation of
    America 250
Polen-Petit, Nicole 195
political economy 183–85
Pollard, Amy 51
polycystic ovary syndrome (PCOS) 135
population growth 268
porn 37
post traumatic invasion syndrome 68
Prism 40
production 187–88
profit 187–88
Program of All-Inclusive Care for the Elderly
    (PACE) 244
proximal stressors 278
psychotherapy 153–54
public health 305–11
    bodies 306–7
    community participation and ownership 311
    critical sexuality in 307–8
    disease prevention 306–7

public health (*cont.*)
  evidence 307
  health promotion 306–7
  local articulations of 308–10
  programs 308
  regulatory scope of 307–8
  sexual literacy in 308

QPOC. *See* queer people of color
queer 213
  meccas 213
  online recognition 225–26
  pedagogical practices 17–18
  politics 184–85
  theory 6, 159, 183–85, 188, 272–73
  visibility 223–27
queer people of color (QPOC) 271–72

racism 37, 57, 59, 124–28, 225,
    238–39, 267
rape 45–46, 164
Ratjen; Dora 133
Reddit 224
relationalities 29
repression 197
reproduction 188–89
reproductive justice 8, 271–73
  Birth Justice Movement 271–72
  black feminism 272
  decolonizing feminism 272
  definition 271
  intersectional feminism 272
  matricentric feminism 272
  queer theory 272–73
Reproductive Rights 8, 267–70, 273
  limitations of 270–71
  usefulness of 270–71
ritualized homosexuality 198–99
Roberts, Dorothy 38
Roman Catholic Church 96
roughcasting model 52
RRTTR strategy 229
Rubin, Gayle 81

SA. *See* situational analysis
Saint Patrick's Day Parade 242
Sambia 198–99
Samsung 219
San Francisco 43–47
Sanger, Margaret 96
SAR. *See* sexual attitude reassessment

Scientific-Humanitarian Committee 241
SDGs. *See* Sustainable Development Goals
Semenya, Caster 136–37
SESTA. *See* Stop Enabling Sex Traffickers Act
    of 2017
sex 8, 80
Sex Discrimination Amendment Act
    (Australia) 110
sex diversity 106–7
sex panics 7, 93–102
  challenge 102
  emotional reaction and 94
  examples 95–96
  glocal sexual discourse and 94–95
  HIV pandemic and 100–101
  incidence/frequency of 101
  #MeToo Movement and 99
  Nazi ideology and 97–98
  sexual abuse of children and 98
  social life and 98–99
  Socrates and 94
  of sodomy 97
  in twentieth century 98–99
  in United States 95–96
  in Western countries 99–100
sex positivity 291
sex trafficking 83–84
sexual abuse of children 98
sexual assault 45, 49–53
sexual attitude reassessment (SAR) 302
sexual attractions 58
sexual competence 8, 287–94
  agency and structure 291–92
  choice 292–93
  definition 288–89
  framing 287–88
  individual 287
  performance 293–94
  properties/attributes of 288–91
sexual essentialism 81
sexual fluidity, psychotherapies for 58,
    153–60
  common issues in therapy 156–58
  historical overview 153–55
  useful modalities 158–60
  well-trained therapist 155–56
sexual freedom 196–97
sexual harassment 49–53
sexual health 260–63
sexual identities 8
sexuality 1–4, 8, 13, 29, 183–86, 252

decolonization/decolonizing 67, 69–70
definition of 80–81
education 7, 13–18
fluid 58
glocal for 4–5
local articulations of 308–10
women 43–47
sexuality education within United States 13–
18, 116
Black 35–40
challenge for 18
goal of 17
historical context of 13–16
myths about 33–34
queering pedagogical practices 17–18
teaching 16–17
Sexuality Information and Education Council
of the United States (SIECUS) 14–15
SEXUALITY (poem; Frazier) 35–36
sexuality research, decolonization of
embodied reflexivity and 75–76
impacts of 76
white fragility and 74–75
sexual liberation 184
sexual literacy 1–6, 46–47, 195–203,
259–64
advocacy for 323–31
barriers to 93–102
intersex people 105–10
moral panics 93–102
sex panics 7, 93–102
Black 35–40
cancel culture in journey of 123–28
characteristics of 3–4
childhood and 113–20
critical 5–6, 23–29
definition of 3, 250
in diverse communities 8
education and research 7, 13–88
epistemic violence in 83
exercise 302–3
in fieldwork preparation 49–53
gay men and 143–50
genealogy of 2–3
global, challenges to 263–64
glocal 4–5, 197–200
health, well-being and practice 8
lifelong 249–54
moral panics and 93–102
non-consensual sexual interactions
and 168–69

in older gay men 235–39
in Papua New Guinea 198–200
pedagogy (critical) in 13–18
policy and social discourse 7
praxis of 2
public health and 305–11
sex panics and 7, 93–102
sexual health and 260–63
sexual minorities/majorities, universal
human right for 249–54
social networking sites and 216
and sports 131–38
student 13–18
surrogacy and 143–50
in Thailand 230–32
within United States 13–18
sexually transmitted diseases (STDs) 229
sexually transmitted infections (STIs) 3, 14–17,
36, 168, 170, 229–31, 237, 260
sexual minorities/majorities, universal human
right for 249–54
sexual orientation 58, 60, 154, 209, 213–15,
238, 242, 244–45, 281, 290
sexual science 197
sexual sovereignty 67–71
sexual well-being (SWB) 1–2, 8, 167–68
efficacy 167–68
as human right 168–69
messaging in sexual literacy campaigns 169
in treatment 168
sex workers 83–84
shunga 195
SIECUS 14–15, 250, 253
situational analysis (SA) 23–29
affordances of 27
Clarke's (revised) situational matrix 24
for glocal sexuality studies 27
mapping situation, strategies for 26
capacities for participatory, decolonizing
and related research, capacities
for 28–29
differences, marginalities and "epistemic
diversity," attentiveness to 27
distinctive power analytics 27–28
relationalities 29
sexualities 29
theoretical foundations of 24–25
Snapchat 213
SNSs. See social networking sites
social constructionism 81
social media 221, 231

social networking sites (SNSs) 213–17
  definition 213–14
  future 216–17
  for LGBQ youth 214–15
  sexual literacy and 216
  for TGD youth 215
  for young adults 214–15
Society for Human Rights in Chicago 241
sodomy ("unnatural sex") 97
Spivak, Gayatri 3
sports 7
  biological advantages 134
  current governing policies 137–38
  female participants, exclusion of 132–33
  for future (inclusive and equitable
      policies) 138
  GSVT policy in 135–37
  intersex/DSD athletes 135
  as male heterosexual domain 131–38
  MtF transgender athletes 134–35
  nonbinary athletes 133
  policy per competitive level 137–38
  sexual literacy and 131–38
Spyer, Thea 241
Stacey, Kevin 99
Staley, S. 127
*The Statistical Manual for Use of Institutions of the
    Insane* 301
STDs. *See* sexually transmitted diseases
STIs. *See* sexually transmitted infections
Stop Enabling Sex Traffickers Act of 2017
    (SESTA) 84
stress 278. *See also* minority stress, LGBT
stressors 278
Structuration Theory (Giddens) 292
student sexual literacy 13–18
surrogacy 143–50
  clinics 7
  egg donation 146–48
  expenses 145
  gay men and 145–50
  laws 148
  sexual literacy and 143–50
  traditional *vs.* gestational 144
Sustainable Development Goals (SDGs)
    13, 269
SWB. *See* sexual well-being

Takacs, David 37
TGD. *See* transgender and gender-diverse
Thailand

bisexuality in 220
  errancy in 229–32
  Gay Both in 220
  HIV/AIDS prevention campaign in 230–31
  Internet and 221
  karma in 229–32
  Kathoey 219–20
  phu chaai 220
  sexuality/gender- scape 221
  sexual literacy in 230–32
  social media and 221, 231
  United Nations Program on HIV/AIDS
      (UNAIDS) 229
*Thinking Sex: Notes for a Radical Theory of the
    Politics of Sexuality* 81
Thorpe, Shemeka 38
*Through Our Eyes: Perspectives and Reflections from
    Black Teachers* 39
Tolman, Deborah 44
Towards a Feminist Theory of the State 43
transgender and gender-diverse (TGD)
    213, 215–17
Trobriand Islands 305–11
Trump, Donald 175, 243–46
Tumblr 215, 224–25
Twitter 224
Two-Spirit community 67–71

UNESCO. *See* United Nations Educational,
    Scientific and Cultural Organization
United Nations Convention on the Rights of the Child
    (1989) 113
United Nations Educational, Scientific and
    Cultural Organization (UNESCO)
    259–60, 262–65
United Nations Program on HIV/AIDS
    (UNAIDS) 229
United States, sexuality education
    within 13–18
  challenge for 18
  goal of 17
  historical context of 13–16
  queering pedagogical practices 17–18
  SFSU 43
  teaching 16–17
  youth's sexuality in 14
Universal Declaration of Human
    Rights 267–68
UN Millennium Development Goals
    (MDGs) 268–69
Unorthodox, Netflix series 200–203

unwanted pregnancies 14
U.S. LGBT rights struggle, glocality in 241–46
US Mexico City Policy 315
US *National Sexuality Education Standards Core Content and Skills K-12* 110
US PEPFAR program 246

vagina 107, 109, 164, 178, 199, 270
vnokeckv 67–71

Ward v. Wilbanks, 2010 244
Waria, Indonesian 219
Weinstein, Harvey 99
Welfare Reform Act of 1996 15
White fragility 73–75
whiteness 73–75
White-norm sexuality 37–38
White sexuality 61
White supremacy 76
WHO. *See* World Health Organization

widows 95
Windsor, Edie 241
WOC. *See* women of color
women
    in COVID-19 pandemic 318–19
    oppression for 43–44
    sexuality 43–47
The Women of Color Sexual Health Network 40
women of color (WOC) 271–72
Woodhall, Victoria 96
working-class families 184
World Health Organization (WHO) 116, 163, 177–78, 261, 270, 290, 314

Yogyakarta Principles 268
young adults, SNS for 214–15
YouTube 213, 215, 224

Žižek, S. 271

CPSIA information can be obtained
at www.ICGtesting.com
Printed in the USA
LVHW030853260821
696089LV00006B/294